THE HORROR FILM

New Approaches to Film Genre

Series Editor: Barry Keith Grant

New Approaches to Film Genre provides students and teachers with original, insightful, and entertaining overviews of major film genres. Each book in the series gives an historical appreciation of its topic, from its origins to the present day, and identifies and discusses the important films, directors, trends, and cycles. Authors articulate their own critical perspective, placing the genre's development in relevant social, historical, and cultural contexts. For students, scholars, and film buffs alike, these represent the most concise and illuminating texts on the study of film genre.

1   *From* Shane *to* Kill Bill: *Rethinking the Western*, Patrick McGee
2   *The Horror Film*, Rick Worland

Forthcoming:
3   *Hollywood and History*, Robert Burgoyne
4   *Film Noir*, William Luhr

THE HORROR FILM

AN INTRODUCTION

RICK WORLAND

Blackwell
Publishing

© 2007 by Rick Worland

BLACKWELL PUBLISHING
350 Main Street, Malden, MA 02148-5020, USA
9600 Garsington Road, Oxford OX4 2DQ, UK
550 Swanston Street, Carlton, Victoria 3053, Australia

The right of Rick Worland to be identified as the Author of this Work
has been asserted in accordance with the UK Copyright, Designs, and
Patents Act 1988.

All rights reserved. No part of this publication may be reproduced,
stored in a retrieval system, or transmitted, in any form or by any means,
electronic, mechanical, photocopying, recording or otherwise, except as
permitted by the UK Copyright, Designs, and Patents Act 1988, without
the prior permission of the publisher.

First published 2007 by Blackwell Publishing Ltd

1   2007

Library of Congress Cataloging-in-Publication Data

Worland, Rick.
    The horror film : an introduction / Rick Worland. — 1st ed.
        p. cm. — (New approaches to film genre)
    Includes bibliographical references and index.
    ISBN-13: 978-1-4051-3901-4 (hardcover : alk. paper)
    ISBN-10: 1-4051-3901-3 (hardback : alk. paper)
    ISBN-13: 978-1-4051-3902-1 (pbk. : alk. paper)
    ISBN-10: 1-4051-3902-1 (pbk. : alk. paper) 1. Horror films—History and criticism.
I. Title. II. Series.

    PN1995.9.H6W64 2007
    791.43′6164—dc22

                                                                    2006017117

A catalogue record for this title is available from the British Library.

Set in 11/13pt Bembo
by Graphicraft Limited, Hong Kong
Printed and bound in Singapore
by COS Printers Pte Ltd

The publisher's policy is to use permanent paper from mills that operate a
sustainable forestry policy, and which has been manufactured from pulp
processed using acid-free and elementary chlorine-free practices.
Furthermore, the publisher ensures that the text paper and cover board
used have met acceptable environmental accreditation standards.

For further information on
Blackwell Publishing, visit our website:
www.blackwellpublishing.com

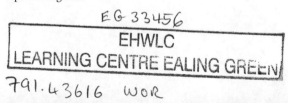
EG 33456
EHWLC
LEARNING CENTRE EALING GREEN
791.43616   WOR

CONTENTS

List of Illustrations   vii

Acknowledgments   xi

1 Introduction: Undying
   Monsters   1

2 A Short History of the
   Horror Film: Beginnings
   to 1945   25

3 A Short History of the
   Horror Film: 1945 to
   the Present   76

4 Monsters Among Us:
   Cases of Social Reception   118

5 Edges of the Horror Film: Lon Chaney, Tod
   Browning, and *The Unknown* (1927)   144

6 *Frankenstein* (1931) and Hollywood Expressionism 157

7 *Cat People* (1942): Lewton, Freud, and Suggestive
   Horror   176

8 Horror in "The Age of Anxiety": *Invasion of the
   Body Snatchers* (1956)   193

9 Slaughtering Genre Tradition: *The Texas Chain Saw
   Massacre* (1974)   208

10 *Halloween* (1978): The Shape of the Slasher Film   227

11 *Re-Animator* (1985) and Slapstick Horror   243

12 Demon Lover: *Bram Stoker's Dracula* (1992)   253

13 Afterword: Our Haunted Houses   266

Appendix: Horror Auteurs   273
Notes   279
Index   304

ILLUSTRATIONS

1 Expressionist distortion:
  Dr. Caligari (Werner
  Krauss) tends his enslaved
  somnambulist Cesare
  (Conrad Veidt) in *The
  Cabinet of Dr. Caligari*
  (1920)   45

2 Theatrical flair: Lon
  Chaney as *The Phantom
  of the Opera* (1925)   53

3 *Doppelgänger*: Fredric
  March in the classic film
  version of *Dr. Jekyll and
  Mr. Hyde* (1931)   60

4 Horror stars of the genre's
classic period: the Frankenstein Monster (Boris Karloff)
gently attends his late friend Ygor (Bela Lugosi) in *Son
of Frankenstein* (1939)   68

5 Sequels and series in the World War II era: the
Frankenstein Monster (Bela Lugosi) and Larry Talbot
(Lon Chaney, Jr.) in *Frankenstein Meets the Wolf Man*
(1943)   72

6 Atomic terrors: the most famous of many radioactive
monsters in the post–World War II years, Japan's
Godzilla (1954)   79

7   Hammer updates the classic genre movies: the (first) destruction of Count Dracula (Christopher Lee) and the start of a new series featuring more graphic violence and sexuality in *Horror of Dracula* (1958)   83

8   Poe goes to the drive-in: in the flashback of Roger Corman's *The Pit and the Pendulum* (1961), the Inquisitor Sebastian Medina (Vincent Price) lures his unfaithful wife and brother to their dooms   89

9   Essence of exploitation: American International Pictures (AIP) ad slick for *The Thing With Two Heads*, combining elements of the 1970s "Blaxploitation" cycle and the outlaw biker movies of the 1960s (1972)   98

10   Postmodern quotation: *The Funhouse* opens with self-conscious reference to *Psycho* by way of *Halloween*. A parodic "rehearsal" before the "real" violence later in the movie (1981)   110

11   The slasher cycle and a new monster pantheon in the 1980s: Jason does it again, and again, and again in *Friday the 13th Part VII – The New Blood* (1988)   116

12   Defending the gothic home front: Andreas (Matt Willis) repels the vampire Armand Tesla (Bela Lugosi) revived by Nazi bombs in a publicity shot from *Return of the Vampire* (1943)   133

13   Alonzo the Armless (Lon Chaney) and his diminutive alter ego Cojo (John George) in *The Unknown* (1927)   145

14   Jack P. Pierce's makeup for Boris Karloff as the Monster in *Frankenstein* (1931) became one of the iconic images of twentieth-century culture   158

15   Simone Simon as the troubled Irena, flanked by the symbolic statue of King John impaling a cat in Val Lewton's production of *Cat People* (1942)   177

16   Subterranean realms: Dr Miles Bennell (Kevin McCarthy) discovers the duplicate pod of Becky forming in a coffin-like box in the cellar. *Invasion of the Body Snatchers* (1956)   194

17   Family portrait: post-*Psycho* horror films increasingly blurred distinctions between monster and family. *The Texas Chain Saw Massacre* (1974)   209

18   Final girl: Laurie (Jamie Lee Curtis) prepares to fight as Michael Myers breaks into the closet where she has hidden. *Halloween* (1978)   228

19 Going head to head: Herbert West (Jeffrey Combs) revives his decapitated nemesis Dr Carl Hill (David Gale) to initiate the absurd and gory climax of *Re-Animator* (1985)   244

20 Androgynous and orientalist motifs: Gary Oldman's introduction as the shape-shifting Count in *Bram Stoker's Dracula* (1992)   254

ACKNOWLEDGMENTS

Since the mid-1990s, several academic writers on the horror film have begun their books with more or less ironic declarations of whether their interest began in childhood or fairly recently, implicitly arguing that one's credibility to speak about the genre was somehow either enhanced or hurt by just when the writer's interest began. Such statements indicate that horror may be the original "guilty pleasure"; and underscore again the genre's roots in the psychological jungles of childhood. I am among those whose fascination started early. In October, 1967, I asked my grandfather for a "loan" of 75 cents to buy a strange magazine I had spotted at the drugstore, one with silly puns accompanying photos of Godzilla, the Phantom of the Opera, and a still shocking image of a woman with a hatchet buried in her forehead. Realizing this last item might prejudice my case, I told Grandpa the money was for a "Halloween magazine." The description was true enough and it skipped over extraneous details. The pitch worked; and though my interest in the genre has changed and deepened, its multi-faceted appeal endures.

Scholars and critics of varied backgrounds whose passionate work on the horror film have both inspired me and informed this study include the late Carlos Clarens, R. H. W. Dillard, David J. Skal, Linda Williams, Tony Williams, and Robin Wood.

Special thanks to Barry Keith Grant, who initiated an earlier version of this project and provided much valuable editorial commentary and support throughout.

Harry Benshoff, Sean Griffin, and Brian Taves gave their support and encouragement and freely shared their knowledge and insights on the horror film and other aspects of film scholarship at important points in the book's development. Thomas Graham graciously lent his insight and research on Aurora model kits that enhanced Chapter 4.

My friend and colleague Kevin Heffernan was a constant source of information, insight, and invaluable critique that strengthened this study. His work on the economic and formal history of post-World War II horror kept me aware of the importance of industrial context to the development of the genre overall.

At Southern Methodist University, I must thank Carole Brandt, Dean of the Meadows School of the Arts; Tinsley Silcox, Director of the Hamon Arts Library; and David Sedman for their personal and professional help in the research and writing of this book.

At Blackwell Publishing, Ken Provencher and Jayne Fargnoli provided steady professional advice and encouragement in finally bringing this project to fruition.

Two extraordinary teachers and friends fired my passion for the study of movies and American culture, Dr James M. Curtis at the University of Missouri, Columbia; and Dr Howard Suber at UCLA. Thank you for your examples.

Many thanks to my wife Kathy, and our wonderful children Emily, Julia, and Ethan for their love, support, and patience. I could not have done this without you.

Finally, I dedicate this book to the memory of my father, C. I. "Ike" Worland, Jr. The last farmer.

RW

CHAPTER 1

INTRODUCTION: UNDYING MONSTERS

A stranded group approaches the ancient house where a dim light burns in an upper window. As the full moon rises a pain-wracked man gasps at fur growing on his palms. Thunder crashes and lighting illuminates the operating table lifted into the night sky. Eager for furtive sex on a dark night, a young couple hear twigs snap as a hooked blade rises above them. Seated in a movie theater, these sights and sounds can only mean you are watching a horror film – paradoxically prepared, even eager to see things that may make you to avert your eyes. Ominous places, grotesque semi-humans, or outright monsters await, ready to make you confront your own fragile mortality. Who would go here willingly? Millions have, for decades; centuries, if we recognize the basic shape and themes of horror narratives in media long preceding motion pictures. Many explanations for the perennial appeal of horror have been advanced, yet most probe similar points: the psychological and emotional reactions of the individual viewer/consumer, most importantly the evocation of mortal fear, one of our most primordial instincts; the dread of a radically nonhuman monster; events that challenge traditional conceptions of morality and/or the social good. The horror tale compels us to contend with a particularly violent and uncanny disruption of our unremarkable, everyday experiences, one that carries both individual and social implications.

Say that you seriously enjoy horror movies and you are likely to elicit reactions that seldom occur should you express affection for love stories or even science fiction. Unless you are with other like-minded people – and horror is a broadly popular, not elite form – those reactions may range from amused condescension ("kids' stuff," "camp"); to quiet opprobrium ("Aren't there enough real horrors in the world?"); or even suspicions about your emotional health ("You're drawn to images of women being murdered? Let's explore that . . ."). Still others may respond that they avoid horror movies either because they find them too upsetting to be "entertainment," or reject the entire form on moral or political grounds. Those wary of horror films surely understand part of the story: the psychology of the horror-film viewer, or at least the particular emotional reactions such works can provoke, are central to the genre's construction and reception. The monsters in horror stories are powerful and truly immortal beings because no matter how many times they are killed or destroyed, our fear and desire for their company compel their return.

This book surveys the history, stylistic development, and social reception of the American horror film from the earliest period of the genre's importance to the present. While we will touch on antecedents of the horror film in art, literature, and theater for the themes and motifs they share, cinematic horror will remain the major focus. We examine ways in which horror movies have been produced, received, and interpreted by filmmakers, audiences, and critics throughout the medium's history. Though horror has proved popular in many media (witness the phenomenal success of the novels of Stephen King and Anne Rice), the mass audiences long attracted to cinematic horror have made it the most prominent cultural source for frightful tales of monsters, madmen, and supernatural evil. Characters and scenes from horror movies permeate our cultural consciousness: the flat-topped Frankenstein Monster; the Phantom of the Opera unmasked; Bela Lugosi's black-caped Dracula; Janet Leigh's fatal shower in *Psycho*; Linda Blair's demoniacally rotating head in *The Exorcist*; or more recently, an unholy trio of implacable stalkers with preppy names – Michael, Jason, and Freddy – in the slasher series of the 1980s and beyond. The horror film draws together and transforms mythic and literary traditions, forming a pool of images and themes that filmmakers reference, vary, or revise. Probing such a vibrant yet often controversial genre brings us closer to understanding the functions, meanings, and pleasures of that form as it circulates in changing historical circumstances.

Since the mid-1970s we have seen increasingly specialized writing on the horror genre. Individual films, auteurs, and stylistic sub-groups have been critiqued from various critical perspectives (by feminist writers especially), submitted to the rigor and variety of analysis previously devoted to the Western, Film Noir, or the cinema of Alfred Hitchcock. Over this same period, however, discernible shifts occurred in intellectual conceptions brought to bear on horror. Critics moved from suggesting that this modern form continues the traditional concerns of ancient mythology and canonical literature for confronting fundamental, even universal philosophical and moral questions about human mortality and the nature of evil; to emphasizing the psychological processes either reflected in or stimulated by horror's frightening narratives; to probing the genre for allegories of contemporary social and political ideology. Some would argue this is clear evidence that comprehension of the horror film, indeed of all popular forms, has grown steadily more sophisticated, but in any case, recent approaches have tended to become more historically and culturally specific. Still, the production of historical or critical knowledge is as much related to the intellectual framework one builds, the assumptions or omissions made, as it is to the establishment of empirical facts. Critics tend to combine and borrow pragmatically from various approaches because different insights can result from different interpretive methods.

Horror often achieves its greatest impact when it exposes or flaunts cultural taboos. Yet, over time, movies proven to have scared audiences in their day and beyond did so because they succeeded first as movies – through cinematic renderings of characters and stories that skillfully manipulated the range of film technique. In this regard, although the very concept of artistic canons has been the subject of intense intellectual and political debate for over thirty years, canon formation remains both inevitable and essential to provide any framework for analysis, regardless of the conclusions or interpretations at which one finally arrives. Simply to describe works of interest does not automatically legitimate these and only these texts as important, valuable, or worthy of consideration. One of the most salient facts about fictional horror is the generally low regard in which it is held – at least publicly – by proponents of "good taste" and higher intellectual and aesthetic aspirations. Such disdain invites closer investigation, as it likely obscures a wealth of ideological assumptions. Moreover, when dealing with the popular arts, canons may be formed from both the enduring commercial appeal of certain texts (e.g., the many incarnations of Frankenstein's Monster) as well as from the received wisdom of critical tradition, wisdom that can be more readily challenged if one has a broader grasp of the genre as well as the conventional terms of valuation and debate. Danish director Carl Theodor Dreyer's brooding and difficult *Vampyre* (1932), for example, though often championed as a genre landmark, is really a highbrow "cult movie," one we might now categorize as an example of the international art-cinema style; and though a distinguished film filled with uncanny imagery, not remotely a popular work like contemporaneous Hollywood efforts such as *The Mummy* (1932) or *Dr. X* (1933). Self-conscious attention to canon formation that seeks rapprochement between audiences and critics, which acknowledges that each side has something important to tell us about a given movie or period, seems likely to produce a more complete account of a genre and its most significant works.

In the 1960s and early 1970s, a rich period of formal innovation throughout the film medium (e.g., the French New Wave, Direct Cinema documentary, the avant-garde "New American cinema," and directors of the "New Hollywood" grappling with these forms) stimulated increasingly sophisticated popular criticism that enhanced cinema's cultural prestige. This artistic and intellectual activity meshed with the political and social tumult of that same period from the Civil Rights movement to increasing opposition to the Vietnam War, a subsidiary effect of which was to shift attention to the social dynamics of cultural, especially popular cultural forms. Significant work on film also began to emerge from established academic departments of language and literature, art history, or theater. Partly owing to the need to justify such work to culturally conservative administrators and traditionalist colleagues, these writers analyzed popular movies with steady reference to the canons and concerns of High Culture. For them, film versions of *Frankenstein*, *Dracula*, and *Dr. Jekyll and Mr. Hyde* were ripe for analysis because of their roots in nineteenth-century novels that had some (though not wholehearted) literary cachet. These initial efforts sought to prove that such sensational fare might not only be redeemed but also incorporated into the canons of the humanistic tradition. The effort was as sincere as the task was formidable since it often failed to satisfy neither traditional cultural elites nor the unabashed fans of movie monsters; or after the early 1960s, account for the lurid exploitation movies that increasingly made up the genre's most dynamic works.

The fine 1972 anthology *Focus on the Horror Film* typifies the humanistic criticism I am describing. At what they recognized as a significant transitional moment in the genre's history after the end of censorship in 1968, the writers collected in this volume sought to present a critical and historical overview of horror's development. The essays are grouped into categories including "The Horror Domain," "Gothic Horror," "Monster Terror," and "Psychological Thriller," indicating major genre patterns. Titles of two essays in the initial category reference Shakespeare and Yeats. The third essay, by literary critic R. H. W. Dillard, begins:

> I suppose that all significant Western art, at least since the medieval period, has been directly concerned with the original fall of man and the consequent introduction of sin and death into the world . . . The horror film is, at its best, as thoroughly and richly involved with the dark truths of sin and death as any art form has ever been, but its approach is that of parable and metaphor – an approach which enables it . . . to achieve a metaphysical grandeur, but which also may explain why its failures are so very awful and indefensible.[1]

Dillard walks a fine line here, beginning an analysis of the genre's particular mediation of the confrontation with mortality and asserting its importance as a cultural voice while dismissing the likes of *I Was A Teenage Frankenstein* (1957) or *Billy the Kid vs. Dracula* (1966), movies "obviously" more suited to the drive-in than the classroom. Yet how, then, to reconcile serious considerations with the positively thrilling sense of partaking of something that is low, vulgar, and offensive to paternalistic authority, the things that more often than not give the horror film its charge and appeal? This work would have to come a bit later.

Overall, perhaps the greatest contribution of humanistic critics was to take horror films seriously, a simple act that opened many doors. They did so in part by riding the high tide of auteurism, the controversial but suggestive critical notion that certain outstanding directors ought to be considered the principal creators (authors) of their films. In discussing James Whale or Tod Browning as auteurs, critics were insisting on the analysis of these directors' work as cinematic art as opposed to earlier rejection of *Frankenstein* (1931) and *Dracula* (1931) as shallow mass-cultural travesties of their literary predecessors; or, closely related, dismissal on the grounds that monster movies were simply and obviously juvenile entertainment that ought not to impress or engage any "serious" person above age 12. Considered in terms of typical settings, characters, and themes (key components of any genre), horror movies could indeed suggest parallels with ancient myth, gothic literature, and other artistic forms. But to the extent such critics began to focus attention on the formal properties of the films, they brought a new aesthetic vocabulary to bear on visually rich works produced from at least the 1920s German Expressionist period onward. One might argue that analyses that proceeded from High Culture models or appeals to film-as-art were superfluous or even distracting from the subject at hand, but at certain points such appeals were entirely necessary.

About two decades later, however, freed of the need to rationalize the object of study, James Twitchell's *Dreadful Pleasures: An Anatomy of Modern Horror* (1985) still considers the horror film a continuation of themes in art dating from prehistoric times. But for Twitchell this is merely the starting point for other analyses, including his argument that horror stories "carry the prescriptive codes of modern Western sexual behavior."[2] A similar notion that the horror film both assimilates and secularizes persistently important cultural and philosophical motifs appears in Walter Kendrick's *The Thrill of Fear: 250 Years of Scary Entertainment* (1991). The broad, inclusive approaches of English literature professors such as Twitchell and Kendrick remain important to contextualize prevalent issues in horror criticism. Scholars had noted even earlier that the flowering of gothic literature, if dated from the publication of Horace Walpole's *The Castle of Otranto* (1764), roughly coincides with the Age of Enlightenment, marked in this case by secularization that increasingly rivals or replaces traditional religious explanations and earlier or coexistent folk superstitions and practices with skeptical philosophical and scientific inquiry.[3] In a period largely stripped of literal belief in the supernatural, a new form of literary expression arose based on confrontations real or presumed with the occult, a form that endures to the present. Why? And what are the implications of this cultural response and its persistent popularity? As I will suggest, these and other analyses of the horror film often seek to map and understand the genre in relation to four major questions, large issues that can be subdivided into more specific areas.

First, just what is a "horror film"; or what are the typical settings, characters, and narrative problems that structure and define this genre? Second, what are the psychological functions of horror? Writing about gothic literature in the twentieth century took it as axiomatic that its "true" meanings were to be found in psychological (particularly Freudian psychoanalytic) conceptions. Because the horror genre is defined by the emotional response it provokes – apprehension, fear, and terror – critics have pursued questions about the individual reader/viewer's psychological reactions. Third, how has this form evolved over time, or, what does the history of the horror film tell us about both its relatively stable and constant aspects and of those that change historically? Finally, what are the social functions of horror? Recent commentators would agree that the psychological and social implications of the genre are closely related, even inseparable, reasoning that the individual is a subject of social formation and conditioning whose personal responses must be mapped onto larger social questions raised by horror as entertainment. Most public discussions of fictional horror center around issues of censorship, the violation of social standards of morality and conduct, and the potential deleterious results from exposure of some members of society, especially children and the socially disadvantaged, to violent, disturbing, and destabilizing horror narratives. But there are other issues to consider in regard to horror's social meanings; and historical conditions shape reception as well as the genre's formal features. I will defer discussion of the genre's social impact to Chapter 4. Yet throughout this book, we will suggest ways in which all of these basic questions or areas of analysis overlap.

Tracking the Thing

What do we mean when we use the term "horror film"? An important part of the definition is self-evident: it is a movie that aims foremost to scare us. But the fear it evokes and how it goes about it are particular. While we are likely to experience anxiety and fright in other violent genres – a war story, disaster movie, or crime drama, for instance – a horror film evokes deeper, more personal psychological fears in the starkest terms. The most basic fear in the horror story is the fear of death. But this is only the beginning of its impact and appeal. The fate of horror's most unfortunate characters usually comes down to two possibilities, which a given story may or may not consider synonymous – death, the physical fact of the end of life; and damnation, a metaphysical conception that describes a state in which the immortal "soul" is condemned to eternal suffering and punishment. Creatures in horror stories, as well as their victims, often straddle these two domains in a horrible state that is neither death nor life – the threat of becoming one of the "living dead" or "undead." The monster can be seen as the personification of Death itself which, like the traditional figure of the Grim Reaper, is an ultimately unstoppable opponent relentlessly committed to the destruction of healthy and vibrant human beings. As the perfect title of a sporadically effective horror movie of 2000 had it, seemingly, *The Dead Hate the Living*. Such stories depict death as the possible start of an even more terrible fate.

As regards the omnipresence of death in horror tales, however, these stories threaten or present us with images not merely of death but of an especially grotesque and painful end, what Stephen King sardonically dubbed "the bad death," which he considers a fundamental aspect of horror tales.[4] Marion Crane wasn't simply stabbed, she was sliced to pieces; the zombies in *Night of the Living Dead* (1968) disembowel and eat their victims; opponents of the shadowy corporation in *Scanners* (1981) don't just suffer strokes, their heads explode; *The Texas Chain Saw Massacre* (1974) – well, the title says it all. Horror in all periods has thrived on depictions of "bad deaths," the kind that make us dwell on physical agony. To learn that someone "died instantly" can provide a certain comfort. But suffering occurs over time, its dread that the pain will be drawn out indefinitely. (Hell is often depicted as endless physical torment, lavish "bad deaths" extended through eternity.) Despite widely varying tones, the deathtraps in *Peeping Tom* (1960), *The Abominable Dr. Phibes* (1971), and *Saw* (2004) frighten not just with the mortal punishment the victims endure but from the soul-killing depression of knowing that the perpetrator is all-too human and drawing a sadistic thrill from the victim's agony. These examples and others wring additional intensity from allowing the victims to contemplate their impending deaths. To depict atrocious acts on screen may be decried as gratuitous or tasteless; but when violence is intermingled with sexual sadism it is likely to raise charges about potential harm in the real world.

As such, another significant dimension of the horror tale is its affinity for the lesson, often metaphysical, implicitly social. Though we will never encounter such unnaturally powerful monsters in the material world, such stories serve as parables or convey a sharp message of warning. As the American horror genre took shape in the early 1930s, censors inside and beyond Hollywood vigilantly insisted that its monsters and transgressing scientists either perished or lived long enough to recant. Regardless, horror stories seem to form a secular, parallel narrative to the essentially religious traditions of the cultures that generate them. Their plots describe situations that carry ultimate consequences for certain characters, which by analogy offer similar alternatives for the reader/viewer regardless of narrative plausibility. Avoid the vampire and we will walk in the sun tomorrow; but should we fall victim to its bite, we may be damned forever. Accordingly, the undead creature can often be checked or wounded by the most familiar Judeo-Christian religious symbols, the cross, holy water, or a prayer that invokes the Almighty. Even though gothic novels were originally formulated in a skeptical age whose most vibrant minds aimed to question and reject traditional religious dogma, these tales still affirmed the power and persistence of the uncanny, the inexplicable, and the irrational in most aspects of individual and social life.

Besides intending to scare the viewer by presenting images that most people would certainly not wish to see in real life, a major component of the horror film is its star, the monster. Most genres contain a collection of stock characters that appear in assorted variants and combinations and the horror film is no exception: the mad scientist and his deformed servant, the scoffing authority figure, a wise elder who recognizes the evil, the screaming (usually female) victim, among others. Still, no one goes to a horror movie to enjoy another pair of typical characters, the sturdy hero and wilting heroine often pursued by the monster, the earnest heterosexual couple hoping to put all this behind them the morning after. No, the audience comes to see the creature, the thing, the supernatural menace in whatever near-human or non-human form it assumes. Most sub-genres of horror are built around specific monsters: the zombie, werewolf, vengeful ghost, or psychotic slasher, to name a few. As I suggest later, particular monsters can be thought of as embodying particular threats or fears. The monster is often a liminal figure, an uncertain amalgam or transitional form between living and dead; human and animal; male and female. The most potent character in the genre, the paradox of the monster is that it incites our fear, compels our attention, and quite often courts our empathy and fascination, even though it remains the most remote from any possible reality.

As such, perhaps the most important aspect of the horror story is that its situations and sources of fear are largely irrational. (We will talk more below about the varied possibilities of irrational powers in the related forms of horror, science fiction, and fantasy.) Horror tales can evoke genuine fears; frequently these consist of scenarios common in nightmares of being pursued, trapped, and slaughtered by an overwhelmingly powerful figure. In fact, one of the most complimentary things to say about a gripping horror story is to call it "nightmarish." Yet in most horror tales, the agents of destruction are purely imaginary creatures, essentially the products of lingering pagan superstition. Put it this way: Though we might check into an out-of-the way motel and be murdered by a maniac while showering – and for this reason, *Psycho*, by the way, was generally not considered a "horror movie" upon its 1960 release – it is impossible for us to ever be bitten by a vampire, chewed by a decaying zombie, or torn up by a werewolf. Nevertheless, movies featuring these creatures are among the best known and most lasting works in the horror genre. It is this central irrationality that allows the mass-mediated horror story of the modern technological age to seem a logical extension of monster and hero stories from mythology, folklore, and fairy tales, the last usually intended for young children at a developmental stage at which distinctions between wish and reality, or make-believe and material, are not so clear.

A supernatural basis is only apparently absent in the slasher films that appeared in the late 1970s where the monster at least begins as a human psychopath, yet the most enduring of these series, such as *Halloween* and *Friday the 13th*, quickly developed their invulnerable killers as virtual immortals. Still, stressing the irrationality of the threat in the horror genre, many movies may gather under its umbrella even if the monster remains fully human from start to finish. Some of the best of these, however, use so much time and atmosphere to convince us that the weird occurrences are the work of ghosts or a curse that even, when finally told, they are not (e.g., in *Rebecca* [1940], *The Pit and the Pendulum* [1961], or *Dead Ringers* [1988]), our sense that this was all fundamentally uncanny remains. The cultivation of fear and a sense of the psychologically bizarre they evoke is what most aligns these stories with the horror genre.

For at least a generation now, the term "horror movie" has likely evoked acts of graphic violence rather than subtle constructions of ominous atmosphere. Yet over time, horror stories have often differed by how much or how little their atrocities were hinted at or shown directly. In this regard some have sought to distinguish between "terror" and "horror," arguing that the former is more artful and unsettling than the latter, which is condemned as aesthetically cheap, perhaps even ethically suspect. Author Ann Radcliffe, one of the central figures in the formation of gothic literature, believed the distinction between terror and horror to be an important one, as did actor Boris Karloff, who preferred the term "terror pictures" to describe the work he did for nearly forty years after he played the Monster in *Frankenstein*. Radcliffe insisted that "Terror and horror are so far opposite, that the first expands the soul, and awakens the faculties to a high degree of life; the other contracts, freezes, and nearly annihilates them."[5] Nearly two centuries apart, Radcliffe and Karloff agreed that terror was a more refined and difficult performance to achieve than the quick shocks of mere horror – effects that simply disgusted the audience rather than engaged it in the more psychologically complex anxiety of terror. Terror evolved from the careful construction of suspense; it disturbed by creating apprehension that something awful was *likely* to happen to characters we cared about. Also, it was more effective, or so this argument went, because it required the audience to participate intellectually, to actively create the frightening thoughts in their individual minds. In the 1940s, producer Val Lewton became a master of such suggestive effects in finely crafted movies that lacked visible monsters or on-screen violence. The issue was not censorship, though Hollywood movies were heavily censored at that time, but taste. "Terror" became a conscious aesthetic approach.

Horror, then, is seemingly distinguished by the opposite of restraint. Horror is an emotionally overwhelming form that produces not mere anxiety but revulsion, a sensation that might be literally stomach-churning: explicit scenes of gory violence and the decay of the grave paraded into view. In the sadistic German film *Mark of the Devil* [*Hexen bis aufs Blut Gequaelt*] (1970), about eighteenth-century witch-hunting, we see a young woman's tongue ripped out of her mouth by Inquisitors. Nothing is spared or left to the imagination. If terror makes us worry what might happen to a potential victim, horror shows us, it realizes our worst fears of victimization. However, the claim that the impact of graphic horror is easily achieved and inevitably less effective than a more restrained approach is not upheld by the history of the genre since the mid-1960s, where complex works from *Night of the Living Dead* and *Last House on the Left* (1972) to *The Fly* (1986) or *The Ring* (2002) combine grisly effects and unsettling themes whose dark implications outlast their shock value. True, graphic horror with little else to recommend it can be quite dull. *Mark of the Devil* is a less interesting or skillful work than an earlier one that inspired it, Michael Reeves' *Witchfinder General/Conqueror Worm* (1968). Careful writing, direction, and performance usually carry the day in a horror movie, as in any other. As I suggest in Chapter 10, John Carpenter's *Halloween* (1978) became such a popular and influential movie owing to its balance of suspense and explicit violence. Nevertheless, in the 1980s a horror sub-genre (often called "splatter movies") appeared (e.g., *Dead and Buried* [1981], *The Burning* [1981], *Scalps* [1983]), largely intended to showcase increasingly gory and spectacular illusions of dismemberment, impalement, and decomposing flesh that drew audiences largely for the craft of the makeup artist. If we simply want to see astonishing demonstrations of gross-out effects, these movies succeed, too. In any case, the genre is flexible enough to accommodate a range of possible styles.

The final distinguishing mark of the horror film I will describe pertains to its construction of a steadily growing mood of foreboding derived from the story's setting. In fact, this was the principal form and appeal of its major literary predecessor. Arising in late eighteenth-century

England, gothic fiction formed the basis for the modern horror story. So named because of their typical settings in medieval (gothic) castles, manors, or abbeys, novels such as *The Castle of Otranto* (1764), *The Mysteries of Udolpho* (1794), *The Monk* (1796), and *Melmoth the Wanderer* (1820) built their plots around restless spirits, ageless monsters, and unresolved sins of the past that reappear to bedevil modern characters. The gothic novel conventionalized many of the plots, characters, and themes still found in surprisingly similar forms in horror movies. The ghost-plagued fortress in *The Castle of Otranto*, written a decade before the American Revolution, established a dark setting to contain guilty family secrets. Castle, ghost, secrets: these gothic tropes were widely familiar by the time Edgar Allan Poe evoked them in "The Fall of the House of Usher" (1839); knowingly manipulated in Henry James' eerie psychological tale "The Jolly Corner" (1909), where the association of the dwelling's architecture and the anatomy of a disturbed mind becomes explicit; subtly parodied in Universal's *The Old Dark House* (1932); used to juxtapose a banal postwar motel with the sinister Victorian house behind it in *Psycho*; or disguised in the vicious thing stalking the dark passageways of a futuristic spaceship in *Alien* (1979). Though gothic elements grew to define Euro-American horror stories, we should not assume these settings and themes are essential or natural to such tales, not in the way that supernatural monsters or fear of the bad death seem to be. Rather, gothic imagery is both historically and culturally particular to the Western world. Horror stories from Asia, Africa, or the Middle East draw on cultural traditions for which the decaying medieval castle or shadowy Victorian manor have no strict parallel. Western societies gradually developed the gothic setting as horror's most familiar realm.

It's All in Your Mind

Like other writers on horror, I assume that the underlying irrationality of its scenarios – the certainty that this *thing* is not real, this situation could not actually occur – provides an allegorical cushion allowing us to contemplate, both intellectually and emotionally, the implications of a variety of threatening, painful, and finally individually and socially important conflicts. Critics have recalled from Greek mythology the polished shield of Perseus that permitted him to look indirectly at an awful monster, the Gorgon, and thus slay it. Freud's theories that dreams are a visually and narratively coded form of self-communication that address ongoing emotional traumas have proved perennially attractive for considering many aspects of cinema; for horror, we need only emphasize the symbols as if in a terrible nightmare, and seemingly we're off on a variety of analyses. Indeed, the nightmare analogy suggests itself because horror's realm is a profoundly nighttime world. Many horror films signal the passing of danger with the rising sun. In any case, these analogies offer explanatory possibility because while the monsters in horror stories are decidedly unreal, the implications of the stories told about them can offer insights into the material world. Here I am presenting only a few basic ideas about possible psychological ramifications of the horror film, a complicated topic further explored in other sections of this book and in the work of various critics cited in accompanying discussions.

The horror film represents a contemporary instance of an apparently universal phenomenon. As with comedy and pornography, frightful stories and images can be found in all human cultures. Moreover, these three seemingly distinct modes frequently intertwine.[6] At least since Freud's work became widely popularized around the time of World War I, audiences have taken for granted the ever more direct mixing of horror and sexuality: Count Dracula is at once seducer and murderous fiend. Yet it's hard to find a character (or characterization, especially Bela Lugosi's tuxedoed vampire) more frequently lampooned. This may suggest that humor often provides horror-film viewers with a psychological escape from on-screen terrors, an emotional defense that can be wielded as effectively as a crucifix against a vampire. Yet if horror stories existed solely to be subjected to condescending laughter, they would have disappeared long ago. Laughter in the face of something awful is likely an outward sign of other more troubled reactions. The desire to seek out terror or revulsion in the ultimately safe confines of the movies must serve certain psychological and ultimately social functions. Such questions have occupied a variety of thinkers since antiquity.

In the perennial debates about the social functions of art, Aristotle is frequently evoked in relation to his theory of catharsis, an idea that seems particularly germane to analysis of the horror film. Aristotle implied that art ought not be subject to censorship because by experiencing vicariously a range of events and emotions in an artwork – especially fear and pity – the reader/viewer was purged of the desire to act out any such natural but dangerous tendencies in the real world. For Aristotle the proper work of tragedy produced a purification (catharsis) of all such emotions for the audience, whether the resolution was "happy" or not. The individual experience of catharsis through art functioned as a social safety valve. This most traditional model generally applies to the experience and narrative trajectory of what we will call the classic horror film. Aristotle's ideas conflict with the social theory of his mentor, Plato, who so distrusted the emotionally seductive powers of drama that he argued that in the ideal republic, one of the first actions of the rulers should be to drive all the actors from the city. Plato and many later theorists and censors feared that depictions of antisocial acts and immoral behavior in art were socially dangerous because they stimulated our baser emotions and instincts rather than appealing to our higher faculties of reason and analysis. The obviously more complex ideas expressed in this simple sketch have nonetheless formed the basis for much subsequent theory, debate, and conflict over the social impact of art.

Aristotle's theory of catharsis was memorably restated in relation to horror by Stephen King:

> I like to see the most aggressive [horror films] as lifting a trapdoor in the civilized forebrain and throwing a basket of raw meat to the hungry alligators swimming around in that subterranean river beneath. Why bother? Because it keeps them from getting out, man. It keeps them down there and me up here.[7]

On the other hand, latter-day proponents of Plato's view might say the dangerous alligators ought to be killed, not fed. Such critics can be called "determinists"; that is, they argue that art can cause the acceptance, or even imitation of emotionally and socially dangerous behavior or attitudes reflected in artworks. (Behavior and attitudes – i.e., beliefs, values – are not the same, of course; and the debate often continues over these no less tricky distinctions.) Deterministic arguments have existed throughout the history of the film medium but became more acute as formal censorship waned and established social standards of all sorts underwent political challenge and change in the 1960s and 1970s. Indeed, one of the hallmarks of horror movies of those decades was an increasing tendency to deny catharsis and/or to present monstrous evil as an unstoppable force. Critics and commentators since then have given divergent interpretations of such films, as we will see.

Freud, who considered caves, cellars, and other underground realms to be metaphors for the unconscious mind itself, would have quickly grasped King's image of the subterranean river. Indeed, one must think the doctor inspired it. The many schools of Freudian criticism, both scholarly and popularized, present an important avenue into the horror film long accessible to artists, viewers, and critics. Chapter 5's discussion of *The Unknown* (1927) and Chapter 7's analysis of *Cat People* (1942) describe how filmmakers sometimes consciously introduced a Freudian framework into psychological horror. One of Freud's basic tenets was "the return of the repressed": psychosexual traumas and conflicts experienced both in childhood and as adults are never fully resolved; yet if left unrecognized or untreated such problems are bound to fester and return as neurotic symptoms, behaviors, and phobias. The gothic form is ripe for Freudian critique, as many such stories involve a guilty secret that cannot be acknowledged or reconciled. The antique and evil house is the genre's physical representation of this theme. Inside are monsters frequently described as germinated from past events, however remote. Broadening this theme to a sociopolitical critique, recent horror critics have described the genre as resonating the return of any number of actions and desires repressed by the dominant social order. The monster itself is but the most obvious manifestation of the repressed, of which the divided psyche of *Dr. Jekyll and Mr. Hyde* might be the most explicit example. The analogy between the symbolically coded nightmare and the fearful world of horror fiction is highly suggestive, regardless of how fine the application of psychoanalytic theory. A horror film may conjure private fantasies and dreads; its reception and interpretation remain a public and social phenomenon.

The Horror Film as a Genre

Though horror films may seem exceptional in some ways, for the particular kinds of villains or violence they depict, as genre movies, they share much with other story types far removed from their gloomy moods and death-dealing monsters. A genre can be simply defined as a large category of stories united by their particular settings, characters, themes, and narrative conflicts. The word comes from the same root as the words general and generic, terms meant to describe a broad category of things. A supermarket often has an aisle of lower-priced generic or "plain-label" products, commonly used items like toothpaste, cat food, and beer. Typical of capitalist consumer society, there are also numerous brand-name products that, through a combination of differing ingredients, quality of materials and manufacture, or often just differences in packaging and advertising, seek to stand out as distinct individual examples of this primary category. This is roughly the relationship between a given genre and individual movies within that form. Genre study tries to balance analysis and description of the larger, common attributes of the form with the smaller, unique aspects of individual movies.

Similarly to the Western, the combat film, the "woman's picture," or television sitcom, the horror film seems to exist in a fictional world at once highly familiar and quite removed from the everyday experience of most people. One can easily describe typical characters and problems in these genres, even though such familiar forms are still capable of originality and broad variation. Indeed, one of the crucial features of any popular genre is its ability to balance the familiar and the novel. Although an individual genre movie must stand on its own, it draws much of its meaning, effects, and inferences from its relation to other stories of its type. Good or bad, complex or simplistic, a genre movie simultaneously participates in an ongoing tradition and creates precedents for the future. As we will see, the horror film is a particularly self-reflexive form, one that often tacitly or directly references its forebears and acknowledges its place in a larger tradition, if only to invert or undercut the assumptions and expectations of those earlier works. Genre movies communicate with each other as much as with their audiences.

The particular terms that have evolved to name genres often emphasize one aspect of the form over another: The Western is identified primarily by its setting in space but the time is important, as well (the western American frontier some time in the second half of the nineteenth century). A "hospital drama" names a specific setting but is really about the occupations and roles of its typical characters – primarily doctors, nurses, and patients. A "romantic comedy" is a hybrid of those stories that either offer dramatic takes on romantic love or those meant to be funny generally. Romantic comedy will look for laughs in the difficulties a couple has getting together. Similarly, the "private detective," "gangster," or "cop" drama tells stories about crime (the central conflict) which vary in their emphasis on particular characters within that larger situation. Genre designations may be incomplete: A "musical" describes what the movie's major attraction and experience will be, the performance of songs, yet these films usually feature intricately choreographed dance as well, a genre highlight which somehow didn't make it into the genre name. Even so, it is important to pay attention to a genre name, however arbitrary it might seem. Though "gothic novel" emphasized a setting, "horror movie" stresses the emotion of fright experienced by both the characters and the audience, which remains this genre's primary distinguishing feature.

Genres usually depend upon a set of established conventions, familiar elements of these stories that filmmakers regularly include – and then try to vary while still remaining recognizable. Walter Kendrick calls this process genrefication, the gradual but steady production of assorted literary and cinematic works that establish stock characters, plots, and conflicts that producers successfully repeat and audiences soon expect to be found in particular story forms.[8] Some people disdain certain genres (or all genres) because of their ritualized sameness and predictability; more often, audiences are drawn to individual genres precisely because of these features. Multiple aspects of a genre become conventionalized: the recurrently employed settings of such tales; a constellation of character types that populate many examples of the form; in plots, obligatory and common scenes that usually appear; and fairly circumscribed dramatic and ideological conflicts that erupt in its narrative. Horror films, foremost, revolve around the monster and its threat to individual characters. The stakes are high because the struggle, as suggested above, is often not only a mortal but a metaphysical one. The horror story turns fear, whether personal or social, into a specific type of monster; and seeks to contain and destroy it.

Many examples of the vampire sub-genre, for example, are highly dependent on specific aspects of Bram Stoker's novel *Dracula* (1897). These include a discovery of the seemingly human monster by an unsuspecting person; the creature's lair in an isolated, rotting castle; the vampire's gradual draining of the blood of a virgin; a wise elder who leads the hunt for the creature; and the monster's eventual destruction by wooden stake, silver bullet, or exposure to sunlight. Dracula's (blood)lust for Lucy Westerna and Mina Harker underscores the primarily sexual nature of the threat this monster represents. Other versions of the myth flaunt their deviations from Stoker's model. In *The Lost Boys* (1987) the vampire is not one but several contemporary American teenagers, friends who gradually join the ranks of the undead. In *From Dusk Till Dawn* (1996) a veritable horde of vampires must be destroyed in an involved combat scene. In the comic parody *Love at First Bite* (1979) a Jewish doctor (Richard Benjamin) amuses Dracula (George Hamilton) by pulling out an evidently harmless Star of David to defend himself. These variations work by conscious reference to the "normal," i.e., conventionalized version of the story familiar to the audience.

Genres are also identified and vary in relation to their manipulation of particular iconography. The word literally means "picture writing" and here refers to the visual shorthand that films (or paintings, theatrical productions, etc.) muster to quickly communicate a set of meanings that have gathered around this character, object, or setting over time. This may include typical costumes, props, and locations the stories employ (cemeteries, dark castles, shadowy cellars, lonely woods, etc.) and the events that often transpire there (hesitant exploration, stalking, bloody murder). In one aspect of what Thomas Schatz calls "the feedback circuits" of genre popularity, iconography is also developed gradually through an indirect process – offerings by producers followed by acceptance or rejection by readers and viewers.[9] Gothic locales, along with their requisite shadows, cobwebs, and antique décor, constitute important horror iconography; as do the specific appearance or costuming of certain monsters, looks often derived from particular movies. The widely recognized image of the Frankenstein Monster, an icon in and of itself, comes directly from Universal's 1931 version; a child wearing a hockey mask on Halloween is dressed not as a goalie but as Jason from *Friday the 13th*. Iconography is a powerful determinant of how viewers both recognize and respond to a genre; so powerful, in fact, that filmmakers can also trick viewers by playing off such codes and conventions. Hitchcock intensified the impact of *Psycho* by spending nearly an hour convincing the audience they were watching a contemporary crime story before abruptly shifting into the iconography of gothic horror. Like genre itself, iconography is a culturally coded language system that is developed through many statements, repetitions, and variations that audiences have come to understand and accept through exposure to assorted works.

The Growth and Development of Genres

Like language itself, two intersecting axes structure genres: those aspects that remain relatively stable over time (which linguists call synchronic) and those that change and evolve (called diachronic). Major aspects of popular genres have stayed much the same over the decades but some have changed, responding to forces industrial, social, and historical. Adapting a model from art history to theorize the historical transformation of artistic styles to the analysis of movie genres, Schatz presents a taxonomy of genre evolution: the experimental, classical, refinement, and baroque phases.[10] These stages describe structural changes in both form and content within a genre. Early film adaptations from gothic or gothic-inspired literature such as Edison's *Frankenstein* (1910) or Thanhouser's *Dr. Jekyll and Mr. Hyde* (1911) mark experimental attempts to create a distinct horror genre (though the "experiment" is rarely conscious on the parts of producers at this phase) and offer some elements that will come to be conventionalized and some that won't. (This is Kendrick's genrefication process at work.) The first uses of the term "horror movie" by critics and industry commentators appeared in 1931–2 upon release of Universal's *Dracula* and *Frankenstein* and similar productions by other studios, as observers noted the arrival of something new and groped for a commonly accepted name. Indeed, they often put the term in quotation marks or referred to "so-called horror movies" to indicate their uncertainty and suspicion of the entire enterprise. Yet we now recognize that the early 1930s marked the start of the horror genre's classic phase, that in which "the conventions reach their 'equilibrium' and are mutually understood by artist and audience."[11] This phase was relatively stable; the classic period stretches into the 1960s and exerts a great influence still on films that came after.

The third stage is refinement, "during which certain formal and stylistic details embellish the form."[12] This phase involves conscious experimentation, filmmakers in search of novelty and original flourishes pushing and testing the limits of the classic conventions. In the late 1950s, Britain's Hammer Films released new color versions of *Frankenstein* (*Curse of Frankenstein* [1957]) and *Dracula* (*Horror of Dracula* [1958]) that enhanced the classic models established by Universal with greater gore, more open sexuality, and harsher tones. In Hollywood, an odd but interesting movie seemingly refined the classic conventions of two genres at once: Universal's *Curse of the Undead* (1959), despite a clear "horror-movie" title and plot involving a vampire, is actually set in the Old West; the monster is a gunslinging enforcer in the employ of a greedy cattle baron. The movie is a riot of contradictory genre icons, with scenes including a midnight visit to the vampire's coffin in a mausoleum and shootouts in the street where the "outlaw" laughs off bullets striking him in the chest. Is *Curse of the Undead* so outlandish and exceptional that it spilled over from mere refinement into what Schatz terms a genre's baroque stage?

The baroque is characterized by increasing stylistic adornment and self-consciousness in which the genre's classic conventions are sharply revised or inverted. This may extend so far as to make the genre itself, its history and conventions, the major subject of the work. A genre's baroque stage presents the classic conventions only to reject or ridicule them as inadequate, obvious, and outdated. *The Texas Chain Saw Massacre* tortures the audience as well as its characters by refusing most of the classic elements, especially the cathartic destruction of the monster. *Re-Animator* (1985) evoked the Frankenstein myth but only as a backdrop for a mix of outrageous gore and black comedy. *Scream* (1996) is about almost nothing except the often-simplistic formula of the slasher cycle of the early 1980s, including a notable scene in which a character smugly lists the trite conventions of those earlier movies. Here the classic elements have become so familiar they can no longer be considered natural but rather inevitably noticed as artificial and played out.

Although this model of genre development permits a variety of explanatory insights, it also has some problems. Its structure can seem rigid, making it difficult to account for the many subtle differences created through formal aspects of individual movies. In Chapter 6, I argue that *Frankenstein* exemplifies the classic-style horror film. However, I also suggest that crucial elements of that classicism, the climactic destruction of the monster and formation of a couple, are compromised because Dr Frankenstein seems a dubious combination of hero and monster. As such, classic should not be construed to mean either naïve or "pure." Moreover, though the model accurately describes important genre changes, it is not historically specific. While I believe horror's classic phase started in 1931 and "ended" some time in the 1960s, it is important to recognize that such phases – understood as differences in form and narrative structure rather than chronology per se – can and do overlap. Dr Van Helsing destroys his nemesis as usual at the end of *Horror of Dracula*; and the literally bloodthirsty gunman of *Curse of the Undead* also perishes. Such movies stretch the classic patterns without breaking them. The evolutionary process is not always so linear; nor is it a one-way street.

Assuming the horror genre entered its baroque phase at least thirty years ago, is it impossible now for audiences to accept a movie that largely fits the contours of the classic type? No. Such movies can be made and have been commercially successful: *The Sixth Sense* (1999) revamped an old-fashioned gothic tale and garnered Academy Award nominations. The remake of *The Texas Chain Saw Massacre* (2003) still gave us lots of gore but steadily worked to produce a cathartic and relatively "happy" ending. Since the early 1980s we have perhaps seen the start of a "neoclassical" phase of genre development. Yet we can concur with Schatz's larger idea that most genres do display "patterns of increasing self-consciousness" over time. The creation as well as comprehension of a genre is an indirect but ongoing process of communication between producers and consumers influenced by a variety of cultural and historical factors.

Since the 1980s Robin Wood has been perhaps the single most influential and insightful critic of the horror film. In his 1979 essay "An Introduction to the American Horror Film," Wood's nuanced distinction between what he terms "classical"- versus "contemporary"-style horror employs elements of formalist, Freudian, Marxist, and feminist analysis.[13]

His idea of horror's classic form is roughly equivalent to Schatz's definition, emphasizing a stable set of conventions and ideological assumptions mutually understood by producers and audiences. Wood's contemporary films, however, which he dates from the appearance of *Psycho*, subvert the norms of the classic type. Although concerned with history, Wood also considers these differences to be matters of internal structure and theme, of plot development rather than of strict chronology. More importantly, he argues that horror's classic model represents a strongly conservative tradition, which, like many other cultural and political traditions, was sharply contested in the 1960s and 1970s. For Wood, horror carries profoundly political ramifications.

As a radical social critic Wood contends that horror holds particular interest to critics of ideology because it opens a direct "pipeline to the unconscious," giving expression to that which is repressed in both individual and social circumstances. By this Wood means not only to probe horror's psychological functions but to unite these ideas with a theory of the genre's political implications. Rather than seeing classic-style horror films as somehow socially destabilizing, the fear that had always fueled calls for censorship, Wood argues they worked to uphold the status quo. He offers a fruitful beginning to analysis of the genre by applying the simple formula "Normality is threatened by the monster" to the narrative and stylistic aspects of a given film.[14] This leads to an assessment of how and what the film defines as the normal; the nature of the monster; and the specific threat it represents. However varied these terms may be, classic horror films end in a certain way: The monster is definitely destroyed in a manner that permits a sense of catharsis; and the restoration of "normality" is usually signaled through the formation (or preservation) of a heterosexual couple or family group.

By the late 1960s, Wood indicates, the most intense and aggressive horror films were more or less directly reflecting the radical momentum of the counter-culture and social liberation movements for blacks, women, and gays. This conflict can first be seen in *Psycho*'s image of monstrosity gestating within the nuclear family itself; in the resilient African-American hero of *Night of the Living Dead* assumed to be a zombie and shot down by the all-white posse at the end; with a bourgeois couple in *Last House on the Left* succumbing to the same savagery as the outcasts that killed their daughter; and as Wood and various feminists argued, in reactionary violence directed against sexually independent women in the slasher cycle of 1978–84. Wood argues that low-budget, exploitation-style horror movies carry greater progressive potential than glossy, big studio productions which are likely to be both formally and politically conservative if only because of the need to recoup far larger investments. (Both left and right condemned the low-budget slasher films.) The interest and energy were to be found at the cultural margins, not the staid mainstream. Accordingly, horror's exploitation variant is the most disdained by "respectable" arbiters of dominant taste. Lacking major stars and slick production values, with by definition only a lurid premise of sex and violence as its chief selling points, exploitation horror is the dominant ideology's id exposed and unleashed. Though again stressing the importance of narrative structure and formal style (e.g., graphic versus "tasteful" effects) over historical period, Wood's "contemporary" horror primarily describes the exploitation movies of the 1960s and 1970s ignited by the social and political strains of the Vietnam era. Still, unlike the humanistic critics of those same years who began to take horror seriously, Wood presents a way to account for and understand the "subterranean river" of ideological conflict that has always fed the genre.

Family of the Fantastic Film

It has been my observation (and experience) that many people who become seriously interested in making or studying film and television often do so through fascination at an early age with one or more of the related genres of horror, science fiction, and fantasy. I think this is because while it soon becomes apparent that the vampires, aliens, and dragons of these stories are decidedly unreal, their fascination is supplemented by increasing recognition of the art and artifice that went into their creation. Even while mundane crime stories and domestic sitcoms can still be thought "realistic," we plainly see the hand of writers, set designers, makeup artists, and visual effects technicians behind Darth Vader, Godzilla, or Freddy Krueger. And this may lead to increasing interest in film aesthetics and curiosity about the history of these genres. The common appeal of the three main branches of the fantastic film is their distance from everyday life and reality, the possibilities they open for imagination, creativity, and speculation about other lives, times, and worlds.

Though all these genres usually feature monsters, the nature of their unnatural creatures varies substantially. Yet it behooves us not to create too strict a division between these forms that might actually inhibit analysis. Initially, the variance between horror, science fiction, and fantasy can be found in relation to the narrative, and ultimately, sociopolitical nature of *power* governing their respective universes. Power can be defined simply as the ability to effect and change the world around us. While in our everyday lives we are bound by the laws of Newtonian physics, these limitations are easily overcome in the fantastic film. Though qualifications can be represented by individual works, I will call the three motives of action, the power, in the three genres by the following terms: In horror, the source of power is the supernatural; in science fiction, science and technology; in fantasy, magic. For horror, I use supernatural in the sense of the malevolent powers of the occult, or the "black arts." Horror involves instances and figures of evil, however defined, and death. In fantasy, the irrational forces I call magic are not necessarily evil or dangerous.[15]

Fantasy has its roots in two other related narrative forms, mythology and fairy tales. The latter are usually teaching stories aimed at children and touch on issues of morality and conduct yet also evoke the psycho-sexual conflicts and fears that animate the horror genre. Fairy tales are ultimately about children and parents. The strict definition of mythology is stories about the relations between men and gods. In particular this would include such ancient epics as the *Iliad*, *Odyssey*, and *Aeneid*. In mythology, incredible power is invested in the gods, though they sometimes share some of their amazing abilities with humans. One of fantasy's major branches is often called "sword and sorcery," which reveals its origins in ancient myth. In general, if a story features magic and characters wielding swords, it falls into the fantasy category. Thus the *Star Wars* saga is more closely related to fantasy than science fiction, despite the prevalence of robots and spaceships. Indeed, its central element of magic, The Force, is shown throughout to be superior to mere technology. As in the ancient epics, fantasy stories are often variations of the quest myth (e.g., *The Lord of the Rings*), or involve an incredible journey to exotic lands (*King Kong*, *The Wizard of Oz*), or even to the realm of the dead. Importantly, magic power is often neither intrinsic-ally good nor evil; much depends in these stories on how such power is used and by whom and to what ends.

Science fiction is largely a product of the Industrial Revolution and modernity. Early literary examples appear in the second half of the nineteenth century in England, France, Germany, and the United States, the most advanced industrial nations. This genre's fictional wonders are assumed to be rational and understandable by people. The Martian invaders who attack the Earth in H. G. Wells' novel *The War of the Worlds* (1898) used highly advanced science, knowledge possibly acces-sible to humans, though not just yet. The hypothetical things of science fiction are often extrapolations from known scientific principles or emerging technologies. There is no guarantee, of course, that such things will ever come to pass. Based on what science thinks now, faster than light travel, a staple of many space-faring stories is no more possible than werewolves. The key point is that science fiction postulates that such developments could occur, and if they did would come from dogged research and discovery, not divine intervention. This returns us to *Frankenstein*, long considered one of the major works of gothic fiction and central to the definition of the horror film in the early 1930s. Frankenstein's creature was born through scientific not supernatural means. The same is true of the titular scientist and his nasty alter ego in *Dr. Jekyll and Mr. Hyde*. These stories and characters have become associated with horror rather than science fiction in part because of their treatment on stage and screen, but also in relation to other factors that distinguish the two genres.

As Vivian Sobchack argues, one of the most significant differences between the dreadful creatures or events in horror versus science fiction is the site and scale of the threat. In horror the danger is personal and individual; in science fiction, social and collective, the threat rapidly expanding from the local to the global. Horror stories usually take place in remote locations (in a mountain castle, on a secluded island, at a deserted summer camp). This parallels the view of the haunted house as a metaphor for an individual human mind. Science fiction often depicts public and social spaces under threat. Thus, "The horror film deals with moral chaos, the disruption of natural order (assumed to be God's order), and the threat to the harmony of hearth and home; the SF film . . . is concerned with social chaos, the disruption of social order (man-made), and the threat to the harmony of civilized society."[16] Science fiction's origins in utopian literature and its common allegorical bent often make its social and political intentions apparent. Horror returns us to the basics of individual mortality and/or damnation. Yet the example of *Frankenstein* argues again for critical flexibility, despite the advantages of a fairly specific demarcation between these genres. Qualifications are made not for the sake of consistency but analytical open-mindedness that allow us to consider issues or experiences whether or not a particular work fits easily into a predetermined category.

CHAPTER 2

A SHORT HISTORY OF THE HORROR FILM: BEGINNINGS TO 1945

Fear has always existed, and each century has stamped upon its literature the mark of the fears that tormented it, but the primitive caveman and the contemporary businessman have not shuddered for the same reasons. The sources of fear have varied, but not fear itself, which is eternal and immutable . . .
— playwright André de Lorde, 1927[1]

Horror is universal. It has appeared in a variety of forms and media in most every human culture. What we now consider horror stories for commercial entertainment were for many centuries the stuff of religious belief and practice. In traditional cultures, demons, monsters, evil spirits, or the Devil himself were immanent and deeply feared. After the mid-eighteenth century an increasingly secularized Western culture progressively altered many of these assumptions and practices, but horror as an emotion and a form of cultural expression endures. At the end of the nineteenth century, the new motion-picture medium joined an ongoing tradition of frightening narratives that run through mythology, painting, literature, popular theater, and other cultural forms. Without suggesting a direct, linear connection between the arts of the past and the latest horror sequel playing at the multiplex, we can begin by noting the prevalence of particular images and themes in past representations that persist today.

The fear of death, acute awareness of human mortality, surely underlies every horror tale. One might choose different terms, but blending the material facts and transcendental yearnings of human life, the horror story, ancient or contemporary, typically narrates two major themes: the destruction (or preservation) of the physical body, and the damnation (or salvation) of the soul. The intertwining of these two fears, these two hopes, structures the horror tale. Notably, the predominance of the darker, more fatalistic terms of each pair virtually defines and identifies the world of horror. This may simply expose the understood but deeply denied knowledge of the inevitability of death, and the fantasy of ultimate salvation. Yet the value of struggle, the persistence of a germ of hope, however defined, is equally important in most horror stories. Though the emotional experience of horror is universal, the particular forms it assumes – especially the nature and definition of the monster, the genre's most significant character – are historically and culturally shaped.

In Christian tradition, one of the most moving scenes often chosen to decorate the interior of major cathedrals depicts the Last Judgment as described in the book of Revelation. The Judging Christ dominates the center of symmetrically divided compositions showing the ascension of the elect toward Heaven on one side; the condemnation of the damned to Hell on the other. Paradise is usually depicted as peaceful and static, a gathering of prophets, apostles, and churchmen in neat rows of orderly abstraction. Visions of Hell and the fate of the damned, however, were highly specific, violently dynamic, and recognizably human.[2] The soul's eternal damnation is rendered in perhaps the only possible terms as the hideous, excruciating torture of the physical body. The styles vary with the skills and traditions of the artists, but the message, especially when situated in the commanding form of large frescoed walls and ceilings, is clear and direct: Follow the teachings of the Church and receive eternal life or suffer unimaginable pain and mortification of the flesh forever. One of the most vivid tableaux of this type appears in huge scale beneath the enormous dome of the cathedral in Florence, where amid tortures including figures rent by chimerical beasts, the artists Vasari and Zuccari (1570s) depicted a muscular demon with a flaming pike anally impaling an unfortunate man while another demon similarly rapes a nude woman. Sexual violence such as this, whether hinted or explicit, figures in most horror narratives.

In an evident burst of macabre inspiration in 1431, Fra Angelico painted a small but detailed Last Judgment on the back panel of a wooden bench used for sung masses at the church of Santa Maria degli Angeli in Florence. With hairy, apelike demons busy at their awful work, Angelico depicts a schematic view of the pits of Hell in which consumption is the dominant motif. The uppermost segment depicts a human slaughterhouse. Naked, blood-soaked bodies hang upside down like beef carcasses, as demons feed the "meat" into the open mouth of a monstrous crocodile, blood spraying from its sharp teeth. In the bottom panel, a huge, apelike beast is devouring people, body parts dropping from its mouth as it chews, a bloody mess. In between, people boil in an iron cooking-pot above a roaring fire. A woman kneeling alongside is forced to extend her tongue to the pot's searing rim. In perhaps the most horrific scene, the damned consume each other, throttling and chewing their fellows, while one agonized man bites off his own fingers. The fates of those who committed the Seven Deadly Sins turn on consumption: Demons melt down gold coins as one pours the molten liquid into a greedy man's mouth with a dipper. Another section shows five bound men seated around a table. Gleeful demons grab the gluttons, forcing their heads into plates full of – what? Human entrails? The dark brown color of their meal suggests otherwise. These images surely reminded congregants of the importance of the Mass! As visions of horror and hopelessness they are stunning.

Gothic Literature

The foundation for the modern horror genre was laid in late eighteenth-century England when a taste for what came to be called gothic literature – stories of terror, mystery, and the supernatural – first gained relatively wide popularity. As gothic is a synonym for medieval, novels of this type became so identified because they were set in decaying castles, manors, towers, or other medieval structures. Typically an antique dwelling comprising several stories and many eerie rooms, the foreboding castle of gothic fiction became the haunted house of countless pulp romances and Hollywood B movies. (As late as 1976, interior design of the protagonist's grim frame house in Brian De Palma's *Carrie* included an otherwise incongruous row of pointed archways, a characteristic feature of medieval architecture.) Important gothic novels included Horace Walpole's *The Castle of Otranto* (1764), often considered the classic work that defined the form; Matthew Gregory Lewis's *The Monk* (1796), which contains grotesque scenes of physical degradation that can still provoke revulsion; and *A Sicilian Romance* (1790), *The Mysteries of Udolpho* (1794), and others by the prolific Ann Radcliffe. Edgar Allan Poe entered American literature in the mid-nineteenth century as an author of somber poetry and macabre short stories built on the gothic tradition.

A gothic tale is foremost a story that intends to frighten or unnerve the reader and does so through evocation of ominous atmosphere and supernatural threats. England's vogue for gothic literature coincided with the turmoil of the American Revolution and the more radical French Revolution. This was a time of change, upheaval, and uncertainty. In an increasingly secular and skeptical age, gothic literature insisted that the religious and pagan mysteries of the past were not as easily rejected or vanquished as rationalists believed. Sometimes in gothic literature apparently supernatural events may be exposed as hoaxes or misunderstandings, given rational explanation. In this the gothic tale was also a forerunner of detective fiction. (Poe wrote several stories of this type such as "The Purloined Letter" [1845] that solidified the detective genre.) But the classic gothic tale maintains a commitment to irrationality and the fantastic. Demons, ghosts, and vampires are understood to be "real" within its fictional world. Crucially, eroticism and fear intermingle in gothic stories. The gothic villain is usually a violent, sexually predatory male. He may or may not have supernatural abilities (Ambrosio, the title character of *The Monk*, sold his soul to the Devil for such power), but his threat of sexual violence against women and weaker males remains.

The symbolic importance of architecture in gothic tales cannot be overstated. Foremost, placing modern characters within the walls of a medieval edifice signifies a clash between the present and dark secrets of the past. Indeed, the gothic plot is characterized in large part by the violent eruption of an unresolved or irreconcilable past of which the haunted castle is the concrete symbol. As such, the ghost is the gothic threat *par excellence* – the restless spirit of a victim or villain from long ago. Gothic manors or haunted abbeys were also signs of class conflicts, identified with the arbitrary power and dangers of corrupt nobility, hypocritical religious authority, or rapacious plutocrats. Calling the castle "a multivalent symbol" in gothic tales, that is, one with multiple and complex meanings, Valdine Clemens argues that the castle

> may be associated with the maternal or the sexual body, the human psyche, or the patriarchal social order. The dark tunnels and underground passages of Gothic edifices represent descent into the unconscious, away from the socially constructed self and toward the uncivilized, the primitive. Violence, pursuit, and rape occur in these lower depths, yet they are also the realms where valuable discoveries are made.[3]

Most of these elements appear in Walpole's *The Castle of Otranto*, whose villains are Prince Manfred, a wicked nobleman, and his wife Hippolita. Their son was betrothed to a young woman, Isabella, but died in mysterious circumstances after being crushed by a huge helmet. Manfred now lusts after Isabella. After repeated manifestations by the ghost of the castle's original owner, the novel climaxes with Manfred's pursuit of the frightened woman through the castle's lower recesses, during which he mistakenly stabs to death his own daughter, Matilda. Isabella finally marries Theodore, a nobleman who has been helping her, and from whose family Manfred had stolen the castle and title years before. Repentant and in despair over the deaths of their children, Manfred and Hippolita depart, leaving the estate to the deserving young couple. Isabella's role is typical in that women are frequently the central characters of gothic fiction, much of it not only read by women but also written by female authors. Clemens claims: "One aspect of the ritual of descent in gothic fiction that undoubtedly appealed to women readers of the day was its suggestion that the above-ground, or conscious, public version of reality is incomplete; if one dares to venture into the strange and uncanny world below the surface, one finds a different story."[4]

In the finale of *The Castle of Otranto* the ghost makes the castle walls collapse. The destruction of the dark house often climaxes gothic fiction, as in Poe's "The Fall of the House of Usher" (1839), where it splits and sinks into a bog; and continues in a variety of twentieth-century writing, including the fire that engulfs the haunted manor in William Faulkner's modernist novel *Absalom, Absalom!* (1936), a work laden with gothic motifs; the inferno closing Daphne Du Maurier's bestseller *Rebecca* (1938), vividly realized in Alfred Hitchcock's 1940 movie version; or the finale of *Carrie*, in which the heroine's house implodes and disappears into the earth. So many horror stories end with survivors fleeing a collapsing, burning, exploding, or sinking gothic structure that it became one of the most characteristic images (and common clichés) of the genre. The catastrophic finale may mark liberation from the injustices, debaucheries, and crushing guilt of the past. Destruction of the evil edifice may not necessarily portend catharsis, however, the triumph of some universal justice. Characters may emerge alive but chastened, even shattered such that the story conveys an impression that the horror has only been transferred to a new locale, the psyches of the survivors. In any case, there is little doubt the experience has taught them important truths about nature, society, and human destiny. This need not be merely an affirmation of staid traditional values but an opportunity to challenge them and remake the world. Gothic narratives involve both a descent and a return.

Terrible Trio

Three key cultural antecedents of the horror film emerged from gothic literature in nineteenth-century English novels that not only found contemporary fame but also formed the basis for much of the genre's popular development in the following century's mass culture. If the impact of books like *The Castle of Otranto* persists primarily through example, Mary Wollstonecraft Shelley's *Frankenstein, or The Modern Prometheus* (1818), Robert Louis Stevenson's *The Strange Case of Dr. Jekyll and Mr. Hyde* (1886), and Bram Stoker's *Dracula* (1897) established iconic characters that gave modern context to ancient myths. These tales have since proved highly adaptable to evolving historical trends. Various critics have argued that these three figures represent *the* major archetypes of modern horror, going so far to suggest that most popular horror tales can be considered variations on one of these enduring stories. Novelist Stephen King claimed "the Vampire, the Werewolf, and the Thing Without a Name [i.e., the Frankenstein monster] . . . stand at the foundation of a huge skyscraper of books and films – those twentieth-century gothics . . . known as 'the modern horror story.'"[5] James B. Twitchell's *Dreadful Pleasures* devotes a separate chapter to each character, titling one "Dr. Jekyll and Mr. Wolfman" to emphasize the basic similarity of the man–into–beast pattern in the werewolf myth and Stevenson's book.[6] Moreover, later adaptations sometimes intertwine the themes and narrative situations of the different icons. David J. Skal calls them the "shape-shifting entities that move in the modern imagination like dream carvings on a dark carousel . . . if one looks long enough, one monster eventually blurs into another."[7]

Further discussion of these novels, their varied adaptations, and changing thematic implications will continue below and in other chapters of this book. As we will see in numerous examples, however, it is precisely in particular variations from the original story – in setting, style, tone, or emphasis on some motifs at the expense of others – that the analytical interest may lie. However, the basic themes of each work can be stated briefly here.

Frankenstein considers the moral, philosophical, and ultimately social implications of increasing human mastery of the natural world, extending here to speculation about the consequences of man usurping the powers of God or nature in the creation of life itself. Despite common confusion, the title of Shelley's novel refers to the doctor, not his monster; its subtitle, *The Modern Prometheus*, compares Dr Frankenstein to the Titan of Greek mythology who stole fire from Mount Olympus for the benefit of mankind but was punished by Zeus with endless torture for his affront. The impact of a story about a scientist who creates an artificial being that then runs amok was bound to increase through the nineteenth and twentieth centuries, as it contemplates the responsibilities, limits, and potential costs of advancing scientific and industrial technology.

The double remains a persistent theme of horror literature. *Dr. Jekyll and Mr. Hyde* is now the most famous version of the literary figure called in German the *Doppelgänger*, literally, "double-walker," but meaningfully translated as dark alter ego. Stevenson's monster expresses the lustful, cruel, and violent side of Jekyll's nature that the proper Victorian gentleman wishes to *hide* from public view. The figure of the divided self, which both predates and exceeds the limits of Stevenson's novel, has variously been described in terms of simple morality (tendencies toward good or evil); in evolutionary language as a conflict between our human and animal natures, though invested in premodern times with supernatural fear; or, through most of the twentieth century, explained by increasingly psychological, especially Freudianized, conceptions.

The vampire is by far the most sexually charged of the major archetypes (though all contain important psychosexual implications). Dracula is not just a murderous fiend but a seducer who appears in the bedrooms of young virgins at midnight, embraces them, and sucks their blood, leaving them limp yet eager to invite him back the following night. The vampire's deadly kiss, a source of both pleasure and fear focused on oral eroticism, calls forth a variety of sexual interpretations. The vampire is also the most unabashedly supernatural, which is to say, ancient myth. Appearing at the end of the rationalist nineteenth century, *Dracula* pits the monster against a team of young investigators led by a wise scientist, Dr Van Helsing, such that modern and archaic beliefs collide. Moreover, Dracula's bite is both toxic and contagious; his victims become vampires too, the curse threatening to spread like a plague. Later commentators suggest Stoker's novel expressed a racist fear (mixed with guilt) that Imperial Britain might succumb to a "reverse colonization" by foreign cultures.[8] As powerfully fixed as the Dracula character became, the vampire may be the most malleable of the three horror archetypes.

Georges Méliès and the "Trick Film"

No nation or individual can accurately claim the sole invention of motion pictures, not even Thomas Edison, who is often credited. Though technicians under Edison's direction made major advances in 1891–4, the development of motion-picture technology was a truly international phenomenon. Working independently with varying approaches, inventors in the United States, Britain, France, and Germany all made important technical breakthroughs at about the same time. Edison demonstrated an individual viewing device for film loops, called the Kinetoscope, in 1894. In France, however, Auguste and Louis Lumière, operators of a photographic manufacturing business, made crucial strides in the development of projected motion pictures, exhibiting short films shot on their Cinématographe camera/projector system to a paying crowd for the first time in Paris on December 28, 1895.

Present in the Lumière audience by special invitation the night before was a prosperous stage magician named Georges Méliès, the owner and principal performer at *Le Théâtre Robert-Houdin*, a house that featured assorted magic acts and illusions of great sophistication. An experienced showman and illusionist who had used magic lanterns (optical slide projectors) in his act for years, Méliès immediately grasped a different potential for the new medium beyond its ability to capture and record the space and time of everyday reality – an accomplishment sufficiently astounding in itself, at least initially. Instead, he sought the camera's ability to distort and transform reality, stopping and starting time and motion at will, manipulating physical space in heretofore undreamed of ways in conjunction with techniques of stage magic.

Beginning in 1896, Méliès led a troupe of actors and technicians in a large glass-enclosed studio on the outskirts of Paris in the production of over 500 short films, most in the category of what were soon called "trick films": those that combined stop-camera substitution effects with careful editing, double exposures, superimpositions, or other photographic effects to create instantaneous materializations or disappearances, sudden transformations, and other impossible occurrences. Méliès also built miniature models and marshaled the full range of stage technique including elaborate props, costumes, makeup, and pyrotechnics, all arrayed before ornate theatrical backdrops and settings to create fantastic self-contained worlds. His intricate multi-scene production *The Impossible Voyage* [*Voyage á travers l'impossible*] (1904) contains all these techniques. Sales catalogs issued by early producers called such films by different names – tricks, magical, mysterious, ghostly, etc. – testifying to both the genre's popularity and its association with the fantastic. Motivation for trick effects was ascribed to acts of supernatural beings, wizardry, nightmares, or pure whimsy. Méliès was not the first to realize these potentials of the motion-picture camera. Indeed, transformation illusions had been possible even earlier, using magic-lantern projectors in tandem. But because of his methodical exploration of innumerable trick effects in hundreds of short films, Georges Méliès is rightly considered the most creative and influential pioneer of cinematic sleight of hand, the father of special effects in the fantasy film.[9]

Borrowing a metaphor derived from the circus or carnival, film historian Tom Gunning coined the term "the cinema of attractions" to describe the dominant style of films produced in the medium's earliest phase, roughly 1894 to 1907.[10] In this period, movies were not conceived primarily as a storytelling medium. Rather, in their conception and exhibition to audiences, early films were more like the discrete, unconnected acts in a three-ring circus or the assorted games, rides, shows, and other attractions on a carnival midway. A program of several short (one-shot) films typically made up a performance, which might include slapstick comedy, filmed vaudeville acts, coverage (or reenactments) of recent news events, and trick films. The miraculous transformations or mischief of fairies and imps were the self-sufficient "attractions" in Méliès's films, regardless of narrative motivation. Trick films were not intended to horrify as much as astonish and amuse the viewer with images of absurd or physically impossible events. Yet from Méliès forward, horror, science fiction, and fantasy cinema has remained heavily dependent on the orchestration of spectacle alone, the display of visual effects, whether wondrous or repulsive, for their own sake. Such is their very reason for existence in the motion-picture medium, perhaps more so than for any other genre.

The "haunted hotel" plot, often performed in nineteenth-century magic shows, was a popular subject reworked many times by Méliès and others. Most follow the plot of a guest shown to a room, his nocturnal torment by ghosts or enchanted objects, and subsequent eviction for making too much noise. Méliès made this the subject of one of his earliest films, *A Terrible Night* [*Une nuit terrible*] (1896), in which common bedbugs pester the hotel guest but the tortures quickly became less mundane, as indicated in the title of *The Bewitched Inn* [*L'Auberge Ensorcelée*] (1897). The ambiguity between the waking world and the dream was often evoked in such films including *The Inn Where No Man Rests* [*L'Auberge du bon repos*] (1903), in which a traveler's boots walk up the wall after he retires; and *The Apparition* [*Le Revenant*] (1903), where an elderly guest (Méliès) tries to read a newspaper by the light from a candlestick that keeps moving away from him. When it slides across the table and sets fire to his newspaper, he jumps up to fight the blaze, only to see a beautiful woman appear in the flames. The old man begs for her favors but, via double exposure, she turns into a shimmering ghost. He leaps at the specter but only tackles the maid delivering a tea tray, resulting in the usual ejection. This play with illusion and reality, eroticism and death underpins the horror/fantasy film throughout its history.[11]

Illustrating the common convergence of fantasy formulas, Méliès often appeared not only as a stage magician but alternately as a scientist, wizard, or even Mephistopheles, the devil from the Faust legend that he portrayed several times. Weirdness ensues again when the alchemist Méliès plays in *The Mysterious Retort* [*L'Alchimiste Parafaragaramus ou la Cornue infernale*] (1906) falls asleep in his laboratory beside a large glass retort. While he dreams, a prop serpent crawls out and transforms into the Devil. He expands the retort to great size, within which we see an almost surreal spider with a manlike head leering from a web, until another beautiful woman materializes. The retort begins spraying sparks that yield a floating phantom. At this, the alchemist awakens but then collapses in fright as the retort explodes. When his assistants try to rouse him, the Devil appears on a flaming throne and scares them away, coming to stand in triumph over the supine alchemist. Many dream-motivated trick films conclude with a startled awakening. This one suggests a deathly image, of ancient evil crushing scientific ambition.

In 1902, Méliès released his longest and most ambitious trick film to date, *A Trip to the Moon* [*Voyage dans la lune*], the first science-fiction film, and one of the single most influential works in the medium's history. Méliès plays a scientist who conceives the first journey to outer space, supervising the construction of a bullet-shaped capsule that is fired from an immense cannon. For one of the most famous images in screen history, Méliès cast an actor as "the man in the moon," the planet imagined as a cream-pie face shown blinking and smiling in close-up. Méliès depicts the lunar landing as the capsule splatting into one eye. In the first of innumerable cinematic clashes between humans and hostile aliens, the space travelers are attacked by the Selenites, crustacean-insect creatures played by costumed acrobats who bound and somersault all over the scene. Taken to the hall of the Selenite king, Méliès breaks free and hurls down the king, who explodes in a burst of smoke. The astronauts escape and board the capsule, as the pursuing Selenites knock it over the edge of a cliff, sending it hurtling back to Earth. Landing in the ocean, a passing ship rescues the crew and takes them home to be lauded with the dedication of a statue to their achievement.[12]

In loosely adapting a novel by fantasy author Jules Verne, Méliès again primarily considered creating opportunities to display his trick effects. But other filmmakers, in a time of intense competition and rapid stylistic change, grasped something else in this widely screened, often illegally duplicated and stolen film – a continuous, sophisticated narrative running over 12 minutes in 16 scenes. The important American filmmaker Edwin S. Porter (*The Great Train Robbery* [1903]) later explained: "From laboratory examination of some of the popular films of . . . Georges Méliès – trick films like *A Trip To the Moon* – I came to the conclusion that a picture telling a story in continuity form might draw customers back to the theaters and set to work in this direction."[13] Porter's output for the Edison Company included the Méliès-inspired *The Dream of a Rarebit Fiend* (1906), in which a man's late-night ingestion of heavy food and drink sparks a seriocomic nightmare, including tiny demons who attack his head with picks and a nocturnal flight across the roofs of the city as he clings to his soaring bed.

Méliès's business began to decline after 1910, by which time the stylistic and industrial practices of motion pictures had changed substantially, even though his painstaking, artisanal mode of filmmaking had not. One of his last productions, *The Conquest of the Pole* [*À la conquête du pôle*] (1912), although a characteristically delightful film, was not significantly different in story or technique from *A Trip to the Moon*. Here international teams of explorers in wondrous flying machines vie to reach the North Pole. Méliès and his group must confront "the Snow Giant," a shaggy, pipe-smoking polar monster. Realized through a large mechanical puppet, the creature rises from the icy ocean and gobbles up several men. A few gunshots and firebombs cause the monster to spit out his victims and return to the frigid depths, and the explorers return home in triumph. The ultimate triumph of Méliès himself would be posthumous. After losing his company, the magician suffered more financial reversals and disappeared, though not before angrily destroying his stock of film prints and original negatives. (Thanks to the diligent work of international film archives, about 175 Méliès titles survive today.) Méliès and his work enjoyed a brief rediscovery and celebration around 1930, but he ended his life selling candy and toys from a stand in a Paris train station. Still, his contributions to cinema are great and enduring. His tomb reads simply: "Georges Méliès, creator of cinematic fantasies."

The Grand Guignol Theater

At almost the same time Méliès began making motion pictures, the Montmartre district of Paris saw the opening of one of the most bizarre and unique theaters in history. While Méliès produced fantasy films to showcase visual tricks, *Le Théâtre du Grand Guignol* staged hundreds of one-act plays devoted to tales of terror, insanity, and murder. The special technical feature, the major "attraction" of the Grand Guignol, was its realistic presentation of shockingly graphic mutilations, eviscerations, stabbings, beheadings, electrocutions, hangings, rapes, and other atrocious acts performed live on stage. The sadistic and bloody plays produced at the Grand Guignol from 1897 until its closing in 1962 established important precedents for popular horror entertainment that took the cinema many years to match. Under the guidance of its second and more important owner, Max Maurey, the theater's reputation and fame spread internationally, attracting a variety of curious patrons including European royalty and other celebrities. The phrase *grand guignol* is still commonly used to describe particularly graphic horror in the arts.

The Grand Guignol was founded by playwright Oscar Metenier, who had helped develop the *Théâtre Libre* in the 1880s, an experimental theater catering to lower-class patrons that produced so-called *rosse* (or "crass") plays set in the Parisian underworld, works influenced by the new aesthetic style of naturalism propounded by novelist Émile Zola. *Rosse* plays were often based on tabloid newspaper reports called *faits divers*, brief items that reported lurid accounts of violent and unusual occurrences. Unlike popular melodramas, which depicted innocent lower-class people victimized by ruthless upper-class villains, but which usually ended happily, *rosse* plays featured darkly ironic conclusions that not only mocked middle-class life and mores, but flaunted the triumph of injustice, cruelty, and lust. As theater historian Mel Gordon contends, "Here, none of the normative values of French society – good and evil, simple 'right and wrong', the hierarchy of one class over another – existed. Nothing *had* to happen in a *rosse* play. Any conclusion was possible. Naturally, these amoral and unsettling naturalistic dramas proved to annoy the pundits of establishment mores."[14]

The Grand Guignol would embellish this thematic and aesthetic strategy. Metenier took the name of his new theater from the medieval puppet character called Guignol, a rough peasant type usually featured in violent, slapstick comedy. By the nineteenth century, "guignol" had become a synonym for puppet shows of all kinds, so by inference, Metenier's theater would feature "grand," or large, guignol plays, that is, aimed at adult audiences and featuring live performers. In order to maximize emotional manipulation of the audience during the evening, the terror plays were alternated with comedy, usually sex farces. The technique was referred to as "hot and cold showers," the idea being that one intensified the other.

The success of Max Maurey's odd theater was due in part to his keen handling of publicity. Reports of patrons vomiting or fainting during performances were prominent in popular press accounts and in the word-of-mouth lore of the theater, reports whose veracity remain difficult to assess. For example, one of the major human taboos, the gouging out or cutting of eyes, is still rarely enacted in popular horror movies, even those awash with gory effects. Yet eye mutilation was frequently a climactic shock-effect in Grand Guignol plays. This, coupled with other intricate effects of facial disfigurement, burnings, and torture, carefully rehearsed and skillfully executed by actors on stage, may well have produced physical as well as emotional revulsion in the audience, especially when presented in a context of dramatic irony where innocent people suffered punishment from amoral forces of fate, chance, or insanity. Some Guignol plays ended with a rough poetic justice, but others seemingly staged the narrative as an excuse for shock effects.[15] *A Crime in the Madhouse* (1925) depicts female mental patients almost pointlessly mutilating each other. A wrongly hospitalized woman has her eyes gouged out by other patients who fear she has a cuckoo hiding behind her face. Then one of the attackers forces another's face onto a searing hotplate that melts it into blackened goo.

André de Lorde was the most prominent figure associated with the Grand Guignol, writing or co-writing over one hundred plays for the theater, many among its most popular, some repeatedly staged in repertoire for decades. De Lorde's plays defined the theater's typical fare: *The Dead Child* (1918) concerns a man who discovers that, in his absence, his wife has left him for another man and abandoned their baby to die. The father steals the baby's bones, hair, and nails from the grave and creates a wax mannequin of the child, forcing his wife to cradle it in her arms before he strangles her. Surgical settings were often used to motivate amputations, ill-fated transplants, and other medical atrocities. In *The Horrible Experiment* (1909), a doctor resurrects his betrothed with electrical apparatus after her death in an auto accident but the ferociously reenergized body arises and strangles him.

De Lorde's *At the Telephone* [*Au téléphone*], written with Charles Foley in 1902, contains no visceral effects but was one of the Grand Guignol's most popular and influential plays. Marex, a prosperous businessman, has moved his household to a country estate. On a stormy night when he leaves on business to stay with friends, he receives frantic calls from his wife, who hears tramps breaking into the house. Marex must listen in impotent terror to the screams of his wife, child, and elderly servant being strangled by the intruders. The end! *At the Telephone* prompted several movie adaptations, including one of the most celebrated works in traditional film history, D. W. Griffith's *The Lonely Villa*, produced for the Biograph Company in 1909. The film's climax cuts between the besieged wife and children barricading doors against the robbers while the desperate father and policemen race to the rescue by wagon. Will they arrive in time? Yes, Griffith's bourgeois family is saved when the good guys burst in and subdue the attackers. Not so in de Lorde, where the father's utter helplessness as he listens over the telephone to his family's slaughter ends the play. The contrasts between these two versions are instructive in their respective treatments of class distinctions as well as traditional morality. The primarily working-class patrons of the Grand Guignol could be horrified but perhaps also secretly thrilled that a bourgeois gentleman pays for an elegant evening with the lives of his loved ones. Griffith's movie, made for a growing industry that was actively courting a "respectable" middle-class clientele, ends with the sanctity of the family upheld by the forces of patriarchy and the law. One is melodramatic suspense that affirms dominant values; the other a horror vignette that thwarts those very assumptions.

The Grand Guignol made a certain impact on the horror film, though its influence was neither immediate nor direct. The prolific André de Lorde wrote several movie scripts in the 1910s that drew on his association with the theater, including his adaptation of Poe's *The System of Dr. TarrTarr and Professor Fether* [*Le Système du Docteur Goudron et du Professeur Plume*] (1912). Evidence of exchanges between this peculiar theater and the movie industry appeared in de Lorde's 1925 adaptation of the seminal German horror film, *The Cabinet of Dr. Caligari* (1920), for the Grand Guignol stage; and in MGM's *Mad Love* (1935), part of Hollywood's Depression horror cycle, which opens with the villain attending a performance of a theater of horrors clearly modeled on the popular Parisian attraction. The Grand Guignol's method of intense visceral shocks and disturbing amorality would not be fully adopted by Hollywood horror films until after the end of formal censorship in 1968.

Nickelodeon Nightmares, 1908–14

Increasingly after 1904, story films became the major product of film producers internationally. The years from approximately 1906 to 1914 are marked as the "Nickelodeon" (nickel theater) era because the period witnessed the rapid proliferation of hundreds of cramped, storefront theaters exhibiting programs of short narrative films to eager patrons seated in straight-backed chairs. Since most nickelodeons played at least two films on each bill and changed programs two or three times weekly, an insatiable demand for new product now drove the industry. Even so, few films we would consider horror/fantasy were screened in the nickelodeon period. Conceptually, the horror genre itself did not yet exist in the way we now think of it, despite precedents in literature, theater, and early film. One would only develop gradually as the industry changed in the 1910s.

Walter Kendrick's notion of the genrefication process stresses how a new category evolves through repetition and variation of similar story types as authors, playwrights, painters, and later, filmmakers draw on a variety of sources each of which is itself influenced by those other works being created around it. Early contributions to popular horror came from gothic fiction, notably Poe's short stories, or more typically, now obscure work published in mass-circulation magazines. Various theatrical adaptations of *Frankenstein* and *Dr. Jekyll and Mr. Hyde* presented these characters in alternative forms even before the advent of motion pictures. The trick films of Méliès provided a method and certain themes to the development of such a movie genre, as did the Grand Guignol, whose vivid displays of gore assaulted its audience with shock. Yet plays successful with middle-class audiences remained a common source of movie fare at a time when live theater of all sorts was more prominent in the cultural experience of average people than it is now. Examples of screen horror that appeared in the nickelodeon era were often derived from literature via the stage.

Adaptation of well-known literary and dramatic properties not only provided a hook for movie versions; it surrounded a new and socially suspect entertainment medium with the sheen of genteel culture. Producers were cautious about fright tales and shock effects because the nickelodeon boom precipitated growing social anxiety and censorship owing to adverse effects on women and children that habitual moviegoing allegedly promoted.[16] It was in this context that director J. Searle Dawley, working for the Edison Company, produced the first film version of *Frankenstein* in 1910.[17] Edison publicity emphasized that it had "carefully tried to eliminate all the actually repulsive situations and to concentrate . . . upon the mystic and psychological problems that are to be found in this weird tale. Whenever . . . the film differs from the original story it is purely with the idea of eliminating what would be repulsive to a moving picture audience."[18] The 15-minute film starred Augustus Phillips as the Doctor and Charles Ogle as his artificial creature.

The first *Frankenstein* film may draw our attention today primarily because of the enduring impact of the 1931 version starring Boris Karloff, but it remains an interesting production in its own right. Dr Frankenstein is a young medical student who dreams of creating "the most perfect human being the world has yet known." The film follows Shelley's tale by intermingling Frankenstein's work with his impending marriage, directly contrasting notions of natural versus "unnatural" pro-creation. Shelley throws away the creation scene, which nonetheless became the central image of movie versions. Here the monster is gestated in a vat of bubbling chemicals. Through a series of dissolves, we see the creature's bony outline slowly form and emerge from the cauldron. Ogle's appearance as the monster is still striking – a tall, skeletal frame with improbably broad shoulders, elongated fingers, and head topped by a mane of wild hair. Thin legs and heavy feet give it the look of an animated scarecrow.

Edison's claim that its telling of *Frankenstein* emphasized the story's "mystic and psychological problems" is notable. Despite popular con-fusion, Mary Shelley's title refers not to the monster but to its creator. Yet Dawley's *Frankenstein* conceived the monster as a projection of the doctor's own dark psychological drives through repeated use of mirror reflections, a motif that would appear again and again in the horror genre. After its creation, the monster's next appearance begins with the doctor catching sight of it in a mirror while reading in his library. It sees its own reflection and flees in revulsion, but later returns to threaten Frankenstein's bride, Elizabeth. When the doctor fights to protect her, a title says this demonstrates his choice of the wife over the artificial man. In the climax the monster opens his hands beseechingly to his creator (a gesture Karloff would imbue with great pathos in the classic version) while reflected full-figure in a mirror. Rebuffed, the creature itself slowly fades away. Frankenstein looks in the mirror as the monster's lingering reflection is gradually replaced by his own. This visual con-ception of the creature as the doctor's doppelgänger marks this surpris-ingly sophisticated film's most engaging contribution to the Frankenstein myth.[19]

Chicago's Selig Polyscope Company filmed the first *Dr. Jekyll and Mr. Hyde* in 1908. Screen versions were numerous in the 1910s, with more than a dozen produced on both sides of the Atlantic. Thanhouser's 1911 adaptation starred James Cruze as Jekyll and Henry Benham as Hyde, evidently the only time two different actors played the parts. Like Selig's, this version was modeled on a 1904 American play. Universal's 1913 rendition with King Baggot was an important early success for the rising studio. The trend climaxed with two ambitious Hollywood feature productions in 1920, the most famous made by Paramount, starring John Barrymore.[20] Brian A. Rose argues that across more than a century of adaptation, the double personality of Stevenson's 1886 novel was initially treated as a moral allegory, then gradually given over to psychological interpretation, the latter emphasis becoming dominant after 1920.[21] Despite the novel's gothic trappings, adaptations of *Dr. Jekyll and Mr. Hyde* also chart evolving social attitudes about the efficacy of science, which, for example, became much more pessimistic and fearful following World War II.

The 1911 Thanhouser film begins with a medical text stating the tale's basic elements: "The taking of certain drugs can separate man into two beings – one representing evil, the other good." The transformation is accomplished simply through stop-camera substitution and dissolves the first time, or thereafter, via brief cutaways to other locations, after which Hyde appears. While Cruze's Dr Jekyll is a distinguished young man with light hair, Benham's fanged Mr Hyde is depicted with a tangle of shaggy black hair and dark eyes, walking with the stooped gait of an ape. The conception of Hyde as bestial primitive remains so basic to the popular iconography that Spencer Tracy's decision (1941) to play the role on screen with little makeup became a showy exception that proved the rule.

In thematic parallel to *Frankenstein*, Stevenson's novel concerns a scientist who loses control of his experiment with tragic personal consequences. Although female characters are not significant in the book, women figure prominently in film adaptations of *Jekyll and Hyde* after the example of two successful plays staged in 1887 (British) and 1904 (American). These versions further paralleled *Frankenstein* as Jekyll's impending marriage became a major plot thread in adaptations between 1887 and 1920, when the story was reconfigured as a domestic melodrama.[22] As in most traditional horror tales, the monster threatens the family, the most basic social institution. Thanhouser included a discrete rendering of the shocking episode that opens Stevenson's book in which Hyde coldly tramples a child in the street, as direct an attack on "family values" as one could imagine. Here the good Doctor's fiancée is the prim daughter of a minister; later versions would add the figure of a prostitute Hyde terrorizes, restating the ancient virgin/whore dichotomy, which echoes the doubling of the male protagonist. The experiment and Jekyll's love life converge when, after several ingestions of the formula, Hyde begins to manifest spontaneously. Jekyll courts his beloved on a park bench, yet when he is compelled to leave and return as Hyde, he lustfully grabs at her. When her father comes to her aid, the monster clubs him to death. Finally, with no more transforming potion available and the police at the door of his lab, Hyde gulps poison and dies without physically returning to his better self, implicitly the final punishment for sinful acts in a clear moral fable.

The steady transition from moral to psychological themes in the *Jekyll and Hyde* story as well as in other proto-horror films attended the crystallization of a distinct film genre. An illustration of this shift can be found in D. W. Griffith's *The Avenging Conscience* (Mutual, 1914), made by one of the emerging Hollywood industry's leading directors as producers were starting to increase the length of feature films to around one hour or longer. *The Avenging Conscience* related a plot familiar in the realm of popular melodramas but deepened the characterization of its protagonist by drawing on the repertoire of visual effects explored in trick films to depict his growing madness. A young man's (Henry B. Walthall) passion for a woman he nicknames Annabel after the idealized love in Poe's poem "Annabel Lee" is thwarted by the opposition of his rich, doting uncle. After reading "The Tell-Tale Heart" and observing natural scenes in which a spider devours a fly trapped in its web and swarming ants dismember the struggling spider, he plots to murder his uncle. Griffith obtained startling shots of the battle for life in the natural world abstracted into symbolic inspiration for the nephew's murderous anger.

The film adapts motifs from "The Tell-Tale Heart," starting with the uncle's black eyepatch, analogous to the old man with one dead "vulture eye" that Poe's mad narrator comes to fear. After killing his benefactor and walling up the body in the fireplace, the nephew is grilled by a suspicious detective in a manner derived from the central scene of Poe's story. The "tell-tale heart" is of course the murderer's own, not his victim's, that the narrator hears pounding in his head until he is driven to confess. Griffith creates visual correlatives for the aural hallucinations to impart the nephew's increasingly frantic, psychologically subjective perceptions. Stylized closeups of the detective's penetrating stare intercut with shots of a hooting owl and the nephew's nervously twisting fingers portray the torment of his "avenging conscience." Shots of a clock's swinging pendulum intensify his agitation, while the inspector's impatiently tapping foot and pencil rapping on a table substitute for "the beating of his hideous heart" that deranges Poe's narrator. The nephew sees his uncle's vengeful ghost emerge from its makeshift tomb and is seized by visions of half-animal demons and a skeleton's embrace. "I heard many things in Hell," reads a title card, quoting Poe.

Fully mad after confessing, the young man flees, is tracked by a posse and hangs himself to avoid capture, after which Annabel hurls herself over a cliff. Yet in an ending Griffith seemingly meant to deliver a stern moral warning but which is bound to disappoint contemporary viewers, the nephew abruptly awakens in his study to find the uncle busy at his ledgers, and the dreadful experience only a nightmare. Everyone quickly becomes reconciled and the film ends happily in the melodramatic manner. Still, Griffith and other filmmakers of the nickelodeon and early features period had made important inroads into the constitution of a distinct horror genre by yoking the discrete fantasy effects of the "cinema of attractions" to emotionally involving narratives that developed literary sources of the past into particularly cinematic expressions of terror.

German Expressionism in the 1920s

High on the cliffs of a steep volcanic crag in central Italy sits the small town of Orvieto. Thriving since the Middle Ages, Orvieto has long been famous for its spectacular Late Gothic cathedral, white wine, and decorative ceramics. When Italy entered World War I on the side of the Allies in May, 1915 the official population of Orvieto and its surrounding municipal district was 19,242. When the fighting ended less than four years later, 490 men from Orvieto were dead. Of these, 54 were missing in action, their bodies never recovered. Of the 490 dead, 419 were lifelong residents of the town.[23] The effects on every aspect of life in a small, tightknit community of losing nearly 500 fathers, sons, brothers, and friends cannot be easily cataloged, but one must assume they were profound. Orvieto's catastrophe was repeated and multiplied in greater or lesser proportions all over Europe and parts of the Middle East. The American toll in the war, about 105,000 killed, was relatively light. Some twenty million people died in the Great War of 1914–18, and millions more were wounded and maimed physically and emotionally. Not surprisingly, the decade following the war was crucial to the development of the modern horror film.

In late 1917, as the war began to turn against Germany after fresh US troops entered the fighting, the Kaiser's government consolidated most commercial film production companies into a single government-controlled entity charged with producing propaganda films to boost morale at home and for distribution in neutral countries. The new body was called *Universumfilm Aktiengesellschaft*, or Ufa, as it was known by its German acronym. When the war ended, Ufa returned to private hands, fully capitalized and employing much of the country's finest film-making talent. Despite major social upheaval and a devastated economy, German producers also benefited from a 1916 ban on the importation of foreign films, a restriction not lifted until 1921. Throughout the period of postwar Germany's Weimar Republic (1919–32), Ufa represented Hollywood's greatest competition in Europe.[24]

A weirdly atmospheric horror drama called *The Cabinet of Dr. Caligari* [*Das Cabinet des Dr. Caligari*], opening in Berlin in February, 1920 (US release April, 1921), helped make German cinema world-famous.[25] *Caligari* initiated a decade of innovative and distinguished films that were widely proclaimed to mark the most advanced developments in the state of motion-picture art. (*Caligari* was produced by Decla, not Ufa. Within two years of its completion, however, Decla merged with the larger concern, bringing its creative personnel and state-of-the-art studios at Neubabelsberg, near Berlin.) The film's impact was such that it can rightly be considered important as both a commercial movie and as the first widely circulated avant-garde film. Besides creating an international sensation, *Caligari* and other German fantasy films of the 1920s strongly affected Euro-American horror films for the next 30 years.[26]

What so distinguished *The Cabinet of Dr. Caligari* was not its story but its style. The film achieved a unique and influential look by basing the design of sets, lighting, costumes, and even acting performances on the tenets of modern art, particularly the branch arising in Germany in the 1910s called Expressionism. *Caligari*'s settings, some simply painted on canvas backdrops, are weirdly distorted, a jumble of clashing, oblique angles, with caricatures of narrow streets, misshapen walls, odd rhomboid windows, and leaning doorframes. Effects of light and shadow were rendered by painting black lines and patterns directly on the floors and walls of sets. The idea for designing the film in expressionist manner came from art directors Hermann Warm, Walter Reimann, and Walter Rohrig, who emulated the settings of avant-garde plays first cropping up in Berlin near the end of the war.[27] Although ample precedents for modernist design existed in German experimental theater and painting, even in the commercial graphic art of the day, nothing like it had

FIGURE 1 Expressionist distortion: Dr. Caligari (Werner Krauss) tends his enslaved somnambulist Cesare (Conrad Veidt) in *The Cabinet of Dr. Caligari* (1920, Decla)

ever been seen in movies. Bolstered by the designers' presentation of preliminary sketches, director Robert Weine and Decla producers quickly approved the concept. Shot completely within studio walls, *Caligari* evoked particularly Germanic ideas of *Stimmung*, "mood" or "atmosphere" that would become central to the classic horror film.

After a brief framing scene, Francis (Friedrich Feher) relates, in flashback, the plot describing the arrival in Holstenwall of Dr Caligari (Werner Krauss), a traveling hypnotist who appears in a carnival with a "somnambulist," or sleepwalker, named Cesare (Conrad Veidt). Francis learns that the wicked doctor controls Cesare as a slave, at night dispatching him to kill and terrorize. Dr Caligari is finally discovered to be the director of a mental asylum, though possessed by the delusion that he is an evil eighteenth-century mystic of the same name. Cesare was an afflicted patient he exploited. Exposed, the doctor is wrestled into a straitjacket and the reign of terror ended. Yet the return to the framing story reverses this apparent ending: Francis is revealed as a mental patient who hallucinates that the institution's benign head is the monster Caligari. "I know how to cure him now," says the smiling doctor after the agitated Francis is safely restrained. The film's shadowy, off-kilter settings were generally understood to represent the world as conceived by the mind of a madman.

"Expressionism" is not easy to define and has often been applied to a group of only loosely related twentieth-century styles in painting, literature, and theater. We can say that, like other modernist art movements such as cubism, surrealism, and futurism, it aimed to break decisively from past traditions in both form and content, and was strongly anti-naturalistic, exploding the smooth linear perspective of post-Renaissance art. Some expressionist works attempted to visualize (or evoke) interior psychological states and emotions, that is, subjective perceptions that cannot be "pictured" as such. Norwegian artist Edvard Munch's famous painting *The Scream* (1893) is close to the idea of expressionism sketched here. On a bridge under a thick, blood-red sky, Munch depicts a traumatized, androgynous figure, open-mouthed with terror, the landscape behind its undulating body forming quivering arcs that suggest radiating waves of psychic torment, as two vaguely threatening figures pass in the background. Similarly, *Caligari* sought to make its settings, décor, and acting reflect no reality other than its characters' anxious psychological states.

Caligari partly originated in the mass carnage and despair that four years of trench warfare had spread across Europe. Hans Janowitz, the film's co-writer, had served in the Austrian army, and lost his beloved brother in the fighting. Like millions of their generation, the war experience left Janowitz and his collaborator Carl Mayer angry and resentful of the established authorities that had led European youth to pointless slaughter. Years later Janowitz claimed that the writers did not originate the framing story and that its inclusion by director Weine and studio heads subverted their intention to make the doctor a symbol of mad, authoritarian evil, one that used men as Caligari used Cesare, a helpless robot wound up and ordered to kill or be killed. Noted scholars have persuasively refuted much of this traditional account, but the unique vision of *The Cabinet of Dr. Caligari* evoked the pain and confusion of postwar Germany and much of the continent.[28] For all its visual abstraction, the film seemed psychologically accurate.

Werner Krauss and Conrad Veidt give the film's two most stylized, non-naturalistic performances. So effective is their presentation in conjunction with the bizarre sets, it is hardly certain that the twist ending can fully reverse the emotional effect of the film's main body as quickly and decisively as Janowitz and many subsequent writers have claimed. We remember the glaring, furtively scheming Dr Caligari of Krauss's portrayal in black cloak, top hat, and spectacles, not the kindly healer who appears on screen for less than two minutes at the end. Similarly, Veidt's Cesare, lithe and sinuous of movement in his black leotard, a look of helpless terror on his own face as he slides along walls or raises a knife to strike a victim, evokes a monster both frightening and strangely compelling.

A 1921 program magazine for Ufa theaters declared: "The strength of the German film lies in the fantastic drama," and indeed many (though certainly not all) of its most influential works of the 1920s fell into this category.[29] Although expressionist style evoked psychological subjectivity in *The Cabinet of Dr. Caligari*, in about two dozen films thereafter it was employed to lend an oddly distinct look to the distant, heavily mythological past, to depict exotic foreign lands, or to embellish gothic tales. German filmmakers produced expressionist works that became hallmarks in the fields of horror (e.g., *The Golem* [1920], *Nosferatu* [1922], *The Hands of Orlac* [1924], *Waxworks* [1924]); science fiction (*Metropolis* [1927], *The Woman in the Moon* [1928]); and fantasy (*Der Müde Tod* (US title, *Destiny*) [1921], *Siegfried* [1923], *Faust* [1927]) for their often flawless synchronization of lighting, camerawork, scenic design, and acting.

Artists who worked repeatedly in the fantasy form enriched the German cinema. Paul Wegener starred in three film versions of the Golem legend, a proto-Frankenstein tale about a mystical rabbi who sculpts a hulking man of clay to protect the Jewish community of medieval Prague from oppression by the Christian monarchy. *The Golem: How He Came into the World* [*Der Golem: Wie Er in die Welt Kam*] (1920) employed expressionist sets including the tower of Rabbi Loew, strewn with half-formed limbs and torsos, where the statue comes to life. Wegener's collaborator on *The Golem* was writer-director Henrik Galeen, contributor to several important fantasy films. The movie was shot by distinguished cinematographer Karl Freund, who was to make major contributions to German and American cinema into the 1950s. Galeen teamed Veidt and Krauss again in *The Student of Prague* [*Der Student von Prag*] (1926), a doppelgänger tale based on Poe's *William Wilson*. Hans Janowitz scripted another Jekyll and Hyde variation called *Der Januskopf* ["the two-faced Janus"] (1920), a much lamented lost film directed by the innovative Friedrich W. Murnau that featured expressionist design, Freund's camerawork, and the acting talents of Conrad Veidt and a young Hungarian named Bela Lugosi in a supporting role.

Murnau's *Nosferatu, A Symphony of Terror* [*Nosferatu, Eine Symphonie des Grauens*] (Prana-Film, 1922) was the first major vampire film. For what emerged as a visually remarkable rendering of the legend, one still quoted and copied in modern films, the project had a rather tawdry beginning as an illicit adaptation of *Dracula*.[30] Henrik Galeen's script called the vampire Count Orlok, but name changes could not hide the origin of major characters and narrative events lifted from Stoker's novel, including Thomas Hutter's (i.e., Jonathan Harker's) journey to the spooky mountain castle of the vampire; his ensuing victimization and imprisonment while Orlok/Dracula travels to Hutter's hometown by ship; and the vampire's fascination with Hutter's wife. Bram Stoker's widow, Florence, was fiercely protective of the famous literary property whose royalties produced most of her income. Learning that an unauthorized German film version had been produced, she set lawyers to work seeking to have all existing prints destroyed. She eventually won the case, but fortunately copies of *Nosferatu* survived.[31]

What was thoroughly original in *Nosferatu* ("the undead") was its visual realization by Murnau and the film's co-producer, scenic designer Albin Grau. Unlike most studio-bound productions of the 1920s, *Nosferatu* was shot on locations including a ruined castle that served as the vampire's lair. Murnau creates expressionist stylization through careful shot composition and lighting rather than distorted sets, as in the vaulted chamber where Hutter discovers the monster resting in his rotten-topped coffin, wide eyes staring up at the terrified man. The passage of the ship unknowingly carrying the creature in its lower decks is perhaps the film's most eerie sequence as the spreading "sickness" that claims the crew one by one gradually turns it into a ghost ship. From a low-angle shot taken through an open hatch, we see the vampire stalking the main deck, framed against the ship's rigging to suggest a malignant spider. Murnau obtained similarly vivid effects with the vampire's gnomelike shadow creeping up a staircase to attack Ellen Hutter, who contorts as the shadow of his clutching hand falls across her heart.

As in *Caligari*, acting in *Nosferatu* is non-naturalistic and heavily mannered, particularly that of the fly-eating madman Knock (the Renfield character) and rightly, Max Schreck as Count Orlok. The plot begins rather slowly for contemporary taste, but, as in many horror films, picks up pace and interest once the monster appears. Schreck's vampire became the film's most enduring image. Unlike the familiar impression of Dracula as a suave, tuxedoed gentleman, Orlok's gaunt frame and beady eyes accentuate an almost alien visage with pointed ears, bald head, sharp nose and chin, and two little fangs set close together. Elongated clawlike fingers complete the effect of the vampire as expressionist rat-man. Hordes of rats emerging from the docked ship to spread pestilence and death through the town as the monster takes up residence extend the motif.

Fritz Lang, Germany's most acclaimed director of the Weimar period, made several important fantasy films in expressionist style. In the 1921 allegory *Destiny/Der Müde Tod* ("the weary death"), Death (Bernhard Goetzke) promises a distraught woman (Lil Dagover) that he will spare her lover if she can save the life of any one of three other men in different period settings. She confronts Death in an otherworldly room filled with flickering candles, each symbolizing a human life. Unlike the painted flats they designed for *Caligari*, Warm and Rohrig, assisted by Robert Herlth, created an array of detailed settings depicting nineteenth-century Germany and fairy-tale versions of Persia, Renaissance Venice, and an Imperial China reminiscent of Méliès, complete with a wizard's tricks realized through clever optical effects. Lang's moody, *chiaroscuro* shot compositions combine sets and actors in evocative tableaux. The film set the pattern for Arthur Robinson's *Warning Shadows* [*Schatten*] (1923) and Murnau's extravagant *Faust* (1927), with its expressionist vistas of Hell. Germany's national epic myth, the Niebelungen saga, came to life in Lang's elaborate sword and sorcery films *Siegfried* and its sequel *Kreimheld's Revenge* [*Kreimheld's Rache*] (1924).

After a notable Soviet film *Aelita, Queen of Mars* (1924), which screened in Germany, Lang's *Metropolis* (1927) was the first major science-fiction epic. The story of class conflict and a workers' revolt in a twenty-first century city-state emerged as a politically confused muddle of Christian, socialist, and fascist themes, but was often no less than stunning visually. A large camera department headed by Karl Freund broke new ground for special visual effects, particularly Eugen Schufftan's process to photograph detailed miniature models reflected off mirrors to depict visually dense cityscapes of the future. The wild-eyed Engineer Rotwang (Rudolph Klein-Rogge), with his black leather jacket and single gloved hand, defined the movie mad scientist, hatching schemes from his shadowy gothic house ensconced in the glimmering city. The still impressive sequence in which he brings to life a female robot amid pulsing electrical arcs prefigured the famous tableau of the monster's birth in Universal's *Frankenstein*. Though commercially unsuccessful, in part because of its great cost, *Metropolis* represented a high point of the German silent cinema, soon fated to be overtaken by technological innovations associated with the coming of sound in 1927–8, and especi-ally, the wrenching historical upheavals brought by the ascension of

Nazism in 1933. Even so, by the time *Metropolis* debuted not only the visual techniques of German films, but German filmmakers in increasing numbers were migrating to Hollywood. Their important contributions to the American horror film are considered further below.

Lon Chaney and Hollywood Horror, 1920–30

That *The Cabinet of Dr. Caligari* had immediately established a striking new look for horror/fantasy that was at once artistically ambitious and commercially viable was indicated not only by the expressionist movement it inaugurated but also by the times it was more or less directly imitated. Paramount's ghost story *The Bells* (1926) and MGM's now-lost vampire film *London After Midnight* (1927) depict Boris Karloff and Lon Chaney, respectively, wearing close copies of Dr Caligari's costume. Karloff even plays an itinerant carnival hypnotist, sporting Caligari's black-framed glasses and threatening glare. Chaney's top-hatted vampire lost the glasses in favor of a grinning corpse-face filled with rows of sharp fangs, but apparently retained Dr Caligari's hunched, scuttling walk. Universal's *The Cat and the Canary* (1927), directed by German émigré Paul Leni, applied the full range of Ufa style to a haunted-house comedy, including a weird doctor with Caligaresque top hat and spectacles. Style and themes in these three films reflect major trends in Hollywood's tentative adoption of gothic horror in the 1920s.

It is a mark of the emotive power of the horror film that Lon Chaney is primarily remembered today for his work in this form. Chaney was a major star in the 1920s, appearing in dozens of films billed as "The Man of a Thousand Faces" owing to the ease with which he obscured his features behind a seemingly endless array of character makeups, most of his own design. Chaney's skills with makeup and pantomime defined his two most lasting roles, the deformed bellringer Quasimodo in *The Hunchback of Notre Dame* (1923) and the ghastly Erik in *The Phantom of the Opera* (1925), the most famous Hollywood horror film of the silent era. Though he is sometimes called the first "horror star," this was not the impression of critics and audiences of his day, who knew Chaney as a versatile creator of offbeat but not necessarily macabre characters.[32] Even *The Hunchback* was really a big-scale costume picture, not a horror film.

Why, then, is Lon Chaney now considered a major figure in the horror field? It is not on the strength of *The Phantom of the Opera* alone, despite the film's often haunting imagery and Chaney's bold performance, which dominates every scene in which he appears. Rather, the impression derives from the cumulative effect of a gallery of grotesque roles and masquerades of which the Phantom and the Hunchback remain the most vivid examples. Chaney played a legless tyrant heartlessly driving factory workers in *The Penalty* (1920); an apeman in *A Blind Bargain* (1922); a one-eyed pimp in *The Road to Mandalay* (1926); an armless circus performer in *The Unknown* (1927); a vengeful, wheelchair-bound carnie in *West of Zanzibar* (1928). He also liked to enact multiple roles such as a Chinese centenarian and his grandson in *Mr. Wu* (1927); a police inspector and the (ultimately fake) vampire in *London After Midnight*; and a sideshow ventriloquist who masquerades as a kindly old lady in order to rob homes of the rich in *The Unholy Three* (1925), remade as Chaney's only talking picture in 1930.

At his best, though, Chaney was always more than just a scary face. In most of these roles, even when playing outright villains, he was given moments of pathos and sympathy that explained the roots of his emotional fixations, often deep anger over injustice or physical injury. Chaney's natural features were thick and rough-hewn, which, coupled with a commanding screen presence, could be powerfully intimidating even if he was hobbling on crutches or sitting in a wheelchair. Yet his crooks and outcasts cried easily, expressing a yearning for love and compassion that had universal appeal. Deformed body, sensitive soul was the key to Lon Chaney's star persona. This formula accounts in part for the paradoxical appeal of many enduring monsters in fiction and cinema.

Art historian Sidra Stich has argued that surrealist art's fixation with twisted, misshapen, and fragmenting human forms in the 1920s responded to the sudden appearance of thousands of mangled veterans in the cities and towns of Europe and North America after World War I.[33] Extending this analysis to explain Lon Chaney's unique appeal at this same time, David J. Skal argued that Chaney's legless character in *The Penalty* "spoke suggestively of the impotent rage of maimed war veterans," and notes that "War wasn't mentioned explicitly in *The Phantom of the Opera*, but since no explanation was given for the Opera Ghost's hideous appearance, Chaney's skull-like face could pluck at the culture's rawest nerves, unbridled by rationale."[34] To this we might add that Hans Janowitz's stated intention to make Cesare a symbol of all the victimized youth betrayed in a fruitless war may have missed not because studio bosses disarmed a radical theme, but because *Caligari*'s expressionist style made the point obscure. Chaney's play on this theme was also indirect but physically glaring in film after film.

Universal Pictures, headed by German-born Carl Laemmle, was one of Hollywood's pioneer film companies and Chaney's frequent employer to 1925. Throughout the 1920s the studio wavered between a conservative business strategy that stressed modestly priced program pictures and stabs at more extravagant movies. Universal's success with *The Hunchback of Notre Dame*, a project Chaney helped develop in order to play Quasimodo, led to *The Phantom of the Opera*, which featured impressive sets of the Paris Opera House, its lobbies and backstage areas, plus the Phantom's hidden lair reached via underground canals. The masked-ball sequence, where the Phantom grandly enters costumed as the Red Death, was used to show off the early Technicolor process. Gaston Leroux's 1908 novel concerns Erik, an elusive "ghost" who terrorizes the Paris Opera while secretly directing the career of Christine, a young singer for whom he composes original music and carries out violent threats to force her promotion to leading roles. Despite clashes with director Rupert Julian, Chaney gave a classic performance in a sumptuously mounted film.

As he had with the Quasimodo makeup, Chaney went to the source novel for ideas on the Phantom's basic look – a living skull with lumpy, parched skin and sunken eyes, sparse hair, jagged teeth, a nearly missing nose. With flowing black cape accentuating gestures both sinuous and athletic, the gaunt Phantom is by turns murderous, debonair, and a sad wretch hungry for love. The film's most famous scene depicts the Phantom unmasked by his kidnapped beloved (Mary Philbin) after being seen only in shadow or covered with a plain mask. The frightened woman creeps up behind her bizarre benefactor, lost in an organ recital of "Don Juan Triumphant." When the mask comes off, the shock cut to Chaney's hideous face in huge closeup was, by all accounts, electrifying. After previewing the film, Universal ordered a bravura ending to replace Erik's passive death at the organ keyboard with an action sequence in which the fleeing monster overturns his carriage and is chased through the streets by a mob. The Phantom dies, though not without theatrical flair. Cornered, he clenches an imaginary bomb in his upraised fist. The crowd halts in fright, upon which he opens his empty hand with a big smile, extending his arms and reveling in his performance just before he is overwhelmed.

Critics have often noted that, unlike the German cinema, Hollywood hesitated to embrace truly supernatural horrors in the 1920s, fearing either that audiences would not accept such nonsense or that gothic horror might prove too morbid for conventional tastes. This observation seems generally correct but does not fit the Phantom, who looks like

FIGURE 2 Theatrical flair: Lon Chaney as *The Phantom of the Opera* (1925, Universal)

nothing so much as a walking corpse, and one with a vampiric obsession for a beautiful young woman. If the Phantom is not a supernatural being, neither is he given banal back-story to explain his grotesque face or his musical talent, information first included in Universal's 1943 remake and continued in subsequent adaptations, including Andrew Lloyd Webber's hit musical. Where most gothic-flavored films of the 1920s end with the ghosts and ghouls exposed as frauds perpetrated to hide criminal activity, Chaney's Phantom enters and exits the film as a cipher.

The haunted-house comedy was a well-worn formula of commercial theater by the time Hollywood adapted several such plays in the 1920s. Plots typically featured a group of characters trapped in a gothic manor and forced to confront ghostly threats that turn out to be illusory. The format gave theatergoers a variety of entertainment experiences, with romance and chills in addition to comedy. Movie versions of Broadway's spook-house comedies contributed to the development of a full-blown horror genre in the way they flaunted a heavily shadowed visual style that seemed to clash with and sometimes overwhelm the basic comic intentions. As such, these films represent an important transitional form.

MGM's *The Monster* (1925), well directed by Roland West, features Lon Chaney as eccentric Dr Ziska, a mad scientist conducting weird experiments in a combination electrical laboratory and medieval dungeon beneath a sanitarium. Three young characters caught in a love triangle are repeatedly chased and caught from secret panels by Ziska's ghoulish henchmen, but finally solve the mystery. Despite some clever slapstick, the sanitarium sequences are played on dark, foreboding sets whose mood predominates. The discovery that the doctor and his men are themselves escaped mental patients only intensifies the scene in which Ziska lingers over the heroine's lithe body tied to an operating table, impulsively flexing his fingers as if torn between science and rape.

What the Hollywood trade press referred to as "Ufa shots" or "German lighting" began to appear in a variety of American films in the mid-1920s.[35] Hollywood was not only assimilating Ufa techniques but also importing German directors, cameramen, set designers, and actors. The aura of artistic excellence surrounding German cinema was its initial appeal for Hollywood, one that could be both emulated and promoted in prestige productions. Fox lured F. W. Murnau to direct the allegorical love story *Sunrise* (1927) from a Carl Mayer script, virtually a "German art film" made in the United States. Carl Laemmle hired Paul Leni to adapt *The Cat and the Canary*, another Broadway haunted-house comedy. Leni had been a Ufa scenic designer before directing the expressionist horror film *Waxworks* [*Das Wachsfigurenkabinett*] (1924), which told multiple, fatalistic stories like Lang's *Der Müde Tod*. *The Cat and the Canary* featured the hallmarks of the German style, *chiaroscuro* lighting, stylized sets, moving camera, and symbolic montage sequences with overlapping dissolves. The hit film laid the groundwork for Universal's horror tradition.

Starting with a gloved hand that wipes away cobwebs and dust to reveal the film's title, Leni's visual flamboyance invigorates a shopworn plot about a group of greedy relatives gathering at a rich uncle's hilltop mansion to hear the reading of his will. The opening describes the uncle's death in similarly high style, with a symbolic tableau of the enfeebled old man sitting beside an array of tall medicine bottles and dodging three gigantic cats representing the relatives grabbing at his fortune. A title card suggests his ghost still haunts the mansion and Leni cuts to a moving shot, the camera gliding quickly down a dark hallway flanked by fluttering curtains, implicitly the ghost's point of view. An impressive range of high and low angles and eccentric framings joined with sharp editing keep the film from exposing its stage origins. Yet it still contains every cliché of the formula, as when the lawyer is just about to tell the heroine who will inherit the money if something happens to her, when a hairy hand emerges from behind a false bookcase and drags him in.

Leni next directed *The Man Who Laughs* (1928), a fog-shrouded drama with *Caligari*'s Conrad Veidt as Gwynplaine, a Scottish noble forced to become a sideshow freak after a cruel childhood mutilation fixes his mouth in a horrible, clownish grin. Veidt played what would have seemed a perfect role for Lon Chaney, who had since departed for MGM. Absent Chaney's wizardry, Veidt's creepy grin was designed by Universal's chief makeup artist Jack P. Pierce, whose indelible work would visualize the studio's (and ultimately American culture's) most famous monsters of the next two decades. Leni's final film, *The Last Warning* (1929), was another Ufa-style comedy thriller set backstage in a Broadway theater. Between *The Phantom of the Opera* and the films of Paul Leni, Universal had demonstrated major interest and success with stylish mystery-horror. Leni's untimely death in 1929, quickly followed by those of Chaney (1930) and Murnau (1931), undoubtedly deprived us of further wonders of horror and fantasy, but even at the moment of their passing, the stage was set for the genre's flowering.

The "Golden Age" of Hollywood Horror, 1931–9

One of the most fruitful and important periods of the American horror film came soon after the arrival of sound and the Crash of 1929. The year before, Carl Laemmle, Sr had turned over control of Universal to his 21-year-old son. "Junior" Laemmle wanted Universal, by now a second-rank studio, to begin competing with Hollywood's major studios (primarily MGM, Paramount, and Fox) in the market for expensive, first-run movies. Commercial and critical success with the powerful war drama *All Quiet on the Western Front* (1930) emboldened him further. Building on the precedents of Paul Leni's work, the studio planned to make *Dracula* as a major production and hoped to star Chaney. The actor's death ended that dream but they engaged Chaney's frequent director, Tod Browning (*The Unknown, London After Midnight*, etc.). Though the production was finally scaled back due to the steadily worsening economy, Universal touched off Hollywood's first gothic horror cycle in the depths of the Great Depression when *Dracula* and then *Frankenstein* scored substantial hits in 1931.[36]

A given phase of the horror film often reveals something about the times that produced it, exposing the anxieties and outright fears of those days, though doing so in a roundabout or thoroughly unintentional way. Weimar Germany was riven by severe economic and political crises in 1920–4, for example, when many horror-fantasy films appeared. To interpret the predatory monsters of Hollywood's horror boom as metaphors for the Depression is tempting, though similarly indirect. Still, the fundamental aim of the genre in whatever medium is to invoke fear, an emotion that was socially widespread at the time horror became popular in America. In this, we might recall the famous words of Franklin D. Roosevelt's first inaugural address in 1933: "the only thing we have to fear is fear itself – nameless, unreasoning, unjustified terror." The President may have been right, but at Universal, and then most other Hollywood studios, inchoate fears had taken tangible shape.

Dracula begins swiftly with the coach bearing real-estate agent Renfield (Dwight Frye) bumping through the Carpathian mountains. Locals are stunned into frightened silence when the Englishman casually reports he is to meet Count Dracula at midnight. Browning cuts to the film's finest and most macabre sequence, deep in the vaulted cellars of Castle Dracula, where the camera glides up to see a probing, clawlike hand emerge from a coffin as fog clings to the damp ground. One of Dracula's brides stirs from another box, followed by a surreal closeup of a large bee climbing out of its own tiny coffin. A huge rat (actually, an opossum) pokes its snout from a coffin; a dull clattering is heard as it steps around crumbling bones. On the rat's squeals, we cut to a track-in on Dracula himself, swathed in black cape, eyes aglow with wolfish menace. In a burst of inspiration lasting for barely longer than a minute on screen, Browning renegotiated the thematic expectations of Hollywood horror. After this there would be no jokes, no last-minute revelation of a criminal scheme. Dracula drank blood.

When Bela Lugosi, appearing to a startled Renfield at the top of a crumbling staircase, first intoned "I am . . . Dracula", he was and remains. Stoker described Dracula as a tall older man with white hair and long mustache. Today this is trivia. Lugosi's performance, accented by his dark good looks and Hungarian-accented speech, his costume and gestures, cemented the popular image of Count Dracula to the present day. Actor and director combined for a fine moment in the dinner scene where Renfield cuts his finger. Browning reframes to a quick track-in on Lugosi in semi-crouched position, staring off-screen, his eyes wide, the impression of a sharp intake of breath. The moment conveys hunger, lust, and Dracula's near-loss of mastery over mortals. The Lugosi image, here at the moment of its cinematic birth, is of suave charm and self-restraint, the outer appearance of a courtly gentleman covering a pitiless monster beneath. Careful editing and Lugosi's perfectly realized performance reveal human weakness beneath Dracula's uncanny bloodlust.

Still, considering Tod Browning's flair for odd, sexually unsettling material, and with Ufa veteran Karl Freund behind the camera, *Dracula* should have been much better. Instead, after a fine 25 minutes, much of the rest seems like a filmed record of *Dracula: The Vampire Play*, the 1927 stage success that earned Lugosi good notices on Broadway and in a national tour. A second *Dracula* made with a Spanish-speaking cast for distribution in Latin America provides an idea of the material's possibilities. Filmed at nights on the same sets after Browning's crew had wrapped for the day, the Spanish *Dracula*, directed by George Melford with Carlos Villarias as the Count, emerged as a technically smoother, often more engaging production, one which, ironically, borrowed visual ideas from *Nosferatu*.[37] Despite its dramatic flaws, Browning's *Dracula* performed impressively at the box office after its February, 1931 release and boosted Universal's Depression-ravaged profits.

Frankenstein was planned as a follow-up. The film was originally assigned to French-born Robert Florey, a feature director and avant-garde filmmaker steeped in the trends of European experimental cinema. With writer Garrett Fort, Florey began work on a script and shot a test sequence with Lugosi as the monster. The actor finally declined the part because it had no dialog and required heavy makeup. Shortly afterwards, however, Florey was replaced by Englishman James Whale, a stage director who had just filmed *Waterloo Bridge* (1931) for Universal. Whale adopted Florey's idea to do *Frankenstein* with expressionist settings and, in preparation, screened German fantasy films including *Caligari*, *Nosferatu*, and *Metropolis* – actually an unsurprising approach, given the strong German influence in Hollywood movies since 1926. For the monster, Whale cast fellow-Briton Boris Karloff. The actor's subtle characterization, aided by Jack Pierce's unforgettable makeup, created one of the lasting icons of twentieth century culture.

From the opening scene of a twilight graveside service, mourners weeping softly, a bell tolling in the distance, Whale takes cinematic command of the story. Dr Frankenstein (Colin Clive) and his hunchbacked assistant Fritz (Dwight Frye) lurk behind an iron fence, waiting for the body to be buried so they may immediately uncover it for the doctor's experiments. The entire hilltop cemetery, with its leaning headstones, gnarled trees, and a skeletal figure of Death standing watch, was built on a sound stage. *Frankenstein* used *Caligari*'s approach of immersing the audience in a fantastic setting, rarely shooting exterior locations. With

Fritz's already twisted body bent into an L-shape when they fall on the fresh grave to begin digging, Dr Frankenstein pointedly flings a shovel of dirt right into the face of Death. The film's formal terms were set: Whale would interpret Mary Shelley's themes in the visual language of German expressionism.

Frankenstein is one of those classic movies like *Casablanca* or *Shane* that has been quoted and parodied so often that the original may now strike us as naïve or even (ironically) derivative. Yet the film retains much of its original punch, particularly in its most famous scene, the creation of the monster in an impossibly angular gothic tower, electrical machinery buzzing, thunder crashing, and Clive's Dr Frankenstein shrieking, "It's moving! It's alive!" when the monster's hand begins to twitch. Scenic designer Charles D. Hall, another key contributor to Universal's original horror series, created visually arresting sets for horror films, from *The Phantom of the Opera* through *Dracula's Daughter* (1936). Frankenstein's tower laboratory, with its tall chimney-like design, stone walls and barred windows leaning in every direction, is Hall's most famous set here, though the graveyard at the opening and the windmill where a torchbearing mob surrounds the creature at the climax are similarly impressive. As in *Caligari*, black shadows and clashing angles convey a world out of balance, a fitting abode for Dr Frankenstein's uncanny ambitions and his creation's agony.

Pierce and Whale fashioned the Monster's now instantly recognizable look. Early sketches depict conceptions wavering between a Neanderthal man and a metallic robot. Of the latter, the only element retained became one of the most iconic – bolts in the neck to indicate the head mechanically fastened to the body. Facial scars and clamps at the hairline further suggest a patchwork project. Another distinct feature, the monster's flat-topped head, implies a crude operation to insert a new brain. To make the monster seem not only taller, but both strong and ungainly, Karloff wore bulky, thick-soled boots. Cutting his coat sleeves several inches too short, a brilliantly simple trick, attained a further illusion of height. But the Frankenstein Monster was more than the makeup. A number of actors wore this basic costume in later years, but none matched the power and pathos of Boris Karloff's performance in which the inarticulate monster is both killer and victim, cunning brute and helpless child.

Whale followed *Frankenstein* with two more important horror films. *The Old Dark House* (1932) featured Karloff as a sinister mute butler in what now became a knowing send-up of *Cat and the Canary*-style thrillers, yet still conveyed an undercurrent of creepy gothic perversity.

The Invisible Man (1933), starring Claude Rains, set the standard for all subsequent invisibility tales, with still convincing special effects by John P. Fulton that depict the invisible man as only an empty pair of pants skipping down a road, or in a famous scene, quickly unwrapping his bandaged-covered face to appear headless before a terrified throng. Though his face went unseen until the movie's final moments, Rains gave a gripping performance as the idealistic scientist gradually succumbing to megalomania and murder as the invisibility potion drives him insane. Rains is darkly malevolent when he ties a helpless man into a car and then cheerfully explains to his victim how his arms and neck will break when he sends it over a cliff. And then he does.

Paramount was first to capitalize on Universal's success with *Dracula* when Rouben Mamoulian directed Fredric March in what is generally considered the classic film version of *Dr. Jekyll and Mr. Hyde* (1931). A commercial and critical hit, it remains one of the few horror films to win an Oscar (Best Actor) since the Academy Awards began in 1927.[38] Mamoulian, already acclaimed as an innovative filmmaker for his early experiments with sound in *Applause* (1929), produced a visually impressive film to match March's fine performance. To accomplish Jekyll's first transformation into Hyde without stopping the camera, cinematographer Karl Struss (a German émigré who had shot Murnau's *Sunrise*) contributed an inventive technique using red makeup on March's face, then slowly changing from red to blue filters, undetectable in black-and-white photography. The aura of artistic prestige may have permitted the film greater latitude with its frank sexuality and violence.

The film begins with subjective camera movements that identify the audience with Jekyll's vision and the movements of his head and hands as he plays the organ. The technique continues for several minutes with our first look at Jekyll occurring, appropriately, in a mirror reflection. This visual strategy appears at key points to encourage the audience to consider itself the protagonist; that is, to recognize Jekyll's dilemma as our own. Jekyll's frustration by General Carew, the stuffy, upper-crust father of his beloved Muriel (Rose Hobart), directly underpins the experiments that release Mr Hyde. Here the double is not a manifestation of some innate human evil but the clear result of Jekyll's struggle against social, and ultimately sexual, repression. Jekyll's plea that the couple marry before Carew's arbitrary engagement period ends is rebuffed by the stern father's assertion that "It isn't done!" Angrily departing Carew's home with his friend Lanyon, Jekyll rescues the prostitute Ivy (Miriam Hopkins) from an aggrieved client. When they return to her apartment, she playfully undresses, and totally nude under

FIGURE 3 *Doppelgänger.* Fredric March in the classic film version of *Dr. Jekyll and Mr. Hyde* (1931, Paramount)

the covers (as we can see from a discreet side view), lustfully kisses her eager benefactor. Lanyon's sudden reappearance aggravates Jekyll's social embarrassment and sexual frustration.

Victor Fleming's *Dr. Jekyll and Mr. Hyde* (MGM, 1941) with Spencer Tracy is often praised for updating the Victorian moral fable with the popularized Freudianism of the 1940s, but the approach was already evident in Mamoulian's 1931 film. When Jekyll first drinks his chemical brew, a subjective montage sequence establishes unambiguous connections between sexual repression and the release of Mr Hyde. Images of Muriel poised to kiss him while her father angrily repeats, "It isn't done!" blend with Ivy's bare leg swinging seductively and her voice calling, "Come back soon!" Hyde later enacts Jekyll's revenge on Carew by beating the elder man to death with a walking stick, the phallic associations of the murder weapon and the Oedipal nature of the crime strongly implied.

Despite the hairy face and fangs that give Hyde an unreal, animal visage, Fredric March is brilliant, especially playing off Miriam Hopkins. With brutish intensity that can still make audiences wince, Hyde relishes torturing her emotionally and physically, reducing the self-possessed streetwalker to a cringing child, invoking the true horror of domestic violence. The killing of Carew pales beside the vicious murder of Ivy, Hyde cooing loving words as he slips below the frame, simultaneously raping her and strangling her to death. At the climax, the police trail Hyde to Jekyll's laboratory and shoot him, causing him to revert back to the good doctor, to the shock of all. However, Mamoulian ends the film with a pullback from this tableau to a pot boiling over on the stove. Unlike most traditional horror films, this ending offers no real catharsis. Hyde may be dead but the pot is still boiling; the social conditions that whelped him persist.

By 1932, a profitable horror cycle was in full swing at Universal and rival studios. *Murders in the Rue Morgue* (1932), often described as Robert Florey's "consolation prize" for losing *Frankenstein*, is the most under-rated film of Universal's original series. Aided by expressionist sets and Karl Freund's mobile camera, Florey turned Poe's detective tale into a Hollywood reworking of *The Cabinet of Dr. Caligari*, with Bela Lugosi as the mountebank and a murderous ape as the somnambulist. Lugosi's performances would grow increasingly broad in coming years, but here he linked Dracula's mesmeric powers with fully human undertones of sadism and madness. The scene in which his Dr Mirakle drains the blood of a trussed-up prostitute for his evolution experiments saw Hollywood approaching the graphic intensity of the Grand Guignol. *The Mummy* (1932) marked Freund's tepid directorial debut. Already the studio was cannily recycling proven elements from its initial hits, especially the stars. Karloff played the ancient Egyptian priest Im-ho-tep, pursuing his reincarnated beloved in the modern world, with *Dracula*'s Dr Van Helsing, Edward Van Sloan, as the scientist combating the mummy. They even repeated the haunting "Swan Lake" theme over the opening credits as in *Dracula* and *Murders in the Rue Morgue*. Fine sets, makeup, and Karloff's quietly methodical monster offset a low-key introduction to what became another iconic horror character.

Bela Lugosi portrayed a malevolent voodoo priest who controls mindless slaves brought back from the dead in *White Zombie* (UA, 1932), a stylish, if low-budget independent film by brothers Victor and Edward Halperin. Filmed on the borrowed sets of *Dracula*, this was Hollywood's first foray into the zombie theme. It was also the first of many Lugosi performances as minor variations of Dracula, emphasized as in the original, with spotlit closeups of his hypnotic stare. Paramount offered *The Island of Lost Souls* (1933), based on fantasy author H. G. Wells' novel *The Island of Dr. Moreau*, about a crazed, whip-wielding scientist (Charles

Laughton) conducting grim experiments in vivisection and evolutionary acceleration to transform animals into proto-humans. (Lugosi played a supporting part as one of the "manimals.") The film contained barely disguised undertones of sadism, torture, and even bestiality. Moreau's greatest success has changed a female panther into a woman, one who's clearly in heat for the male lead. RKO's *The Most Dangerous Game* (1932) was a creepy tale of a mad Russian count (Leslie Banks) who has turned his South Sea island into a hunting preserve where he stalks human prey. The pulp adventure tale's convergence with the horror genre begins when a shipwrecked traveler (Joel McCrea) stumbles up to the imposing gothic fortress the Count calls home and continues with a descent to his awful trophy room decorated with the mounted heads of earlier victims. Such dreadful images, alongside the villains' salacious designs on the women in all three of these movies, indicate Hollywood actively probing the limits of permissible content as it embraced this newly popular form.

Metro-Goldwyn-Mayer's reputation for glossy production values and glamorous stars made Tod Browning's *Freaks* (1932) a highly unlikely project, yet it somehow got made. *Freaks* is a work whose reputation may outstrip the film itself at first viewing. Browning was ultimately not a visual stylist on a par with Leni or Whale, but images and episodes from his psychosexually bizarre films can linger in the mind nonetheless. What made the movie unique (or notorious) was that for performers in its circus setting, Browning cast actual "freaks" – physically or mentally disabled people who made their living in sideshows, including midgets (Harry Earles), a man with no lower body who walked on his hands (Johnny Eck), a pair of Siamese twins (Daisy and Violet Hilton), several "pinheads" (microcepholites), and a man born without arms or legs (Prince Randian). Browning had worked in carnivals in his youth and used its demimonde for some of his most striking films. Condemned as either exploitative for the display of its exceptional cast or grossly repellent to "normal people" for the same reason, *Freaks* was heavily censored or banned outright from some locales.

Freaks boldly reverses the common assumptions of the horror film in its definition of monstrousness. Here the freaks are the highly sympathetic and engaging figures while the hyper-masculine strongman, Hercules, and the voluptuous trapeze artist Cleopatra (Olga Baclanova) are the clear villains. Scheming with Hercules, Cleopatra marries the midget Hans (Earles), intending to poison him and steal his money. The physical frustration of normal sexuality underpins almost every relationship in the film.[39] Hans is the ultimate "little man" who will never satisfy the "big woman." Cleopatra's scheme is revealed at a wild engagement celebration where the freaks pass around a wine goblet (comparison with Communion ritual fully intended), chanting: "Gooble-gobble, gooble-gooble, one of us!" Repulsed, she rebukes them as "You dirty, slimy freaks!" as the room falls angrily silent. Before the plot can be carried out, the freaks rally to defend Hans. As a midnight storm rages, Hercules is knifed and crawls, wounded, along the ground. Images of the sideshow avengers silently stalking him on their bellies or on all fours beneath the wagons, the limbless Prince Randian slinking through the mud with a knife clenched in his teeth, are unforgettable. A coda reveals a legless Cleopatra exhibited in a sideshow herself, as a squawking human chicken, an image both comic and nightmarish.

Fritz Lang's *M* (1931), a stylish psychological thriller usually considered the last great work of the pre-Nazi German cinema, introduced Hungarian-born Peter Lorre as a haunted child murderer. With his pop-eyes and distinctive nasal accent, Lorre became a fixture in horror and mystery films after immigrating to America in 1935. His Hollywood debut in MGM's *Mad Love* (1935), directed by Karl Freund with a surer touch than he had shown in *The Mummy*, combined black comedy with psychosexual undertones. The story was adapted from the French novel *The Hands of Orlac*, about a concert pianist (*Frankenstein*'s Colin Clive) who loses his hands in an accident and has them replaced by those of an executed knife-throwing killer, hands which continue their murderous ways. *Mad Love* emphasizes the surgeon Dr Gogol (Lorre) and his obsession with Orlac's wife, Yvonne (Frances Drake), an actress at the *Théâtre du horreur* whose on-stage torture on the rack provokes Gogol's sadistic delight in the movie's first scene. A visually sophisticated film abounding in motifs of doubles and artifice versus reality, *Mad Love* continued the interwar period's obsession with physical mutilation. Here the symbolic interplay of knives, hands, and amputation evokes castration anxiety in the Freudian tradition.

Perhaps the maddest love of the decade was that of a giant gorilla for an unemployed actress. RKO's *King Kong* (1933) became one of the landmarks of old Hollywood.[40] Manic movie producer Carl Denham (Robert Armstrong) discovers his new leading lady, Ann Darrow (Fay Wray), stealing a grocer's apple while awaiting a soup-kitchen meal, underscoring the fantasy's grounding in its own hard times. An undaunted American dreamer, Denham hopes to strike it rich by making the most extraordinary movie ever, leading Ann and a crew of merchant seamen on a voyage to discover a legendary island god called Kong. Skull Island is a primordial realm where dinosaurs still roam and Kong, a towering ape, reigns supreme. More an adventure fantasy than a horror film, *King Kong* set the pattern for 1950s science-fiction movies about prehistoric giants rampaging through urban landscapes. The script neatly counterpoints events on the ancient island, with Kong's ill-fated trip to the modern island of Manhattan. The image of the defiant, suddenly sympathetic beast fending off attacking airplanes atop the newly constructed Empire State Building invoked the powerful ambivalence toward the monster often at work in the most effective horror-fantasy.

Kong was actually an articulated, 18-inch model filmed alongside dinosaur miniatures on tabletop sets. The monsters came to life through the painstaking process of stop-motion animation, a technique going back to the trick-film era in which a model was photographed one frame at a time, moved very slightly, and then another frame exposed. The more subtle the movement between shots, the smoother the effect on screen, so technicians led by Willis O'Brien (who had wrought similar miracles with dinosaur models in Goldwyn's *The Lost World* [1925]) were fortunate to shoot more than 10–20 seconds of usable footage per day. These shots were blended with the actors and normal sets via optical compositing. The titanic battle between Kong and a Tyrannosaurus Rex, the roaring ape thumping his chest while the lizard hisses and swings its tail, ranks as one of the great triumphs of movie special effects.

Warner Bros. joined the horror vogue cautiously, producing *Svengali* (1931) with John Barrymore as a malevolent, Caligari-like hypnotist amid distorted sets derived from the famed German silent.[41] The versatile Michael Curtiz directed Lionel Atwill and Fay Wray in *Dr. X* (1932), a darkly suggestive science-fiction gothic about a mad doctor-turned-serial killer, shot in the two-strip Technicolor process for novelty appeal in an increasingly crowded field. The same team turned out *Mystery of the Wax Museum* (1933), perhaps the studio's most original contribution. The film's carnivalesque confusions of artifice and reality in the wax museum setting starred Atwill as a mad artist who can no longer sculpt wax figures after his hands are burned in a deliberately set fire and so must turn to coating the bodies of murdered victims. When the heroine (Wray) finally smashes Atwill's wax face-mask to expose his horribly burned features, the film nearly trumped *The Phantom of the Opera*. As surely as *White Zombie* did for Lugosi and Dracula, Warner's *The Walking Dead* (1936) confirmed Karloff's close identification with the Frankenstein monster in a tale about an executed criminal who is scientifically resurrected. The film's contemporary art-deco rendering of the laboratory complements the characteristic style of the studio that innovated the gangster film, here featuring wisecracking reporters and gun-toting hoods as Karloff's supporting cast.

The horror trend was nearing its peak when Universal teamed Karloff and Lugosi in *The Black Cat* (1934), one of the cycle's best films. Directed by German émigré and former art director Edgar G. Ulmer, *The Black Cat* was a dark salute to the Ufa tradition. Early on we see a mustachioed hotel porter in ostentatious uniform carrying a lettered umbrella — a figure nearly identical to the protagonist of Murnau's acclaimed 1924 drama *The Last Laugh* [*Der Letze Mann*], on which Ulmer had worked. The villain was named Hjalmar Poelzig, after Ulmer's former colleague Hans Poelzig, art director of *The Golem* (1920). Karloff's Poelzig has built a gleaming modernist house on the foundations of a fortress he once commanded above a bloody World War I battlefield. The house's clean lines, porthole windows, and recessed lighting emulate the Bauhaus school of Walter Gropius, contemporary architecture Ulmer admired. Our first view of the house shows its smooth, horizontal form sitting atop a dark hill below which tilting crosses mark the graves of hundreds of soldiers. The importance of the Great War to the rise of gothic horror in Europe and Hollywood was never more directly illustrated.

The Black Cat's creepy high point comes when Poelzig leads his former wartime comrade Dr Vitus Verdegast (Lugosi) on a tour of the dark lower chambers containing the glass-coffined bodies of a half dozen women displayed in upright position. The gallery includes the doctor's former wife Karen, whom Poelzig married after claiming the imprisoned Verdegast was dead. His morbid crimes don't stop there. Poelzig is now married to Verdegast's adult daughter, also named Karen, to imply a perverse combination of necrophilia and incest. This is but the prelude to Poelzig's conduct of a Black Mass for members of his satanic cult on an expressionist altar of inverted crosses. Lugosi helps a young American couple escape the *moderne* madhouse before surgically flaying the skin from Karloff's body and blowing up the place. Universal combined Karloff and Lugosi again in *The Raven* (1935) and *The Invisible Ray* (1936), to far less memorable effect.

In 1931–3, just as the horror cycle began, movie attendance dropped by one-third as the economy nearly collapsed. With a quarter of the workforce unemployed, the entire social system strained under the effects of the Depression. In this climate, a grassroots lobbying group, the Catholic Legion of Decency, denounced what it perceived as Hollywood's assault on traditional social and moral values in a perilous time. The powerful film-industry trade press empire of Martin Quigley, who had coauthored a stringent though less enforced regulatory code in 1930, actively supported the group. Along with Warner Bros.' violent gangster movies and the bawdy comedy of Paramount's Mae West, horror films were obvious targets. Movies like *Frankenstein*, *Freaks*, and *Island of Lost Souls* were indeed testing the limits of violence and morbid sexual suggestiveness. In mid-1934, in direct response to pressure and threatened boycotts from the Legion of Decency, Hollywood instituted a strict new regime of censorship governed by the industry's Production Code Administration (PCA).

Although the censors actually treated *The Black Cat* rather leniently, much of its disturbing content would have been prohibited entirely a year later. The effects of public complaint and PCA control were increasingly evident after 1934. *The Werewolf of London* (1935) was Universal's take on Jekyll and Hyde, with Henry Hull as a scientist bitten by a Tibetan werewolf. Reviewing an early script, the PCA warned Universal "that if this story is photographed in a fashion to create nervous shock among women and children, it might be held up as contrary to the good and welfare of the industry."[42] Where Rouben Mamoulian had produced a violent, sexually energized fable in 1931, *The Werewolf of London* felt restrained, despite another fine monster makeup by Jack Pierce and a good performance from Hull. Interesting and effective horror films would still be made in the next 20 years until PCA power began to fade, yet they would always have to reckon with the authority of a censorship office that actively disliked the genre.

Still, Universal was about to produce its horror masterpiece. James Whale admired the films of Paul Leni for their blend of gothic atmosphere and humor. He had a chance to make such a film himself when Universal decided to produce *Bride of Frankenstein* (1935), the first sequel to the 1931 hit. Whale pushed the expressionist visuals even further this time with outlandish set design, lighting, and canted framings in a brilliant variation of the *Frankenstein* story as black comic fantasy. Colin Clive returned as the doctor, with Boris Karloff's Monster speaking dialog for the first and only time. While the creature's plight became more pathetic, his longing for love more acute, the film abounded in camp humor, particularly in the performance of Ernest Thesiger as fey Dr Pretorius, a scheming medico who forces Frankenstein to make a mate for the creature. The sequel opens with an approximation of the novel's origin, depicting Mary Shelley (Elsa Lanchester), husband Percy, and Lord Byron recalling her great horror story, as illustrated by quick highlights from the 1931 film.

Bride of Frankenstein's most poignant interlude finds the Monster taking refuge in the cottage of a blind hermit where the creature finds his first true friend, learns to enjoy music and wine, and smokes a cigar. Compare this to the weirdly funny moment in which the monster, seeking shelter in a catacomb, comes upon the grave-robbing Dr Pretorius, also savoring a cigar and drinking wine, using a bone-covered coffin lid for a table. "Oh. I thought I was alone," the doctor deadpans, greeting the man-made monster as if they were businessmen at a sidewalk café. In a tale about man usurping the power of creation and resurrecting the dead, Whale audaciously composed visual comparisons of the Monster with the persecuted Christ, showing him captured by the villagers and trussed up in cruciform imagery. Elsa Lanchester reappears briefly at the end as the Bride, decked out in a flowing white wedding gown/shroud, and wild, electrified hairdo inspired by the famous Egyptian bust of Nefertiti.

Dracula's Daughter (1936), starring Gloria Holden, was the last entry in the original Universal series. "She gives you that *weird* feeling," claimed the ads, though the general feeling among recent critics is that here vampirism was a metaphor for lesbianism.[43] The homoerotic undertones of the vampire myth seem to come directly to the surface when the vampire is female. (The potential was no less rife when Dracula bit Renfield, but might still be disavowed.) Attention focuses on the scene in which Holden's Countess Zaleska (née Dracula) corners a young woman and entices her to model nude for a painting. Everyone probably understood that the bite on the neck (discretely off-screen) was really foreplay. Hollywood has a long history of equating homosexuality with criminality, perversion, and morose self-destruction, but Zaleska still emerged as an engaging, partly sympathetic character. Fully awake to the sexual undercurrents of *Dracula's Daughter*, the PCA's persistent demands for script changes smothered the story's more subversive elements.

That same year, Laemmle family control of Universal ended owing to financial reversals from the failure of Junior's first-run picture strategy. With or without the taming effects of the PCA, the horror vogue had seemingly run its course anyway, and Universal's new owners were not inclined to keep it alive. Foreign censorship was a factor as well. In 1932, the British Board of Film Censors created a new ratings category, the "H" (for horrific), largely restricting such films to adults.[44] Likely to be heavily cut if permitted to be shown at all, horror films were increasingly unwelcome in the British market, a major source of Hollywood profits.[45] After 1936, the genre disappeared for about two

FIGURE 4 Horror stars of the genre's classic period: the Frankenstein Monster (Boris Karloff) gently attends his late friend Ygor (Bela Lugosi) in *Son of Frankenstein* (1939, Universal)

years until a curious phenomenon occurred in August, 1938 when a neighborhood theater in Los Angeles booked a triple feature of *Dracula*, *Frankenstein*, and RKO's *Son of Kong* (1933). Lines went around the block and the program was held over for weeks, attracting press attention. This prompted Universal to re-release a *Dracula/Frankenstein* double bill nationally that fall that returned handsome profits, while the studio set to work on an ambitious new sequel titled *Son of Frankenstein* (1939), with Karloff as the Monster and Bela Lugosi in scene-stealing support.[46]

For a movie that commenced shooting without a completed script, *Son of Frankenstein* emerged as a triumph and a great favorite of horror fans. Roland V. Lee assumed the director's chair, maintaining the blend of horror and humor Whale achieved in the previous film. The highly capable Jack Otterson's rich, angular sets for the interior of the Frankenstein castle and the ruined laboratory blended gothic and expressionistic motifs to produce exciting compositional possibilities for Lee's inventive direction. Basil Rathbone starred as Wolf von Frankenstein, who returns to his ancestral home with wife and child to face a hostile greeting by local villagers victimized by his father's handiwork years before. Wolf resists temptation at first, but is soon drawn to continue the family business. Seeing his father's crypt desecrated with the scrawl, "maker of monsters," he strikes it out and writes, "maker of men." The broken-necked Ygor (Lugosi), who stalks the castle grounds after surviving a hanging for grave robbing, pressures the doctor to revive his friend, the Monster. Affecting a gravelly voice, Lugosi gave a vivid performance, by turns menacing and droll, and without the Dracula mannerisms for once. Lionel Atwill was Inspector Krogh, a policeman with a wooden arm who describes the Monster tearing off his real arm in childhood. Karloff played the Monster for the last time, wisely suspecting the creature would hereafter decline into a plot device, a killer robot without nuances. He retained much of the character's richness here, however, particularly in his conspiratorial friendship with Ygor. *Son of Frankenstein* made an outstanding finale to the American horror film's most seminal decade.

The Horror Film in the World War II Era

After the success of the lavish *Son of Frankenstein*, Universal renewed its commitment to the genre with which it was most identified but would do so by recycling its 1930s hits as more modest programmers – medium-budget movies that could serve either as headline attractions or to fill half of a double feature (an exhibition practice born of economic necessity in the mid-1930s) in some theaters. In 1940, the studio initiated a series of horror sequels, which, although solidly produced and not without interest, were clearly less ambitious than the originals. Some representative titles – *The Invisible Man Returns* (1940), *The Mummy's Hand* (1940), *Frankenstein Meets the Wolf Man* (1943), *Son of Dracula* (1943) – suggest that breaking new ground was not the goal. Universal's demotion of horror movies from feature attractions to programmer status mirrored what happened at other studios. The only A-budget horror films made during the decade were MGM's *Dr. Jekyll and Mr. Hyde* (1941) and Universal's Technicolor remake of *The Phantom of the Opera* (1943) with Claude Rains, a disappointment that seemed more interested in opera than the Phantom. Moreover, where *Frankenstein* et al. had been pitched to adults, the sequels were increasingly aimed at juvenile audiences, which, coupled with the PCA's firm hand, made the more violent, sexually outlandish horror of the previous decade even less likely.

Lon Chaney's son, Creighton, worked as a character actor under his own name at RKO in the late 1930s before reluctantly agreeing to be billed as Lon Chaney, Jr. After a touching performance as the retarded Lennie in the film version of Steinbeck's *Of Mice and Men* (1939), Universal signed him for a long series of horror vehicles. The first, *Man-Made Monster* (1941), was an entertaining diversion but Chaney, Jr's signature role as the tragic Larry Talbot in *The Wolf Man* (1941) highlighted a film on par with the best efforts of the 1930s. With George Waggner's smart direction of Curt Siodmak's original script, and special promotion to commemorate the studio's tenth anniversary of horror productions, *The Wolf Man* became Universal's biggest money-maker of the season. Once more expressionistic visuals held sway on the fog-shrouded forest set where Chaney's werewolf prowls, now cleverly used as much to disguise its modest budget as to invoke a nightmare world.

Chaney played the estranged son of an English lord (Claude Rains) who returns home from America after the death of his elder brother. The ubiquitous Lugosi briefly appears as the gypsy fortune-teller and werewolf whose bite inflicts the curse on Larry, while Maria Ouspenskaya made a vivid impression as Maleva, Larry's surrogate witch-mother. *The Wolf Man*'s literate script and sharp direction pack visual and thematic complexity into its 70-minute running time. Like many 1940s dramas, the movie abounds in Freudian motifs. Flirting with Talbot in her antique shop, Gwen Conliffe (Evelyn Ankers) selects a slim cane with a little dog on the handle for Larry, who instead prefers a big one with a snarling wolf's head. These phallic elements coalesce in a swirling delirium montage at Larry's first transformation that reiterates the similarities between the werewolf myth and the Jekyll and Hyde story. Jack Pierce created a more fully animalistic concept here than he had designed for *Werewolf of London*, emphasizing the high sweep of the wolf's hirsute forehead and thick covering of fur on feet and hands. Chaney walked on upraised feet with back bent, stalking the misty woods with a startling blend of animal cunning and recognizable insanity in his eyes.

Following *The Wolf Man*, Universal promoted Chaney, Jr as "The Screen's Master Character Creator" in a series of uneven turns as the studio's most famous monsters: assuming the Karloff part (and becoming the robot Karloff foresaw) in *The Ghost of Frankenstein* (1942); enacting a slow-moving menace in three outings as the mute, bandaged-swathed Kharis beginning with *The Mummy's Tomb* (1942); and rather miscast as the mysterious Count Alucard (get it?) in *Son of Dracula*, a suggestively eerie film in which the King Vampire is virtually a supporting player. (The elder Chaney's retrospective identification as the first "horror star" stems in part from Universal's active direction of his son's career in just such roles.) Fortunately, the studio let him reprise his favorite part, with the Wolf Man maintaining a certain anguished dignity in four increasingly unlikely tales.

Frankenstein Meets the Wolf Man, despite the shabby title, was an enjoyable sequel with Larry Talbot seeking Dr Frankenstein's legendary secrets of life and death in hopes of ending his own cursed existence. Lugosi finally portrayed the Monster, the part he had proudly refused a dozen years earlier. The creature was originally to speak in Ygor's voice, after a brain transplant in *Ghost of Frankenstein*, but when the Lugosi accent emanating from the monster provoked laughter in post-production screenings, all his lines were cut. The movie Universal proclaimed "The beast battle of the century!" ends with a listless 30-second tussle between the monsters, cut short by the floodwaters from an exploding dam. Accepted on its own terms, however, it is a well-mounted affair, as in the opening scene where a pair of grave robbers break into the Talbot family mausoleum on a moonlit night and accidentally revive the werewolf, a hairy hand emerging from a coffin to strangle one of them.

Critics have suggested that the perceived aesthetic decline of the horror film in the 1940s must have been an effect of the war experience. That is, the real and mounting horrors of global war overwhelmed fake movie scares and made them irrelevant except as purely escapist, increasingly puerile entertainment. *Variety*'s review of *The Wolf Man*, which was released the week after the Pearl Harbor attack, suggested it might offer welcome relief: "Here is a film that will take the minds of patrons off the Japanese war, thoroughly and effectively – at least for the time they are in the theater." Yet under the headline, "Possibly Too Much For the Present Day," *The Hollywood Reporter* worried the movie might now be too disturbing: "[Universal] . . . dresses it all up with the craft of a studio practiced in spinning horror yarns. Still it is impossible to guess how the public will accept 'The Wolf Man' in these times."[47] The war so quickly and radically shifted national priorities, overflowing into almost every cultural experience, that even gothic horror could take on implicit war associations, regardless of intentions. Only a few months later in *The Ghost of Frankenstein*, Ygor (Lugosi) schemed to transplant his cunning brain into the Monster's invincible body, using timely language: "I will live forever!" he exults. "My brain in that body would make me a leader of men. And we would

FIGURE 5 Sequels and series in the World War II era: the Frankenstein Monster (Bela Lugosi) and Larry Talbot (Lon Chaney, Jr.) in *Frankenstein Meets the Wolf Man* (1943, Universal)

rule the state and even the whole country!" Now even gothic trolls were nurturing Hitlerian dreams of thousand-year Reichs and world domination.

Still, several B horror movies tried a frontal attack. Universal offered *Invisible Agent* (1942), a wartime variation of the Invisible Man series that finds scientist Frank Griffin (Jon Hall) using his amazing powers to infiltrate Germany, where he steals a list of Japanese spies operating in America and destroys Nazi bombers primed to attack New York. "Poverty Row" chillers including PRC's *The Mad Monster* (1942) and Monogram's *Revenge of the Zombies* (1943), respectively, pictured Nazi scientists laboring to create invulnerable monster-soldiers or raise armies of the walking dead to fight for Hitler. In Columbia's *Return of the Vampire* (1943), Bela Lugosi, reprising Dracula in all but name, stalks Britain during the Blitz after Luftwaffe bombs blow open his crypt and civil defense workers remove the stake they perceive as a bomb splinter from the vampire's corpse, bringing him to life. Remarkably, the film places a woman, Lady Jane Ainsley (Frieda Inescort), an aristocratic medico, in the Dr Van Helsing role of vampire-hunting savant. In its portrayal of a strong female protagonist assuming a traditional male role, the movie retooled the vampire tale for wartime propaganda tasks, as if casting "Rosie the Riveter" in horror-genre terms.[48]

Critics who roll their eyes at the likes of *Ghost of Frankenstein* and *Revenge of the Zombies* typically agree that a slate of nine low-budget horror films produced by Val Lewton at RKO between 1942 and 1946 encompass the genre's finest achievements of the decade. The studio gave Lewton a list of preselected titles. As long as storylines reasonably matched with exploitable titles such as *Cat People, The Leopard Man, Isle of the Dead*, etc., and did not exceed a budget of $150,000 per picture, he would enjoy considerable creative freedom.[49] Lewton gathered a unit of creative collaborators, including screenwriter DeWitt Bodeen; directors Jacques Tourneur, Robert Wise, and Mark Robson; and cinematographer Nicholas Musuraca. The impressive results typified the higher-quality B product of a major studio, which could draw on a better infrastructure of facilities, standing sets, and technical personnel than comparable efforts at Columbia or Monogram.

Tourneur's *Cat People* (1942), the unit's first release, reportedly returned over two million dollars on its small investment. In contemporary New York, a young Serbian artist, Irena Dubrovna (Simone Simon), believes she will turn into a marauding were-cat if sexually aroused, leaving her unable to consummate her marriage to architect Oliver Reed (Kent Smith), and pushing him toward Alice (Jane Randolph), a friendly co-worker, for platonic solace. Lewton disliked the Universal style of horror predicated on tangible monsters and heavy makeup and sought to make his horror effects more suggestive than overt, the motivations of plot and characters implicitly more psychological than supernatural. *Cat People* abounds in images and figures of cats, yet setting the precedent for subsequent Lewton films, its shadowy visuals waver between rational and uncanny explanation for Irena's increasingly threatening behavior. In a standout sequence Irena, who we believe may turn into the cat woman at any moment, follows Alice down a dark street. Suspense builds through careful cutting and sound effects until the screeching brakes and whooshing door of a suddenly appearing bus become the climatic "attack" that jolts Alice and audience alike.

As such, Lewton's films may initially disappoint contemporary viewers because they are neither as obviously art-directed as the expressionist films of the 1920s and 1930s, nor remotely as violent as post-1968 horror films. Yet particularly in *Cat People, I Walked With a Zombie* (1943), *The Seventh Victim* (1943), *The Ghost Ship* (1943), *Curse of the*

Cat People (1944), and *Bedlam* (1946), Germanic cinematography and sharp editing combine to invoke strange moods of guilty torpor and inevitable doom. Rather than monsters that could be run to ground by angry mobs, characters in Lewton films are haunted by unspecified sins or beset by ominous, undefined threats. This air permeates Tourneur's *I Walked With a Zombie*, a sly adaptation of *Jane Eyre* transplanted to the West Indies, concerning a naïve Canadian nurse come to care for a rich planter's wife suffering a catatonic malady possibly brought on by a voodoo curse. Direction and performance suggest that the emotionally abusive husband, his dissipated brother who also loved her, or the oddly detached mother-in-law may be equally culpable.

Robson's *The Seventh Victim* follows another young innocent, Mary Gibson (Kim Hunter), into contemporary Greenwich Village in search of her missing sister, eventually uncovering a decadent coven of satanists. The claustrophobic tone dominates a chilling scene in which, alone on a subway car at night, she watches two men wrestling an apparently drunken friend to a seat. When his hat falls off, she sees it is actually the corpse of a detective who had been helping her. An almost abstract sequence depicting her sister's pursuit by cultists through the dark streets accentuates the threat of cold, urban indifference. The film also includes an unsettling episode in which Mary is surprised while showering by an intimidating older woman – seen only as a shadow hovering behind the translucent curtain – that has been claimed as a possible inspiration for the most famous scene in Hitchcock's *Psycho* (1960). (Lewton and Hitchcock were friends from their days working for producer David O. Selznick.)

Less a horror sequel than a lyrical tale of a lonely, imaginative child, Wise's *Curse of the Cat People* concerns Oliver and Alice's daughter, Amy (Ann Carter), who becomes fascinated by a photograph of her father's first wife. Irena appears as the girl's spectral playmate and confidante, though typically, we never quite know whether she is a ghost or a figment of the child's imagination. Amy's involvement with the emotionally tormented residents of a dark, gothic house leads to a surprisingly moving conclusion. Robson's *Isle of the Dead* (1945), a brooding period drama about a random group seeking island refuge from a plague, displays the Lewton team's economical craft. Along with a premature burial subplot, it features a taut performance from Boris Karloff, who could convey deep cruelty with or without stitches and neck bolts. Karloff's sinister intensity also dominates *The Body Snatcher* (1945) and *Bedlam*, the final Lewton release, a beautifully shot drama with compositions derived from the grim asylum drawings of William Hogarth.

Back at Universal, the studio's second horror series ended with two "monster rally" films, *House of Frankenstein* (1944) and *House of Dracula* (1945), in which the Wolf Man (Chaney, Jr) and Count Dracula (John Carradine) vie for screen time with the Frankenstein Monster (Glenn Strange). Karloff plays a mad scientist continuing Frankenstein's experiments in the former, while the latter features Onslow Stevens as a selfless scientist afflicted by transfusions of Dracula's blood. Although a quick knock-off, *House of Dracula* still managed an impressive Freudian nightmare sequence in which the doctor, succumbing to vampiric evil, sadistically unleashes the Frankenstein Monster to attack the innocent. If 1940s horror had a characteristic theme aside from the war, it was this increasing psychoanalytic undercurrent rivaling supernatural rationales for monstrous doings. Robert Florey's eerie *The Beast With Five Fingers* (Warner Bros., 1946), another *Hands of Orlac* tale with Peter Lorre, is fully predicated on an uncertain, subjective tension between reality and delusion. The horror film was about to enter a decade of hibernation, but when it reemerged in the late 1950s, psychosexual themes would grow increasingly common.

CHAPTER 3

A SHORT HISTORY OF THE HORROR FILM: 1945 TO THE PRESENT

Teenage Monsters and the Rise of Science Fiction, 1948–60

In 1948, after years of antitrust litigation, the US Supreme Court handed down a verdict in what is now called the Paramount case. The high court ruled that the five largest Hollywood studios had indeed engaged in monopolistic activities. In particular, their ownership of nationwide chains of first-run movie theaters had kept other producers out of the market. As a result, the major studios were forced to divest their theater holdings and cease other anticompetitive practices. The Paramount decision came at a bad time for Hollywood. After a tremendous box-office take in 1946, theatrical attendance began to decline annually. (The slide continued through the 1960s.) The beginning of national television broadcasting in 1948, and the new medium's rapid adoption by American households, is often considered the reason. Yet changes in larger social patterns in the postwar years, especially the explosive growth of suburbs and the "baby boom," which made critical demands on disposable income and leisure time alike, were the more important factors that kept Americans away from movie theaters. These social and industrial shifts had long-term effects on the kinds of movies produced after the war.

Universal's *Abbott and Costello Meet Frankenstein* (1948), pitting the popular comedians against Dracula (Lugosi), the Wolf Man (Chaney, Jr), and Frankenstein (Strange), is often bemoaned by purists as the final insult to the 1930s horror tradition, but is really a fine genre burlesque where everyone is in on the joke. Still, its symbolism for the genre is hard to avoid. The beasts that haunted the Depression and war years had become the butt of jokes, their terrors far outstripped by colossal horrors of world-historical proportion. The staggering death toll in World War II, over 50 million people killed, included the numbing revelation of the Nazi Holocaust and the atomic bombing of Japan at the war's end. In the 1950s, though Americans were enjoying an economic boom while much of the world still lay in the rubble of war, a persistent fear shadowed the new prosperity. The communist government of the Soviet Union, America's wartime ally, soon became a nuclear-armed, international rival, as tensions seemed to increase daily. Against this background, it seems likely that the 1950s might have seen an outpouring of terror-tinged cinema exceeding that of the 1920s. This is indeed what happened, but the fear favored a new genre form.

Through most of the 1950s, science fiction abruptly supplanted the horror film. Previously, science fiction rated even lower than horror with dominant critical tastes and was not popular with movie audiences young or old. Even weekly sci-fi serials for kids such as Universal's *Flash Gordon* (1936) were fairly rare. Yet after the war, science fiction became the newest and perhaps most apt genre for what pundits dubbed, after poet W. H. Auden, "the age of anxiety." In quick succession, the Soviet Union's successful atomic bomb test and the victory of Mao Zedong's communist forces in the Chinese Revolution in the fall of 1949, followed by the outbreak of the brutal Korean War (1950–3), stoked American fears of an apocalyptic World War III with the communist bloc. That science fiction became a viable Hollywood genre for the first time in the midst of the Cold War hardly seems coincidental considering its two major themes in the 1950s: invasion of Earth (that is, the United States) by aggressive, often technologically superior aliens; and the pervasive dread of atomic weapons, typically imagined as a revolt of nature in which irradiated monsters ravage entire cities.

Alien invasion movies appeared after US forces entered the Korean War, which had begun with a surprise invasion of South Korea by North Korean communist troops. *The Thing* (UA, 1951) depicted a literal "cold war" at a remote arctic base where a group of soldiers and scientists must fight off a radioactive alien that thrives on human blood, a combination of technological and gothic terror. *The Day the Earth Stood Still*

(20th Century-Fox, 1951) opens with a flying saucer landing on the Mall in Washington, DC, then quickly surrounded by tanks and jittery troops. While it was ultimately the rare 1950s SF movie that preached tolerance over paranoia, the alien visitor Klaatu (Michael Rennie) delivers an ultimatum that Earth must learn to live in peace or face annihilation. More typically, in Paramount's *The War of the Worlds* (1953), a montage sequence describing the nations of Earth joining forces to battle the Martian invaders conspicuously omits the Soviet Union from the roll call, implying that the marauding aliens were metaphorical stand-ins for communists. "Flying saucer" had entered the national vocabulary in 1947 after a rash of reported sightings of alleged extraterrestrial vehicles. The Cold War undercurrent of this popular fixation was exposed in a low-budget movie simply called *The Flying Saucer* (Colonial, 1950), in which American agents investigate UFO reports in Alaska and discover the unscrupulous assistant of a brilliant scientist scheming to sell his chief's advanced experimental craft to Soviet spies. No metaphor here. The flying-saucer threat was directly tied to the Russians.

Hydrogen bomb testing, which continued throughout the decade, was the timely motive behind the resurrection or mutation of gigantic monsters in matinee features such as *Them!* (1954), *The Beast From 20,000 Fathoms* (1955), *It Came From Beneath the Sea* (1955), *Tarantula* (1955), *The Beginning of the End* (1957), *The Deadly Mantis* (1957), and *The Amazing Colossal Man* (1957). To signal evidence of the monster, the geiger counter became one of the genre's standard props. Japan, the only nation ever attacked by atomic bombs, produced the decade's most famous radioactive giant. *Godzilla* (Toho, 1954) opens with somber images of a city in smoking ruins after the creature's rampage, scenes that, absent a mutant dinosaur, were still painfully familiar to most Japanese. With added footage featuring Raymond Burr as a visiting American journalist, *Godzilla* was a hit with US audiences, too.[1] The decade's two most elaborate science-fiction productions, *This Island Earth* (Universal, 1955) and *Forbidden Planet* (MGM, 1956), climax with the protagonists witnessing the explosive disintegration of alien worlds in contexts that suggest visions of Earth's possible fate. It seemed that the further science fiction went toward ever less plausible fantasy in the 1950s, the more clearly it revealed immediate and tangible fears.

Invasion of the Body Snatchers (Allied Artists, 1956), a seemingly un-assuming programmer that has since achieved cult status, became one of the most famous movies of the sci-fi boom. Though seedpods from outer space are blamed for the gradual enslavement of an average American town, the film retains the look and feel of traditional horror with its

FIGURE 6 Atomic terrors: the most famous of many radioactive monsters in the post-World War II years, Japan's *Godzilla* (1954, Toho)

expressionistic visuals and emphasis on the hero's psychological terror. Director Don Siegel's compelling vision of quotidian reality gradually transformed into nightmare continued the genre's invasion anxiety yet also condemned the paranoia and passivity of the early Cold War years. Siegel wanted to end the movie with a hysterical Dr Miles Bennell (Kevin McCarthy) screaming, "You're next!" into the camera after failing to stop the alien menace. But the studio insisted on framing scenes that show skeptical doctors and policemen finally convinced he is telling the truth. "Get me the Federal Bureau of Investigation!" one barks into a phone, promising that traditional values and institutions still represent the solution, not the implicit cause of emotionless social conformity.

Universal's newest monster debuted in *The Creature From the Black Lagoon* (1954), made during Hollywood's brief experiment with 3-D movies, one of several technological innovations intended to entice audiences back to theaters. Similar to *King Kong*, the movie followed a scientific expedition to the Amazon in search of a prehistoric missing link, an amphibian hominid who still haunts a remote lagoon. Along with requisite 3-D effects of fish swimming over the audience and spear guns fired into the camera, lyrical underwater photography captured the Creature swimming in fascinated, balletic parallel with the expedition's lone female member, played by Julia Adams. The monster became strangely sympathetic, despite his fishy face. The repetitious *Revenge of the Creature* (1955) was followed by the more interesting *The Creature Walks Among Us* (1956), where the "gill-man" is subjected to evolutionary surgery to turn him into an air-breathing proto-human. Forced into bulky coveralls, the post-operative Creature paces his cell, gazing out at the beckoning ocean. The beast's suicidal escape into the water where it can no longer live became another indictment of risky tampering with nature. The Creature became one of the most widely circulated pop icons of the 1950s.

Hollywood's disappearing audience indirectly sparked the rise of many small, independent production companies. As attendance waned, the major studios cut back production sharply. This left many theaters with a shortage of new movies to show. The independents (and foreign producers) helped fill the gap. Moreover, a specific demographic cohort drove the postwar popularity of science fiction and horror. Throughout the 1950s, not only did the American movie audience get smaller, it also got much younger. By mid-decade, the industry's most reliable customers were teenagers and young adults (roughly aged 12–24), a pattern that largely holds today.[2] Not coincidentally, the postwar period was also the heyday of drive-in theaters, which sprang up by the hundreds in small towns and cities alike. Drive-ins usually offered two or three movies, typically a mix of major studio releases and low-cost quickies made by the independents for just these exhibition circumstances. Teenagers eager to escape parental controls and young parents wanting a cheap night out with their little ones in tow usually made up the audience. (A set of playground equipment below the screen was a common feature of drive-ins.) While mainstream Hollywood was slow to capitalize on the youth audience, smaller, hungrier producers were catering almost exclusively to teens by decade's end, as indicated by a sampling of genre titles: *I Was A Teenage Werewolf* (1957), *I Was A Teenage Frankenstein* (1957), *Teenage Caveman* (1958), *Teenagers from Outer Space* (1959), *Teenage Zombies* (1959), *Monster on the Campus* (1958), *The Ghost of Dragstrip Hollow* (1959).

Most of those teen titles were produced by American International Pictures (AIP), a small but prolific company formed in 1954 by Samuel Z. Arkoff and James H. Nicholson to produce exploitation movies for neighborhood theaters and drive-ins. The term "exploitation movie," like the older "B movie," is often used inaccurately. The industry took the former to mean a low- to medium-budget genre movie lacking major stars but compensating with relatively high degrees of sex and violence. Such movies were built around a concept, sometimes just a title that could be easily "exploited," that is, incessantly promoted by distributor and exhibitor alike. Exploitation included lurid posters, frantic preview trailers, radio and TV spots, or eye-catching stunts tied to the movie's plot staged outside a local theater.[3] Remarkably, AIP, Allied Artists, and other exploitation outfits often invented catchy titles and advertising come-ons first and only then began thinking of a particular story to accompany the promotion. Arkoff often praised Nicholson's knack for dreaming up bankable titles, including *I Was A Teenage Werewolf*, one of AIP's most characteristic and successful movies.[4]

Teenage Werewolf starred Michael Landon as Tony, a troubled high-schooler deeply bugged by parents, peer acceptance, and sexual frustration. Adult authority figures were usually the villains in all the teen genres. Tony's inattentive single father passes him off to a sinister psychiatrist played by Whit Bissell, an indispensable character actor who made a career playing assorted mad scientists and oily officials. Ostensibly seeking to solve Tony's problems through hypnosis, the shrink regresses him to a primitive state of consciousness that manifests itself as a shaggy werewolf. That one transformation occurs as Tony watches a buxom gymnast on a balance beam indicated that lycanthropy was a little-disguised symbol for adolescent sexual anxiety. The movie's surprising grosses (more than $2 million) prompted *I Was A Teenage Frankenstein*, in which Bissell played a doctor with even greater disdain for the welfare of his teenage monster-victim. *Teenage Frankenstein* was also relatively gory, dwelling on the literal assembly of the monster from body parts of teens killed in a wreck. The doctor, who uses a hungry alligator to dispose of discarded bodies, is himself tossed into its jaws at the end by the tragic young monster.

Releasing through Allied Artists and Columbia, producer-director William Castle was the king of exploitation stunts in postwar horror. Beginning with *Macabre* (1958), which offered a $1,000 life-insurance policy from Lloyd's of London to any patron who died from fright during the movie (unlikely!), Castle's succeeding pictures featured highly exploitable gimmicks that helped sell, and often outshone, the movies themselves. *The House on Haunted Hill* (1958) introduced "Emergo," a literal exploitation breakthrough – a plastic skeleton that emerged from the screen and sailed "menacingly" over the heads of delighted kids in attendance. *Thirteen Ghosts* (1960) required moviegoers to don special viewers similar to 3-D glasses to see ghosts materialize in color at certain points in the black-and-white film. Castle shot only one ending for *Mr. Sardonicus* (1961), yet ostensibly allowed the audience to decide the fate of the partly sympathetic monster by a "Punishment Poll" taken in the theater before the climax. *The Tingler* (1959) used Castle's most notorious gimmick. A scientist (Vincent Price) discovers that a large centipede-like organism that attaches itself to a victim's spine causes death from fright. Unless people scream loudly when they feel the tingling sensation, death is inevitable. Here Castle arranged for some theater seats to be rigged with buzzers to produce a mild vibrating shock on cue. Near the climax, as the screen went dark, Price's voice warned the audience the tingler was loose in the theater; the shocks were administered and set off shrieks throughout the auditorium. (Joe Dante's 1993 comedy *Matinee* starred John Goodman as a fast-talking showman modeled on William Castle.)

Innovative work in Britain also hastened the revival of the horror film in 1957. Hammer Films, an older company reorganized in 1949 by producer-distributor James Carreras, produced a range of conventional genres but enjoyed substantial success in 1955 with a literate science-fiction film, *The Quatermass Xperiment* [US title: *The Creeping Unknown*].[5] After this, Hammer decided to try a new version of *Frankenstein*. Terence Fisher's *The Curse of Frankenstein* (1957), with Peter Cushing as the doctor and Christopher Lee as his misshapen experiment, substantially altered the horror genre. Trade announcements about the project had led to warnings from Universal threatening legal action if any of its copyrighted elements, especially Jack Pierce's famous makeup design, were violated. So Jimmy Sangster's inventive script sought to create as original a variation of the tale as possible. Against the monster's friend-ship with the blind hermit in *Bride of Frankenstein*, for example, when Lee's mindless brute comes upon a blind man and his grandson he kills them both. Notably, *Curse of Frankenstein* (and the six sequels that followed to 1973) returned to Mary Shelley's focus on the doctor rather than the creature. Peter Cushing's brilliant but malevolent Baron Frankenstein was the center of Hammer's vision, his monster a different shape and look (or even gender in 1967's *Frankenstein Created Woman*) in each retelling.

Hammer's most immediate contribution was to ratchet up the gore and graphic violence and to include more, and often more cynical, sexuality in its horror films. Bringing the Grand Guignol aesthetic to the screen, Hammer horror was typically most effective when flaunting sex and violence in combination. Preparations for the Monster's birth in *Curse of Frankenstein* involve collecting a rotting corpse from the gallows, the casual removal of its head with a scalpel in the laboratory and disposal in a vat of acid, and close views of a pair of eyeballs floating in a jar, effects heightened by vivid color photography. Moreover, Peter Cushing imbued the Baron with undercurrents of sadism, for example, dallying with his maid until she becomes inconveniently pregnant, then locking her in a room with the creature, and listening at the door with relish to what is implicitly a rape-murder. Where some versions of *Jekyll and Hyde* depict a saintly Dr Jekyll laboring to heal wretched indigents in a charity hospital, the Baron's work with the poor in *Revenge of Frankenstein* (1958) is a contemptuous cover for his aim to harvest body parts from helpless patients. The doctor was the true monster of this saga.

Hammer followed the international success of its new *Frankenstein* with Fisher's *Horror of Dracula* (1958) [simply *Dracula* in the UK], in which Peter Cushing portrayed Van Helsing while Christopher Lee, aristocratically elegant and physically intimidating with his considerable height, became the Master Vampire. Like its predecessor, *Horror of Dracula* was shot in color with detailed sets and period costumes. Although a

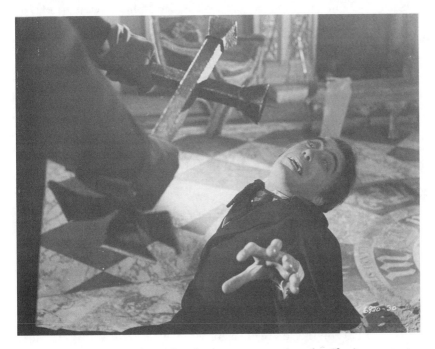

FIGURE 7 Hammer updates the classic genre movies: the (first) destruction of Count Dracula (Christopher Lee) and the start of a new series featuring more graphic violence and sexuality in *Horror of Dracula* (1958, Hammer)

memorable grotesque in *Curse of Frankenstein* in a part far more limited than Boris Karloff's, Lee brought a fresh approach to Dracula. A sense of coiled anger that quickly gives way to red-eyed rage bolstered by athletic strength distinguished his interpretation. When Lee's Dracula, hissing through bared fangs and bloodstained lips, shoves down a vampire bride advancing on Jonathan Harker, then sweeps her into his arms, he decisively separated from the quietly sinister mesmerist Lugosi perfected. The film, which includes Harker's gory staking of the brides, appropriately concludes with physical combat between Van Helsing and Dracula, the doctor barely triumphing by bounding across tables to tear down drapes so the sun's rays scar and burn the vampire to dust. (Thanks to censorship and greater reticence in 1931, Lugosi's Dracula was discreetly staked off screen.)

Shortly after completing *Curse of Frankenstein*, Hammer negotiated a shrewd distribution deal that allowed the British studio to proceed with new accounts of Universal's horror classics without legal trouble.[6] In addition to a steady supply of Frankenstein and Dracula sequels through the early 1970s, this first resulted in Terence Fisher's retelling of *The Mummy* (1959) with Cushing as an archaeologist and Lee as Kharis, injecting Lon Chaney, Jr's mute robot with Lee's physical vitality; and an uninspired remake of *The Phantom of the Opera* (1962) with Herbert Lom. Fisher's finely produced *Curse of the Werewolf* (1961), starring Oliver Reed, was more original. Imprisoned by a lecherous nobleman, a young servant girl is raped by another prisoner and conceives a son born on Christmas Day, an affront to Christ according to the script that curses him with lycanthropy in adulthood. The mother's bloody dispatch of her male oppressors in the prolog prefigures how Hammer's wolf man becomes a driven, class avenger rather than anguished victim like Larry Talbot.

Screen Gems, Columbia's television division, enhanced the growing popularity of horror from AIP, Columbia, and Hammer by making a lucrative deal to acquire broadcast rights to hundreds of Universal's pre-1948 titles. In late 1957, Screen Gems began syndicating a package of classic horror movies of the 1930s and 1940s called *Shock!* Stations typically broadcast them after 10:00 PM on Friday or Saturday nights, introduced by a local host got up as some campy, Halloween variation of Dracula, a zombie, or mad scientist.[7] New York's WOR-TV featured one of the most famous, a droll, funereal ghoul named Zacherley. Since the Universal features ran for only 70–75 minutes, they fit comfortably into 90-minute slots filled out with comedy shtick from the hosts and plenty of commercials. Often aired under the name *Shock*

Theater, the old movies found a new, highly enthusiastic audience. In the age of home video and dozens of cable channels, it is worth recalling that prior to the late 1950s most movies were never seen again after they played their final runs at neighborhood theaters. Television introduced younger viewers to the horror movies, characters, and stars of the previous generation as they aired again and again. The gothic world entered into popular consciousness as never before, merging with a steady stream of new productions.

In February, 1958, publisher James Warren of Philadelphia and Los Angeles-based editor and literary agent Forrest J. Ackerman launched a one-shot magazine unsubtly titled *Famous Monsters of Filmland*. Ackerman, a lifelong fan of horror and science fiction, brought his knowledge, passion, and huge collection of publicity stills to the project of celebrating horror/fantasy cinema for a core of young readers assumed to be between 8 and 15 years old. The first issue quickly sold out, was reprinted, and sold out again. The monster fan magazine was born, spawning more than two dozen imitations in the 1960s and 1970s. *Famous Monsters* reported on new horror movies and spotlighted genre classics with emphasis on the careers of Lon Chaney, Boris Karloff, and Bela Lugosi. The magazine's first issue suggests that a shrewd gauging of major trends had made such a peculiar publication viable at just this point. Under the title, "TV Means Terrifying Vampires," Ackerman penned a long, characteristically punning and digressive report on the coming of Screen Gems' *Shock!* package to the nation's airwaves. The feature included publicity shots of an actor in Frankenstein costume promoting the program, a Los Angeles television guide ad for the show (called *Nightmare* there), and an alphabetical list of 35 markets from Atlanta to Youngstown where the Universal monsters could be seen.[8] The magazine was directly acknowledging its link to the national circulation of these vintage movies. Published until 1983, *Famous Monsters* also inspired important figures in the subsequent development of horror/fantasy, including directors Steven Spielberg, George Lucas, John Carpenter, Joe Dante, and Tim Burton, makeup artist Rick Baker, and writer Stephen King, who all acknowledged its influence on their formative years.

Hitchcock's Psycho *and Genre Transitions, 1960–8*

With exploitation horror playing well at the box office in the late 1950s, director Alfred Hitchcock, known for some of the slickest and most visually complex thrillers of the decade, including *Rear Window* (1954) and *Vertigo* (1958), turned his fertile mind to an offbeat project. He decided to follow the huge success of his suspenseful blockbuster *North By Northwest* (1959) with a quickly produced, modestly budgeted adaptation of Robert Bloch's 1959 novel *Psycho*, inspired by the shocking depredations of Wisconsin serial killer Ed Gein.[9] Bolstered by a sophisticated ad campaign, a high-dollar version of the teasing come-ons beloved by AIP and William Castle, *Psycho* (1960) became Hitchcock's most famous film, and a rare individual work like *Dr. Caligari* or *Dracula* that rearranged the thematic assumptions and stylistic priorities of the genre.

Psycho detailed the fatal, chance encounter between secretary Marion Crane (Janet Leigh) and lonely motel-keeper Norman Bates (Anthony Perkins) that exposed a grisly world beneath an unremarkable surface. Hitchcock subverted the fundamental conventions of Hollywood narrative by spending *Psycho*'s first 45 minutes with Marion, her impulsive theft of cash from her boss, and flight to join her lover. Played by the glamorous Leigh, Marion is the sympathetic protagonist we guiltily hope will get away with the crime. Traditional genre scenes, including narrow escapes from the police, lead us to assume we are watching a crime thriller up to her arrival at the out-of-the-way Bates Motel. Here the film jarringly switches to the conventions of gothic horror when Marion is brutally butchered while showering by a figure we assume is Norman's insane mother. Hitchcock foreshadows the impending collision of characters and genres by contrasting the low, horizontal line of the motel with the dark, vertical form of the Victorian house on the hill behind it.

The shocking spree of bloody violence inflicted on a woman in *Psycho*'s shower murder was virtually unprecedented in Hollywood cinema. The scene, which shows only flashes of contact between the plunging knife and Marion's nude body, lasted only 45 seconds but became indelible through expert editing set off by Bernard Herrmann's screeching violin theme. Where earlier Hitchcock had steered us to sympathize with Marion's theft, after her murder, we are uneasily stranded with Norman as the new protagonist. When he sinks Marion's car in a swamp with her body inside, we listen anxiously to the gurgling sounds as it begins to disappear, then catch our breaths when it won't go down. The second we fear Norman's exposure and sigh with relief when the gurgling resumes and the car disappears, the director has aligned our empathy, however unwittingly, with Marion's killer. That Hitchcock, an acclaimed director working for a major studio (Paramount) rather than an exploitation producer like William Castle, had made such a powerful and disturbing film, helped propel it to the forefront of cultural consciousness and influence.

Psycho signaled the start of a major shift in the American horror film, the full import of which would become increasingly significant after 1968. Hereafter, the popular definition of a horror film would be routinely understood to encompass predatory sexual psychopaths stalking everyday, domestic settings as much as supernatural doings in gothic manors. Marion had been cut to ribbons in a motel shower, after all, not some medieval dungeon. A substantial social and emotional barrier had been crossed thereby, implying a general condition in which average people felt less safe. Moreover, rather than a vampire or rotting zombie, *Psycho*'s monster was a shy, boy-next-door type; the very name Norman ironically suggested "normal." Perhaps most importantly, in the blood-soaked battle between Norman and the cruel, jealous mother pathologically absorbed into his psyche, *Psycho* located monstrosity squarely within the nuclear family itself – that is, the key social institution marked for zealous defense in traditional horror.

Back in Hitchcock's native England that same year, Michael Powell, one of Britain's most esteemed directors, released a visually elegant film that mined similar thematic terrain. *Peeping Tom* (1960) told the disturbing tale of another milquetoast whose benign exterior hid a tormented madman. The first murder is conveyed through the viewfinder of a 8-mm movie camera as the operator solicits a prostitute, who is then forced down and killed, we know not how exactly, as light plays across her face. We soon realize that amateur photographer and professional cinematographer Mark Lewis (Carl Boehm) is the lens-obsessed killer, his camera tripod concealing a retractable blade and mounted mirror so that the horrified victim is photographed while gazing up at the act of her own murder. The movie abounds in witty and unsettling equations of cinema, sex, and murderous violence. Like Norman Bates, Mark is a sadly sympathetic protagonist shattered by the heartless abuse of his late father (played by Powell himself), a psychologist who not only bugged and filmed him incessantly in childhood but deliberately terrified the boy in nasty experiments to study the effects of fear on the nervous system. Powell's somber palette and a consistently understated tone only amplified the dread. Clearly a work ahead of its time, *Peeping Tom* was critically savaged and not widely recognized for the brilliance of its methods until the 1980s.

When William Castle cast Vincent Price in *The House on Haunted Hill* and *The Tingler*, he inaugurated a new career as exploitation horror star for a journeyman character actor working in mainstream movies for 20 years. With his mellifluous voice and often over-the-top acting, Price won new fans with his unique combination of charm and menace. He had made an important foray into the genre a few years earlier when Warner Bros. remade *Mystery of the Wax Museum* in 3-D as *House of Wax* (1953), but the Castle pictures caught the attention of AIP, which was in the midst of an important change in its business plan. According to Samuel Z. Arkoff, AIP's difficult decision in 1959 to begin producing fewer but more expensive color movies came in response to growing competition in the market they had opened for exploitation horror and other genres aimed at teenagers.[10] *House of Usher* (1960), the first of director Roger Corman's eight adaptations of Poe tales, marked the beginning of this new phase in the studio's history and the start of Vincent Price's busy 15-year association with AIP.

The Pit and the Pendulum (1961), perhaps Corman's most effective adaptation, owed little to Poe save its central image of a prisoner strapped to the torture device of the title, yet emerged as a dynamic variation of the more faithful *House of Usher*. Continuing the Hammer precedent of gothic horror envisioned through moody color cinematography, *Pendulum*'s sixteenth-century Spanish setting featured period costumes and atmospheric set design. A showcase for Price, the movie first lets him play the hollow-eyed wretch then move to wild gesticulating and shrieking when his Don Nicholas Medina is seized by the delusion of becoming his father, an infamous Inquisitor. Even with budgets higher than usual for AIP, Corman's Poe pictures still sought to satisfy the exploitation market's increasing penchant for shocks. When the principals break open the crypt of Nicholas' late wife and discover her contorted corpse clawing at the coffin lid after being accidentally buried alive, AIP moved decisively into Hammer-style Grand Guignol.

Corman's *Tales of Terror* (1962) capitalized on the European vogue for anthology films made up of three or four short episodes. A traumatized Vincent Price flees from the ghost of "Morella" and melts into putrid goo at the climax of "The Case of M. Valdemar," while "The Black Cat" segment was mainly comic, at one point pitting a fussy Price against Peter Lorre's drunken sot in a wine-tasting duel. The casting of Peter Lorre and Basil Rathbone (*Son of Frankenstein*) beside Price in *Tales of Terror* indicates how heavily the medium-budget horror feature leaned on the star system after *Curse of Frankenstein*. The trend lasted through the early 1970s as Cushing, Lee, Price, and veteran boogeymen such as Lorre, John Carradine, and Lon Chaney, Jr appeared repeatedly in European and American chillers. The aging but still vital Boris Karloff worked in horror throughout the 1960s, including Corman's comic

FIGURE 8 Poe goes to the drive-in: in the flashback of Roger Corman's *The Pit and the Pendulum* (1961, American International Pictures), the Inquisitor Sebastian Medina (Vincent Price) lures his unfaithful wife and brother to their dooms

rendition of *The Raven* (1963) opposite Price and Lorre, and the brooding *The Terror* (1963), featuring a young Jack Nicholson.

Darkly beautiful Barbara Steele, a supporting player in *The Pit and The Pendulum*, was the compelling star of Italian director Mario Bava's stylish vampire tale *Black Sunday* [*La Maschera del Demonio*] (1961), which scored international success. In a chilling seventeenth-century prolog, Steele is a convicted witch tied to a stake by frightened villagers, before a spike-filled metal mask is placed on her face and then hammered in by a hooded executioner. Reborn as a viciously seductive vampire in the nineteenth century, she wreaks vengeance on the descendants of those who persecuted her. When the marble vault of the vampire/witch blows apart leaving her writhing in murderous arousal on a slab, it brought the sexual undercurrent of the vampire myth fully into the open. Feminist criticism has argued that the fear and containment of potent female sexuality centrally structures the horror genre. Steele's defiant rage alongside the archly phallic means by which she was attacked lends support for such interpretations. Bava returned with the visually expert anthology *I Tre Volti della paura* ("The Three Faces of Fear"), which was recut and dubbed in English by AIP for US release as *Black Sabbath* (1963). Besides introducing the tales, Boris Karloff delivered one of his finest performances in "The Wurdulak," about the complete destruction of a landowner's household. Karloff is fearsome as the pitiless monster of the title, a Russian variation of the vampire. "The Telephone" was a capable suspense tale, while "The Drop of Water," about a greedy woman's theft of a ring from a corpse and her subsequent torment when the old woman's spirit seeks revenge, was cinematically inventive and genuinely unsettling.

The major Hollywood studios remained aloof from horror, conceding the genre and its youthful audience to the independents and foreign producers.[11] Slick efforts like MGM's *The Haunting* (1963), a suspenseful ghost story based on Shirley Jackson's novel *The Haunting of Hill House*, were rare. Directed by Val Lewton alumnus Robert Wise, *The Haunting* was one of the last suggestive horror films that depended on careful construction of foreboding mood rather than bloody, violent shocks, attractions the big studios were not quite ready to provide. Still, the steady demand for product in drive-ins and urban neighborhood theaters presented opportunities for "off-Hollywood" producers with far fewer means than AIP. As mainstream Hollywood hovered on the verge of major breakthroughs in permissible content, ad man-turned-exploitation filmmaker Herschell Gordon Lewis helped pioneer the semi-underground genre of "nudie films" (e.g., *Lucky Pierre* [1961]) before making the first examples of what Lewis termed "the gore film," *Blood Feast* (1963) and *Two Thousand Maniacs* (1964). Filming in lurid color with blood spurting and viscera flopping, Lewis proclaimed the commonsense philosophy of the exploitation producer: "if you cannot titillate [an audience] with production value, you titillate them with something else."[12] Hammer wouldn't approach such violent extremes for another five years or so.

Two Thousand Maniacs was a bloody *Brigadoon* about the ghostly inhabitants of a small southern town who arise a century after the Civil War to hold a communal celebration in which travelers, all northerners, are lured in and butchered. One victim is actually barbecued and eaten. Released at the height of the Civil Rights struggle – this was the summer three young Civil Rights workers were murdered by the Ku Klux Klan in rural Mississippi – *Two Thousand Maniacs* depicts a hospitable, back-slapping populace of a town adorned with Confederate flags who are really ghouls and merciless sadists. That it raked in profits from play dates mostly in southern drive-ins suggests a powerfully conflicted response to the movie and the unfolding events it paralleled. Conscious or not, political allegory was not what patrons came to see. After a leisurely buildup, the scene in which two locals suddenly hack off a young woman's thumb and then her entire arm still shocks.

Despite their offbeat energy and episodes of extreme gore, atrocious acting and technical roughness mar Lewis' movies. *Carnival of Souls* (1962), the lone feature-film effort of veteran industrial filmmakers Herk Harvey and John Clifford of Lawrence, Kansas, was far more polished. Here midwestern locales took on a dreamlike mood through sumptuous black-and-white cinematography and crisp editing in a tale of a woman who narrowly survives a car crash only to be stalked by a threatening, chalk-faced man. *Carnival of Souls* has acquired a cult reputation and garnered lavish comparisons to the European art cinema of Carl Theodor Dreyer and Ingmar Bergman. Yet with its eerie atmosphere and twist ending, the film was more reminiscent of the well-crafted horror/ fantasy tales of the popular *Twilight Zone* television series.

From only a few thousand television sets in the nation at the end of World War II, the new medium had penetrated 90 percent of American households by 1960. Network television became a source for influential horror/fantasy storytelling with the anthology series *The Twilight Zone* (CBS, 1959–64) and *The Outer Limits* (ABC, 1963–5). Strong writing, acting, and direction distinguished both. Introduced by writer-producer Rod Serling, most *Twilight Zone* tales build to a twist ending in the manner of O. Henry, or perhaps more aptly, the famous horror tale "The Monkey's Paw," with its emphasis on human frailties and the intercession of fate. Memorable episodes included "It's A Good Life" (originally aired 11/3/1961) about a spoiled child (Billy Mumy) with godlike powers who arbitrarily remakes the world in his own image; "Eye of the Beholder" (11/11/1960), which used expressionistic visuals to describe a future society where a congenitally "deformed" woman undergoes surgery to transform into the "normal" appearance of her misshapen, pig-faced doctors and nurses; "To Serve Man" (3/2/1962), whose punning title describes seemingly friendly aliens actually scheming to feast on gullible humans; and the cautionary "The Monsters Are Due On Maple Street" (3/4/1960), about a suburban neighborhood that succumbs to paranoia and mob violence when a series of inexplicable power failures afflict the area. Fantasy novelist-turned-screenwriter Richard Matheson (who also wrote several Corman/Poe pictures) contributed numerous scripts to the series.

In an era of repeated Cold War confrontations and crises, *The Twilight Zone* aired several warnings of nuclear Armageddon (e.g., "Time Enough at Last" [11/20/1959], "The Shelter" [9/29/1961]). Yet *The Outer*

Limits, created by Leslie Stevens and *Psycho* screenwriter Joseph Stefano, going into production only a few months after the terrifying 1962 Cuban Missile Crisis, took the nuclear threat and dawning fear of the military-industrial complex as its most persistent themes. "The Man With the Power" (10/7/1963) was a Jekyll and Hyde story complete with psychosexual undertones about a meek professor with an electronic implant in his skull that generates a fearsome energy cloud to incinerate anyone who stands in his way; in "The Architects of Fear" (9/30/1963) an idealistic scientist is surgically transformed into a bogus alien invader to frighten the nations of the world into peaceful coexistence; "It Crawled Out of the Woodwork" (12/9/1963) depicts malevolent energy gestating inside a common vacuum cleaner at a shadowy government research center; "The Forms of Things Unknown" (5/4/1964) was a suggestively eerie psychodrama shot in expressionist style about a controlling rich man and his two mistresses who experiment with a scientist's time-, and implicitly, mind-altering device.

As a cult of monster toys, model kits, movie magazines, and TV programs from *Shock Theater* to *The Twilight Zone* flourished in the early 1960s, the networks offered two parodic gothic sitcoms, CBS's *The Munsters* and ABC's *The Addams Family*, both telecast between 1964 and 1966. *The Munsters* was a Universal project, so family patriarch Herman could appear as a grinning copy of Karloff's Frankenstein monster. Silly domestic sitcom plots were put over by standout performers in both casts. In *The Munsters*, Fred Gwynne's bumbling Herman played off the Borscht Belt mugging of Al Lewis' vampiric Grandpa; in *The Addams Family*, John Astin's pop-eyed Gomez lusted after Caroline Jones' weirdly erotic Morticia, supported by Jackie Coogan's anarchic madman, Uncle Fester. Derived from Charles Addams' macabre magazine cartoons of the 1940s and 1950s, *The Addams Family* was the darker, stranger of the two. While the Munster clan was ultimately a pleasant bunch one could invite to a church bazaar, with the Addams family you could never quite shake the suspicion there were traumatized victims writhing in some hidden dungeon of their creepy house.[13] The monster family sitcoms subconsciously reinforced the growing equation between the world of gothic horror and the middle-class American family itself.

The 1960s also witnessed the popular run of the odd but engrossing soap opera *Dark Shadows* (ABC, 1966–71), in which a diffident vampire presided over a daytime *danse macabre* of familiar monsters and recycled genre plots. Producer Dan Curtis sold the series, revolving around the ancestral New England mansion of the wealthy Collins family, as a variant of the traditional soap-opera format, with gothic ambiance recalling

Jane Eyre or *Rebecca*. Several months later, with ratings in decline, Curtis tried an experiment, introducing a short-term plotline about an ancestor who returned as a vampire. Playing the revived bloodsucker Barnabas Collins, Jonathan Frid became an overnight sensation and the show's central character. After this, the writers plunged headlong into the supernatural with storylines about witches, werewolves, demons, ghosts, and time travel. *Dark Shadows* was surely the first network soap that addressed two distinct audiences simultaneously. Viewers divided between the traditional daytime target of middle- and working-class housewives and a juvenile cohort of approximately 8–15-year-olds of both sexes, enthralled by a world in which every day was Halloween.[14]

Against the backdrop of social and political tumult in the late 1960s, harsh reality that never directly entered the land of *Dark Shadows*, Barnabas Collins evolved from monster to tragic hero as the sometime-vampire and his ally Dr Julia Hoffman (Grayson Hall) fought to protect the Collins household from ceaseless supernatural threats. Its weird, camp appeal aside, *Dark Shadows* furthered the breakdown of barriers between daylight world and gothic darkness. After directing *House of Dark Shadows* (MGM, 1970), a successful feature-film version of the series that indulged increasing trends for graphic violence, Dan Curtis returned with tautly produced made-for-television movies from Richard Matheson scripts including *The Night Stalker* (ABC, 1972), a ratings topper about a vampire terrorizing Las Vegas, whose undertones of Watergate-era political conspiracy continued the genre's move toward contemporary parable.

Rosemary's Baby (Paramount, 1968), helmed by itinerant director Roman Polanski, culminated gothic horror's absorption into the family structure that ran through the decade. "Pray for Rosemary's Baby," pleaded the ad line over a shadowy baby carriage, but it really meant pray for us all when the hapless Rosemary (Mia Farrow) gives birth to the antichrist in modern-day New York after a ritualistic rape by the Devil himself. A Polish Jew who lost his entire family in the Nazi Holocaust, Polanski could easily locate the uncanny and horrific in the most ordinary settings. His *Repulsion* (1965), shot in London with Catherine Deneuve, was another psychosexual descent, perhaps more unnerving in spots than *Psycho*. *Dance of the Vampires* (1967), released in a reedited US version as *The Fearless Vampire Killers*, was less a genre parody than a grimly pessimistic comedy that demonstrated how traditional heroes were not simply obsolete but helpless in the face of pure, determined evil. Similarly, Rosemary feebly resists a scheming coven of satanists that includes her greedy husband and elderly neighbors before agreeing to suckle the hell-spawn in the film's serio-comic conclusion. *Psycho* had announced that henceforth things would be different in the horror genre. *Rosemary's Baby* confirmed it.

"American Gothic": Sex and Violence, 1968–80

Hollywood censorship had been waning since the Paramount decision in 1948. Absent a distribution system based on direct ownership and control of first-run theaters, the major studios had less incentive to continue the strictures imposed in the 1930s, particularly as box-office revenues continued to fall after the war. The Production Code endured but its power steadily weakened. Moreover, although the Supreme Court had only extended clear First Amendment protection to motion pictures for the first time in 1952, prevailing social standards began to change, too. By the late 1960s, exploitation movies were competing with escalating levels of sex and violence in mainstream features. *Bonnie and Clyde* (1967), *Bullitt* (1968), *Midnight Cowboy* (1969), *The Wild Bunch* (1969), et al. included nudity or flaunted intense, bloody violence in prestigious Hollywood releases. In late 1968, in the midst of immense social shifts crystallizing around the Civil Rights movement and growing protests against America's immersion in the Vietnam War, Hollywood eliminated prior restraint of content and adopted the first ratings classification system. Critics extolled and debated "the new freedom of the screen." Exploitation producers now unleashed outrageous scenes of gore, sadism, and sexual violence in often coldly ironic films that seemed to feed off the energy and fears of the times. Indeed, horror films throughout the 1970s can be seen as both a reaction to, and assimilation of, the social traumas of the Vietnam era.

Pittsburgh-based industrial filmmaker George A. Romero revolutionized the exploitation field with the brilliant *Night of the Living Dead* (1968) just as censorship was lifting. The first assault by a shuffling, resurrected corpse occurs less than 10 minutes into the movie and the carnage and desperation only increase thereafter. Romero filmed much of the story at night and shot in black and white with heavy shadows to evoke the classic horror films. Shadows would not be used suggestively in the Lewton manner, however. A young couple burned inside a pickup while trying to escape are set upon by the ghouls, their flesh slurped and gobbled in graphic closeups. The movie was extremely gory throughout, with victims eviscerated by an army of walking dead; corpses zapped back to half-life by what the script breathlessly explains as some alien plague brought back by a space probe. Like a ravenous vampire mob, the zombies' victims join the walking dead and move mindlessly to kill and devour the living.

The movie's central scenes, a frantic group barricaded inside a house while a vicious horde tried to break in, seemed derived from *The Birds* (1963), Hitchcock's gripping if enigmatic thriller with the zombies substituted for swarms of attacking birds. As apocalyptic scenarios of total destruction both could be read as allegories of nuclear doom. Yet *Night of the Living Dead* carried a strong undercurrent of the racial turmoil convulsing America at the time. Ben (Duane Jones), the lone African-American character in an otherwise all-white group, played the film's reluctant hero. Ben struggles for leadership with angry, white father Harry Cooper in bitter exchanges where racial animosity is tangible but unspoken. Contrary to traditional horror films, in the climax, courageous and resourceful Ben dies a meaningless death and the movie ends on a note of nihilistic despair. *Night of the Living Dead* mapped major new directions for the American horror film of the next 10 years.

A young British director named Michael Reeves made several original horror films in this milieu. In *The Sorcerers* (Tigon, 1967), an elderly scientist (Boris Karloff) and his wife use a consciousness-transfer process to regain their youth by taking over the minds and bodies of young people. That the elders seem mostly interested in sex, drugs, and violence spoke to the generational anxieties of the times. By the late 1960s, AIP was shooting films in Britain and co-producing or distributing Hammer and other British movies domestically. This included Reeves' *Witchfinder General* (Tigon-AIP, 1968), a stark drama set in the English Civil War featuring an icy Vincent Price as Matthew Hopkins, a corrupt and merciless witch-hunter. AIP retitled it *Conqueror Worm* (a Poe poem) for US release to imply it was a continuation of the Corman series, though it was far grimmer than those earlier movies. A genre-bender without supernatural elements, the beautifully shot but disturbing film graphically depicts sadistic torture and burning of innocent women condemned by Hopkins. In the end, the stalwart soldier-hero not only fails to rescue his beloved from the witchfinder but also succumbs to maniacal blood lust himself.

Night of the Living Dead and *Witchfinder General* had shown that horror films might end anticlimatically with moral boundaries erased, or even with clear victory for the monster, family and society crumbling – tendencies that would characterize horror films of every stripe through the 1970s. Peter Bogdanovich's *Targets* (Paramount, 1968) posed the question of whether an older, and suddenly tamer style of horror retained any power whatsoever in a society consumed with the real horrors of the Vietnam War and attendant domestic upheavals. Boris Karloff appeared as famed horror star Byron Orlok, who confronts a psychotic serial gunman at the drive-in premiere of his latest movie (actually clips from Corman's *The Terror* [1963]). *Targets* replaced the *chiaroscuro* of European expressionism with a mundane setting, the smoggy haze of a southern California suburb. Here the new "monster," a seemingly average mid-century everyman, inexplicably slays his entire family before venturing out to shoot at cars on the freeway. Cousin to Norman Bates, the character was based on Charles Whitman, the 1966 bell-tower sniper at the University of Texas. Bogdanovich's finest inspiration is the sniper shooting from behind the movie screen at unsuspecting victims sitting isolated in their cars, a horribly literal extension of William Castle's "Emergo" gimmick in *The House on Haunted Hill*.

Even post-1968 horror films with familiar gothic settings sought, with varying degrees of sincerity, to express and exploit the major shifts in gender roles and sexual identities that were unfolding. Hammer's Dracula series was characterized by increasingly open sexuality. A telling image in *Taste the Blood of Dracula* (1969) depicts a young woman sleeping in implicit post-coital languor on a marble slab above Dracula's half-exposed coffin. Hammer then turned out a cycle of lesbian vampire movies that bordered on soft porn. *The Vampire Lovers* (1970) was the best of the lot, starring sultry Ingrid Pitt as the undead seducer and Peter Cushing as a vampire-hunting nobleman. *Lust for a Vampire* (1971) and *Twins of Evil* (1971) were graphically violent but equally committed to filming female stars topless as often as possible. (*Daughters of Darkness* [1971], a Belgian–French production, was a more sophisticated and visually interesting variation of the theme.) AIP's release of Hammer's well-produced *Dr. Jekyll and Sister Hyde* (1972) cried, "Warning! The sexual transformation of a man into a woman will actually take place before your very eyes!," a wonderfully bold lie that nonetheless indicated the conflicts, confusions, and liberating possibilities of the sexual revolution of the 1960s and 1970s.

When Hollywood began targeting urban black audiences in the early 1970s, one result was a rash of low-budget movies with African-American casts, dubbed "Blaxploitation" by the media. Mainly identified with violent urban crime thrillers such as *Shaft* (1971), *Superfly* (1972), and *Foxy Brown* (1974), the cycle also yielded several horror variants. AIP's *Blacula* (1972) starred William Marshall as a nineteenth-century African prince bitten by a bigoted Count Dracula then revived in modern-day Los Angeles. Like most Blaxploitation antiheroes, the vampire remained highly sympathetic throughout. In the finale, Blacula slays a posse of white policemen before discovering that his reincarnated wife (Vonetta McGee) has been staked by the Van Helsing figure, Dr Thomas (Thalmus Rasulala). Crushed, he chooses a suicidal walk into the sunlight, destroyed neither by white authorities nor his black establishment foe. In addition to the sequel, *Scream Blacula, Scream* (1973), other examples included the gimmicky *Blackenstein* (1973), the interesting *Sugar Hill* (a.k.a. *The Zombies of Sugar Hill*) (1974), about resurrected slaves taking revenge on oppressive white gangsters, and *Abby* (1974), concerning a young woman's demonic possession, made in response to *The Exorcist* (1973).[15]

The Blaxploitation cycle was condemned by black opinion leaders across the political spectrum for its criminal stereotypes and rightly identified as mainly the product of white studios, writers, and directors, yet the movies proved highly popular with inner-city audiences.[16] Expert at varying proven formulas, AIP produced its most characteristic Blaxploitation picture by combining its outlaw biker movies (e.g., *The Wild Angels* [1966], *Chrome and Hot Leather* [1970]) with its horror tradition. *The Thing With Two Heads* (1972) was a jaw-dropping affair about a racist white scientist (Ray Milland) who winds up sharing the body of a black convict (former NFL star Rosie Greer). "They transplanted a white bigot's head onto a Soul Brother's body!" explained the ads, which pictured the enraged two-headed freak astride a leaping motorcycle, police cruisers in pursuit – a scene that weirdly encapsulated Blaxploitation's fundamental nature as a running struggle between black and white for control of images and stories.

Vincent Price concluded his horror career in the early 1970s with AIP's stylish *The Abominable Dr. Phibes* (1971), and three variations on its themed serial murder formula, *Dr. Phibes Rises Again* (1972), UA's *Theatre of Blood* (1973), and *Madhouse* (1974), an AIP co-production with Amicus, Hammer's leading British rival in the horror field. Skillfully directed by Robert Fuest, *The Abominable Dr. Phibes* straddled major genre trends of the 1960s and 1970s. Displaying the graphic violence energizing exploitation and mainstream movies alike, *Dr. Phibes* satisfied AIP's drive-in aesthetic while continuing to assimilate the stylistic marks of Hammer's sumptuous gothic horror of the previous decade. Along with its art-nouveau décor, *Dr. Phibes* includes slyly self-reflexive humor that references Price's status as horror icon.

Price plays Dr Anton Phibes, renowned organist and theologian, whose injured wife dies in surgery following an auto accident. Racing to her side, Phibes himself is burned in a crash and presumed dead. Though

FIGURE 9 Essence of exploitation: American International Pictures (AIP) ad slick for *The Thing With Two Heads*, combining elements of the 1970s "Blaxploitation" cycle and the outlaw biker movies of the 1960s (1972, AIP). *Producer:* Wes Bishop. *Director:* Lee Frost

terribly disfigured, he resurfaces several years later and begins systematically eliminating the nine members of the surgical team he madly blames for her death. Using motifs derived from the Old Testament curses on the Pharaoh (blood, boils, frogs, death of the firstborn, etc.), Phibes slays the doctors in a series of witty, occasionally gory set pieces. The doctor worships at the shrine of his late wife who is seen only in photographs, slides, and other graphic renderings, and channels his artistic impulses into elaborate episodes of murder-as-performance-art. A complex play of artifice and actuality, being and imitation runs throughout the movie, starting with Phibes himself, a knowing combination of Lon Chaney's Phantom and Price's first major horror role as the mad sculptor concealing a grisly face behind a mask in *House of Wax* (1953).[17]

Further indication that the genre was entering a volatile period of transition came from parodies of its traditional forms that appeared in mid-decade. Mel Brooks' *Young Frankenstein* (1974) was an affectionate tribute to, and lampoon of, Universal's 1930s horror films, sporting lush black-and-white photography and detailed sets derived from the classic designs of Charles D. Hall. Gene Wilder, who played Dr Frederick Frankenstein ("That's *Fronkensteen*"), said that his inspiration for the screenplay came from the unlikely image of the Frankenstein monster in top hat and tails, an idea realized with the Monster (Peter Boyle) on stage growling out "Puttin' on the Ritz." Wilder's anarchic juxtaposition complemented the camp explosion of musical and horror film in *The Rocky Horror Picture Show* (1975). Based on an off-Broadway hit, *Rocky Horror* soon sparked an enduring cult phenomenon as the original "midnight movie." Its opening number, "Science Fiction Double Feature," tartly recaps horror and science-fiction highlights from the 1930s through the 1950s.

Following the path of *Night of the Living Dead*, however, most low-budget horror films of the early 1970s showed that raw social and sexual conflicts could be expressed in ways that were anything but funny and reassuring. Wes Craven's *Last House on the Left* (1972) opens with a pair of teenage girls leaving home for a rock concert only to be abducted, raped, and relentlessly tortured before being killed by a hippie band inspired by Middle America's worst nightmares of the counter-culture in the wake of the 1969 Charles Manson "family" atrocities. The killers unknowingly seek refuge at the home of one girl's parents, who eventually discover what happened to their daughter and exact a methodical and equally savage revenge. Dad splatters one killer with a roaring chain saw, while Mom, using a vicious ruse, castrates another with her teeth while performing oral sex. The ads warned: "To avoid fainting, keep repeating, 'It's only a movie', It's only a movie,'" advice that for once wasn't just hype.

Tobe Hooper's *The Texas Chain Saw Massacre* (1974) was a more visually sophisticated but no less harrowing work that genuinely shocked and offended while earning great profits and attracting appreciative fans, including a growing number of intellectuals. The movie begins with the grim discovery of grave robbing and ritualistic arrangement of corpses in a cemetery, then descends into a truly hellish nightmare. Like *Psycho*, *Last House on the Left*, et al., *Chain Saw Massacre* refused to indulge in a supernatural conception of its monsters, a family of unemployed slaughterhouse workers who annihilate a group of young travelers. Reminiscent of Romero's zombies, Hooper invests his butchers with an aggressive malevolence approaching the apocalyptic. Combining motifs from *Last House* and *Chain Saw Massacre*, Wes Craven's *The Hills Have Eyes* (1977) was a similarly relentless inversion of traditional genre structures about an extended suburban family in mortal combat with their *doppelgängers*, a degenerate cannibal clan in the southwestern desert, where once more the distinction between monster and family evaporates.

The collapse of traditional social and ideological barriers in these gory movies paralleled the erosion of institutional barriers between major studio releases and exploitation horror exemplified by Warner Bros.'

The Exorcist (1973). A big-budget movie with an Oscar-winning director, *The Exorcist* brought explicit horror firmly into the mainstream. Based on William Peter Blatty's bestselling novel, William Friedkin's film describes the inexplicable satanic possession of 12-year-old Regan MacNeil (Linda Blair), and the efforts of her frantic mother Chris (Ellen Burstyn) and a pair of priests to drive the Devil from her soul. The possessed child levitates off her bed, spews green vomit, turns her head around backwards, and masturbates with a crucifix while screaming a string of obscenities unimaginable in a big studio movie only a few years earlier. Along with such blockbusters as *The Godfather* (1972), *The Sting* (1973), and *Jaws* (1975), *The Exorcist* was one of the most profitable movies of the decade.

Set in Washington, DC, and released at the height of the Nixon administration's immersion in the Watergate conspiracy scandal, *The Exorcist* abounds with Vietnam-era references. Early on we see actress Chris MacNeil on the set of a campus protest movie, shooting a scene in which a crowd of student demonstrators shouts down her character, the voice of moderation and compromise; Chris cynically describes the picture as "a Walt Disney version of the Ho Chi Minh story." Meanwhile, wise old Father Marin (Max Von Sydow) has been living in Woodstock, New York, presumably trying to exorcise its countercultural demons. These topical references not only grounded the story's uncanny events in everyday reality, they signaled the precise hot-button political anxieties underlying the movie's phenomenal reception. The climax, with the girl saved but the priests dead, resonantly suggested that the battle between good and evil as the film defined it had ended at best in an exhausting and uneasy draw.

The Exorcist inspired a spate of glossy horror films, none as interesting as it or remotely as unnerving as contemporaneous exploitation movies. Suspenseful and effective, *The Omen* (1976) combined *Rosemary's Baby* and *The Exorcist* to describe the birth of the antichrist to the American ambassador to Britain (Gregory Peck) and his wife (Lee Remick). In one memorably grotesque scene, the boy's bewitched governess hangs herself before the horrified guests at his birthday party. John Boorman's *Exorcist II: The Heretic* (1977) was a box-office disaster but an enigmatic and visually atmospheric spectacle. Other demon-child movies included *Burnt Offerings* (1976), *Audrey Rose* (1977), and the positively old-fashioned *The Changeling* (1980). Revisionist trends shaped another major studio offering, John Badham's *Dracula* (1979). Often more genteel costume drama than horror film, it starred Frank Langella as the Count with Laurence Olivier as Van Helsing, rewriting the story as an Oedipal contest for the soul of Van Helsing's daughter (Jan Francis). In synch with many other movies of the period, though, this time Dracula wins.

The stylistic and thematic influence of Hitchcock's *Psycho* appeared in a number of 1970s horror films (e.g. *Carrie* [1976]), but perhaps most directly in John Carpenter's *Halloween* (1978), one of the most profitable sleepers in film history. Jamie Lee Curtis (daughter of *Psycho*'s Janet Leigh) starred as a naïve high-school babysitter who becomes the target of a silent madman in a white rubber mask. *Halloween* continued *Psycho*'s transformation of banal Americana, here a tree-lined midwestern neighborhood, into a haunted gothic wilderness. Less raw than *Texas Chain Saw Massacre* but as carefully rendered in its portrait of a relent-less sexual psychopath and his terrified victims, *Halloween* quickly became widely influential itself. The movie's huge grosses (an estimated $47 million on a $340,000 investment) spawned a flood of derivative quickies that coalesced into an altogether new subgenre variously called "slasher," "stalk and slash," or "body count" movies. Simultaneously, the slasher cycle also attracted highly negative mainstream media attention for the next several years.

Halloween popularized one of the most controversial visual elements of post-1968 horror, a subjective camera prowling through streets and houses that puts the audience into the optical point of view of the killer. Nationally syndicated columnists like Roger Ebert and Janet Maslin charged that this technique represented the ultimate degradation of humane cultural and moral values in that it forced, or worse, encour-aged the viewer to identify with the murderer rather than his victims.[18] This condemnation occurred, moreover, after several years of increas-ingly vocal and well-organized opposition to media images of violence against women emerging from the women's liberation movement of the 1960s and early 1970s. Yet the vexed issues of audience "identification" are hardly as straightforward and one-dimensional as the critics claimed. In any case, the slasher cycle and the surrounding controversy under-scored the increasingly brutal gender combat that was always more or less at the surface in the genre but seemed to be a particular feature of the 1970s horror film.

Science fiction's popularity languished after the late 1950s until Stanley Kubrick's breathtaking *2001: A Space Odyssey* and 20th Century-Fox's more conventional *Planet of the Apes* scored critical and commercial hits in 1968, reviving the genre with expensive, effects-laden releases. A second science-fiction boom accompanied the horror upsurge in the 1970s. Most dreaded the future, predicting everything from nuclear Armageddon (the *Planet of the Apes* series [1968–73], *The Omega Man*

[1971], *Zardoz* [1973], *A Boy and His Dog* [1975]); and environmental catastrophes (*Silent Running* [1972], *Soylent Green* [1973]); to the victory of totalitarianism (*A Clockwork Orange* [1971], *Rollerball* [1975], *Logan's Run* [1976]). Still, the emotional distance between George Lucas' stark *THX-1138* (1971) and *Star Wars* (1977), an effusive salute to 1930s adventure serials, could not have been greater. Along with Steven Spielberg's *Close Encounters of the Third Kind* (1977), *Star Wars* reversed the trends for socially critical, revisionist genre filmmaking which had animated Hollywood since the mid-1960s. Its heroes are born-again innocents who decisively defeat the cartoon villains and restore the traditional order. The horror film, based in social disruption and terror, did not fully succumb to this return to conservative tradition, however.

The lines between horror and science fiction instructively blurred in Ridley Scott's nerve-wracking *Alien* (1979), promoted with the tagline, "In space, no one can hear you scream." Costly post-*Star Wars* visual effects highlight a chilling contest between a spaceship crew and a marauding beast they unwittingly release in their midst. *Alien* played like a slasher film with toothy crustacean in place of demented killer. Sensuously gothic production design by surrealist artist H. R. Giger infused the story with sexual symbolism. Dressed in helmeted space-suits that suggest spermatozoa, three astronauts walk into the distinctly vulva-like openings of a derelict spacecraft and inadvertently "fertilize" an egg that hatches the alien. The larval monster's explosive, gut-splattering burst from the chest of one unfortunate astronaut is a sequence of frightening gore. As in *Halloween*, *Alien*'s bold heroine (Sigourney Weaver) narrowly survives after all her compatriots have died; both films conclude on unsettled notes that denied complete catharsis. The implication was heavy – that, like *Halloween*'s implacable psycho, the alien horror would inevitably return. (Both did, several times.)

Gothicism's central motif, the haunted house, was carried to its logical end in *The Amityville Horror* (1979), where the dwelling itself becomes the monster. When an urban family buys a country house where a young man had slain his own family years before, it turns against its new owners in frightening acts of aggression. One of the last AIP releases before Sam Arkoff sold his company to Orion Pictures in 1979, *Amityville Horror* was a surprise hit. The movie got to the box office ahead of Stanley Kubrick's long-awaited adaptation of Stephen King's *The Shining* (1980). When frustrated writer Jack Torrance (Jack Nicholson) takes his wife Wendy (Shelly Duvall) and psychic son Danny (Danny Lloyd) to winter at a closed mountain hotel he gradually goes mad and tries to murder his family. Kubrick's acolytes assumed the maestro was simply slumming in this tawdry genre and could not have regarded it with anything other than ironic detachment. Indeed, as in most of his work, Kubrick used familiar genre conventions as jumping-off points for other themes. Still, the director's command of cinematic technique delivered a gripping horror tale. *The Shining* proved a solid hit, despite mixed reviews.

The effect was all the more remarkable because Kubrick avoided shadows, cobwebs, and antique trappings. The Overlook Hotel was often photographed in even lighting or bright daylight that emphasized its modern banality. Menacing atmosphere built from long stretches without dialog such as the camera closely trailing Danny as he pedals a tricycle through the empty hallways (the film featured one of the first uses of the Steadicam). Still, *The Shining* brought out the sexual insecurity and rage at the heart of many gothic tales. Danny's vision of a slow-motion cascade of blood pouring from the doors of an elevator evoked gothicism's principal theme, sins of the past that can no longer be contained. Nicholson's quipping, wild-eyed pursuit of his terrified wife ("Wendy, I'm home!" he calls, after smashing through a door with an ax) is both comic and chilling. Not since Fredric March's Mr Hyde tormented Ivy had so harrowing an image of domestic violence been presented in such a fantastic setting.

The Vietnam War's near-complete absence from movie screens for more than a decade still produced some roundabout commentary in popular genres, including horror. *Night of the Living Dead* referenced TV news coverage of the war with its paramilitary posse hunting zombies recalling an army patrol on a search-and-destroy mission. A few exploitation movies broached the war more directly. The monster in *Blackenstein* was a demolished black soldier resurrected by a white mad scientist; Bob Clark's grisly *Deathdream* (1974), featuring makeup by recently discharged combat veteran Tom Savini, concerned a Vietnam casualty who returns to his parents' home as a decomposing vampire-corpse. Starting from the climactic image of *Planet of the Apes* in 1968, the Statue of Liberty half-buried in the sand, 1970s science fiction repeatedly presented images of American society in ruins. Early in the film, stranded astronaut Taylor (Charlton Heston) mocked a fellow-spaceman dutifully planting the Stars and Stripes on a barren world. That same year, the height of the Vietnam War, a small flag loomed in the foreground above a veteran's grave (and behind Romero's directing credit) at the opening of *Night of the Living Dead*. The social and political aftershocks of the post-Vietnam years, including Watergate, the energy crisis, and the 1979–81 Iranian hostage crisis, were also accompanied by ironic insertions of American flags in horror films. In *The Shining*, a flag adorns the realtor's desk when Jack Torrance accepts the caretaker job at the Overlook Hotel and hangs above his head in the room where he does his mad "writing." In the opening of *Poltergeist* (1982), Old Glory waves on a TV screen as the national anthem plays. Between these two pairs of flag imagery in horror/science-fiction cinema lay the era of ideological breakdown and cultural confusion President Jimmy Carter called America's "malaise"[19]

On movie screens in those years, the American family had been assaulted by demons social, sexual, and implicitly political in a series of widely discussed horror hits – *Night of the Living Dead, The Exorcist, Halloween,* and *The Shining.* Ronald Reagan ascended to the White House in 1980 on a pledge to restore a glorious American past. But the social and cultural aftershocks of the most politically divisive period since the Civil War could not be simply banished by fiat. The bumpy collaboration of director Tobe Hooper and producer Steven Spielberg on *Poltergeist* wavered between whiz-bang special effects and displays of its suburban family's acquisitive superficiality. In a neighborhood erected by greedy developers atop a desecrated Indian burial ground, goblins whisper to a little girl from inside a television set and pull her into the netherworld. As the house finally collapses in a raging storm, empty-eyed corpses bob to the surface of the half-built swimming pool. The family narrowly survives but the suburban tract home had become America's *Castle of Otranto.*

Slashers, Splatter, and Postmodern Horror, 1980–95

Although there had been precursors to the slasher movie before 1978 such as Bob Clark's chilling *Silent Night, Deadly Night* (a.k.a. *Black Christmas*) (1974) and AIP's heavily promoted *The Town That Dreaded Sundown* (1977), *Halloween*'s triumph sent big studios and small producers scrambling to cash in. Many unabashedly lifted major elements from Carpenter's hit. The gripping *When A Stranger Calls* (1979) starred Carol Kane as a babysitter terrorized by the phone calls of a madman who seemingly sees her every move. *Prom Night* (1980), *Happy Birthday To Me* (1981), *My Bloody Valentine* (1981), and *Graduation Day* (1981) exploited the "horror holiday" premise. Jamie Lee Curtis kept screaming in formula slashers including *Prom Night, Terror Train* (1980), and *Halloween II* (1981). Released by Paramount, the most successful variant was Sean S. Cunningham's *Friday the 13th* (1980), where a group of summer-camp counselors are bloodily dispatched by what is thought to be the ghost of Jason Voorhees, a boy drowned in the lake years before due to his counselors' neglect. Yet in a reversal of *Psycho*, the climax reveals the killer as Mrs Voorhees, the boy's mother. Still, Jason's rotted corpse rises from the lake to grab a last victim in a shock coda derived from *Carrie* as well as *Halloween*'s final moments when Michael Myers suddenly seems supernaturally powerful. With *Friday the 13th Part 2* (1981), Jason himself, now a hulking, hooded figure (the hockey mask arrived in *Part III* [1982]) became the relentless slayer in sequels that stretched into the early 2000s. Coming full circle, Universal produced two surprisingly well-mounted sequels to Hitchcock's milestone, in which Anthony Perkins returned as Norman Bates, released from the mental institution after 20 years to resume his quiet life as motel proprietor, though his old problems – and mother – soon reappear. *Psycho II* (1983) and *Psycho III* (1986), though essentially typical genre entries, attested to the degree to which this unique character and film had become icons nearly on a par with Dracula or Frankenstein.

The slasher cycle quickly solidified into a repetitive formula. *Friday the 13th* and others recycled *Halloween*'s stalking, subjective camera and musical motifs from Bernard Herrmann's *Psycho* score. After the example of Norman Bates, the slashers were usually sexually confused or otherwise feminized males enacting some psychotic revenge for traumas suffered in childhood; their victims usually teenagers, stand-ins for the audience the films themselves targeted. In true exploitation-movie fashion, sex and violence were closely intertwined. The victimization of young women was common, yet slasher movies also depicted randy couples slaughtered in the midst of sexual romps or just afterwards. (The crass exploitation of female nudity followed by bloody murder led to the crude but accurate description of these films as "show your tits and die.") The madman butchered his victims with a variety of primitive hand weapons – knives, spears, machetes, bludgeons, axes, torches. (*The Toolbox Murders* [1978] and *Driller Killer* [1979] played up this convention.) The killer's ancient weapons, often used for beheadings and eviscerations, underscored an atavistic binge of revenge-fueled brutality. While few examples were of more than passing interest – it's hard to believe a movie called *Friday the 13th Part V: A New Beginning* (1985) will really contain anything new – the slasher cycle's popularity, along with its highly sexualized violence, kept the phenomenon on the public radar through the mid-1980s.

Although the sexual-revenge angle drove most slasher films, the killer in the *Friday the 13th* series remained a ghostly figure that was virtually immortal. Jason became another Dracula, destroyed and resurrected in film after film. The opening of *Jason Goes to Hell: The Final Friday* (1993) sees the monster ambushed by a troop of heavily armed policemen and shot to pieces. He doesn't stay down long. The change from human psychopath to supernatural menace signaled a return to gothic tradition, providing a cushion of aesthetic and emotional distance between viewer and on-screen horrors that the most unnerving exploitation horror of the 1970s had stripped away. Indeed, the completion of the first slasher cycle can be marked by Wes Craven's *A Nightmare on Elm Street* (1984), which projected the serial killer formula into solidly supernatural territory. With increasing reliance on elaborate special effects, *A Nightmare on Elm Street* and its sequels brought back those fantasy elements, and in the process became less unsettling, certainly as compared to Craven's own work in the 1970s.

Freddy Krueger (Robert Englund), a serial child murderer, was hunted down and burned alive by a mob of enraged parents. Years later, he begins to haunt the nightmares of neighborhood teens he had terrified as children. This time, Freddy is a malicious ghost of amazing power who aims to complete the destruction of his victims when they sleep. Often a fount of macabre wit, Englund's Freddy was a nasty if engaging villain. Like many classic monsters, he wore a unique costume – his face and body a mass of scar tissue, Freddy sported a porkpie hat and brash red and green striped sweater. Most famously, he wore a make-shift glove with long metallic blades/fingers he scraped along walls or used to rip into victims. The first *Nightmare on Elm Street* recalled *Halloween* in that a resourceful teenager, Nancy (Heather Langenkamp), was Freddy's nemesis, and the evil again appeared unstoppable. With Freddy seemingly destroyed, a daytime coda has Nancy and friends picked up in a vintage convertible. As she gets in, the windows roll up and the covering top displays Freddy's trademark stripes. Transformed into the car itself, he apparently drives her away to her doom. Still, the eerie interplay between dream and reality underpinning the tale made it easy to begin a *Nightmare on Elm Street* franchise that proved enduringly popular.

The contradictory pull of attraction and repulsion in the Freddy character sparked several horror series built around charismatic monsters. British horror novelist and director Clive Barker's *Hellraiser* (1987) was a visually baroque and not a little campy work featuring an ancient monster known as Pin-Head, a sadomasochistic demon pierced with thousands of nails. *Child's Play* (1988), featuring a wisecracking devil-doll named Chucky, tapped horror's deep roots in childhood fears.

Taking off from the slasher cycle, Chucky is really the repository of a serial killer's evil spirit. *Candyman* (1992), adapted from a Clive Barker story, was a rare play on American racism in the horror genre. In three movies to date Tony Todd played Daniel Robitaille, a black artist lynched in the 1890s for falling in love with the daughter of a white patron. After his hand was sawed off and his body covered in honey he was stung to death by swarms of bees. Reborn as the ghostly Candyman, he guts victims with a sharpened hook in place of his hand. In the original, a graduate student (Virginia Madsen) researching urban legends learns about Candyman, who is said to appear if you repeat his name five times while looking in a mirror. The *doppelgänger* motif evoked by the mirror opened intriguing possibilities, but the movie was finally an ideologically contradictory jumble.

A related subgenre John McCarty dubbed "splatter movies" paralleled the slasher cycle. Splatter, a term borrowed from George Romero's wry description of his zombie pictures, referred to vivid spectacles of bloody violence rooted in the Grand Guignol.[20] Perhaps only a new term for what Herschell Gordon Lewis had called gore films in the mid-1960s, splatter might also be understood as a further move toward the "cinema of attractions" mode of early cinema. A splatter film's main interest laid in its construction of detailed, often breathtakingly gross effects of bodily destruction, decomposition, or mutation. Story and character-ization became secondary. *Phantasm* (1977), an effective sleeper with surreal undertones, set an example. In a mortuary concealing the en-trance to a netherworld, a flying metallic ball sprouts blades to grind out the victim's eyes, blood spraying. The result was literal "splatter." While pointing out that certain exploitation films were indeed flaunting higher degrees of carnage, McCarty's definition of what is or is not "splatter" is porous. In terms of plot structure, the low-budget *Maniac* (1980), featuring grisly effects by Tom Savini, was closely aligned with the slasher cycle. Still, the early 1980s often hailed makeup artists and special-effects technicians as auteurs in their own right. Developments in makeup techniques, especially the refinement of latex and foam-rubber appliances plus sophisticated mechanical effects, lay at the center of movies such as Carpenter's *The Thing* (1982), Romero's *Living Dead* sequels, and the work of David Cronenberg. Yet these movies were much more than just showcases for effects.

Rick Baker and Tom Savini were two of the most accomplished makeup artists of this era. Baker, who initially specialized in realistic ape costumes, playing the monster in the 1976 remake of *King Kong*, had started at AIP. For *The Thing With Two Heads* (1972), he designed and played the mad doctor's first experiment, a two-headed gorilla. Baker's gory effects for *The Incredible Melting Man* (1977) exemplify the splatter concept in a movie with little to recommend besides the increasingly hideous decomposition of an astronaut infected with a space virus. An acclaimed industry professional, Baker was the first winner of Hollywood's long overdue Academy Award for Best Makeup Design for his work on *An American Werewolf in London* (1981). (He credited the inspiration of Jack Pierce in his acceptance speech.) Tom Savini has rendered exceptionally gruesome effects for numerous horror films, including most of George Romero's since the mid-1970s. His work on *Dawn of the Dead* (1979), featuring assorted zombie eviscerations, axings, gobblings, and beheadings, defined an important moment in the splatter film. He also contributed to the original *Friday the 13th* and other slasher movies. *Maniac* contains some of Savini's most nauseating – and amazing – effects, including the repeated scalping of female victims and a man decapitated by a shotgun blast.

Stuart Gordon's *Re-Animator* (1985), adapted from a tale by horror writer H. P. Lovecraft, exemplified splatter cinema's fast-paced shocks and vivid gore. A sharp departure from the slasher formula of the early 1980s, *Re-Animator* seemingly marks a return to tradition in its variation of the Frankenstein myth. The film's true accomplishment lies in its deft negotiation of the often sought but seldom realized balance of gross-out horror and macabre humor, efforts that culminate in a scene of attempted rape so outlandish and shocking it shatters the seemingly clear boundary between revulsion and laughter. As the obsessive but dryly comic visionary Dr Herbert West, Jeffrey Combs delivered an adroit performance that made him a minor cult figure in low-budget horror thereafter. Gordon's *From Beyond* (1986) was a creditable follow-up, with many of the same talents adapting another Lovecraft tale combining grotesque special effects and dark humor.

Re-Animator includes elements of what has been called "postmodern" horror. Postmodernism is not easy to define, and since the 1980s has become so broadly applied to such a variety of cultural forms and social practices as to become nearly meaningless. Still, the proliferation of mass-media forms (especially television) and the resulting recycling of myriad other forms of high and popular culture through multiple media venues have led some critics to suggest that this aesthetic may signal an entirely new stage of social and cultural development. Though cultural theorists have made large if provocative claims for postmodernism, it is still probably too early to proclaim a new epoch in human history and consciousness. However, theorists seem to have identified significant elements of style that make such films (and other contemporary cultural forms) sharply different from traditional predecessors.

First, postmodernism is characterized by pastiche – consciously grabbing elements from other films and genres in a seemingly random fashion, intermingling sounds, images, narratives, and icons from a variety of cultural sources. Postmodernism is thus defined by an overwhelming historical self-consciousness, signaled by many direct quotations and allusions to earlier, well-known texts such that a movie may repeatedly call attention to itself as an artificially constructed work rather than something "real." (Indeed, more extreme theories of postmodernism argue there is nothing "real" whatsoever, just an endless series of linguistic references without beginning, center, or irreducible meaning.) This notion of acute historical self-consciousness can be distinguished, though not easily, from outright genre parodies such as *Young Frankenstein*. That is, horror dramas featuring strong undercurrents of self-conscious humor may tend toward the postmodern aesthetic. *Fade To Black* (1980), a novel variation of the slasher story, concerns a disturbed movie fan (Dennis Christopher) who slays victims in imitation of famous genre scenes from *Psycho* to *Dracula*. (The title refers to a common screenwriting term to mark the end of a scene.) The opening sequence of *The Funhouse* (1981) recaps the evolution of the contemporary horror film. Donning a mask (through which we watch the scene unfold as in *Halloween*), a boy sneaks up on his sister while she is showering and attacks her with a rubber knife. This play with quotation and audience expectation serves as a kind of "rehearsal" before the "real" murders later in the film.

Premised on a complete breakdown between movie and reality, *Wes Craven's New Nightmare* (1994) represents a more direct example of postmodern horror. Here Craven, Heather Langenkamp, and Robert Englund appear as "themselves" during production of yet another *Nightmare on Elm Street* sequel, as the cast and crew are stalked by the "real" Freddy Krueger. Moreover, as opposed to the resolution and closure in traditional narrative forms of all kinds, postmodern works tend toward open-endedness. Indeed, for exploitation horror, the many roman-numeralized sequels that keep bringing audiences back for the same basic tale for years or even decades (the *Friday the 13th* series has entered its third) present the lack of catharsis and closure considered characteristic of postmodernism. Each sequel more or less directly states that the monster lives and will inevitably return. Theorists disagree on the implications of this kind of aesthetic experience, however.

FIGURE 10 Postmodern quotation: *The Funhouse* opens with self-conscious reference to *Psycho* by way of *Halloween*. A parodic "rehearsal" before the "real" violence later in the movie (1981, Universal). *Producer:* Steven Bernhardt. *Director:* Tobe Hooper

As in *Re-Animator*, comedy mixed with extreme violence and gore often feature in postmodern horror. Dan O'Bannon's *Return of the Living Dead* (1985) was a bloody but humorous revision of Romero's nihilistic and genre-changing work, in which we are tacitly encouraged to root for the zombies instead of their witless victims. After the living dead devour an ambulance crew responding to a distress call, for instance, a zombie radios their dispatcher to "Send more paramedics" – as if ordering pizza. Sam Raimi's *Evil Dead 2* (1987), the middle part of a trilogy (1981, 1987, 1993), may be one of the truest examples of post-modern horror. A swiftly paced, absurdist comedy, *Evil Dead 2* contains an astonishing sequence of slapstick mayhem in which, plunged into a nightmare world, the quirky protagonist Ash (Bruce Campbell) suffers a zombie bite on his hand. The appendage suddenly acquires a mind of its own, a nasty little voice, and determination to kill its owner. Increasingly enraged, Ash must battle his own hand and finally slice it off with a chainsaw. Undaunted, the hand "walks" away on its fingertips and must be trapped under a can.

Michael A. Arzen notes that the sequence contains direct and implicit allusions to *Night of the Living Dead, Texas Chain Saw Massacre, The Hand* (1981), *Gremlins* (1984), and *The Addams Family*.[21] (Moreover, the scene's premise might also reference Peter Sellers' brilliant slapstick battles with his own willful hand as the title character in Kubrick's *Dr. Strangelove* [1964]). Yet in treating skeptically the claim that post-modernism represents something entirely new and unprecedented, we might recall that in the early twentieth century, the Grand Guignol typically mixed humor with spectacles of excessive gore that reportedly not only provoked fear but sometimes laughter as well. A similar reaction to *Evil Dead 2* signals shock and disbelief, along with delight in the audacity of the technique. The notion of postmodernism applied to the horror genre remains an intriguing, if not altogether definitive development in the form.

The slasher's popularity notwithstanding, the vampire has apparently become our favorite monster since the mid-1980s, a phenomenon critics have associated with the age of AIDS. *The Hunger* (1983), a visually sumptuous and enigmatic tale of vampires locked in an erotic bisexual triangle, exploited and contrasted the sexual personae of its shimmering stars, David Bowie, Catherine Deneuve, and Susan Sarandon. *Fright Night* (1984) was a fairly traditional tale with a touch of genre self-consciousness. Roddy McDowall plays a timid TV horror-show host reluctantly drawn to help kids plagued by a vampire next door. The old story was given a wide range of new interpretation in *Near Dark* (1987), *The Lost Boys* (1987), *Bram Stoker's Dracula* (1992), and *Buffy the Vampire Slayer* (1992). (*Buffy* spawned a clever television series that rose above the movie's one-joke premise.) James Bond III's *Def By Temptation* (1990) recalls 1970s Blaxploitation with an African-American cast battling a vampiric female sexual demon. Robert Rodriguez's *From Dusk Till Dawn* (1996) was a fast-paced, postmodernist jape with a gory, climactic shootout between a ravenous vampire mob and a desperate group armed with crossbows and squirt guns filled with holy water. With the vampire as a resonant metaphor for many forms of sexual identity, anxiety, and desire; the symbolic transfer of blood; and the potential geometric expansion of the plague through those very avenues of sexual contact and blood/fluid exchanges, it seems logical that the AIDS crisis might find cultural expression in this malleable myth. This is not to say that AIDS fear is the "real" meaning of every recent vampire movie, only to suggest that the escalating tragedy may have rekindled popular interest in this particular monster since the mid-1980s.

As horror films have done since AIP made *I Was A Teenage Werewolf* in 1957, these recent vampire yarns sought to address the experiences and concerns of their youthful audiences. With the American divorce rate climbing in the 1980s, *Fright Night* and *The Lost Boys* depict fatherless households where mom's new beau turns out to be the monster. (*The Step-Father* [1987] was a *Psycho*-based treatment of this theme.) Though *The Lost Boys* portrays vampires as a disaffected youth gang, its title associates vampirism with the *Peter Pan* story. Indeed, recall the shadowy, expressionist introduction of Peter as a mysterious figure alighting on a rooftop near the beginning of the 1955 Walt Disney animated version. Dracula also underpins one of the most enduringly popular comic-book superheroes. In *Batman Forever* (1994), the caped hero (Val Kilmer) appears in dark silhouette at Nicole Kidman's window as she lies resplendent in a diaphanous white gown – exactly the way Dracula is usually portrayed in the act of stealing sex/blood from beautiful virgins. These ambivalent portrayals may signal the embrace of the vampire as a complex power figure as well as a talisman against death.

Gregory A. Waller's study of the vampire film, *The Living and the Undead*, points to the 1979 Frank Langella version of *Dracula* as a significant revision of the myth in which Dracula triumphs, impaling Van Helsing with the stake. This version paralleled Anne Rice's 1976 bestseller *Interview With the Vampire*, in which the monster is essentially the hero, and there is no Van Helsing figure in the story at all. Warner Bros.' 1994 film version starring Tom Cruise ends with the vampire LeStat driving away in a vintage Mustang, "Sympathy for the Devil" blaring on the radio – Dracula as Bondian playboy. Anne Rice publicly blasted the casting of Tom Cruise, then later apologized, saying she liked the film. Her resistance turned on Cruise's image as a hunky male ingénue, rather than the world-weary decadence her character exuded. Still, this 1990s image of the vampire was something new.

Recent Genre Trends, Mid-1990s to the Present

When *The Silence of the Lambs* (1991) captured the 1992 Best Picture Oscar, it was the first major award for a horror film since Mamoulian's *Dr. Jekyll and Mr. Hyde* (1931). Despite grotesque violence and Anthony Hopkins' chilling performance as the dreadful Dr Hannibal Lecter, it was not conceived as horror per se. Rather, *The Silence of the Lambs* marked the Hollywood debut of gory, Italian-style detective drama

– American *giallo*. Gothic tropes predominate when FBI agent Jodie Foster first meets "Hannibal the cannibal," a madman so dangerous the government keeps him locked up in what appears to be a stone-walled dungeon. The immeasurable influence of Hitchcock's *Psycho* recurs in the film's adroit audience manipulation and in its second killer, "Buffalo Bill" (Ted Levine), a vivid take on the psychopathic Ed Gein. Other films of this type included *Se7en* (1995), a downbeat drama about edgy detectives (Morgan Freeman and Brad Pitt) trailing a serial killer (Kevin Spacey) whose victims die in gruesome scenarios tied to the seven deadly sins; and *The Bone Collector* (1999), with Denzel Washington and Angelina Jolie in a plot derived from Hitchcock's *Rear Window* (1954). For crime stories, these movies depict a level of unnerving sexual violence and gore drawn from the most uninhibited horror films of the 1970s.

Wes Craven entered a third influential phase of his horror career with the surprise success of *Scream* (1996) from a script by Kevin Williamson, a postmodernist revival of the slasher film. With sexuality and violence restrained in comparison to its forebears, *Scream* may be notable primarily for a blasé teen's ongoing recitation of the hackneyed conventions of those earlier movies ("Never say, 'I'll be right back,'" "the virgin never dies," etc.), while a group watches *Halloween* on videotape, oblivious to the shadowy killer stalking them. The monster appears as the iconic figure from Munch's painting *The Scream*, cloaked as the Grim Reaper and converted from terrified victim to ruthless butcher. Honoring all ancestors, *Scream* opens with a sly allusion to *Psycho* in which popular star Drew Barrymore, the apparent protagonist, quickly succumbs to a grisly death. The hit spawned two highly repetitive sequels. Williamson also scripted *I Know What You Did Last Summer* (1997), the story of teenage friends who accidentally run down a fisherman and then try to disguise the death, only to be haunted by a vengeful killer who may be a ghost. It took over half a century, but *I Still Know What You Did Last Summer* (1998) finally surpassed *Frankenstein Meets the Wolf Man* for perhaps the laziest title ever for a horror sequel.

Built on the urban legends concept, *The Blair Witch Project* (1999) was surely the most profitable horror film in relation to cost ever. Conceived by a clever group of university film students, the no-budget movie was cannily promoted on an internet site months before its release, making many believe that its fictitious premise (the disappearance of three student filmmakers researching a local legend, and chance discovery of their video documentary footage several years later) was an actual occurrence. The movie became a word-of-mouth hit in art houses, then opened in hundreds of regular theaters, grossing some $245 million. Remarkably, *Blair Witch* is devoid of violence, gore, or even a monster, relying entirely on the buildup of eerie atmosphere and suspense. Though it is unlikely a similar trick will ever work again, *Blair Witch* added an original notion of style to the genre – horror effects based on a technical and ontological appeal to truth and reality. The ready availability of consumer-grade video cameras in middle-class homes since the 1980s has greatly affected how a younger generation thinks about film and television. As such *Blair Witch* may be less related to the horror film per se than to "reality-based" television shows of the 1990s such as *Cops, America's Funniest Home Videos,* and *Unsolved Mysteries.*

In addition to creating an immediate demand for, and renewed interest in movies of the past, the 1980s home-video revolution encouraged the theatrical and/or video release of the "director's cut" or other "special editions" of some movies. Since the advent of Digital Video Discs (DVDs) in 1997, additional memory compression has allowed "deleted scenes" and features on the film's production. For the horror genre, these technology-driven shifts in exhibition have yielded varying results. The release of original foreign-market versions of movies on DVD has permitted wider access to previously hard-to-see films by European directors like Mario Bava, Dario Argento, and Jess Franco, some of which were never distributed theatrically in the United States. However, when an altered version of *The Exorcist* appeared in September, 2000, the *New York Times* noted that this digitally enhanced revision of the 1973 horror milestone was the first "writer–producer's cut."[22] William Peter Blatty, author of the original novel, pushed for this edition, which runs 11 minutes longer with footage trimmed, in most cases wisely, from the original. Digital "enhancements" are limited to scary faces placed on walls that pointlessly reiterate the impending menace.

In the original, our first realization that something is seriously wrong with Regan occurs during the dinner party when she appears before her mother's guests in her nightgown and releases a stream of urine on the floor. In the new version, the shock of this moment has already been dissipated by a lengthy doctor's office visit where Regan is alternately grouchy and disassociated in flat staging and performances that do nothing but telegraph the approach of the uncanny. The ending is also substantially affected. Blatty never liked *The Exorcist*'s original ending because he said it gave some viewers the impression that evil had triumphed. So now we are treated to a longer coda after Regan and her mother pull away in the taxi, where another priest plays some shtick with Inspector Kinderman (Lee J. Cobb), concluding with the chuckling pair strolling off to dinner and a movie. It's as if we are suddenly watching a romantic comedy about a gay detective indulging his hapless attraction to Catholic priests. In any case, the extended ending fulfills Blatty's desire for a more traditional genre finale.[23]

For the first time in many years, major Hollywood studios have been releasing expensive, star-driven fright films. Most were ghost stories that followed on the profitable heels of M. Night Shyamalan's *The Sixth Sense* (1999), where psychologist Bruce Willis counsels a traumatized boy (Haley Joel Osment) tormented by malignant spirits. Variations of haunted-house stalwarts like *The Uninvited* (1944) and *The Haunting* (1963), these films returned to the genre's gothic foundations for plots while adding special effects displays. High budgets tend to make for conservative filmmaking, however, and truly disturbing moments were rare. Others of this type included glossy remakes of *The Haunting* (1999) with Liam Neeson, and old William Castle titles (minus the charm) such as *The House on Haunted Hill* (1999) and *Thirteen Ghosts* (2001). *What Lies Beneath* (2000) features Harrison Ford and Michelle Pfeiffer in another exercise from the book of Hitchcock. *The Others* (2001), starring Nicole Kidman, was a comfortably spooky outing while *Dragonfly* (2002), with Kevin Costner, used gothic trappings in a familiar romantic fantasy. *The Skeleton Key* (2005) was a more charged but devoutly traditional gothic tale about a young caretaker (Kate Hudson) investigating voodoo rites in a creepy New Orleans manor.

The most popular slasher series of the 1980s stumbled along their profitable but uninspired paths for 20 years but showed some vigor at the millennium through increasing self-consciousness. *Jason X* (2001) was the tenth *Friday the 13th* outing, a clever if unabashed remake of *Alien* with Jason as the deadly thing prowling a futuristic spaceship. The best bit is when the desperate survivors distract him with a virtual-reality simulation that seemingly returns Jason to Camp Crystal Lake circa 1980 where two young women extol the joys of drugs and premarital sex before gleefully peeling off their tops. Commercial logic compelled the two most iconic monsters of the Reagan years to face-off in New Line's long-delayed *Freddy vs. Jason* (2003), with fight choreography derived from Asian movies, and directed by Hong Kong horror veteran Ronny Yu (*The Bride With White Hair* [1993]). Indeed, Asian cinema provided the latest foreign influence on American horror when DreamWorks released *The Ring* (2002), a remake of the eerie Japanese horror hit *Ringu* (1998), about the malevolent ghost of a little girl that kills successive victims who watch a weird videotape filled with surreal

FIGURE 11 The slasher cycle and a new monster pantheon in the 1980s: Jason does it again, and again, and again in *Friday the 13th Part VII – The New Blood* (1988, Paramount). *Producer:* Iain Paterson. *Director:* John Carl Buechler

imagery. More atmospheric than gory, *The Ring* used digital effects sparingly to conjure stark nightmare landscapes that obscured the boundaries between media and reality, while again situating atrocity and evil within the family. The cross-pollination continued as Hideo Nakata, director of the Japanese original, was tapped to direct the effective sequel *The Ring Two* (2005).

As the digital revolution has begun to reshape Hollywood, experimentation is palpable in a variety of films and genres. Digital manipulation has only reinforced the postmodernist aesthetic. In *Queen of the Damned* (2002), from Anne Rice's *The Vampire Chronicles*, LeStat (Stuart Townsend) rises from the dead to front a rock band. A music-video segment depicts him costumed as Cesare and seamlessly blended into scratchy, black-and-white images from *The Cabinet of Dr. Caligari*. The look, and thus far, the contexts in which digital effects have been applied have been largely derived from the fantasy conventions of cel animation and the breakneck pace of Asian action movies, though washed-out digital cinematography added to the sepulchral tone of the zombie tale *28 Days Later* (2003). While we might expect new visual technology to enhance fantasy epics like *The Lord of the Rings* trilogy (2001–3) and science fiction such as *The Matrix* (1999) and *Star Wars Episode II: Attack of the Clones* (2002) – the first blockbuster shot entirely with digital cameras – spectacular digital effects have also driven horror-cum-action movies like *Blade* (1998), *The Mummy* (1999), *Dracula 2000* (2000), and *Van Helsing* (2004). Such films would have delighted Georges Méliès. Effects aside, the need and appeal of frightful and disturbing stories that get under the skin will no doubt continue. The history of the horror film suggests that state-of-the-art technology is hardly its major appeal; and that the most distressing individual and social fears will continue to seek cultural expression in tales of terror.

CHAPTER 4

MONSTERS AMONG US: CASES OF SOCIAL RECEPTION

A genre as rich in psychological, cultural, and social resonance as horror has been received and evaluated in assorted ways. Despite or perhaps because of the genre's popularity, the average horror film, like the Western programmer of the past, is accorded little cultural respect. As producers often flaunt social and moral taboos in the creation and promotion of their wares, public responses to the horror genre often become sharply politicized. At regular intervals, in fact, it has been attacked from both right and left, and greeted by many with a mixture of suspicion and condescension focused around the supposed damaging effects that cinematic fright might have on women, children, or the culturally unsophisticated. (A similar scenario arose with the gruesome and sexy EC horror comic books in the 1950s.) And just as predictably, producers and aficionados of popular horror counter that the Bible, ancient mythology, canonical literature, and the daily news teem with stories of monsters, grotesques, and bloody mayhem – arguments that contend this seemingly low form actually holds a venerable pedigree. Producers, consumers, and critics of horror films are frequently engaged in a fierce three-way struggle to a degree not found in the circulation of more prosaic movies. Like death, horror is a fact of (social) life.

Whether particular films rated lush production values and technically advanced visual effects or were turned out on a shoestring for quick profit in the exploitation market, budget figures and mode of production are not reliable predictors of either aesthetic accomplishment or social impact. The horror film, like other popular forms, responds directly or indirectly to currents beyond the film industry itself. Debates about horror often address issues of individual reception, notions of how particular viewers respond to, and perhaps are influenced by, the films they consume. Yet because the genre's basic definition lies in its intention to evoke terror, and because cinema is foremost a mass medium, a particular moment in its history often reveals fears that are social as much as individual. Understanding the changing historical patterns in which horror movies function, as well as grasping the unique properties horror brings to any cultural debate, illuminates vital aspects of the genre as well as the shifting concerns of the larger society.

Social questions about horror often center on issues of censorship, an official response to counter or prohibit the perceived violation of fundamental social and moral standards depicted in destabilizing horror narratives. The aim of censors is usually paternalistic when not overtly authoritarian, acting, it is claimed, to protect some members of society from the potentially damaging results from exposure to cultural expressions of horror (and other possibly antisocial forms such as pornography or "media violence" in the abstract). However, the public scrutiny of horror that sometimes results exists just as often beside an opposite, even paradoxical response – scoffing disdain for any interest in forms that are denounced as childish, time-wasting, and trivial. Horror films invite controversy, and one must also say surely find their popularity, in a rather small range of topics that recur in the genre's themes and narratives, sites that often expose particular social pressure points. Though the range of such areas is arguably fairly circumscribed, the issues they open are complex, even as certain themes or their relative intensity varies over time. Controversial – and appealing – aspects of horror films include: the spectacle of extreme acts of violence; more or less open sexuality that defies conventional norms and attendant assumptions about gender roles; treatment of particular religious and moral values and attitudes about the nature of evil; social and less overtly, political values implied in the portrayal of traditional authorities and social institutions (e.g., government, science, the Church, the family) and a film's ultimate faith in the efficacy of those institutions to protect society from the monster/evil and restore the status quo.

Whether wolf man or madman, the monster is often equal parts repulsive and compelling in the most effective and enduring horror tales. Social fear and condemnation of the genre, its producers, and most avid consumers betray a fear foremost that the monster will step down off the screen into our world; that is, that the distinction between the fictional monster and the reader/consumer of horror stories may be lost, and an otherwise innocent viewer become the most tragic victim by acting out this new identity or compulsion in society at large. Those who most distrust the horror genre fear that at root all fictional monsters are vampires – creatures whose malignant influence expands each time they claim a new victim. Tracing selected public responses to popular horror, that is, points at which the genre provoked concerted institutional reactions, organized protests, or more ambiguous and nuanced uses by genre fans is the subject of this chapter. Each example illustrates areas of controversy and complaint about horror's social impact that were traditional as well as historically specific.

Hard Times and "Gruesome Pictures"

Perhaps it would be wise to obtain an early estimate of the audience reaction and critical opinion concerning *Dracula* and *Frankenstein* by Universal; *Dr. Jekyll and Mr. Hyde* by Paramount; and *Almost Married* by Fox, all of which are in distribution or are about to be distributed. Paramount has another "gruesome" picture about to be put into production and Metro-Goldwyn-Mayer has *Freaks* which is about one-half shot. Is this the beginning of a cycle which ought to be retarded or killed? I am anxious to receive your advice.

    – Jason S. Joy to Will H. Hays, December 5, 1931[1]

Fox's *Almost Married* (1931), an early directorial effort by noted production designer William Cameron Menzies, is rarely discussed in relation to the seminal horror movies of the early 1930s cited by Jason Joy, but it became associated with them, at least in his mind, in part because the parameters of a horror movie were not well defined in the winter of 1931. Though the title might suggest a romantic comedy, *Almost Married* concerns an imprisoned madman who escapes and tries to murder his wife who, in her despair, has entered into a bigamous marriage with a new husband. Otherwise, we now know that Joy, West Coast head of the Motion Picture Producers and Distributors Association (MPPDA), the film industry's trade association, was entirely correct.

These movies were the vanguard of what soon became one of the most perennially popular genres. On top of other problems facing Hollywood in the first years of the Great Depression, "gruesome pictures" would become an irritant and then a more pressing public dilemma for the organization headed by Will H. Hays, that since its inception in 1922, amid embarrassing star scandals, had sought to rein in morally "objectionable" material for the betterment of the industry if not society at large. Hays had to negotiate the fact that horror movies were suddenly returning badly needed profits even as receipts dropped by one-third in the early years of the bust; while attracting the ire of religious lobby groups and conservative state and municipal censor boards around the country, the latter bodies with varying standards and the authority to order maddeningly inconsistent cuts to otherwise well-received films. Writing to censors in Vancouver about *Freaks* (1932), a Hays staff member admitted: "In these times of depression the loss of one play date for a picture is a matter of serious worry."[2]

The growing economic calamity and political crisis including President Hoover's violent suppression of the veterans' "Bonus Army" demonstrators in Washington in the summer of 1932 fed a sense in some quarters that fighting a perceived moral decline in the movies might offer some way to ameliorate widening fears of social breakdown. Hays and Joy actively worked to "retard" the horror cycle (as well as gangster movies, sex comedies, and anything else that might bring complaint) while juggling the competing interests of the studios and small but vocal segments of the public, especially the Catholic Legion of Decency; and its powerful industry allies, particularly Martin Quigley, publisher of the *Motion Picture Herald*, the main trade paper for theater owners, and co-author of the stricter though less enforced Production Code in 1930. The rise of the horror film in 1931–6 overlapped with a major change in the censorship system. By agreement with the studios in 1934, the MPPDA created a new office, the Production Code Administration (PCA), that began to closely supervise film content before, during, and after principal production; and shrewdly chose as its chief Joseph I. Breen, an officer of the Legion of Decency. Universal's horror releases that pushed the limits of violence and perverse sexuality in the early 1930s show a much more subdued approach after 1934.

As *Dracula* was being prepared in 1930, reviewers at the Hays Office (the general term for the MPPDA before and after the formation of the PCA) initially warned of offending foreign nationalist sensibilities, which could hurt profits in those markets. Of an early *Dracula* script Joy advised Universal: "In Scene F-8 Martin [the asylum attendant] says:

'I am going to find a place with some nice normal loonies – Napoleons, Mussolinis and such like.' You will avoid any difficulty which may arise by using characters from ancient history such as 'Alexanders' or 'Caesars.'"[3] Joy's suggestion to omit reference to Italy's fascist dictator had further repercussions because it made the story's setting harder to define. Apart from a couple of shots of Dracula walking the streets of London with automobiles passing around him, little else indicates this is not the gaslit city of the novel's 1897 publication. Like Bram Stoker, Universal meant to keep the story contemporary, hence the offhand reference to Mussolini, which when eliminated from the shooting script sidestepped even implicit allusion to the Depression's grim reality. Possible inferences between this bloodsucking monster and the frightening, truly debilitating effects of the economic collapse would remain oblique here and in virtually all of the decade's horror films.

Outside of Hollywood, politically appointed censor boards could further alter the themes and impact of horror movies. Upon its release in February, 1931, Dracula experienced moderate complaints from state and local authorities. Although the erotic undercurrents of vampirism and the gothic gloom of the movie's early sequences invited complaint, Dracula's steady shift to a stagy, more subdued style and its mostly off-screen violence may have curtailed greater difficulty. However, evidence indicates that Universal originally produced a more unsettling version, particularly in regard to Stoker's key subplot about the vampire's victimization of Lucy Westenra and her ruthless hunt for children when she joins the undead. In mid-March, Joy's report on Dracula's treatment in British Columbia noted that besides deleting shots from the macabre introduction of the Count and his brides rising from their coffins, the Canadians had also cut from Reel 6 "cries of infants, where a woman vampire is evidently sucking their blood."[4] This note indicates that scenes depicting the most disturbing aspects of Lucy's role in the tale were initially included, but eliminated here and likely in other markets. Only a single shot remains of what may have been a longer sequence: a nighttime exterior over which we hear crying children, seemingly not infants. No complete print of Dracula's initial release version seems to exist now, and this gruesome section about Lucy's return is left muddled and unfinished in the film that has been circulating since that time.

Frankenstein, a more effective movie on the whole than Dracula, caused greater problems, alarming censors both inside and outside Hollywood with its grave robbing, hangings, surgical scenes, and the Monster's inadvertent drowning of little Maria. In Britain, Frankenstein became the chief cause of strict censorship of all horror films upon its release there in 1932, culminating in the British Board of Film Censors' creation of a new classification, the "H" (for horrific) that largely restricted their showing to adults.[5] Responding to a script draft in August, 1931, Jason Joy wrote to Universal: "we suggest that instead of having Frankenstein say: 'Now I know how it feels to be God,' he say: 'Now I know how it feels to be a god.'" Universal ignored the advice. But where Joy "suggested," a few years later Breen could insist and know the studio would comply. When *Frankenstein* was prepared for re-release in 1937, the changes demanded by the PCA consolidated complaints from various censor boards that had accrued during its 1931 debut. Breen notified Universal he would approve re-release of *Frankenstein*,

> providing the following eliminations are made: Reel 3 – Eliminate dialog, "In the name of God" and the line "Now I know what it feels like to be God."; Reel 4 – Shorten, as much as possible, the views of Fritz with lighted torch, rousing the fear and fury of the creature. Eliminate view of Doctor jabbing hypodermic into back of the creature; Reel 6 – Eliminate scene in which the creature throws the child into the water.[6]

Universal obeyed and the PCA certified the reissue. It is a testament to the mythic power of *Dracula* and *Frankenstein* as well as to the skills of those involved in their creation that these movies still gripped and disturbed audiences for decades even while circulating in what we now realize are highly altered forms.

Though *Murders in the Rue Morgue* (1932) was among the less profitable of Universal's first batch of horror films, its expressionist sets and gruesome story indicate the major stylistic and thematic directions in which the nascent genre was heading from the outset. The movie's relative commercial failure may have been due to its sadistic themes, which led to heavy censorship in many locations. *Rue Morgue* is filled with racial and sexual inferences, ambiguous yet clearly perverse, as defined by Bela Lugosi's quietly vicious characterization of Dr Mirakle, a sinister sideshow performer who deploys a trained ape as his alter ego.[7] In the opening, scantily clad harem girls perform at a carnival, their foreignness as well as thrilling "wildness" caught in an exchange between two male observers: "Do they bite?" one playfully asks. "Oh yes, but you have to pay extra for that," his friend responds. This dialog disappeared often in local screenings, as did Mirakle's abduction and murder of a prostitute, some of the most disturbing images of 1930s horror. The doctor implicitly aims to mate the woman with the ape in furtherance of weird experiments in evolutionary acceleration or mixing of species for unknown ends. With the sobbing victim bound to a tilted cross, Mirakle discovers she has "rotten blood," presumably syphilitic and unsuitable for his work. "Your beauty was a lie!" he snarls, before dumping her body through a trapdoor. Given *Rue Morgue*'s full running time of barely sixty minutes, it could only have suffered from any cutting whatsoever. Yet even more lenient authorities thought it exceptionally brutal. Joy's staff received a letter from Seattle officials that noted: "For the first time in years we have had action by the Seattle Censorship Board – they ordered 247 feet removed from *Murders in the Rue Morgue*."[8]

By the time Joseph Breen assumed control of the newly formed PCA in July, 1934, the horror cycle had gained momentum with *Dr. Jekyll and Mr. Hyde* (1931), *Freaks*, *The Most Dangerous Game* (1932), and *Island of Lost Souls* (1933), movies that set new precedents for violence and morbid eroticism. Breen had a mandate to curtail it. Universal's *The Black Cat* (1934) was the last full-bore horror show before the PCA clamped down. Though *The Black Cat* included implications of both incest and necrophilia, he claimed its first script would pass the Code, though "there are a number of details which ought to be carefully handled, to avoid mutilation of your picture by the censor boards." One of Breen's biggest objections was the killing of cats by Dr Verdegast (Lugosi), which seems tame in comparison to the habits of Boris Karloff's pathological Poelzig of keeping the bodies of his former wives on display in glass cases. Breen also urged care in the climax in which Verdegast flays Poelzig alive with a scalpel; and advised elimination of views of an inverted cross in the scene where Poelzig conducts a satanic mass. Relations between the PCA and the studios were often matters of negotiation and compromise, however. Each of these episodes got into the film through discreet cutting. For example, an often-published still depicting Karloff in black robes conducting the mass while flanked by inverted crosses is an establishing shot that appears on screen for only a few seconds. "We are particularly pleased with the manner in which your studio and director have handled this subject, and we congratulate you," Breen wrote to Universal upon approving the movie for release.[9]

Breen's seemingly even-handed treatment of horror films would not last. By 1935, his impatience was growing, even as studios voluntarily toned down horror scripts while showing increasing willingness to bow to PCA complaints. Breen's staff conferred closely with Universal as it scripted and shot *The Werewolf of London* (1935), an interesting variation of *Jekyll and Hyde* about a botanist (Henry Hull) bitten by a werewolf while in search of a rare plant. The censors barred showing "the actual transvection from man to wolf," which in the initial story meant depicting a live animal as a werewolf's form. Nor would they approve showing even the menacing shadows of wolves, as "we have been concerned from the point of view of the general good and welfare of the industry, with the use of terrifying screen-sized shadows of wolves, or wolf-like men on the screen, as they effect children particularly." Universal noted later it had scrapped footage already shot for the story's Tibetan prolog showing real wolves and their shadows.[10] Still, Hull appears quite often in the werewolf makeup and transforms repeatedly on screen. Given the religious forces challenging Hollywood of which Breen himself was part, the PCA aimed to enforce the most narrowly traditional moral and sexual precepts, insisting that vice must never win nor be shown to be attractive. Indeed, the besotted, female half of an adulterous couple becomes one of the werewolf's victims. After early script meetings with the PCA, Universal filmed an encounter between the scientist and an elderly Christian missionary who warns him: "There are some things it is better not to bother with." The PCA also believed that Universal would "return to the morality theme through [Hull's] dying confession to his wife that he knew he had violated the laws of God and man and that his death was a deserved one."[11] This last did not exactly occur. As he dies, Hull's Dr Glendon says only that in a few moments he will learn why this had to happen and expresses sorrow to his wife that he did not make her happier. Throughout, however, Universal quickly cut around images of violence, which mostly occurs off-screen, or flashed only momentary shots of shadows of the beast on walls that the PCA had discouraged.

Possibly scaring children with shadows was secondary to the censors' vigilant prohibition against what the Production Code called "sexual perversion," meaning homosexuality. In *The Black Cat*, devil worship seemingly fell within acceptable bounds so long as there was "no suggestion of the performance of any sexual rite," but more importantly, in presenting guests assembling for the Black Mass, the film must "avoid any suggestion of homosexuality or perversion of any of the characters."[12] Recognizing that *Dracula's Daughter* (1936) carried strong lesbian undertones, the PCA closely monitored, one might even say collaborated on the production from script to screen, so great was its involvement, starting with a six-page response to the first screenplay.[13] The early version began with a medieval prolog featuring Dracula himself that soon vanished. Once his daughter appears, "we ask that you eliminate entirely the business of the Countess gathering John into her arms and the slow fadeout. <u>This is important</u>," he emphasized in underlining, as the fadeout in these circumstances was often a 1930s visual code that strongly implied sex would follow.[14] Breen's comments occasioned a major rewrite. Reading a new script three months later, he allowed it would probably pass the Code but used the foreign censorship threat to inhibit production: "political censor boards generally, and very particularly in England, have expressed their intention of scrutinizing all horror pictures very closely in the future." More to the point, Breen emphasized scenes involving "the Countess and the girl Lilli. This will need very careful handling to avoid any questionable flavor."[15]

Universal knew the exact implication of the scene where the Countess hungrily implored the young woman to model for a painting, and meant to leave it in, yet were still cautious. A day before shooting the scene, Universal's Harry Zehner asked Breen "as a special favor" to read a draft immediately. A Breen associate met with company officials the next day and concluded an agreement:

> The present suggestion that . . . Lilli poses in the nude will be changed. She will be posing her neck and shoulders, and there will be no suggestion that she undresses, and no exposure of her person. It was also stated that the present incomplete sequence will be followed by a scene in which Lilli is taken to a hospital and there it will be definitely established that she has been attacked by a vampire. The whole sequence will be treated in such a way as to avoid any suggestion of perverse sexual desire on the part of Marya [Dracula's daughter] or of an attempted sexual attack by her upon Lilli.

Later, though, Breen also worried about Marya's male servant: "Omit Sandor's line: 'You promised there would never be anyone else' as it seems to suggest a possible sex relationship between Sandor and Marya. Such an inference, if left in the finished picture, could constitute a code violation."[16] Poor Marya: vampires aren't allowed straight or gay sex.

Dracula's Daughter seemingly marked the end of a cycle of which Breen strongly disapproved. He could rest easier until Universal's successful fall 1938 re-release of a *Dracula/Frankenstein* double feature threatened to revive the genre and a script for *Son of Frankenstein* landed on his desk. He again played the British card, exchanging correspondence with Brooke Wilkinson, his counterpart at the British Board of Film Censors, to confirm that English opposition to horror was unchanged. Assured that it was, he sent notes of warning to Universal and Columbia, which had announced a new series of B horror movies. In November,

Breen received a long and distressing letter from an administrator of the school district of White Plains, New York, detailing an incident in which she encountered a boy of 9 wandering the streets at dusk, deeply agitated after seeing *Frankenstein*. The Monster's drowning of little Maria had jolted him, even though it was largely cut for this release. Grateful for her letter, Breen responded: "Personally, I dislike these pictures very much. Like yourself, I can hardly sit through them," adding: "It goes without saying that these pictures are not intended for exhibition before children. The best that can be said for them is that they are 'adult fare' – for the kinds of adults who like them."[17]

Breen's initial communication with Wilkinson had revealed an additional worry about the response to horror movies:

> It just so happens that by one of those curious freakish turns in the field of exhibition, the Universal company have been marketing certain re-issues of these "horror" pictures. Audiences, hereabouts, have turned to laughing at them – "spoofing" them – and refusing to take them seriously. These re-issues have been quite successful and two of our companies have in mind making some "horror" pictures, with the thought that this same curious reaction on the part of audiences may turn them into good box-office successes. It was with this thought in mind that I wired you.[18]

It was one thing to draw audiences with sadism and ghoulishness, which could be morally condemned, but if deviance was going to be sweetened with comic irony and made even more engaging, he realized horror would be increasingly difficult to stop. If Breen knew there was an ironic audience eager to laugh at and with horror movies, Universal surely did, which may account for a certain droll undercurrent in *Son of Frankenstein* (1939), despite the moody lighting and distorted sets. Lugosi is comically deft, when, for example, Ygor sheepishly explains to Basil Rathbone's Dr Frankenstein that he had been condemned to hang, "Because Ygor steal bodies . . . they said." Rathbone swings between the reserved English gentleman and manic scientist who spends much of the third act racing about his monster-plagued estate while trying to maintain an outwardly calm demeanor to his puzzled wife and a suspicious police inspector. (Small wonder Mel Brooks drew on this movie for plot and parody in *Young Frankenstein*.) Despite Breen's opposition, the horror genre would experience a resurgence during the World War II years, though seldom with the edge of violence and erotic gloom of the early 1930s. The issues in their production and reception would change, as would the demands of potential regulators.

Will This (Horror) Picture Help Win the War?

The 1940s is often considered a dismal decade for the horror film. Critics contend that the horrors of global war so far exceeded mere anxiety and the capacities of distanced metaphor that the genre ceased to command both wide audiences and critical respect. Disdain for the genre's aesthetic depletion in the war years, however, overlooks how such movies might still yield other historically interesting subtexts, particularly in those that engaged the wartime background. Indeed, a number of horror films produced after Pearl Harbor were influenced by propaganda themes defined by the federal Office of War Information (OWI), the extent of whose impact on wartime filmmaking is often underestimated. While OWI aimed to affect the broad range of Hollywood product, its major efforts were understandably consumed with influencing movies that bore most directly on the war, such as *Air Force* (1943) or *Gung-Ho* (1944). Still, OWI scrutinized many non-war films, being particularly watchful, for example, for racist portrayals of non-white characters and nations, which could potentially damage Allied unity. How could gothic horror fit into this context?

Throughout 1942 Hollywood released dozens of movies that capitalized on war fever and stoked America's collective dread. Lurid quickies like *Remember Pearl Harbor*, *Menace of the Rising Sun*, *Texas To Bataan*, and *The Devil With Hitler* accompanied the first big-studio combat film, Paramount's *Wake Island*.[19] Among this flood was a group of B pictures from the minor studios and major studio B units that combined topical war plots with the horror genre. In Monogram's *Black Dragons* (1942), Nazi doctor Bela Lugosi surgically alters Japanese spies to impersonate and replace prominent American industrialists; like movie gangsters, his ruthless allies reward his efforts with attempted murder. The surgeon escapes and progressively slays the disguised agents, dumping their bodies on the steps of the shuttered Japanese embassy in Washington. Lugosi's star image links the classic 1930s horror films to their wartime variations. A scalpel-wielding Lugosi mutilates the Japanese spy chief just as he had sadistically disfigured Boris Karloff in *The Raven* (1935). Yet in one of the most florid lines of the time, he coolly avers that "Anything I can do to hasten the establishment of our New Order and to destroy the archaic democracies is an honor and a privilege." *Black Dragons* tellingly underscores Lugosi's menace by repeating the inserted closeups of his searing eyes originally used in *Dracula*. In 1942, this directly associates fascism with Dracula's supernatural threat. At the climax, however, his purely personal vengeance complete, the dying Lugosi laughs madly as the Japanese spymaster reveals his now "monstrous" features, and a newspaper headline, "Jap Spy Ring Smashed," lap dissolves over shots of Old Glory and the US Capitol. Here is a movie (and an industry) struggling uncertainly with diverse formulae, genres, and attitudes in the first months of war.

President Roosevelt created the Office of War Information by Executive Order on June 13, 1942, instructing the organization to "undertake campaigns to enhance understanding of the war at home and abroad; to coordinate government information activities; and to handle liaison with the press, radio, and motion pictures."[20] OWI's Bureau of Motion Pictures (BMP) established an office in Hollywood to interact with the studios. Using the guiding principle "Will This Picture Help Win the War?," the staff, directed by publisher Nelson Poynter, reviewed story treatments, script drafts, or completed movies voluntarily submitted by producers; evaluated them for their positive or negative impact on the government's propaganda program; and offered suggestions for changes. OWI had no censorship powers and the studios were not obligated to comply, though most did cooperate in varying degrees. The Bureau's power was mainly that of persuasion based on patriotic appeals to aid the war effort. Poynter's staff drafted *The Government Information Manual for the Motion Picture Industry* that was distributed to the studios, and seriously read and taken into consideration. The *Manual* outlined five major themes producers should address whenever possible: (1) Why We Fight (democracy versus fascism); (2) The Enemy (fascist governments are our enemy, not their peoples per se); (3) The United Nations (stress an allied fight against fascism); (4) The Home Front (emphasize how civilian work and sacrifices underpin the war effort; (5) The Fighting Forces (portray military proficiency and America's multi-ethnic democracy represented by the soldiers).[21]

The Bureau of Motion Pictures was never automatically hostile to, or particularly worried about the negative impact of horror films. The US government contemplated no restriction or ban on horror movies as the British government had ordered in mid-1942.[22] While the British, who had suffered terrible civilian casualties in the Battle of Britain and costly military defeats in 1940–1 saw good reason to minimize cinematic shocks and gore, it was unnecessary for OWI to police this central feature of the genre since depictions of violence and bloodletting were already firmly regulated by the Production Code. Universal's *Son of Dracula* (1943) with Lon Chaney, Jr as the thirsty Count raised no official eyebrows upon review. Analyst Larry Williams wrote: "This is a story of pure fantasy which could not possibly be confused with reality anywhere in the world. In consequence, it has no bearing whatever on the War Information Program, domestic or overseas."[23]

Trying to allay the industry's fear of censorship, *The Government Information Manual* affirmed that despite the profound emergency, purely entertaining, non-war pictures were still needed. However, traditional entertainment should steer clear of war content because "escapism and war seldom, if ever, mix well."[24] Despite the mildly worded advice this was, in fact, one of the Bureau's most strongly held and vociferously argued principles. Regardless of genre, BMP could never abide movies that either used the war simply as a topical backdrop or whose treatment implied that the greatest conflict in human history could ever be rendered with less than total gravity. The greatest potential problem areas for horror films were wartime settings for "fantasy" tales, and racist portrayals of non-white characters, as frequently occurred, for example, in the zombie cycle that proved popular in the war years. When these trouble spots were avoided, BMP seldom objected to horror stories; when they were transgressed, the Bureau tried to modify the movie's content or discourage its distribution abroad.

OWI insisted that Hollywood's depictions of non-Western peoples at the very least ought to avoid characterizing them as backward and superstitious as this carried the unambiguous stigma of white supremacy. BMP's liberal-leaning personnel made the dilution or elimination of racist slurs and stereotypes from Hollywood movies a high priority. The agency regarded the removal of negative stereotypes central to mobilizing African Americans for the war effort as well as to counter Nazi racist doctrines and Japanese propaganda bids to peoples of color. Unsurprisingly, however, government bureaucrats juggling a variety of problems in a dynamic political and military situation could not hope to eradicate centuries of pernicious racial ideology in a few dozen months. Yet the attention the agency devoted to a lurid genre entry like Monogram's *Revenge of the Zombies* (1943), whose zombie/voodoo plot inevitably surfaced the most retrograde imagery, attests to the urgency of the issue for OWI.

Monogram producer Lindsley Parsons and BMP officials corresponded for over two months as the studio scripted its bayou-country horror tale about a covert Nazi scientist named Von Altman (John Carradine) laboring to produce an invulnerable army for his *Führer* by raising corpses as obedient zombies. While the result was scarcely an aesthetic or social triumph (it still included stereotypical shuffling and quaking from comedian Mantan Moreland), OWI's direct influence unquestionably altered the final release in relation to agency propaganda principles. Reading a script submitted in April, BMP regretted the fantasy portrayal of The Enemy, but was more disturbed by the scenario's overt racism. Von Altman murdered his American wife to further his experiments, but the white woman, when reanimated, proves more resistant to the process of subjugation than blacks that he describes as being "of a lower mentality." Worse, the Nazi's attitude hardly differs from that of the white American hero who, in the early version, dismisses local blacks as "a lot of ignorant natives."

Reviewer Lillian Bergquist wrote: "The Negroes . . . are presented as a strange, uncivilized and superstitious group of people living in a world quite apart from that of other Americans. They are either comic servants, zombies, or in the case of Mammy Beulah, a voodoo-ist. There is not one real Negro American in this story."[25] Bergquist stressed that the film's hackneyed, insulting portrayal of blacks "serves to confirm Japanese propaganda which tells dark-skinned peoples that under fascism they will receive fairer treatment than under democracy," and worried too that "[T]his could also have the effect of alienating our dark-skinned allies from the United Nations' cause." In a terse internal memo Ulric Bell labeled the script "the most irresponsible story I have yet seen out of Monogram," and raised the veiled threat of censorship, urging that "Monogram should be advised that it will in all probability be impossible to obtain an export license for *Revenge of the Zombies*," a point duly communicated to Parsons.[26]

Monogram proved particularly attentive to BMP concerns. Reviewing the release print on July 23, a BMP analyst noted that all specific objections raised by the Bureau's appraisal of the early script had been rectified, though one key problem implicitly remained:

> Von Altman no longer makes zombies only of Negroes as was the case in the script. Of his six Zombies, three are Negro and three are white, and references to the Negroes' being "ignorant natives" and of "a lower mentality" have been eliminated. Von Altman now refers to "my country" to which he will return for the creation of his zombie army, and nowhere in the film is his nationality named. The obvious inference, however, is that he is a German. Because the story presents our Nazi enemies unrealistically, the Overseas Branch of OWI cannot recommend its distribution overseas.[27]

This issue aside, when Von Altman's racially apportioned zombie troop predictably turns on him in the climax, *Revenge of the Zombies* affirms a familiar genre pattern. At the same time one also sees a weird compliance with OWI's entreaties for ethnically mixed combat platoons whose melting-pot democracy would defeat an arrogant "master" race.

Columbia's *Return of the Vampire* (1943), in which the monster surfaces amidst the Battle of Britain, presented more direct themes – and problems – relevant to official policy. From BMP's perspective this movie, made without any agency consultation, was a harmful throwback to those pre-Bureau days of early 1942 when reckless producers used the war as an exploitable backdrop or mixed global war with escapist fantasy. Even so, the movie is redolent of the issues, images, and themes OWI sought to introduce into wartime entertainment. Virtually reprising Dracula, Lugosi plays Armand Tesla, an eighteenth-century Romanian scientist who appears as a vampire in 1918 London, aided by his slave Andreas Obry (Matt Willis), whom he has transformed into a werewolf. Professor Walter Saunders and his young protégé Dr Jane Ainsley (Frieda Inescort) pursue and destroy the monster. In 1941, Nazi bombs expose Tesla's grave and civil defense workers inadvertently pull out the stake, restoring him to life. Tesla again mesmerizes Andreas, and stalks Lady Jane's son John and his fiancée Nicki. Sir Frederick Fleet, a stuffy Scotland Yard inspector, hinders Lady Jane's efforts. In the climax, recalling Lady Jane's teachings of "goodness," the wolf man turns on his master – who's been stunned by another timely Luftwaffe attack – and drags Tesla into the sunlight, to his destruction.

Though built around Lugosi's lurking menace, the wartime setting is central to the movie, where, for example, John and Nicki appear in British military uniform and the vampire infiltrates England by murdering and assuming the identity of a continental scientist recently escaped from a Nazi prison camp. Romania, the nation from which Tesla hails, was a minor member of the Axis partnership, and the role of Luftwaffe bombing in the resurrection of the undead links resurgent vampirism with Hitlerite aggression as only an audacious B picture could.

Shortly before Tesla's reappearance, Lady Jane helps smuggle scientists from occupied Europe across the Channel. Even without BMP consultation, her stoic rationale, "I feel we're doing a good thing for humanity, helping a fellow scientist escape the Nazi yoke," bespeaks the kind of One-World, anti-fascist idealism OWI sought to instill in wartime propaganda.

Moreover, a no less insistent message is a strong, independent, and professionally skilled woman placed in a wholly nontraditional role, one implicitly related to wartime necessity. *Return of the Vampire* portrays "Rosie the Riveter" – symbol for one of the most significant

FIGURE 12 Defending the gothic home front: Andreas (Matt Willis) repels the vampire Armand Tesla (Bela Lugosi) revived by Nazi bombs in a publicity shot from *Return of the Vampire* (1943, Columbia)

rearrangements of feminine gender roles to that time – in genre-specific form as Lady Jane, the vampire slayer. Gregory A. Waller argues that while most vampire tales before and after Bram Stoker share common structural elements, individual texts differ historically and ideologically in relation to subtle or significant variations of the basic myth, especially the identity and social place of the vampire hunter.[28] Considering that the woman as screaming victim is the most fundamental cliché of the horror film, *Return of the Vampire*'s investment of the power and authority of the vampire hunter in a woman – with its assumptions of wisdom, courage, and professional expertise – strongly binds this portrayal to its historical moment.

Referring to the unfamiliar yet vital new roles for women in wartime, *The Government Information Manual* suggested that Hollywood's Home Front movies depict "Women driving taxis, serving as street car conductors, filling station operators. In crowds, fewer men in civilian clothes, and more women in uniform. Women who have adapted themselves to living without husbands or sweethearts."[29] As BMP urged, *Return of the Vampire* tacitly acknowledged the shifts in gender roles the war occasioned. In the prolog, the Van Helsing-like Professor Saunders teaches young Jane Ainsley how to kill a vampire, then disappears from the story. In 1941, Lady Jane accomplishes the pursuit and destruction of Tesla with remarkably little male help. Sir Frederick remains the traditional horror-film skeptic, and thus nearly useless. John Ainsley, a decorated Royal Air Force pilot discharged with combat wounds, succumbs to Tesla's bite. Andreas, the Renfield character, is the pathetic victim, a role Lady Jane never assumes. Like Van Helsing before her, Lady Jane remains composed and resolute. In the end, she pointedly leaves the side of her stricken daughter-in-law to take in the spectacle of Tesla rotting in the sun, showing determination to see the thing through. In this, *Return of the Vampire* bears more relation to the Oscar-winning *Mrs. Miniver* (1942) or the nurses-in-combat film *So Proudly We Hail!* (1943) than to *Dracula*.

Traditional gender roles and assumptions persisted in wartime mass media alongside potentially startling renegotiations of the familiar patterns.[30] The notable lack of sexist condescension in Sir Frederick's opposition to Lady Jane's insistence on a supernatural threat characterizes the film as a whole. Though the inspector scoffs at her belief in vampires, his rejection stems from pure rationality – there are simply no such things. Not once does he dismiss her claims out of hand simply because she's a woman, nor impute to her beliefs charges of hysterical emotionalism or childish superstition. Moreover, Dr Ainsley never cries, screams, or faints in the vampire's presence any more than Dr Van Helsing did. "The strength of the vampire is that people will not believe in him," cautioned Van Helsing, so Lady Jane's identification and acceptance of a supernatural menace strongly affirms her genre role as the moral and intellectual authority figure.

Return of the Vampire also repeats the inserted closeups of Lugosi's glowing eyes to signify the vampire's enslaving power. The special resolve of both Van Helsing in the 1931 film and Lady Jane are demonstrated by resisting the vampire's demonic gaze. Van Helsing's resilience prompts a compliment from the Count: "Your will is strong, Van Helsing." In the scene in which Lady Jane confronts Tesla alone the vampire similarly commends her: "You're a very brilliant woman. But a foolish one to pit your strength against mine." Yet both scenes end with the vampire hunters flashing hidden crucifixes to force Lugosi to retreat, covering his eyes. Lady Jane's coolness and bravery prevail in this pivotal moment of the *Dracula*-inspired narrative, the point at which the vampire hunter takes the offensive. In the penultimate scene, Andreas subjectively recalls Her Ladyship's voice assuring him of his fundamental virtue, which swiftly reverses the werewolf curse imposed by Tesla's gaze. Though he, rather than Lady Jane, physically destroys the monster, it is clearly presented as an act of her influence and will.

The ending slightly compromises the image of its strong female protagonist, however. When Dr Ainsley and the police arrive at the war-ruined church that concealed the vampire's coffin, Andreas, returned to human form, is dead, and Tesla is a decomposed corpse. Sir Frederick's skepticism endures. "That, my dear sir, is all that remains of Tesla!" Lady Jane insists. The incredulous Inspector admonishes her one last time, then asks his two detectives, "You don't believe in this vampire business, do you?" The unnerved officers nod quickly, "We do!" He then looks directly into the camera and with a big smile asks, "And, do you people?" as the scene fades. This ending is indebted to both *Dracula, The Vampire Play* (1927) and the 1931 movie, both of which originally concluded with a curtain speech in which Van Helsing offers the audience droll assurance that vampires are real.[31] By such an abrupt turn to comic self-consciousness, this ironic coda's inclusion in *Return of the Vampire* may subtly diminish Lady Jane's credibility. Whether this mocks the entire notion of an assertive female hero as well remains an open question. From BMP's perspective such a far-fetched tale mixed with the true horrors of the Blitz could offer few salutary lessons of any kind.

Though *Return of the Vampire*'s promotion of a woman to the vampire-hunter role stands out to contemporary eyes, no original reviews took notice of it. Horror's lowly status and Bela Lugosi's swirling cape evidently obscured all other considerations.[32] BMP's film-analysis staff headed by Dorothy B. Jones was largely female, and "sharply attuned to what women meant to the war effort and what the war meant to women."[33] Yet in a scathing review of the finished film, Lillian Bergquist saw only the cardinal sin of treating a war backdrop frivolously and failed to note any proto-feminist implication in Lady Jane's role:

> *Return of the Vampire* uses the war as a background for a sensational melodrama, mixing the very real horrors of this war with a fantastic story about the supernatural. Much of the action takes place while London is defending itself against the blitz, and there are numerous shots of ruined buildings and homes. Some documentary footage is used in this film. Besides being in extremely bad taste, a picture of this type suggests that Americans fail to take the war seriously and regard it merely as a convenient peg on which to hang a yarn.

... This picture was granted an export license (10/30/43). However this office cannot recommend *Return of the Vampire* for overseas distribution.[34]

While it's true *Return of the Vampire* did not treat a significant war problem or issue as defined by OWI, its portrayal of a competent and resourceful woman in a nontraditional genre and social role remains an intriguing variation of the horror film in the context of World War II popular culture. Dr Jane Ainsley marks a suggestive instance of the important new functions for women imagined (in more prosaic ways, admittedly) by OWI, and validated and affirmed by a variety of wartime social and political discourses. Hollywood's cooperation with the federal government in the creation of these propaganda messages remains historically unique. Yet grasping the extent of BMP influence in wartime Hollywood aids a more specific assessment of the horror genre in the 1940s, one that seeks an estimation of these films as something other than merely escapist or aesthetically exhausted. From the government's involvement in a zombie movie to the appearance of a distaff Dr Van Helsing, there were many surprises when the monsters went to war.

"Monsters Are Good For My Children"

Monsters particularize individual and social fears. If the terrors represented in horror films represent a society's collective dreads, their coded reflections on contemporary anxieties seldom appear as overtly as they did in World War II B movies. Susan Sontag's 1965 essay "The Imagination of Disaster" argued that the sudden popularity of science fiction after the war represented sublimated Cold War anxiety with radioactive mutants and bug-eyed invaders barely concealed symbols for the hydrogen bomb and the threat of international communism.[35] This analysis, which has been widely disseminated and frequently oversimplified ever since, is both persuasive and incomplete because much popular discourse in the 1950s extolled the many promising aspects of advanced technology. Political, economic, and educational writing, advertising and popular culture alike as often stressed the potentially limitless wonders that could result from scientific and industrial development, including atomic energy, as expressed fears of nuclear war.[36] In any case, for more than a decade after the war, science fiction's flying saucers and marauding behemoths seemed to bury the old-fashioned gothic horror story. How, then, to account for the reappearance of the horror genre at the end of the 1950s, a wave which has not diminished since? Perhaps the new fears of an impersonal, bureaucratic society and catastrophic nuclear destruction actually intensified the appeal of quaint old demons like Dracula and Frankenstein, especially among children and adolescents, groups that made up increasing portions of Hollywood's audience.

Among the vast commercial output for and about the postwar Baby Boom generation was a set of artifacts tied to the shadowy world of gothic horror. We noted in Chapter 3 how television syndication of Universal's studio-era horror classics helped spark this phenomenon in 1957, creating what David Skal calls the "Monster Boomers," youthful fans devoted to horror movies old and new. Skal argues that their avid consumption of horror films, monster toys, and genre fan magazines, especially the first and most influential, *Famous Monsters of Filmland*, and the attendant cult of stars like Karloff, Lugosi, and Vincent Price was also a response to the threat of nuclear doom, fear that reached its terrifying crescendo with the Cuban Missile Crisis in October, 1962. In the era of "duck and cover" drills in grade schools, adult authority figures from parents and teachers to clergymen and politicians blithely assured children that apocalyptic destruction was a daily possibility – and get used to it. In retrospect, it is unsurprising that those same adult authorities were usually the callous, exploitative, or outright mad villains in all the teen-themed genres of the postwar years, epitomized by *I Was A Teenage Werewolf* (1957). Skal points out a grim irony that the number one song played on the radio during the 13 fearful days of the US/Soviet faceoff over Cuba was Bobby "Boris" Pickett's "The Monster Mash," a novelty record featuring comic impersonations of Karloff and Lugosi: "Throughout the Cuban nuclear threat, America's favorite pop song celebrated a mad scientist who presided over a dance of death."[37] Indeed, when director Joe Dante, an early fan of *Famous Monsters*, later contributor to the more sophisticated *Castle of Frankenstein*, came to make *Matinee* (1993), a tribute to postwar horror movies, it was set during the Missile Crisis, and shows a boy perusing a copy of *Famous Monsters*. That many kids would reach for secularized versions of immortal figures that offered some kind of salvation – undying monsters like Dracula and the Mummy – now seems both logical and transparent.

Nuclear terror was not the only motivation for this particular phase of popular cultural history but it formed a crucial part of the historical matrix. It is often remarked and lamented that modern post-industrial society lacks the customs and ritual of traditional cultures to mark a clear break between childhood and maturity. Given that only 100 years ago, children worked 60 or more hours a week in dangerous, back-breaking labor in factories and mines, the notion of adolescence as a recognized stage of physical and social development is a recent concept. Still, James Twitchell believes the most important subtext of the horror genre for children is the simultaneous fear and compelling curiosity about adult sexuality. Children's increasing awareness of the mysteries of sex, surrounded by circumspection and taboo in most cultures, seems easily transposed into horror narratives, where, for example, King Kong, the Frankenstein Monster, and Dracula aim to carry off a virgin bride. This is not to say that experiences of this developmental stage are the same either psychologically or culturally for both boys and girls or for adolescents recognizing their homosexuality. Yet Twitchell notes that typically, "horror monsters are every bit as anxious and confused about sex as their [young] audience." Indeed, monsters are frequently social outcasts because of their physical appearance, or the grotesque trans-formations their bodies may undergo, just as for adolescents, "All of a sudden there is hair emerging in strange places, mysterious bodily fluids being secreted at unannounced times, breasts budding, voices cracking, and, most important, those disturbing, exciting urges welling up inside."[38] For children in many cultures and times, fairy tales, ghost stories, or horror movies helped ease the passage into maturity by negotiating a range of anxieties and fears of the adult world.

The year 1964 marked a crucial point for the Baby Boomers, the year of the Tonkin Gulf Resolution and the Civil Rights Act, of the Beatles' first American tour, the year the oldest of them started college. It was also the year the media recognized the growing monster craze, as toy manufacturers and other merchandisers released a stream of products built around Universal's classic monster characters and other ghoulish figures. Following on the heels of "The Monster Mash," comedian Gene Moss produced a comedy LP titled *Dracula's Greatest Hits*, including "I Want to Bite Your Hand," a Beatles parody sung with the by now stock Bela Lugosi impression. On network TV that fall CBS's *The Munsters* and ABC's *The Addams Family* depicted the American home in terms of gothic weirdness. These creepy postwar clans had children, too, but their presentations of American youth sent decidedly mixed messages, as revealed in publicity photos: Eddie Munster (Butch Patrick) clutched a stuffed wolf man resembling Larry Talbot's beast, while Wednesday Addams (Lisa Loring) carried a headless doll named Marie Antoinette. Strangely, despite his widow's peak, pointed ears, and fangs, Eddie idealized the young viewers of the day – a grinning kid cuddling a vintage Universal monster. Meanwhile, Wednesday's "normal" appearance is deceiving: Her favorite doll is frankly more macabre, seemingly the mutilated victim of this otherwise sweetly pretty girl. Like Lucy in *Dracula*, Wednesday is implicitly a killer of children, not a nurturing little mother in training. Such images both reflected and shaped the meanings of the monster phenomenon in the 1960s.

By 1964, *Famous Monsters* publisher James Warren and editor Forrest Ackerman had been fomenting this wave for nearly seven years. The February 1958 première issue proved unusual for the magazine in that the cover featured a posed photograph rather than a still or illustration from a particular horror movie. In a glossy color shot, a buxom blond in low-cut evening gown casts a come-hither smile at the tall gentleman in dark blazer and red ascot snuggling behind her, an urban sophisticate who just happens to wear a green rubber mask of the Frankenstein Monster. Though the cover also promised "The Screen's Classic Horror Photos" and "Interviews and Articles on the Guys and Gals Behind the Ghouls," it subtly played on associations with Hugh Hefner's *Playboy* which, since its 1955 debut, had helped crack America's puritan façade by bringing female nudity and the pleasures of sex directly into the open, or at least onto public newsstands. This joking association with the *Playboy* mystique appeared again in Warren's *Spacemen Annual* in 1965, whose cover illustration depicts a futuristic male as blasé stud, reclining in a chaise longue with a magazine and pipe, surrounded by an adoring bevy of half-dressed space nymphs. These sexist notes were no more "liberating" than the mainstream trends of the day that Hefner aimed to join, not beat, but they suggested basic truths about "monster mania."[39]

Judging by the photos of young readers printed in every issue of *FM*, the majority of monster fans were boys, but there was no small number of girls too. Still, for the next 25 years *Famous Monsters* remained cautious about exposing those readers (regularly asserted by Warren to be a median age of 12) to sex, but the horror genre's increasingly obvious inundation in matters of Eros could never be fully disguised, despite Ackerman's stream of jokes. The same was true of the genre's increasingly gory violence after 1968. It was five years before Ackerman ran a feature on *Night of the Living Dead*, which was preceded by warnings that the movie was far more disturbing than the stills selected for publication. Mindful of the opprobrium that fell on the comic-book industry in the 1950s when moralists pilloried EC Comics for flaunting sex and violence, in 1965 *Famous Monsters* published an article titled "Monsters Are Good for My Children" by Mrs Terri Pinckard, a mother of four who saw the magazine and its celebration of fictional horrors as both psychologically and socially healthy. Citing the familiar precedents of terror and monstrosity in fairy tales and the Bible, Pinckard never mentions nuclear war but raises other timely fears that movie monsters could help relieve: "As a child learns of the outside world, he learns of *real-life* things to be afraid of. The violence in the South, the murder of our President, these are all things our children cannot be protected from, *must* not be protected from." Describing how she gently answered her 8-year-old daughter's questions about the Holocaust, the mother reported that after the tearful child began to process the ghastly truth, the family sat down and watched *The Twilight Zone*. "For how much better to have her dream of a Frankenstein than of Buchenwald. Yet, in reality, which was the Monster?"[40]

Pinckard ended with remarks from a psychologist who supports her idea that fears embodied as fictional monsters are less threatening than vague, undefined worries. Moreover, "It is difficult to see how a 'monster' which is always destroyed before the eyes of the onlooker could cause [emotionally harmful] anxiety."[41] Notably, the doctor was describing the horror story's most traditional form, at least on movie screens up through the mid-1960s. Plenty of gothic horror tales, as well as the Grand Guignol Theater and EC's *Tales From the Crypt* had long rejected such affirmative endings. The movie genre was about to start doing so as well, which raised new fears about horror's social impact. *Castle of Frankenstein*, which had premièred in 1962 under the editorship of Calvin T. Beck, was more prepared to reflect these changes. Pitched at a somewhat broader readership, by the late 1960s Beck's magazine embraced the genre's sexual undercurrents, often running photos of topless actresses in Hammer movies. Moreover, rather than celebrating a self-contained world of movie magic, *Castle of Frankenstein* made increasingly angry references to the Vietnam War. In a 1972 editorial, Beck republished the infamous news photograph of a scream-ing Vietnamese girl burned by napalm bombs, presenting the "Award for Best Horror Picture of 1972" to "'Napalm Kills Kids on Route One': Above in *CoF*'s own special Theatre of Horror on the big screen is the scene. Real horrorshow. Burnt kids running, screaming. Little girl tearing clothes off in pain, running naked down the road. Fantastic footage. All produced, directed and distributed courtesy of USA Studios (a Pentagon Production)."[42] Not only had *Castle of Frankenstein* routinely exposed the genre's sexual subtext to kids, this editorial coldly announced their imminent assumption of morally taxing adult responsibilities – the real world horrors that the actually more traditional Terri Pinckard had assumed as the parents' right to present to their children. If horror/ fantasy can be considered "escapist," readers of *Castle of Frankenstein* were not always allowed to escape. They didn't always want to, regardless of what parents thought.

Still, there were limits. In 1971, the Aurora toy company, producers of plastic scale models of airplanes and tanks as well as a popular series depicting the Universal monsters, released a bizarre and controversial line of eight related kits called "Monster Scenes." The idea must have seemed promising in that it combined several strains of postwar horror fandom: Universal's Frankenstein Monster, a mad scientist named Dr Deadly and his electric laboratory gear, Warren's voluptuous comic-book heroine Vampirella, created by Forrest Ackerman in 1969. It even included a working pendulum table with swinging scimitar blade right out of Vincent Price's *The Pit and the Pendulum* (1961). This is where the fun got less funny, though, because the final elements were a medieval hanging cage next to which sat a convenient brazier for heating a sword, tongs, and pokers that were clearly intended for use on the series' fourth character, an anonymous woman in halter top and hot pants simply designated "The Victim." Ads in Warren magazines and DC/National Comics presented comic-strip panels describing Dr Deadly's plan to kidnap the woman and bring her back to the laboratory/torture chamber. As the Frankenstein Monster carries away the screaming Victim against a contemporary urban backdrop, Vampirella assures us, "Don't worry, this is New York. No one will help her," evoking the awful case of Kitty Genovese, murdered in her Queens apartment in 1964 while neighbors heard screams and did nothing. The final panel depicted a smiling boy attaching (or dismembering?) the Victim's arm as he towers over the assembled kits of lab and dungeon ware. Aurora's unabashed claim that the series was "Rated X, for Excitement!" incensed both a parents' group formed to protest the toys and the National Organization of Women, which resulted in the models being pulled from toy shelves.[43] "Monster Scenes" was like seeing the unleashed id of a real Addams family minus the irony, confirmation for many that the realm of gothic horror was simply sexual sadism − surely not good for my children or society. America's Vietnam-saturated torment had seemingly overwhelmed the mythic and cathartic functions of fictive horror and provoked a new array of opponents who would now scrutinize the genre even more suspiciously.

Conclusion: Horror and the Culture Wars

The political and cultural rifts that opened in American society in the late 1960s have yet to close. As "women's liberation" transformed into organized feminism in the mid-1970s, pornography and the increasingly open adult entertainment industry became chief targets of the movement. Groups including Women Against Violence Against Women marched against the spread of pornography in accordance with Robin Morgan's famous dictum that "Pornography is the theory, and rape the practice."[44] After decades or even centuries of inequality and oppression, feminism's unleashed political, intellectual, and moral force was angry, polemical, and effective but also scattershot. Statements and rhetoric often refused to distinguish between the soft-core nudity of *Playboy* and sexist images in mainstream advertising, hard-core porn, and horror films. In 1976, feminists rallied against a clumsy horror movie called *Snuff* (1976) that seemingly confirmed their worst nightmares about the patriarchal culture in that it purported to show a genuine on-screen murder and evisceration of a woman. The producers soon admitted this had been a crude if effective exploitation hoax, but it seemingly exposed the connection between misogynistic media and real-world violence. Feminists as well as the religious right particularly despised Larry Flynt's *Hustler* magazine after a notorious 1978 cover that depicted the legs and buttocks of a woman being fed into a meat-grinder, an impulse seemingly paralleling the atrocities of *The Texas Chain Saw Massacre*. (Indeed, eagerly baiting feminists, the image was accompanied by the statement, "We will no longer hang women up like pieces of meat – Larry Flynt.") With these precedents in mind, protesters were primed when *Halloween* (1978) initiated a dubious new phase of the horror genre.

The slasher movies of 1978–84 displeased and alarmed just about everyone but the teenage audiences that flocked to them. Among the unfortunate effects of this outpouring was a growing assumption that the stalk-and-slash model virtually defined the horror film itself. Certainly the cycle thrived on highly sexualized violence, as in *Friday the 13th Part 2* (1981), when Jason impales a post-coital couple lying in bed, driving a spear through their intertwined bodies and into the floor. Brian De Palma's *Dressed to Kill* (1980) provoked feminists to launch a nationally organized boycott over the movie's early sequence in which a sexually frustrated woman (Angie Dickinson) is assaulted while masturbating in the shower, an homage to *Psycho* which is soon revealed as her lurid rape fantasy. This is followed by a long, carefully shot and edited sequence that culminates in her actual murder by a straight razor-wielding maniac following a casual afternoon pickup. The movie's slick production values and patina of sophistication in its knowing allusions to Hitchcock only added to the rancor of protesters.

Feminist energy and activism shifted into other areas in the 1990s, notably the ever rancorous abortion battle, but the porn-is-horror revolt resurfaced 20 years later in a surprising place. During the Sydney Olympic Games in September, 2000, Nike presented a commercial as part of a campaign called "Why sport?" that parodied the slasher cycle by seemingly inverting its violent gender dynamics. American runner Suzy Hamilton plays a woman disrobing in her bathroom when a masked psycho swinging a chainsaw appears and pursues her through the house and into the dark woods in scenes evoking *Texas Chain Saw Massacre* and *Friday the 13th*. The joke comes in how she perseveres. The lithe Olympian puts more and more distance between her and the assailant until he gives up, panting in exhaustion as a title reads, "Why sport? Because you'll live longer." Anticipating trouble that arrived with an outpouring of complaints that the spot joked about violence against women to sell running shoes, NBC pulled it after only three days.[45]

Although a strong intellectual current underpinned the feminist critique of media misogyny, the basic themes were traditional: The weak and innocent were helpless before the deterministic assault of nefarious imagery foisted upon them. In the desperate rush to find rational explanation in the aftermath of the terrible Columbine High School shooting rampage in April, 1999, the news media reported and Americans debated the fact that the teen killers had been immersed in violent computer games and Goth rock music, perhaps becoming obsessed by these macabre subcultures. This notion soon fell away but the framework was familiar: Decadent culture made them do it – an explanation that flies in the face of both Judeo-Christian moral precepts and the Western legal tradition of individual responsibility. The following spring, advertising imagery for *The Skulls* (2000) depicted a group of ominously leering teens, their faces overlaid with grinning death's heads. Actually not a horror film but a crime story about a secret society loosely inspired by Yale's Skull and Bones Society, the image provoked a genuine shudder of post-Columbine dread. The horror genre's perennial popularity has built on the iconography of particular movies and monsters, but the broader emotional experimentation it allows as much as the dark social and psychological truths it reveals keep its interplay of fantasy and reality close in the cultural dance of life and death.

CHAPTER 5

EDGES OF THE HORROR FILM: LON CHANEY, TOD BROWNING, AND *THE UNKNOWN* (1927)

Since the 1960s, director Tod Browning and silent star Lon Chaney have been remembered primarily for their contributions to the horror film – remarkable considering that the supernatural gothic mode was generally not part of their collaborations, and indeed, the term "horror movie" was not used or recognized as a genre category by critics, filmmakers, or audiences in the 1920s. Their reputations have intertwined even though Chaney's most famous films, *The Hunchback of Notre Dame* (1923) and *The Phantom of the Opera* (1925), were not made by Browning; and the director's most famous films, *Dracula* (1931) and *Freaks* (1932), came after Chaney's death. Of their ten movies together, perhaps none better expresses the strengths of their respective talents than *The Unknown* (MGM, 1927), a fantastic work of psychosexual grotesquerie. Chaney plays a pseudo–armless circus performer who decides to have his arms actually amputated to win the love of a frigid fellow-artiste (a young Joan Crawford) who then abandons him. The astounding plot presents a fever dream of phallic symbolism, castration anxiety, and sexual terror. Typically, the film's circus/carnival setting becomes a liminal location between public and private personae, artifice and reality, distraction and terror – one that has defined recurrent preoccupations of the horror film since

FIGURE 13 Alonzo the Armless (Lon Chaney) and his diminutive alter ego Cojo (John George) in *The Unknown* (1927, Metro-Goldwyn-Mayer)

The Cabinet of Dr. Caligari established the motif. Although *The Unknown* is little indebted to the distorted *chiaroscuro* of German expressionism, Browning's stylization through careful composition and editing combines with Chaney's most truly masochistic character for memorably disconcerting effects. Working separately and together, Lon Chaney and Tod Browning managed at once to help define and broaden the parameters of the horror film.

Genre theorist Steve Neale points out that in the 1920s, at least as far as the film industry and critical conception would have it, a large number of movies were grouped under the rubric of "melodrama" for their stock characters and conventionalized, emotionally excessive plots leaning heavily on romance, violence, suspense, or sentimentality. This definition of melodrama, partly derived from popular fiction and drama, combined a variety of forms we would now subdivide into categories as diverse as love stories, horror, action-adventure, and crime.[1] Most of Browning and Chaney's output would thus have fallen into the melodrama category.

As noted in Chapter 2, Hollywood shied away from supernatural gothic tales before 1931, and works seemingly produced in this vein, e.g., Roland West's *The Monster* (1925) and *The Bat* (1926), the former featuring Chaney, or Paul Leni's *The Cat and the Canary* (1927), were heavily diluted with comedy and the goblins finally exposed as frauds. Browning and Chaney's now lost collaboration *London After Midnight* (1927), despite the actor's most arresting horror makeup after the Phantom, also ends with his supposed vampire revealed as a fake. Even so, *The Phantom of the Opera* now fits easily into most any definition of the horror film, and also exceeds the standards of its day, since it has no comic counterpoint, and Chaney's Erik, with his cadaverous visage, remains an enigmatic figure whose possible supernatural origins are neither confirmed nor denied.[2] *The Hunchback of Notre Dame*, based on a classic of historical fiction and brought to the screen as an ambitious costume drama, is no one's idea of a horror film. Yet what Chaney's signature roles share with *The Unknown* is the star's affinity for characters with physical abnormalities or disabilities, figures that might inspire fright, or pity, or both.

Horror films evoke primal emotions. The stark confrontations with mortality they express tease the primitive fight-or-flight reflex. Moreover, it is common to say that many of fiction and cinema's most enduring and compelling monsters are also complex identification figures. In the Frankenstein Monster or King Kong, to cite two iconic examples, viewers quickly turn from fear to sympathy and regret at their deaths, reactions that indicate a recognition of the monster's dilemma as in some way our own. Even Bela Lugosi's icy Dracula, wandering through the ages, courts a moment of pathos when he wistfully allows, "To die – to be really dead. That must be glorious." That adolescents who, to greater or lesser extents, often picture themselves as physically ugly victims of a fearful and punitive society have largely sustained the horror film economically for more than two generations suggests another basis for the genre's steady popularity. These often-ambiguous reactions to the monster are the aspects of the horror film that readily admit the work of Lon Chaney.

The fear of death is reflexively tied to the dread of injury, mutilation, and disfigurement, results that are not only physiological but also strongly bound up with psychological and social factors. Chaney's Quasimodo is a sympathetic, even heroic figure. He is also a martyr, his deformed back stripped for public ridicule and whipped in the film's most famous sequence. A strong parallel with the passion of Christ arises here, reinforced when, tied to a wheel and mocked by the crowd, the Hunchback cries out for water. The Magdalene-like gypsy girl, Esmeralda, to whom he becomes devoted, answers his plea. Though hardly Chaney's entire repertoire, many of the roles for which he is remembered – and celebrated – are exercises in self-abasement and sadomasochistic spectacle. What Browning seemingly contributed to this dialectic was a far darker, more cynical sensibility that drew on his own experiences as a sideshow performer, the capacity to wring disturbing undercurrents from material devoid of gothic detail. Browning was one of the truest cinematic practitioners of the Grand Guignol aesthetic where the universe, both moral and physical, is random and cruel rather than orderly, just, and socially affirmative in the manner of conventional melodrama.

Based on Browning's original story, *The Unknown* is set in a Spanish circus where Chaney, the armless Alonzo who throws knives with his feet, loves Nanon (Joan Crawford), daughter of Zanzi, the circus owner. Only Alonzo's midget friend and assistant, Cojo (John George), knows that Alonzo really has arms and is in disguise to avoid a murder charge. Because Nanon cannot stand any man's arms around her, Alonzo seems a perfect confidante. Yet when Alonzo expresses his affection for her, Zanzi angrily beats and humiliates him. When the enraged Alonzo later strangles Zanzi, the horrified daughter witnesses the murder without seeing the killer's face but notes an unmistakable aberration, a double thumb on one hand. Alonzo begins to look after Nanon, who has also drawn the attention of the strongman, Malabar (Norman Kerry). Given Nanon's dread of men's arms, Alonzo hatches a fantastic plot, blackmailing a doctor to surgically remove his arms to win her love and provide an alibi for Zanzi's murder. But when he returns after the surgery, Nanon's phobia is somehow cured and she is engaged to Malabar. Unhinged, Alonzo sabotages the couple's new act, in which Malabar is tied between horses running on treadmills, trying to tear off the arms of his rival. Nanon intervenes at the last second and Alonzo is trampled to death by the horses.

Considered lost for decades, *The Unknown* has garnered a cult reputation since its rediscovery in the mid-1960s. Even considering Chaney's fabled skills with makeup and bodily contortion and Browning's penchant for the sideshow demimonde, the plot is something else. The usual willingness of protagonists of melodrama to suffer and sacrifice for love wildly exceeds conventions here. Our certainty that Alonzo's decision to maim himself lacks all plausibility sits beside a skin-crawling contemplation of "What if . . . ?" Despite society's fear and revulsion, the congenitally deformed Quasimodo and the regal Phantom accept and even flaunt their "accursed ugliness," as Erik puts it in the famous unmasking scene. The jaw-dropping irony of *The Unknown* is that Chaney, in a role featuring his natural face, chooses this awful dismemberment and to no end. Michael Dempsey argues that the claim that Chaney's grotesque roles replay the myth of Beauty and the Beast is tangibly false: "In all reworkings of the fairy tale, Beauty recoils at first from Beast's physical-visual ugliness but overcomes her repulsion once she appreciates his poetic soul . . . Chaney's films do consistently evoke Beauty and the Beast, but only to insist that its outcome is a wish-fulfillment fantasy, a lie."[3] Indeed, stolid, handsome Norman Kerry ends up with the woman Chaney adores in *The Hunchback*, *The Phantom*, and *The Unknown*.

Chaney's biographer Michael F. Blake, himself a professional makeup artist, refutes the many legends that have grown up around the star by carefully explaining how Chaney technically executed his various designs. Blake has little patience for those who have claimed that Chaney, an accomplished theater professional of many years standing, was so fanatically devoted to his art that he regularly risked serious injury to his face, eyes, and back to create some characters, Quasimodo and the Phantom in particular. To play Alonzo, for example, Chaney did wear an uncomfortable corset to bind his arms to his sides, but the apparent dexterity with his feet, from lighting cigarettes to drinking wine, was accomplished by a concealed double, an actual armless man named Paul Dismute. Just as there is a substantial difference between uncomfortable and dangerous, so too is Blake quick to caution that critics should not assume that because so many of Chaney's most fascinating characters exhibited sadomasochistic tendencies, often rather spectacular ones, in fact, that these were qualities of the man himself.[4] By contrast, David J. Skal and Elias Savada paint an unflattering portrait of Tod Browning, describing a personal and professional life poisoned by alcoholism and a selfish, often misanthropic streak. They also speculate about a drunk-driving accident in 1915 that killed a friend and may have left Browning genitally mutilated at age 34.[5] Admitting the evidence for this is inconclusive, his biographers argue that the director's work nonetheless indicates an archly morbid obsession with stories and characters that play on themes of castration, sexual dysfunction, and pathological vengeance. In any case, a distressing work like *The Unknown* provokes the intense dread of later horror films with little of the aesthetic distance accompanying gothic stagecraft.

Many of Chaney's roles we now associate with the horror genre in fact emulated the heavily psychologized and arty European, especially

German, cinema that Hollywood was steadily assimilating. Viewed simply in terms of Chaney's career at the recently formed MGM studio, *The Unknown* can be understood as another, certainly more grim telling of *He Who Gets Slapped* (1924), directed by Victor Seastrom, part of the Swedish contingent in Hollywood of the late silent era that included Greta Garbo.[6] Here Chaney is a brilliant scientist plagiarized and humiliated by his aristocratic benefactor, finally becoming a clown whose act consists of being comically slapped by all and sundry. Chaney's clown similarly pines for an unattainable woman and contrives a baroque vengeance on those who wronged him by trapping them with a lion, though he is stabbed and dies in the circus ring. Chaney's continental counterpart was Emil Jannings, who played similar roles in Germany and Hollywood as a proud, often vain man brought low by cruel circumstance or a bad woman in *The Last Laugh* (1924), *Variety* (1925), *The Last Command* (1928), and *The Blue Angel* (1930).[7] Jannings could wallow in public degradation as readily as Chaney. Both played psychologically fraught, even aberrant characters in films enhanced by an often self-consciously showy cinematic style.

Moreover, whatever its origins, the Freudian symbolism in *The Unknown* was neither obscure or naïve at the time when Freud's ideas and terminology had increasingly been circulated in the mass media since shortly before World War I. The first movie to attempt a coherent dramatization of psychoanalytic theory and practice, German director G. W. Pabst's *Secrets of a Soul* [*Geheimnnisse einer Seele*] (1926), was shown in New York early in the year of *The Unknown*'s release. In this sense, "Alonzo the armless" (the film's original title) is himself the tale's central motif. In *The Interpretation of Dreams* (1900), Freud argues that the dream-work frequently transposes the upper and lower portions of the body so that, for example, cutting hair or pulling teeth can be symbols of castration. The loss of Alonzo's arms, first faked then genuine, follows this logic. Freud also claims that "stabbing and shooting [are] symbols of copulation, and knives and cigarettes [are] symbols of the penis," terms that apply directly to events in *The Unknown*.[8] Moreover, Skal and Savada point to Freud's later essay "The Uncanny" (1919) for explication of Alonzo's mutant double thumb. As Freud put it, "This invention of doubling as a preservation against extinction has its counterpart in the language of dreams, which is fond of representing castration by a doubling or multiplication of a genital symbol."[9]

The Unknown begins with a bold if coded display of repressed desires. In the middle of a circus performance, Alonzo shoots a rifle and throws knives with his feet – the target, a smiling Nanon, whose outer clothes are progressively shot away, and her near–naked body outlined by the hurled knives. The act situates them on either end of a rotating apparatus that conveys a delirium of enticement and foreplay. Alonzo's lustful grins as he undresses Nanon via displays of a peculiar phallic prowess are set beside the equally assertive Malabar, first seen hoisting a heavy barbell and bending a steel rod with his brawny arms. Yet despite this public tease, in the following scenes, Nanon recoils from the embrace of men's arms, a euphemism for avoiding intercourse: "All my life men have tried to put their beastly hands on me, to paw over me," she fairly shudders, confiding to Alonzo, after pulling away from the patient Malabar. "Yes, always fear them, always hate them," Alonzo coaxes, compulsive and manipulative even before we know he really has arms.

In this sense, the film's most important character outside the twisted triangle is Alonzo's friend Cojo, who functions as chorus, conscience, and alter ego, but alter ego of a particular sort. As Skal and Savada point out, given the story's setting, the character's name is surely a sly diminutive for the Spanish *cojones*, or testicles.[10] Browning used little people in other pictures, especially baby-faced Harry Earles in *The Unholy Three* (1925) and *Freaks* (released in 1932), to mirror and express dark sexual themes that cast doubt on comfortable definitions of the "normal." Cojo sometimes appears dressed identically to Alonzo in flowing cape and round-brimmed hat, but in the opening scene under the big top he assists Alonzo while costumed as a goateed devil, a wry commentary on the psyche of the armless knife-thrower. When Nanon first rebuffs Malabar, she confides to Alonzo, "You are the one man I can come to without fear," hugging his "armless" frame. Browning then cuts to a reaction shot of Cojo, giving a scoffing laugh as he puffs on a cigar.[11] Soon after, Cojo reveals Alonzo's masquerade by helping him unstrap the corset that conceals his arms, the point at which we see Alonzo's bizarre double thumb. After Zanzi's murder, the police take Cojo for fingerprinting while Alonzo sits by quietly, strumming a guitar with his feet. When Alonzo hatches the crazed scheme to amputate his arms, Cojo both provides the germ of the idea and recoils at the realization that he actually plans it. In a weird image paradoxically expressing impotence and hypersexuality, Alonzo sits in a chair with his arms exposed, yet still so accustomed to concealing them that he lights a cigarette with his feet, to Cojo's amusement. Fittingly, Cojo disappears from the movie soon after the operation, and is absent when Alonzo launches his flamboyant attack on Malabar.

The film's careful yet understated visual style uses remarkable sets at the beginning, middle, and end to impart major themes. Two are familiar entertainment venues, the circus tent and a theater, which continue the dialectic between public spectacle and private secret. In between is a brief foray into another kind of performance space, the deserted operating theater with surrounding rows of seats where Alonzo and Cojo meet the surgeon he blackmails to perform the amputation. We never learn exactly what Alonzo holds over him (we see only a cryptic note reading, "Remember Tangiers twenty years ago?") but the doctor, a respected authority pictured in a setting used to teach surgical technique, is just another fraud with a guilty secret in the Browning world. The operating theater's strongly vertical space, emphasized by long narrow windows, parallels the high, enclosed space of the big top in the opening and the tower Nanon stands on during Malabar's stage act at the end. The similarity of these theatrical settings may suggest a measure of self-consciousness but, overall, functions to underscore the public humiliation Alonzo will undergo. In the first two venues Alonzo holds the center of attention and power. His control evaporates in the penultimate scene when he realizes his complete misunderstanding of Nanon's affections, self-delusion that led to almost literal emasculation. In a particularly cruel touch as Alonzo awaits Nanon at the empty theater, Browning positions him standing nervously before the stage, catching sight of her coming down the center aisle – a darkly comic caricature of the wedding ceremony that will never be.

Not the least aspect of *The Unknown*'s nightmare feel is its lack of explanation either for Nanon's initial phobia or its miraculous cure. It is possible that incestuous abuse by her father may account for her fear, though the film provides little evidence for this beyond Zanzi's otherwise unexpectedly fierce reaction to Alonzo's simple gift of a shawl to his daughter, lashing out with violence that could be interpreted as expressions of jealousy and guilt. Skal and Savada contend that implications of incest appear elsewhere in Browning's work. The theme would cohere with the other more certain Freudian implications of the story. Given that Chaney was 44 at the time compared to Joan Crawford's 22, he is visibly old enough to be her father, which read in this way further disqualifies him as her suitor. As Alonzo dreams aloud of marrying Nanon after Zanzi's death, it is Cojo once again who nervously points out that she would inevitably discover his secret on the wedding night – an obvious truth that still results in Alonzo threatening Cojo's life if he ever divulged it to her. The film's fascination resides in such irrational undercurrents.

In any case, with no narrative preparation for Nanon's sudden liberation from her neurosis, Chaney faced a great challenge in conveying

Alonzo's reactions to the grotesque joke fate has played on him. Worse, he initially thinks Nanon is expressing her desire to marry him just as she announces her engagement to Malabar. In another merciless touch, the strongman then appears on a catwalk, waving broadly to the dumbfounded Alonzo. As Malabar's arms encircle Nanon, Chaney transmits Alonzo's sense of horror, sick comedy, and delirium through subtle movements of his face and shoulders. His dawning awareness passes through a clenched rictus grin, conveying a benumbed shock and a faint rage before he finally throws back his head to scream and collapses in tears. At the scene's climax, Alonzo regains his composure in part by wiping his eyes with the handkerchief clutched in his toes, now much more than the skillful illusion he has practiced before. Moreover, Browning holds the camera on Chaney for many seconds straight for each stage of his unfolding reaction, risking that some viewers might simply erupt in laughter at such an absurd predicament. Even so, this short-circuiting jumble of emotions leaves unnerving impressions.

Through careful cutting that creates a slight sense of ellipsis, we gradually notice others present in the theater as Malabar and Nanon, still oblivious to Alonzo's shock, offer to demonstrate their new act. This tableau is no less fraught with erotic overtones than the one at the beginning, similarly involving a spectacular display of phallic skill. The setting places Nanon atop a tower above two horses running on treadmills in opposite directions as the beaming Malabar stands in between with his arms tied to the animals. The arrangement conveys the strength of his arms even more powerfully extended into the galloping horses – another Freudian phallic symbol – with his lover driving them to greater speed with a whip. However, where all were performing before crowds in the first scene, the pathetic and now truly armless Alonzo is forced to simply sit and watch as the strongman takes center stage. Yet Alonzo's vengeance clearly aims to castrate his rival by causing the horses to tear off his arms. With Malabar bound to the racing horses, Alonzo pushes the speed control lever to the maximum, then holds off people coming to help by threatening to hurl knives with his feet – a surreal tableau even with little stylization through lighting or eccentric camera angles. Instead, cadenced montage, including repeated inserts of a timpani player in the pit visually driving the action with a sense of pulsing rhythm builds a suspenseful climax that blurs distinctions between the drama witnessed by the audiences within and outside the movie itself.

Alonzo's death partly redeems him as he lunges forward to protect Nanon, who is frantically trying to calm a rearing horse and instead falls onto the treadmill himself and is trampled. Chaney is once again a monster both lethal and tragic. In brief courting scenes between Nanon and Malabar earlier in the film, Browning used a period convention of a gauzy filter to drench them in a visually excessive aura of storybook romance. The filter's appearance in the movie's final shots showing the happy couple united in a park after Alonzo's demise now seems no less artificial and contrived than the fantastic events that lead up to it. It is possible that this ending felt more conventionally satisfying to its original audiences, though reviews of *The Unknown* indicate that critics in 1927 were as mystified as viewers today by the lingering implications of the dreadful tale.[12] The settings and situations of many Chaney roles in the 1920s seem on the surface to continue the overwrought dramaturgy of the late Victorian era, the popular theater that in fact comprised his early professional training. Instead, Chaney's presentation of physically bent, emotionally tormented characters remains surprisingly contemporary, particularly in its obsession with mutilation and disfigurement in explicitly psychosexual terms alongside shrewd manipulation of sentiment and cynicism.[13] Even without occult basis, bloodletting, or gothic ambiance, without so much as the luxury of a clearly defined category of a horror film, Lon Chaney and Tod Browning helped establish the form in terms more relevant than ever. Indeed, it took "the genre" years to catch up with their most psychically bizarre works of the Jazz Age.

Lon Chaney, Horror Star

In 1997, when the US Postal Service issued a series of stamps commemorating the classic monsters of Hollywood cinema, the group included Boris Karloff as Frankenstein's Monster, Bela Lugosi as Dracula, and Lon Chaney as the Phantom. With the imprimatur of the federal government no less, Lon Chaney was officially designated and honored as a "horror star." Yet writing in 1939, less than a decade after Chaney's death, film historian Lewis Jacobs summarized the actor's career in different terms: "In a stream of films Lon Chaney became famous for his characterizations of the underworld ruler: *Partners of the Night, Black Shadows, The Girl in the Rain, Kick In, One Million in Jewels, Dollar Devils, Boston Blackie, Outside the Law*, and the celebrated *The Unholy Three*."[14] This list seems surprising because we now have a different notion of Chaney's star persona, even in relation to his billing as "The Man of a Thousand Faces" by which he was well known at the time. Indeed, nowhere in several paragraphs devoted to Chaney does Jacobs even mention The Phantom or The Hunchback. Chaney's special place in the small pantheon of actors associated with the horror film was largely carved out after his death in 1930 through actions taken by Universal studios in its evolving corporate incarnations. What's more, despite the range and variety of Chaney's roles, by the early 1960s, the burgeoning monster fan magazines such as *Famous Monsters of Filmland* and *Castle of Frankenstein* had almost exclusively identified him as the first great horror star, maintaining his reputation while introducing him to later generations in precisely these terms.

By the time Universal signed Chaney's son, Creighton, for lead roles in a series of horror programmers in the first half of the 1940s, RKO had already forced him to take the stage name, Lon Chaney, Jr. In a strong review of what became his signature role, *The Wolf Man* (1941), the *Hollywood Reporter* noted: "Lon Chaney assumes the really terrifying make-up created by Jack P. Pierce and bears favorable comparison to his esteemed father."[15] Here the "favorable comparison" still seems to refer to a role involving a grotesque character in heavy makeup, and not to horror per se. This impression would soon change, however. Hailing Chaney, Jr as "the Screen's Master Character Creator" in an awkward approximation of his father's billing in the 1920s, Universal made him integral to their slate of horror sequels, playing characters the studio had created in the 1930s such as the Frankenstein Monster and the Mummy in addition to further turns as the Wolf Man. During this time, Universal also produced the bland Technicolor remake of *The Phantom of the Opera* (1943) starring Claude Rains, using the original's still-standing opera sets. The name "Lon Chaney" was directly fusing with a now fully articulated and recognized notion of horror as a distinct movie genre.

In 1957–8, horror returned to a level of popularity not seen since science fiction eclipsed the genre after World War II, following Hammer's *Curse of Frankenstein* (1957), AIP's *I Was A Teenage Werewolf* (1957), and William Castle's gimmick horror films beginning with *Macabre* (1958); while Screen Gems began to syndicate its *Shock!* package of vintage Universal horror movies to local TV stations. Further transformation of the elder Chaney's image began in this context, embellished by Universal-International's biopic *Man of A Thousand Faces* (1957), starring James Cagney. The film received good reviews and an Academy Award nomination for Best Screenplay. Integral to the Chaney legend is that he was the child of deaf-mute parents and could only communicate with them by sign language, which supposedly honed his abilities with pantomime from childhood. The sympathetic portrayal of his parents in *Man of A Thousand Faces*, and the prejudice their disability provokes in Lon's first wife became an opportunity for a pro-social message. In fact, the US Department of Health, Education, and Welfare chose the movie to be subtitled for showings to the deaf.[16] Since *The Phantom of the Opera* and *The Hunchback of Notre Dame*, two of Chaney's most successful pictures had been made for Universal, behind-the-scenes looks at the making of these movies were crucial to the story, with Bud Westmore creating new, and rather less interesting versions of Chaney's makeups for Cagney. The film concludes with a wholly fictional and anachronistic scene: On his deathbed, Lon bequeaths Creighton (Roger Smith) his makeup case after adding "Jr" to the name. Thus Universal claimed that Chaney, Sr's roles in the 1920s were really precursors to the horror roles his son would play for the studio in the 1940s – that the Phantom was the literal father of the Wolf Man. This marked an important step in Lon Chaney's reconstruction as a "horror star."

Moreover, Hammer's increasingly successful output promoted a new star system with Peter Cushing and Christopher Lee repeatedly cast together or separately in the *Frankenstein* and *Dracula* series and many other horror films. Simultaneously, Vincent Price became a star in tailored horror vehicles, especially AIP's Poe series (1960–5). After *Curse of Frankenstein*, the medium-budget horror feature thrived on the star system as veteran actors like Boris Karloff, Peter Lorre, John Carradine, and Lon Chaney, Jr returned to the gothic fold. With such stars increasingly active in exploitation horror, a sense of both tradition and vitality seemed to animate the genre around 1960. Celebration of the late Lon Chaney in the pages of monster fan magazines both reflected and encouraged this trend. In early 1958, the first issue of *Famous Monsters* contained what editor Forrest Ackerman termed "a kind of history of horror films" that devoted much of the story to three stars: Chaney, Karloff, and Lugosi.[17] For the next quarter of a century Ackerman regularly paid homage to the Man of a Thousand Faces in the pages of *Famous Monsters*. Indeed, the millions of baby-boomer horror fans raised on the magazine learned much about the star largely without seeing his films since silent movies rarely played on television, unlike sound-era films of the 1930s and 1940s. Chaney's transformation into the quintessence of horror stars was a triumph of pure iconography – familiarity created through Ackerman's steady publication of countless stills from his films, most never seen, some unseeable by youthful readers in every administration from Eisenshower to Reagan. Tellingly, one of the most immediately recognizable Chaney makeups comes from a movie long vanished, *London After Midnight*, put on the American Film Institute's "most wanted" list of lost films in 1980 and still missing at the time of writing.[18]

As noted in Chapter 4, David Skal argues that the Cold War nuclear threat partly motivated the rise of "monster culture" among children and adolescents in the early 1960s, fan activity for which monster magazines, *Shock Theater* telecasts, and increasingly star-driven horror films were the prime movers culturally. Chaney was perhaps the most famous of the famous monsters, a hero with, yes, "a thousand faces," who somehow survived devastating physical and emotional traumas to return in film after film. In the age of crises in Berlin, Cuba, and especially Vietnam this was a great comfort. To these postwar audiences, Lon Chaney as "underworld ruler" meant no more than the ancient movies of Francis X. Bushman or Theda Bara; but as Quasimodo and the Phantom, the toothy vampire from *London After Midnight*, or the father of the Wolf Man, he served a new and entirely relevant purpose.

CHAPTER 6

FRANKENSTEIN (1931) AND HOLLYWOOD EXPRESSIONISM

Though conceived in the early nineteenth century, *Frankenstein* became one of the most widely disseminated and culturally resonant myths of the twentieth, a place broadly secured by popular movie adaptations. Remarkably, a single film originated much of the prevalent iconography. Universal's *Frankenstein* (1931) has not only become perhaps the most famous horror film of all time but one of the landmarks of Hollywood cinema. Through the resources of the studio system, a number of important talents – director James Whale, cinematographer Arthur Edeson, art director Charles D. Hall, makeup artist Jack P. Pierce, and unforgettably, actor Boris Karloff as the Monster – coalesced to produce a definitive screen version that every subsequent retelling has had to confront in one way or another. We noted earlier that while Tod Browning's *Dracula* (1931) initiated the Depression horror cycle and solidified an iconic image of the vampire through Bela Lugosi's performance, it remains an often stagy and disappointing film; whereas Rouben Mamoulian's visually inventive *Dr. Jekyll and Mr. Hyde* (1931) capped more than forty years of theatrical and motion picture adaptation. Yet the popularity and varied cultural meanings of Dracula and Jekyll and Hyde were not dependent on any particular version, let alone wide familiarity with the original

FIGURE 14 Jack P. Pierce's makeup for Boris Karloff as the Monster in *Frankenstein* (1931, Universal) became one of the iconic images of twentieth-century culture

novels. The same is true of the Frankenstein myth. Still, specific elements of Whale's film – the manic scientist and hunchbacked assistant, the crackling electrical laboratory with the monster strapped to an operating table, features of Karloff's makeup, especially the squared skull and neck bolts – have since become the unmistakable signifiers of "Frankenstein." *Frankenstein* was both an outstanding and typical product of 1930s Hollywood, particularly in its confident assimilation of German expressionist aesthetics on which horror's "golden age" was founded.

Frankenstein was envisioned in 1816 during a legendary stay at the Villa Diodati near Geneva when Mary Shelley, along with the major Romantic poets Percy Bysshe Shelley and Lord Byron, her husband and close friend, respectively, held a ghost story-writing contest. According to Mary, this came on the night after conversations about the possibilities of creating life or reanimating a dead body using then – current advances in chemistry, magnetism, and electricity. That a ghost-story contest followed a series of speculations about scientific principles suggests how *Frankenstein* came to be regarded as both a tale of gothic horror and a landmark of science fiction. Percy Shelley apparently wrote nothing; Byron only a partial piece about vampires. Another member of the group, Dr John Polidori, eventually published *The Vampyre* in 1819, an unauthorized 9,000-word revision of Byron's 2,000-word fragment. (Bram Stoker apparently read this story while conceiving *Dracula*.) *Frankenstein, or The Modern Prometheus* was published anonymously in 1818 and became a popular success.[1]

Following her husband's death in Italy, Mary Shelley returned to England in 1823 intending to revise the novel for a second edition. There she found the first adaptation of her work, *Presumption: or, The Fate of Frankenstein* by Richard Brinsley Peake, being produced on the London stage. Apart from necessarily streamlining the novel's convoluted plot, that first adaptation made three major changes in Mary's tale that were still evident when Universal released its movie more than a century later. As Shelley scholar Marilyn Butler notes, the play deprived the monster of speech; introduced the comic character of Fritz, Frankenstein's assistant; and perhaps most importantly, made Dr Frankenstein "confess his religious remorse to the audience, 'Oh that I could recall my impious labour, or suddenly extinguish the spark that I have so presumptuously bestowed'." Butler concludes: "Before she had implemented her own changes Mary Shelley had lost control of the plot and specifically over its range."[2] Popularly, *Frankenstein* became a conservative moral lesson rather than the philosophical and, implicitly radical political allegory that Mary wrote and continued to reshape in two subsequent editions.[3]

Universal's *Frankenstein* emerged from the Hollywood studio system's complex organization characterized by division of labor. Director Robert Florey started the project with writer Garrett Fort, preparing a detailed script that included plans for specific shot compositions. Crucially, Florey, an experienced feature director who had also made avant-garde shorts, planned to produce *Frankenstein* in the manner of German expressionism. Florey also shot a test sequence on *Dracula*'s castle sets with Bela Lugosi playing the Monster, supported by Edward Van Sloan and Dwight Frye, who would appear in the final film. (Sadly, the test is lost, a Holy Grail of the horror film.) The assignment soon passed to James Whale, who cast Boris Karloff and worked with Jack Pierce to design the monster's makeup. It takes nothing from Whale's particular achievements to acknowledge that he harnessed the varied contributions of a creative group of specialists, including Florey.[4] *Frankenstein* remains an emotionally engaging work in both performances and visual realization. Major themes of the novel – humanity's attempts to conquer mortality; the vexed relationship between man and God; the moral responsibility of science; the hapless creature as lonely, even existential outcast – are envisioned here in thoroughly cinematic ways.

When Edison's *Frankenstein* appeared in 1910, the nascent motion-picture business was seeking to protect itself from censorship and bad publicity by adapting well-known works from literature and drama, hoping to absorb their cultural cachet. Even in a different industrial context, similar concerns and strategies figured in Universal's creation of *Dracula* and *Frankenstein* 20 years later. By 1930, within the Hollywood industry Germanic lighting, set design, and camerawork were used to evoke bizarre, otherworldly settings as well as to connote an artistically ambitious production. As in *The Cabinet of Dr. Caligari* (1920), *The Golem* (1920), *Nosferatu* (1922), and *Metropolis* (1927), the specific German films Whale and his key collaborators examined before shooting, *Frankenstein* features expressionist stylization at all levels of visual design. The hilltop cemetery in the opening scene with its slanting grave markers, gnarled trees, and mausoleum was constructed on a sound stage, allowing complete technical manipulation of the environment in the German manner. Expressionistic sets highlight *Frankenstein*'s three most recognizable scenes: the cemetery, the gothic tower where the monster is born, and the old windmill where it is trapped and killed by a torch-waving mob at the climax. In each setting, Whale embellishes the off-kilter sets with canted framings, a variety of unusually high or low angles, a mobile camera, and a heavily shadowed lighting plan.

Frankenstein begins in a curious fashion. Before the opening credits, Edward Van Sloan whom we will soon see as Frankenstein's mentor, Dr Waldman, steps out from behind a theater curtain and addresses the audience/camera directly.

> Mr. Carl Laemmle [president of Universal] feels it would be a little unkind to present this picture without just a word of friendly warning. We are about to unfold the story of Frankenstein, a man of science who sought to create a man after his own image without reckoning upon God . . . I think it will thrill you; it may shock you; it might even horrify you. So if any of you feel you do not care to subject your nerves to such a strain, now's your chance to –. Well, you were warned,

he concludes with a smile. These brief remarks synchronize with previous adaptations that presented the tale as a cautionary moral lesson. Moreover, though not apparent today, this prolog was meant to connect the beginning of *Frankenstein* directly to the ending of *Dracula*, released earlier in the year. *Dracula: The Vampire Play* (1927) and the Universal movie in its original release had concluded with a curtain speech by Dr Van Helsing, adapted for film with the same actor, Edward Van Sloan, standing before the proscenium of a blank movie screen. Beginning with seeming concern for the audience's nerves after seeing the frightful tale of Dracula, Van Helsing/Van Sloan sent viewers home with mordant assurance that, "After all, there *are* such things!"[5] (*Dracula*'s coda was snipped off when Universal re-released it with *Frankenstein* in 1938, and never restored.)[6] Along with knowingly promoting a studio "franchise" on horror, Universal was acknowledging that *Frankenstein* might exceed prevailing standards for gruesome subject matter and violence.

Appropriately, a story about man's attempt to defy death opens in a cemetery. In the first shot after the credits, hands pull back a rope just used to lower a coffin into an open grave as a bell peals solemnly.[7] Gently weeping mourners surround the bleak, shadowed grave site; behind them stands a robed, skeletal statue of Death leaning on a sword. Whale's camera pans on to find Dr Henry Frankenstein (Colin Clive) and Fritz (Dwight Frye) skulking behind an iron fence. As the mourners depart and the gravedigger finishes his task, Whale reframes to a longer shot that reveals a second effigy in the foreground – a tilted carving of the agonized Christ on the cross. Moving out from his hiding place, Frankenstein is momentarily flanked by these two symbolic figures personifying the certainty of human mortality and the Christian promise of resurrection and eternal life. Humanity's bold intercession between those icons begins when Frankenstein flings a shovel of dirt into the face of Death. Despite the thematic importance of this gesture it is easy to miss, because just after Frankenstein hurls the dirt, Whale dissolves into a point later in the excavation. This may have been done because strict state and local censor boards around the country were going to be displeased by many aspects of *Frankenstein* anyway, and grave robbing was just the beginning of this movie. (A complementary toss of dirt onto the figure of Christ would have been incendiary and impossible, though in *Bride of Frankenstein* [1935], Whale will make direct visual comparisons between the Monster and the persecuted Christ.)[8] Standing the coffin upright in the reopened grave, Frankenstein virtually embraces it, saying: "He's just resting–waiting for a new life to come." The process of resurrection by science has begun.

In his insightful analysis "What Changes Darkness into Light?", R. H. W. Dillard identifies key visual motifs interwoven through Whale's

Frankenstein. Fire, and its variation with terms of darkness and light is perhaps the most important, as it pertains to Mary Shelley's conception of Dr Frankenstein as "the modern Prometheus." It first appears when the gravedigger lights his pipe and tosses the spent match on the fresh grave, evoking life's fleeting nature and the finality of death. Dillard also finds Whale's articulation of upward and downward movements equally significant, demonstrating many examples in which up/light/ life contrast with the opposite terms, down/darkness/death. For instance, in the shadowy opening shot, a coffin was lowered into a fresh grave; whereas the monster's body will be raised up on the operating table toward the lightning that will give it life in the creation scene. Stressing the film's cinematic qualities Dillard notes: "That the monster's life begins in lightning and ends in fire . . . is a simple enough observation . . . but it would be a misleading one if the whole complex pattern of fire, light, and darkness were not also taken into consideration."[9] Dillard's point encapsulates other patterns in the film as well.

Eyes and ropes become secondary motifs. Eyes, often termed "the window of the soul," and thus pertinent to the question of whether the man-made creature truly possesses a "soul" as understood in traditional religious conception, appear prominently in the opening credits. Over a somber theme, a drawing of the monster's eyes radiating beams of light as clawlike hands stretch toward the viewer dissolves into a field of slowly circling eyes, suggesting at once the Monster's menace as well as its own terror of the existence it beholds. (Another implicit image of the monster's face in the credits, ultimately misleading, resembles *Nosferatu*'s vampire.) In the Monster's first appearance an extreme closeup depicts Karloff's heavy-lidded, watery eyes appearing at once dead and aglow with inhuman light. Similarly, ropes appear at significant points after the opening shot above the grave. This motif may hinge on another verbal metaphor, that of "the slender thread" between life and death, epitomized when Frankenstein and his servant steal the body of an executed criminal dangling from the gallows. Fritz's initial fear of the hanged man foreshadows his own fate at the creature's hands. Soon after the Monster's creation, it must be subdued with ropes, recalling Prometheus bound to the rock for punishment.

When damage to the hanged man's brain necessitates finding another, we move to Dr Waldman's classroom where the elder scientist addresses eager students as Fritz watches at a window. Unlike the lone visionary Henry Frankenstein, these students (including a few women, incidentally) embrace the teachings of sagacious Dr Waldman. His lecture distinguishes between two brains floating in glass jars on his desk, one labeled "normal brain," the other "abnormal brain," that of a criminal who lived a life of "brutality, violence, and murder." Fritz's bungled attempt to steal the normal brain that sends it crashing to the floor and hasty grab of the criminal brain has become one of the film's critically controversial elements. Frankenstein's tragedy is commonly understood to result from a flawed endeavor, not a defective part. The two major interpretations of the tale contend that man's presumption to create life is inevitably doomed; or that man must take ultimate responsibility for the consequences of any such act.[10] Whale's scene seems to confuse both notions; that is, if only Fritz had taken the "good brain" the experiment might have succeeded. Though some have suggested this damages the movie's thematic integrity, its deep impression in the cultural vocabulary argues otherwise. Moreover, the two brains in Dr Waldman's classroom echo the movie's larger visual strategy.

Unlike *Caligari*, *Frankenstein*'s visual scheme does not employ expressionist distortion in every scene. Rather, the film roughly alternates the episodes of horror shot in expressionist style with others staged and photographed in an altogether different fashion. When we leave the nighttime world of crypts and crooked towers, the realm where Frankenstein defies the laws of God and man to create an artificial being, we depart to what the film conceives as the "normal" world. Most of these scenes, characterized by bright lighting (including sunlit exteriors) and conventional, evenly balanced compositions, involve Frankenstein's fiancée Elizabeth (Mae Clarke) and/or Henry's father, the old Baron Frankenstein (Frederic Kerr). Whale often opens such scenes with an establishing long shot that depicts floor-to-ceiling views of sets designed to convey a good deal of overhead space, a sense of openness in contrast to the clashing angles and shadowy, enclosed forms of the expressionist locations. Elizabeth's introduction in her salon begins this pattern, though Whale starts on a closeup of Henry's portrait flanked by a burning candle that reiterates the fire motif and suggests her ritualistic devotion to her future husband. Then, unobtrusive, eye-level compositions and even lighting mark her worried conversation with Victor Moritz (John Boles), which establishes their mutual concern for Henry's health, misgivings about his work, and Victor's unrequited love for her. Though the actors are stranded in a thankless exposition scene, characters and setting establish sharp distinctions between "normal" and expressionist style.

In this, Dr Waldman is a mediating figure. Waldman's domain, the medical classroom and the private study where he later meets Elizabeth and Victor, serves as a bridge between everyday and expressionist spaces.

The well-lighted classroom, hung with anatomical diagrams and a model skeleton, is a spacious theater where draped cadavers are wheeled in and out with ease, a place for the structured dissemination of established knowledge. In his study, however, cluttered with heavy books and racks of test tubes, subtly shadowed compositions are more tightly framed to suggest a cramped environment. Bookshelves prominent over Waldman's head, one row laden with human skulls, evoke an air of sorcery or alchemy. Even as he condemns Frankenstein's experiments as an "insane ambition to create life," Waldman's inner sanctum suggests that he shares aspects of Henry's "mad dream" yet remains dedicated to professional tradition, rationality, and prudence.

From Waldman's transitional space the film returns to expressionist distortion in three quick shots: an establishing shot of a medieval watchtower on a stormy night is followed by a low-angle view of its top showing the convergence of gothic and modern as Fritz busily installs electrical equipment on the roof. A third shot moves to the interior of Frankenstein's laboratory. Whale starts with the floor-to-ceiling composition used for Waldman's classroom and Elizabeth's home but the similarities end there. Our first view of the laboratory typifies the film's application of expressionist design: high-contrast lighting details a stone-walled interior split by a vertical support beam that divides the space into two irregular trapezoids, with the clashing lines of buttresses, alcoves, and highlighting forming triangles and rhomboid protuberances from wall sections and barred window openings. The tower seems to lean in every direction at once, with an undulating effect enhanced by a concave back wall and ceiling which bend and curve forward. A structural impossibility in reality, the tower becomes an outlandish icon of modernist imagination. The floor is cluttered with an operating table, electrical coils, and generators, adding further elements of visual agitation. Frankenstein appears as a small figure relatively unimportant in this complex plan. Yet the set is on the whole strongly vertical, with the wooden beam, narrow electrical latticework, and dangling cables drawing the eye upward to the rooftop opening. When Fritz calls down from above, the camera looks over his shoulder onto his master standing in the cross-hatched pattern of floor planks, Fritz's body enclosed by the door frame, deep shadows all around. Whale presents many variations of these compositions throughout the tower scenes.

Like Dr Waldman, Fritz too, is mediating figure but of a different sort. A carryover from the first stage adaptation, the deformed assistant providing both sadistic menace and comic relief became one of the icons of *Frankenstein* and other mad scientist tales. Walking with back bent and often assisted by a short cane, Fritz symbolically represents the "imperfect" physical body poised between the "normal" human and the totally artificial creature. (In the prolog of *Bride of Frankenstein*, Lord Byron's voice-over calls Fritz "the dwarf.") This semi-conscious equation of physical disability with moral turpitude or madness was a pervasive trope in many cultural forms for centuries. Contemporary sensitivities, however, should not obscure the character's centrality to *Frankenstein*. Dwight Frye (the mad Renfield in *Dracula*) memorably played Fritz as a combination of superstitious cave dweller and comic child with a violent streak – qualities echoed by the Monster. Fritz remains an engaging character, exemplified by the scenes where, angrily muttering to himself, he must trudge up and down the tower's winding staircase to answer the door, while pausing to pull up one loose sock, a comic touch that incongruously thrusts the mundane and recognizable into an uncanny setting.[11] Fritz's eventual hanging by the monster in retaliation for heartless torment still provokes more sympathy than satisfaction.

The unexpected appearance of Dr Waldman, Elizabeth, and Victor interrupts the preparation for the monster's birth, but only briefly as Frankenstein, his fervor growing as the storm's intensity builds, seems determined to both conduct and justify his experiments. Upset by the pain Henry is causing Elizabeth, Victor calls him "crazy," a word that angers Frankenstein and prompts him to invite, almost dare the group to examine his work. Mary Shelley's account of the creation, described in just a few vague sentences, has Frankenstein isolated and alone. The Universal version enhances the ferocity of the coming spectacle by including witnesses both sympathetic and skeptical to the Monster's bizarre birth. As the guests survey his laboratory, Frankenstein, backed against the operating table with its shrouded body, dryly remarks, "Quite a good scene, isn't it? One man, crazy; three very sane spectators." The doctor's language reveals the theatrical audacity and even blatant artificiality of the setting and the subsequent actions, as what follows became one of the most famous scenes in Hollywood history.

At Elizabeth's introduction she told Victor that "the very day we announced our engagement [Henry] told me of his experiments," establishing the close connection between Frankenstein's impending marriage and his fevered efforts to create life artificially. Parallel to the wish to conquer death is the tale's contrast between natural and "unnatural" forms of procreation. Now, with his trembling fiancée, a rival suitor, and surrogate father looking on, Henry Frankenstein and his perpetually agitated manservant (!) are about to create human life without benefit of clergy – or heterosexual union. This homoerotic undercurrent returns us to aspects of Shelley's radical social allegory.[12] Regardless, the story leaves little doubt that science and technology have challenged the fundamental reproductive prerogatives of nature as well as their traditional mediation through social convention.

Unlike *Bride of Frankenstein*, which floats on Franz Waxman's dreamily romantic score, the original film uses no background music at all. Instead, Whale punctuates the creation scene with crashing thunder, the storm's intensity rivaled by the grinding, buzzing, and pulsing of electrical machinery. Flashes of lighting mix with shots of Henry illuminated by pale electrical arcs from his generators as he crouches over a control lever twisting his neck upward to follow the operating table's ascent toward the sky. Whale takes maximum advantage of the set's contradictory angles, juxtaposing eccentric shot compositions through swift editing. As the table returns to the floor, the angle emphasizes the monster's exposed arm dangling over the side. When the hand begins to move slightly and then raise itself, Frankenstein explodes: "Look, it's moving! It's alive! It's alive!," he repeats, a mad grin widening his face while the hovering Fritz looks stricken. "In the name of God, now I know what it feels like to be God!" Frankenstein shouts as he falls against the table, shuddering in what seems a near-orgasmic frenzy of physical and emotional joy.[13] Overwhelmed themselves, Waldman and Victor rush forward to take his arms, unsure whether to restrain him or catch him before he faints. Thunder rolls again as we fade out, Henry's final high-pitched laugh still audible. Quite a good scene, indeed!

An abrupt return to the "normal" world, again signaled by conventional framing and naturalistic sets, occurs immediately after, as Elizabeth and Victor call on old Baron Frankenstein. Whale begins with a long shot of the couple on a sofa in the Baron's sitting room, brightly lit as if by the sunlight streaming through the tall windows in the background. An establishing shot of normalcy once more displays much open, overhead space, a cleanly vertical composition accentuated by the windows and long drapes. (The floor-to-ceiling long shot will appear shortly upon the entrance of the Burgomaster.) Time elapsed since the creation scene is unclear but now Elizabeth and Victor, having recently witnessed something fantastic, are half-heartedly covering for Henry against the questions of his blustering, impatient father. The subject of this scene is marriage, and the father's demands to know why it is delayed. Marriage is not presented as necessary for the emotional needs of the couple but for the continuation of the Baron's aristocratic lineage. The Frankenstein marriage is also a vital public ritual requiring the witness and endorsement of the larger society, indicated when the Burgomaster

(Lionel Belmore) also inquires about the wedding. "The whole village is kept waiting, the bride is kept waiting, and I am kept waiting!," the Baron grouses. Notably it is the patriarchal authority figures, the Baron and the Burgomaster, rather than Elizabeth, who fret over the delay.

The unspoken opposition between natural and unnatural procreation, or here, socially sanctioned versus illicit union, continues. The Baron marvels that his son can stay immersed in mysterious experiments when he's got "a darned pretty girl" waiting for him, drawing an ironically half-correct conclusion: "I understand perfectly well – there's another woman. And you're afraid to tell me. Pretty sort of experiments these must be!," he scoffs. Contrast this with a key scene of Mamoulian's *Dr. Jekyll and Mr. Hyde* where Jekyll pleads with the white-haired patriarch General Carew to give consent for his daughter to marry immediately. Carew's refusal intensifies Jekyll's social and sexual frustration, directly prompting the experiments that bring out the monster. In *Frankenstein*, the scientist has no further interest in marriage once he has brought forth (monstrous) life through other means. In both cases, the intertwining of sexual desire, rigid social custom upheld by stern fathers, and radical experimentation produces a fierce challenge to the status quo. Small wonder these two tales have been regularly interpreted as both conservative, cautionary fables and as populist folklore featuring sympathetic, certainly compelling, monsters and scientific dreamers who give vent to dissatisfaction with the most basic tenets of social and sexual orthodoxy.

A motif important to the rest of the film first appears in this scene. A bowl of cut flowers on a low table between Elizabeth and the Baron is repeated in the floral print of the sofa, vine patterns carved into decorative panels in the background, and similar designs on the drapery framing the windows. This profusion of natural and decorative flora in the Baron's manor culminates with shrubbery and tree limbs visible outside the window. Flowers move from unremarkable décor to substantial motif when the Burgomaster enters and presents Elizabeth with a bouquet – its importance reinforced with a quick closeup of her graciously accepting – before inquiring about the wedding. A traditional symbol for femininity and fertility, flowers simultaneously connote the beauty and fecundity of nature as well as its cultural containment through the social ritual of the wedding. The scene ends with the Baron's determination to find the "other woman" and assert his customary control of the process.

Back in the tower's shadowy interior, a low angle shot depicts Henry seated at a table, confidently smoking a cigar, while Waldman paces on a lower level. Just as the grouchy old Baron is flummoxed by his son's refusal to marry, Waldman is the surrogate father whom young Dr Frankenstein defies professionally. Frankenstein debates with his mentor about the creature in terms that pit youth against age: "Poor old Waldman. Have you never wanted to do anything that was dangerous?" When Waldman reveals that the brain stolen from his laboratory was a criminal one, Frankenstein stops and glances nervously off-screen in the direction from which his creature will soon approach. "You have created a monster and it will destroy you!," Waldman pronounces. "He's only a few days old, remember," Henry insists, half-consciously comparing the creature to a newborn infant. "So far he's been kept in complete darkness. Wait 'til I bring him into the light." At that moment, plodding footsteps sound off-screen. The thing that finally appears is Frankenstein's stubborn riposte to the parental guardians of social and scientific tradition.

As in its German predecessors, expressionist stylization in *Frankenstein* extends to acting performance and costume, most importantly in the indelible design of the Monster. Aided by Jack Pierce's makeup and Whale's supportive direction, Boris Karloff found a range of moods and a subtlety of movement in his performance that has never been equaled. A heavy door opens and the creature backs slowly into the room, then turns around full-figure. We briefly record a tall, yet slightly stooped figure in black, its height and bulk accentuated by thick-soled boots. Whale then cuts to three successively closer views of the creature's face that display its boxlike skull, scarred and clamped hairline, low, protruding brow, metal neck bolts, and pallid skin. (Karloff actually wore green makeup on face and hands that registered as a strange, milky complexion on black-and-white film.) The actor's face is limp, the jaw slack and lowered to give a dull-witted effect. Yet the final insert reveals glowing eyes accented by spotlighting that radiate alertness and menace.

Before the creature's birth, Waldman derisively asked Henry if he really believes he "can bring life to the dead." Frankenstein resolutely replies, "That body is not dead. It has never lived. I created it, I made it, with my own hands from the bodies I took from graves, the gallows, anywhere!" Herein lies the key to how and why this Frankenstein Monster has outshone all others. Whale's Monster is not a "wild man," a robot, or a decomposing zombie but something else entirely – the human form rebuilt and reshaped, stitched and bolted together by successive applications of surgery, mechanics, and electrical current. The trick of making his jacket sleeves too short reveals metal bands and stitches apparently joining hands to arms from which they never previously sprouted. Similarly, the neck bolts reiterate the creature's mechanical construction as fasteners that join separate components of skull and torso.[14] The creature's most distinctive feature, the squared head, suggests the functional but inelegant lines of a cranium altered with the straight cuts of saws and closed with irregular patterns of sutures. As David Skal summarizes this expressionist collision of organic and mechanical design, "The square head . . . powerfully evokes the plight of an old consciousness forced to occupy a new paradigm, a round brain bolted uneasily into a machine-tooled skull."[15]

After the quick montage revealing the creature's face, we return to the full-figure view that begins a 50-second-long take. Here the creature's appearance mirrors its surroundings, the jagged clutter of the tower laboratory. In the low-angle shot, the slight curvature of the doorframe above the creature's head sets off its planar skull, the creature's zigzag form emphasized by Karloff's bent, stiff-legged posture. The monster sways slightly at the knees, unsteadily anchored by its boots like some ugly jack-in-the-box. Frankenstein moves in to steady it, fearing it might fall, or perhaps lunge, then beckons it forward as it stumbles into motion. As the camera tracks right, the creature advances on its maker, throwing a huge shadow on the wall. The monster's halting movements and the doctor's cautious excitement as he gently orders it to sit in a heavy wooden chair invest the scene with compositional as well as dramatic tension.

When Frankenstein opens a ceiling panel to admit sunlight into the gloom, it affords Karloff one of the film's most poetic moments. The creature at first opens his hands and gestures beseechingly toward his maker. As the light falls on its face, he looks up hesitantly, a subtly beautiful expression of innocence and longing crossing the grotesque visage. He rises and stretches his arms toward the ethereal substance that gave him life, seeking to clasp it in his hands. When Henry removes the light the monster sadly repeats the pathetic gestures toward the only "parent" left, Dr Frankenstein, who simply orders it to sit once more. Oblivious to his creature's emotional pain, Henry marvels, "It understands this time. It's wonderful!" This moment of pathos and misapprehension is destroyed by Fritz's frenzied call of "Frankenstein! Frankenstein! Where is it?," as the hunchback races in with a torch, sadistically thrusting it into the creature's face. Fritz's torment of the creature is apparently ongoing. Why Frankenstein permits it is not clear, but can be taken as evidence of his almost immediate neglect of the living thing he boasted of forming with his own hands. The dangerously strong creature erupts in terror, requiring all three men to wrestle it down. As they bind it with ropes, Waldman's angry words close the remarkable scene of the creature's first appearance. "Shoot it!," he demands. "It's a monster!"

The brevity of the following scene can obscure its importance in realizing one of Shelley's major themes. Revived in the cellar (another arresting expressionist set), the growling monster thrashes against chains that hold it to the wall as Fritz continues to torment it with a whip and torch. Here Frankenstein makes his tragic error. In sorrow and disappointment, he abandons the creature rather than take responsibility for it. Paralyzed by indecision, Frankenstein confiscates the whip but will not acknowledge the Monster's grunts of physical pain any more than he recognized its emotional yearning. He merely implores, "Oh, come away Fritz. Leave it alone," before stumbling out, whereupon Fritz immediately resumes the torture. Whale uses off-screen sound throughout to announce major shifts in the narrative, especially violent actions. Sometime later, Waldman and Henry are working in the laboratory when, hearing faint screams, they race to the cellar and find Fritz hanged and the angry creature free. Now it must be subdued again with even greater difficulty.

The monster's subjugation is interrupted by a second visit from a trio of uninvited guests, this time including Baron Frankenstein. The Baron's foray into the expressionist world prefigures the increasing difficulty of keeping these realms distinct in the remainder of the film. ("You'll soon feel better when you get out of here," Elizabeth says to the stricken Henry, shuddering at the bizarre surroundings.) Displaying a rare concern, the Baron declares he will take his son home, presumably to marry, and so the father get his wish. Waldman informs his pupil that he will painlessly dispose of the ill-advised experiment. Thus Henry's "fathers" reassert control of an errant son. Yet, as they will soon learn, Frankenstein's own uncanny son, the Monster, has motives, too – strong impulses to self-preservation and growing recourse to complex emotions, especially revenge.

A high-angle shot looks down on the shadowy laboratory with the monster once more on the operating table where it was born, though Waldman now prepares to dissect and destroy it. Ironically, Dr Waldman, who repeatedly warned of the monster's danger, becomes its second victim when the creature stirs and strangles him. The decision to forgo background music pays off again in the quietly desperate struggle that climaxes with the distinct snap of Waldman's neck. With surprising agility, the creature strides down the circular staircase and pauses uncertainly before yanking open the door and escaping into the night. Immediately following, an exterior location in bright daylight depicts Henry recuperating beneath a spread of trees, seated in a plush chair with Elizabeth by his side and hounds at his feet, as in some Romantic painting. The quiescent dogs imply the squire's relaxed harmony with nature as Henry renounces his work and he and Elizabeth plan their long-delayed wedding. Yet despite the sunshine and sentiment, this is a precarious tableau, given our knowledge that the angry creature is loose.

In Shelley's novel, Frankenstein reluctantly agrees to construct a mate for the creature but then reconsiders and tears apart the new body. Furious, the Monster vows revenge in kind on his maker, promising: "I shall be with you on your wedding night." Universal's adaptation retains the centrality of the Monster's intrusion on Frankenstein's wedding in terms already established at the introduction of the old Baron. The wedding day begins with a closeup of the Baron opening a glass jar containing a tiara of preserved orange blossoms for the bride and boutonnière for the groom, heirlooms worn by three generations of the family on their wedding days. The recurrent flower motif symbolizes the maintenance of social tradition. He toasts his son with vintage wine he laughingly explains his grandmother would not permit his grandfather to drink: "Here's to the health of a son of the house of Frankenstein." Though Henry still does not know the monster is free, a cut to his worried reaction questions the likelihood of that health in the immediate future. Whale repeats a floor-to-ceiling long shot of the spacious room, the very center of normalcy, when the Baron goes to the window to imperiously greet an assemblage of celebrating villagers.

The camera dollies from the Baron's manor into the streets, moving screen right through the crowds drinking and dancing, the movement continued with a quick dissolve into a shot following the Monster pushing through underbrush. The linkage of these two shots suggest he is moving away from Frankenstein's wedding but he will soon be drawn directly back. The creature's first appearance in a sunlit exterior resembles the setting in which Frankenstein and Elizabeth planned their wedding. In one of the genre's most famous scenes, the monster comes upon the lakeside cottage of a woodcutter and his young daughter, Maria (Marilyn Harris). The busy father cannot stop to play and leaves her alone with a kitten, reinforcing her innocent vulnerability. When the monster approaches the girl, gesturing pathetically, she treats the silent hulk as a child like herself. Just as the Burgomaster presented Elizabeth with a bouquet, and the Baron pinned the boutonnière on his son, Maria gives the monster a daisy, which he lightly whiffs, grunting happily. "Two children, both left alone by their fathers," as Dillard observes, sit beside the lake and take turns pulling off petals and tossing them into the water, much to the creature's delight.[16] However, this brief union will result in tragic misunderstanding and death.

The ending of this scene was trimmed for the tougher post-1934 censorship version, which became standard in television and rental prints of the film for many years. Finding no more petals to throw, the Monster smilingly reaches for the girl as she cries, "No, you're hurting me! No!," and tosses her into the water. Karloff always maintained that he preferred what we now recognize as the edited version, where we cut before the monster seizes the girl, because it kept up sympathy for the creature.[17] However, as critics have noted, when the panting monster simply reaches off-screen, the censored print might invite an even more unsavory interpretation of what is about to occur. In any case, struggling under the costume and clumsy boots, the way Karloff drops Maria in the water seems more awkward than chilling. Realizing that he has drowned the child, the panicked monster flees into the woods, heading back, screen left, toward Frankenstein's wedding.

This leftward movement continues as Elizabeth approaches Henry with anxiety over Dr Waldman's absence, the camera tracking laterally through the sitting room, across a hallway, and into Elizabeth's dressing room, each space crowded with bouquets and vases of flowers. Victor's report that Waldman is dead and the monster spotted in the hills prompts Henry, having failed to contain the creature itself, to lock Elizabeth in her room. While the men scour the premises after hearing the monster's low growl, we cut back to Elizabeth, alone in bridal gown with long train, clutching her bouquet. A body of water just outside the window reminds us of how little Maria died, as the Monster appears at the window and stalks into the room. Whereas the killing of Maria was presented as the inadvertent act of a childlike wretch seeking only love and acceptance, the attack on Elizabeth seems a premeditated act of aggression and revenge. Whale's monster behaves like Shelley's here, though definite explanation is lacking. In the novel, the creature murders Elizabeth. Here she is found unconscious and implicitly raped. As Frankenstein and others rush to her aid, we see the room ransacked and Elizabeth draped in a faint across the bed, her train and long hair flowing. A tall vase of flowers tilts against a chair by the open window, suggesting the monster's violent "deflowering" of the bride.

The Monster's threat escalates to society at large when the village celebration gradually falls silent as Maria's father staggers through the streets with her drenched body, and the Burgomaster forms a posse to pursue her killer. Product of an unnatural birth, the Monster has now killed a child and assaulted Frankenstein's betrothed, demolishing a public celebration of social stability. Henry takes belated responsibility for the monster, telling Victor: "There can be no wedding while this horrible creation of mine is still alive. I made him with these hands and with these hands I will destroy him." As the posse sets out, leading bloodhounds, shots of women and children looking on nervously from windows reinforce the monster's threat to the normative values of home and family. The climax returns to dark, expressionist sets of woods and mountains. As the posse searches, the Monster overpowers Frankenstein and carries him an old windmill, a setting that combines the bleak cemetery of the movie's beginning and the dark tower where the creature came to life.

When the posse appears outside, the Monster tosses Henry from the top of the windmill, though a turning vane carries him down. Beginning with *Son of Frankenstein* (1939) society, represented by the enraged villagers, would increasingly direct equal or greater hostility toward scientists reviving the creature. A curious tenderness toward Dr Frankenstein remains here, the mob's fury vented exclusively on the monster. The Burgomaster urges: "Take him down to the village, and let's get him home," as men pick up the wounded Henry, while the rest set fire to the structure. Yelping like a frightened child or wounded animal, and so courting a last bit of empathy, the monster is hemmed in by the flames and felled by a collapsing beam. The burning windmill surrounded by the cheering posse is the scene's final image. The Promethean flames, symbol of humanity usurping the power of the gods, have been seized by society rising to protect itself from the freakish product of human ambition gone wild.

The movie's last scene opens on a group of maids bringing Henry a glass of his great-grandfather's wine, passing through another high, brightly lit foyer set. Henry recuperates in bed with Elizabeth at his side, a scene we observe from outside the bedroom as seen by his contented father. The Baron drinks the wine himself and toasts: "Here's to a son to the house of Frankenstein!" The bastard thing Henry and his servant assembled in a watchtower from parts of stolen corpses was clearly not the "son" the old Baron envisions. With the Monster dead in the twisted darkness of its birth, the Baron will presumably achieve his fondest wish of seeing his son extend the family line. Lying in bed under his wife's care and his father's watchful eye, Henry is simultaneously chastened, infantilized, and strategically located to resume natural procreation. The image lends a powerfully conservative closure to the tale of the doctor's rebellion against religious, social, and scientific tradition.

As discussed in Chapter 1, Robin Wood argues that traditional horror films end with the monster definitely destroyed in a manner that permits a sense of catharsis; and the restoration of "normality" signaled through the formation of a heterosexual couple. *Frankenstein* exemplifies the genre's classical narrative structure. However, if we apply these terms too rigidly, then the hopelessly dull Victor Mortiz might have been the film's center of interest. That is, to regard the ending as a categorical endorsement of the status quo we must forgive and forget a lot about Henry Frankenstein. This is the fellow who, by his own admission, stole bodies "from the grave, the gallows, anywhere!" to make his monster. Are we now to believe he is ready to settle down and become the gentleman physician of the village?

Notably, Universal wavered about what should finally befall Dr Frankenstein. The shooting script had him die along with the Monster, approximating Shelley's conclusion. But when production finished, they switched to a traditional happy ending.[18] Even so, one reason Henry cannot fully assimilate into the normative vision the ending provides is because the film has paralleled scientist and monster throughout. The common confusion that Frankenstein is the name of the monster rather than the doctor reinforces the *doppelgänger* theme, which was explicit in the 1910 Edison version. (While we might assume this confusion resulted from the popularity of Frankenstein movies, the earliest recorded mix-up of Shelley's characters goes back to 1823.) Universal's prolog stated that Frankenstein "sought to create a man after his own image." Repeated dialog in which Frankenstein refers to his hands ("I made it, with my own hands from the bodies I took from graves") parallels repeated closeups of the monster's hands as when it first comes to life, or in the open-palmed, circling gestures Karloff makes to convey the creature's inexpressible longings. In the climactic struggle, Whale shoots reverse shots of the pair facing each other tensely through the turning spindles of the mill wheel, the alternating close ups inviting us to consider monster and creator as alter egos. Yet time and many variations of the tale have proved that these characters, who seem most at home in the realm of expressionist distortion, are far more fascinating than the uninspiring paragons of the normal, Victor, Elizabeth, or the old Baron.

With its story related through Hollywood's adoption of German expressionism, *Frankenstein* defined the classic horror film in the 1930s. Yet its influence persisted. In the late 1950s, television syndication of *Frankenstein* and its Universal cohorts helped popularize the horror film once again, just as new interpretations of the genre were emerging from Hammer, AIP, and Columbia. Although Jack Pierce's makeup design is still closely guarded by Universal's copyright, Karloff's Monster is an instantly recognized and widely circulated icon, even honored on a US postage stamp in 1997. Powerful myths have multiple uses and varied meanings. In the modern age, the monster that threatens or destroys its maker can be a chilling metaphor for nuclear weapons, environmental catastrophe, or any scientific or industrial technology that produces unintended if no less devastating consequences. *Frankenstein* as modern myth, one both strengthened and shaped by Universal's 1931 movie, continues to fascinate; the issues it raises make the story more pertinent now than when first conceived by the 19-year old Mary Shelley in 1816.

CHAPTER 7

CAT PEOPLE (1942): LEWTON, FREUD, AND SUGGESTIVE HORROR

When writer-producer Val Lewton came to RKO-Radio Pictures in 1942 to oversee a string of low-budget horror films, his efforts yielded movies that have come to be considered some of the best of their kind. Forties horror is usually disparaged in standard historical accounts of the genre, with the exception of the nine stylish B pictures Lewton produced from 1942 through 1946. The Lewton cycle has long been a source of discussion and praise by assorted critics for its combination of sophisticated visuals and Freudian undertones. Director Jacques Tourneur's evocative, thematically complex *Cat People*, the Lewton unit's first release, drew on both the expressionist tradition of the 1930s and the popularization of Freudian psychoanalytic theory in 1940s America for its tale of a woman who fears she will transform into a murderous were-cat if sexually aroused. As with subsequent Lewton entries, *Cat People* diverged from Universal predecessors by substituting suggestive horror effects and psychological atmosphere for the attacks of physical monsters. Moreover, with a female protagonist who doubles as the monster, this variation of the werewolf myth illuminates provocative differences in the treatment of gender in the traditional horror film. Combined with its sustained mood of apprehension, these

FIGURE 15 Simone Simon as the troubled Irena, flanked by the symbolic statue of King John impaling a cat in Val Lewton's production of *Cat People* (1942, RKO)

elements invite closer analysis of a movie with a preselected title sold as a routine exploitation "chiller."

Historians of film style often note two major offshoots of German Expressionist cinema in studio-era Hollywood: Universal's gothic horror films of the 1930s; and 1940s Film Noir, a term retrospectively applied to a group of shadowy, pessimistic crime thrillers including *This Gun For Hire* (1942), *Double Indemnity* (1944), *Phantom Lady* (1944), and *Murder My Sweet* (1944).[1] Unlike gothic horror, Film Noir overlaid expressionism's low-key lighting and skewed shot compositions onto contemporary crime stories generally considered "realistic" in their day. Moreover, while the Universal horror films take place in an indistinct European neverland, six of the nine Lewton productions are set in modern America or feature contemporary American characters. Similar to its German predecessors, Film Noir style conveyed a thick layer of psychological subjectivity pertinent to its violent, sexually obsessive, or otherwise deviant characters. As such the Val Lewton cycle provides the clearest link between 1930s horror and 1940s Film Noir.

In his seminal 1972 essay "Notes on Film Noir," critic (and future director) Paul Schrader contends that what finally gathers a large number of 1940s dramas into the discernible group now called Film Noir are commonalities of visual style, mood, and themes.[2] Schrader never mentions the Lewton films, presumably because they were firmly tied to a distinct genre category. Yet the notion of Film Noir, whether considered a genre, a style, or a period, needn't be strained to include the dark, psychologically tangled vistas of *Cat People*, *I Walked with a Zombie* (1943), *The Seventh Victim* (1943), *The Ghost Ship* (1943), et al.[3] Besides its baroque visual style, Lewton's work parallels Film Noir through a similar construction of fatalistic moods and neurotic, angst-ridden characters whose deep disquiet seems to exceed the particular conflicts of the stories themselves. Considering *Cat People* in this vein connects it to contemporaneous Hollywood production as well as to larger social patterns of the World War II years, especially the shifts in gender roles the war occasioned. As such Lewton's B horror films become far less anomalous in the evolution of the horror genre than they have sometimes been considered.

Cat People begins as a love story when nautical architect Oliver Reed (Kent Smith) meets Irena Dubrovna (Simone Simon), a Serbian artist, at a New York City zoo, sketching a prowling black panther. Irena tells Oliver about the legendary cat people of her native village and how Serbia's King John thwarted their satanic perversion of its populace in the Middle Ages. Irena soon divulges her belief that she is one of these cat people and fears she will transform and slaughter any man who kisses her. Despite her phobia, the couple are drawn to each other and wed, though her fear prevents the consummation of their marriage. The anguished Oliver confides in his coworker Alice Moore (Jane Randolph), who confesses her love for him. Seeking to help the couple, Alice recommends a psychiatrist, Dr Louis Judd (Tom Conway). Increasingly jealous, Irena suspects Oliver and Alice are having an affair. Twice Alice is stalked by a threatening figure that may be Irena as a snarling panther. When the unscrupulous Judd later kisses his comely patient, she transforms and kills him. Mortally wounded by the doctor's sword cane, Irena returns to the zoo, opens the panther cage and is felled by the escaping cat, leaving Oliver and Alice together but heartbroken.

Although Lewton insisted on an approach to the genre he considered more sophisticated than the Universal-style "monster movie,"

Cat People, opening in November, 1942, still shows indebtedness to Universal's profitable *The Wolf Man*, released in December, 1941, which in turn bore traces of MGM's tonier *Dr. Jekyll and Mr. Hyde*, from July, 1941. To varying degrees, all three movies use the horror genre as a pretext for stories rich with Freudian implications that invite the attentive viewer to recognize actual psychosexual conflicts and "scientific" explanation beneath the superficial gothic details. Each features an impressive nightmare/delirium sequence filled with phallic imagery and intimations of sadomasochistic violence, with symbolic structures drawn from *The Interpretation of Dreams* (1900), perhaps Freud's most popular and accessible work. Of the three, *The Wolf Man* (its title derived from one of Freud's famous case studies) was the most conventional horror tale, with Lon Chaney, Jr.'s furry werewolf a visible and explicitly supernatural monster; whereas Spencer Tracy's turn at *Jekyll and Hyde* was the least interested in horror effects and indeed, drew praise for its seeming transcendence of the low-status genre with which the story had become identified.[4] *Cat People* floats artfully between clinical and occult explanations for Irena's fears. Yet even *The Wolf Man* carries the imprint of psychotherapy, beginning with closeups of a thick book opening to the definition of "lycanthropy" (werewolfism), "a disease of the mind in which human beings believe they are wolf-men." *Cat People* bears a pseudo-Jungian quotation from *The Anatomy of Atavism* by one Dr Louis Judd, whom we will soon meet as a character in the film: "Even as fog continues to lie in the valleys, so does ancient sin cling to the low places, the depressions in the world consciousness." The epigraph appears over an equestrian statue of King John hoisting up a cat speared on his sword, the same sculpture soon seen in Irena's apartment.

Cat People opens on a black panther pacing its cage in a zoo, the camera pulling back to reveal Irena intently sketching the beast. It is a mark of the film's economical expression that much of its thematic implication coheres in the first shot of the first scene. Besides her fixation on predatory cats, the cage itself is a closely related motif, as are graphic renderings of cats, all of which intimate possible solutions to the mystery of Irena's dread. Oliver observes her as she discards the sketch and starts anew, then catches her eye and playfully indicates a sign reading, "Let no one say, and say it to your shame, that all was beauty here until you came." Given its own closeup for emphasis, the sign's poetic injunction, more resonant than a simple "No Littering" notice, solicits interpretation.[5] Understood as a classic-style horror film, *Cat People* makes Irena the monster, concluding with her destruction and the formation of a heterosexual couple. Yet the film's often sympathetic portrayal of Irena's dilemma would not inevitably imply that "all was beauty" for Oliver before her disturbing presence, though that notion cannot be fully eliminated either.[6]

To Oliver's opening remark that he has never met an artist, Irena replies, "I'm not an artist; I do sketches for fashion drawings." She apparently works as a commercial artist, and although we never see her in an office, she talks about her work experience and draws at home in an important scene. As the couple stroll off together, Tourneur's camera follows Irena's torn drawing blown by the wind, which comes to rest revealing the image of a snarling panther run through with a sword, blood discreetly dripping from the wound. The sketch carries different connotations. It foreshadows Irena's own death on this very spot after she is impaled by Dr Judd's sword cane while in her cat form, and struck down by the panther. Given what we will soon learn about Irena's emotional anxiety, the sword also signals her fear of sexual penetration, with the actual shadows of the cage bars falling across the drawing denoting psychological imprisonment. Irena is equated with the panther in either case.

At Irena's invitation to her apartment "for tea," Oliver laughs, "Oh, Miss Dubrovna. You make life so simple!," implying that a sexual tryst will occur without much effort at seduction on his part. Pausing at her apartment door, which is covered by vertical shadows resembling bars of a cage, the romantic and sexual interplay continues in dialog rich with double meaning. "*I've never had anyone* here . . . ; *You might be my first* real friend," she says sincerely. Inside, Oliver notices the aroma of her perfume: "It's hard to describe – it's not like flowers exactly. It's something warm and alive." As the door shuts leaving the camera outside, the daytime scene dissolves into a point later in the evening with the apartment lying in heavy nighttime shadow. The statue of King John impaling the cat stands in the foreground; silhouetted against light from the window, Oliver sits smoking in a relaxed pose on the sofa while Irena gazes out, dreamily humming. In other movies of the 1940s, this staging and performance would have subtly implied the couple had just had a satisfying sexual encounter. That possibility remains, though Oliver later says they have never kissed, and following the psychoanalytic thread, Irena's inability to sleep with him after marriage might be understood as a deep guilt reaction to having once violated traditional moral precepts. (She is portrayed as strongly religious.) Their initial dialog concerns the roar of lions coming from the nearby zoo. Irena says she finds their sound soothing but, curiously, given where we met her, claims to dislike the panther's shriek: "It screams – like a woman. I don't like that." Irena's preference for the lion ("the king of beasts", i.e., parallel to King John) versus the panther, with its feminine screams suggesting both victimization and sexual passion, continue the film's contradictory presentation of surface events.

Cat People achieves effective – and inexpensive – atmosphere throughout with jungle cats, house cats, or feline figures, illustrations, and references in virtually every scene. When Irena turns on the light, their discussion moves to the statue of King John. Oliver's inquiry about why he is spearing the cat prompts a measured response acknowledging it as simply a metaphor: "Oh, it's not really a cat. It's meant to represent the evil ways into which my village had once fallen." The room features two other cat images: A decorative partition picturing a black panther slinking down a tree limb in the jungle, the same image seen over the movie's opening credits; and a Goya print above the mantel of a young boy with a magpie on a string by his feet, a cage of finches beside, and three house cats eager to pounce.[7] Actually, Irena never mentions the cat people at this point; instead she talks of witches and how the villagers became devil worshipers until King John killed most of them, though some, "the most wicked," escaped into the forest. Like her drawing of the panther, the feline images surrounding Irena reverberate her neurotic obsession, a point later made by Dr Judd, while simultaneously foreshadowing a supernatural fate. A series of episodes similarly intimate Irena's feline nature and/or indicate her growing neurosis, as when the kitten Oliver presents as a gift before their marriage hisses in fright when she tries to hold it. "Cats just don't like me," Irena says sadly. When they return it to the pet shop, the caged birds erupt in squeals of panic when Irena enters, implicitly recognizing her as a threatening predator. ("Animals are psychic," the elderly female proprietor asserts.) Oliver nonetheless buys a canary for her whose fate we can probably guess.

The couple's wedding reception in *The Belgrade* restaurant shifts the meaning of cat symbolism substantially. From an establishing shot outside the window, snow falling, we see Oliver, Irena, and friends inside celebrating as cheerful music plays. Rather than lending a romantic counterpoint to the physical and emotional warmth inside, the snow prefigures the "frigidity" that will soon scuttle the wedding night. Alice brushes aside the concerns of their boss, the Commodore (Jack Holt) that Irena is a strange girl and that their coworker Doc Carver (Alan Napier) is "worried about the marriage." When the Commodore rises to toast the bride, a woman at the bar (Elizabeth Russell) notices the wedding party. "Look at that woman. Isn't *she* something," the Commodore leers. "She looks like a cat," Doc responds, intent on his meal. The deadpan humor actually amplifies our impression of the woman's feline guise – a sequined black dress, wide-set eyes, and hair piled on her head by a headband that suggests raised ears. When the "cat woman" approaches and addresses Irena inquiringly in Serbian, she freezes and crosses herself. "She called me sister," the shaken bride tells Oliver, who of course dismisses her fear. Critics have interpreted this scene as neither a supernatural encounter nor the projection of a troubled mind but the sign of a suppressed lesbian attraction between the women.[8] Indeed, in the next scene, Irena's inability to consummate her marriage suggests the "real" root of her anxiety is the socially mandated repression of homosexual desires. "I want to be Mrs Reed . . . and everything that name means," Irena tearfully asserts, and yet she cannot. As snow still falls outside the window, Irena shuts Oliver outside their bedroom and sinks down in tears in the shadowy, backlit room. The low yowl of the panther, with its "screams, like a woman," resonates from the zoo.

As they have from the start, Irena's periodic encounters with the panther signal her growing discord. Her second zoo visit opens on an aged keeper sweeping in front of the panther cage while singing: "Nothin' else to do / nothin' else to do. I strayed, went a'courtin' / for I had nothin' else to do." (Minor characters often amplify important themes in the Lewton films.) To his remark on her recent absence, she explains flatly, "Been married – almost a month." Their conversation about the panther, which Irena calls beautiful, turns on his belief that it is instead an "evil critter" and a harbinger of doom, via a quote from the Book of Revelation. "'And the beast which I saw was like unto a leopard'. Like a leopard, but *not* a leopard," he insists. But like the "all was beauty here" sign in the first scene, the zookeeper's song comments on the tale as much as the Bible verse. The counterpoint of "nothin' else to do" and "courtin'" proves anything but innocuous. "Best wishes for your marriage, ma'am," he calls as they part, bracketing the scene with talk of matrimony and the deceptive beauty of a caged beast.

Back home, another carefully composed shot opens on the partition depicting a black panther, the image of the big cat covered by the shadow of the canary cage, then pulls back to Irena working at her drawing table. She now hums "Nothin' else to do" while sketching what appears to be either the fashion designs she initially said she drew for a living, and/or another figure on whom she may be fixated – the lithe, black-garbed "cat woman" from the restaurant. As she did in the semi-darkness of her apartment after what may have been casual sex with Oliver when they first met, Irena's contented humming signals a rare moment of joy that here seems directly connected to her work. Happiness is fleeting in the Lewton world, though. When she playfully approaches the birdcage the panicked canary drops dead from fright. Both sad and visibly angry, Irena returns to the zoo and furtively tosses the bird to the panther, a gesture like a sacrifice to a pagan god that seems to mark complete surrender to her supernatural destiny. Still, the act unnerves her. Her confession to Oliver that night, "I had to do it! I had to!," recognizes the act as an unhealthy compulsion. Regarding this as a breakthrough, he asserts, "We don't need a King John with fire and sword. We need someone who can find the reason for your belief and cure it . . . a psychiatrist," to which she readily agrees. From this point, the movie will trade openly in psychoanalytic language and imagery to account for Irena's torment.

Still, it is important to stipulate that at the narrative level *Cat People* (unlike the subsequent Lewton films) finally presents the fantastic explanation as the "truth." We glimpse an actual black panther cornering Oliver and Alice at their office and later see both the shadow and figure of a big cat mauling Dr Judd as he stabs it with the sword cane. "She never lied to us," are Oliver's final words to Alice as they survey Irena's sword-pierced body at the zoo. Some of Lewton's early admirers, noting that the studio insisted on a real leopard in the office scene against the wishes of Lewton and Tourneur, claimed the filmmakers outsmarted their bosses by making the animal virtually invisible with deep shadows and careful editing. Yet such critics seldom acknowledge that a visible leopard appears twice, ignoring the attack on Dr Judd.[9] Even so, the film's preferred meaning remains elusive because so much is communicated at the level of tone and visual style.

As such, *Cat People* adheres to what Paul Schrader calls the "noir principle" that privileges style over content: "the how is always more important than the what."[10] He outlines seven stylistic elements that characterize Film Noir, five of which mark *Cat People*.[11] True to its name, "The majority of scenes are lit for night" and "As in German expressionism, oblique and vertical lines are preferred to horizontal."[12] Tourneur's film plunges into darkness in its third scene inside Irena's apartment; and combines nighttime shadows and high-contrast lighting with assorted high and low angles in the horror episodes, including the two scenes of Alice stalked by an unseen menace and the killing of Dr Judd. These scenes further exemplify Schrader's third point: "The actors and settings are often given equal lighting emphasis."[13] This effect obtains in the stilted love scene where Irena refuses to kiss Oliver, while a wing chair behind them casts a looming shadow resembling a cat's head and ears; and the aborted attack at the office where bounce light from a low drafting table bathes Alice and Oliver in a swathe of brightness as black shadows encroach all around. As Schrader summarizes the effect of such techniques: "When the environment is given an equal or greater weight than the actor, it . . . creates a fatalistic, hopeless mood."[14] In the absence of a visible monster or haunted castle, *Cat People*'s richly shadowed settings echo the psychic dislocation of its characters.

As such, the aforementioned examples also illustrate Schrader's fourth Noir characteristic, "Compositional tension is preferred to physical action."[15] Physical as much as emotional eruptions continually threaten to occur in the Lewton universe, yet rarely do. Instead, *Cat People*'s ominous settings highlight episodes of suggestive horror, the characteristic point that for most critics has made Lewton's work superior to Universal's 1940s monster sequels. For some tastes, horror based on suggestion is more effective than the most grotesque makeup (or graphic violence in later horror films), because it allows fearful impressions to jump from the movie screen into the mind of the individual spectator where his or her particular phobias conjure up visions more disturbing than filmmakers could hope to create. Built on suspenseful incidents surrounded by auras of alienation and doom, Lewton's movies epitomize this aesthetic principle. Still, *Cat People* does not rely on darkness and compositional tension alone. Its two most famous sequences use skillful editing to depict Alice stalked by what is implicitly Irena transformed into the were-cat – implicit because no beast appears in either scene.

The first comes after Irena follows Oliver and Alice to a café. Theirs was a chance meeting, but Irena feels betrayed after learning Oliver told another woman about their marital problems. Beginning with a visual motif common to Film Noir and horror, Irena's surreptitious approach to the café appears as a mirror reflection in a store window. She also wears a long fur coat here and in other scenes, suggesting her feline *doppelgänger*. Alice walks alone down deserted streets passing in and out of darkness, accompanied only by the clicking of her high heels on the pavement. In a series of lateral tracking shots Irena follows, the sounds of their footsteps merging as shots alternate between each woman's feet moving along the sidewalk. Soon, Alice passes out of frame and where we expect to see Irena following, the camera records only movement along the same stone wall (of the zoo as it turns out) before which they have been walking. The editing tempo increases with Alice's panic. Tourneur frames Alice more tightly, restricting our field of vision and investing off-screen space with impending threat – still one of the most effective devices of suspense. As she shelters against a lamppost, a bestial growl suddenly blends with the squealing brakes and whooshing doors of an arriving bus – the truest shock in the film and one without any actual assault, let alone a monster. This sequence became the model for the Lewton treatment of horror, one the producer often alluded to when discussing his ideas about suggestive screen terror, calling such effects "buses."[16]

The justly famous sequence actually continues a bit longer. As Alice hurries onto the bus, the scene moves behind the wall to the caged panther and other cats agitated by the sounds of bleating sheep. A zookeeper discovers several sheep dead and moves his lantern light along the ground revealing the rounded tracks of a large predator. The camera continues following the tracks as the sound of slowly clicking heels resumes and the wet, round tracks become the prints of Irena's shoes. A final shot depicts a tearful, stricken Irena falling against a lamppost, then startled by the sound of a taxi approaching from screen left, the opposite direction of the bus that saved Alice. Irena looks shaken and exhausted, suggesting she fought the impulse, whether psychotic or supernatural, to murder her rival and instead vented her rage on the sheep. Coupled with Irena's obvious pain, the visual rhyming of this sequence with the threat against Alice extends audience sympathy.

Similar scenes appear in *The Wolf Man* but the effects are quite different. Larry Talbot is bitten by a werewolf after coming to the aid of a woman fleeing through the woods from an initially unseen threat finally revealed as a black, four-legged canine; and later, after Larry's first on-screen transformation, the camera follows muddy paw tracks into his bedroom, ending on his bare feet as he lies unconscious on the bed. Neither Larry nor the viewer ever doubts that his change into a terrible monster has actually occurred. R. H. W. Dillard's perceptive essay on *The Wolf Man* points out that although the werewolf that bites Larry appears as an actual canine, Larry's own lycanthropic form is that of a *wolf-man* walking erect, and thus literally embodying his deter-mined, if ultimately futile struggle against evil.[17] In contrast, though Irena never changes before our eyes, the glimpses of her feline form depict a live animal. In Dillard's terms, Irena is no conflicted cat woman, but an immanent leopard – her "true nature" revealed as opposed to Larry's helpless victimization. *Cat People* provides opportunities to sympathize with Irena but with more equivocation than in *The Wolf Man*. Indeed, by the second stalking, when Alice flees into the swimming pool from the growling beast which seemingly lurks nearby, Irena's taunting manner when she appears after flipping on the lights conveys a streak of cruelty, implicitly that of a cat toying with its prey. Her demeanor is now so cold, we would not then need to see Alice's robe shredded as if by sharp claws to realize Irena has become both emotionally unstable and a genuine threat.

In casting a woman as the monster, another significant trait *Cat People* shares with Film Noir is the inversion of gender roles, usually manifested in stories featuring weak, passive males prone to sexual obsession with strong, scheming women. Critics have nicknamed Noir's femme fatale "the spider woman" for her combination of sexual allure and predatory danger. It is easy to consider the "cat woman" a literal variant of the "spider woman" even though Irena is initially sweetly passive and Oliver, unlike the end-of-their-ropes losers in Noir crime dramas, appears more naïve than desperate. The more important point is that *Cat People*, like Film Noir, counterpoints the traditional heterosexual couple and nuclear family to a dark world of danger, vice, and exhilarating if illicit freedom from restrictive social convention.[18]

As such, what if Irena is neither crazy nor a cat woman, nor a lesbian, but just doesn't really want to be a wife and mother? John Berks relates Irena's dilemma to dominant social roles and expectations for women in the early 1940s. Traditionally, many women, especially middle-class women who worked before marriage, were pressured to stop and become homemakers and mothers afterwards; thus it is Irena, a single woman working in a creative occupation when we first met her, who truly has "nothin' else to do" after she weds.[19] Berks notes that *Cat People* was released just as this powerful social custom was being altered by the exigencies of mobilization for World War II, when women were now officially encouraged to take up vital jobs in industrial labor traditionally held by men. Although the script is vague about whether Irena has indeed quit her job, Alice remains a white-collar "Rosie the Riveter" whose work in shipbuilding is indirectly associated with military industry, and retains Oliver's interest (paradoxically) due to the self-confidence and satisfaction she draws from meaningful work outside the domestic sphere. When Oliver expresses gratitude for her emotional support at their café meeting, "Alice, you're swell," her playful reply acknowledges the recent tremor in gender roles: "That's what makes me dangerous. I'm the new type of 'other woman'." Directly after this, Alice herself is endangered while walking alone on the nighttime streets.

Between the two stalking sequences, Tourneur presents another poignant episode in which Irena cannot sleep with Oliver, and instead cries while sitting in her bathtub (the camera tilting up from the tub's claw-foot to her sobbing figure); which is followed by the nightmare sequence in which the cat woman phobia blends with images and discussion from her hypnosis session with Dr Judd. The bathtub and swimming pool connect with Schrader's fifth observation that Film Noir's rain-slicked streets and waterfront locales suggest an "almost Freudian attachment to water."[20] Freud argued that water imagery in dreams can refer to fantasies of embryonic life in the womb, to the experience of birth itself, and/or to giving birth. Analyzing a dream in which a woman described diving into water, Freud claims: "Dreams like this one are birth dreams. Their interpretation is achieved by reversing the event reported in the manifest dream; thus, instead of 'diving into the water' we have 'coming out of the water', i.e., being born."[21] In a related reference, he suggested that "subterranean realms" can refer to the unconscious mind itself and/or to the womb.[22] In Freudian terms, then, when Alice descends to a shimmering pool in the dark basement of the athletic club, she has entered the unconscious; when threatened by an animal, she retreats to the womb (the pool) but by diving in, is actually invoking birth. Notably, the receptionist's new kitten eagerly follows Alice into the basement, in contrast to the one that spit at Irena. "Kitten" probably means "baby" in this context. Alice is imperiled because Irena, instead of consummating her marriage (and potentially giving birth), has succumbed to a violent delusion of becoming a wild beast (which Freud considered an expression of the id's unleashed desires). Something indefinite yet insistent about procreation and unconscious desires underpins another exemplary scene of suggestive horror.

But what are Alice and Irena doing in the pool with Dr Freud anyway? The wider dissemination of Freudian concepts beginning around the time of World War I, even by those strongly opposed to his ideas, holds part of the explanation. Nathan G. Hale, author of two detailed histories of Freud's impact on American psychiatry and culture, writes that by 1940 (usually pegged as the beginning of the Film Noir cycle), "the newspaper and magazine-reading public was familiar with a number of psychoanalytic conceptions defined in widely varied ways: the unconscious, the importance of early childhood and of sexuality, repression, psychological conflict, a continuum between normal and abnormal, dreams as expressions of repressed emotions."[23] According to censor reports, Cat People's first script began not with a fictional citation from Dr Judd but "with a quotation from Sigmund Freud to the effect that 'evil' lives on in our subconsciousness."[24] A Freudian frame of reference was clearly in the minds of the filmmakers from the start, so, for example, Irena's drawing of a cat pierced by a sword in the first scene decodes as the "obvious" sexual imagery Freudian theory often located in dreams.[25] In observing Freudian concepts illustrated in *Cat People*, we are not suggesting anything about the scientific validity of Freud's theories, many of which have long been rejected, refined, or surpassed by later developments in psychiatry and medicine. Moreover, since we are not even talking about actual patients but fictional characters, the point is to consider the filmmakers' highly self-aware transposition of psychoanalytic notions into easily digestible forms for movie audiences in the 1940s.

Earlier, after Irena tearfully pleads for psychiatric help, a quick dissolve reveals her speaking to Dr Judd under hypnosis, her face encircled by light in a darkened, slightly soft-focus composition. Afterwards, he dryly dissects her fears in what contemporary audiences would have recognized as psychoanalytic language (though Freud actually rejected hypnosis as a therapeutic tool). Dr Judd's diagnosis (swift, after only a single session!) attributes Irena's cat-people fantasies to childhood traumas: Her father died in a mysterious accident in the forest when she was small and other children teased her and blamed her mother for his death, calling her a witch and a cat woman. "Childhood tragedies . . . leave a canker in the mind," he explains. Irena leaves her first analysis with a sense of hope but typically this will not last. Returning home, she finds Oliver in their apartment with Alice, who reveals it was she who recommended Judd to Oliver. Irena's embarrassment and anger erase the optimism with which she entered. At another zoo visit she again observes the zookeeper singing "Nothin' else to do" while feeding the leopard. Irena notices the key left in the lock and exchanges intent looks with the black cat, before returning the key to the keeper as Dr Judd appears with another diagnostic opinion at hand: "You fear the panther, yet you're drawn to him again and again." Noting that she vacillated while apparently weighing up whether to release the creature from its cage, he judges her a Pandora figure: "There is in some cases, a psychic need to loose evil upon the world." Hereafter the key in the lock alternately becomes the psychoanalytic "key" to unlocking her repressed emotions, and in Irena's nightmare, another Freudian symbol.

The explicitly Freudian nightmare sequence also originated with the Germans, notably G. W. Pabst's *Secrets of a Soul* (1926), which was adapted from actual cases, cited two of Freud's disciples as technical advisers, and sought to illustrate aspects of psychoanalytic theory and clinical practice in dramatic form.[26] *Secrets of a Soul* contains an extended montage recounting the nightmare of its tormented protagonist (played by Dr Caligari himself, Werner Krauss) that became the model for similar sequences in a variety of Hollywood films thereafter.[27] Pabst's film ends optimistically. By undergoing psychoanalysis, the man discovers the childhood roots of his neurosis and is cured of guilty, morbid thoughts of killing his wife. However, when the Freudian nightmare trope was adapted to 1940s horror like *Cat People* (or, e.g., *Dr. Jekyll and Mr. Hyde*, *The Wolf Man*, *House of Dracula* [1945]), it conveyed the fated destruction of the afflicted monster/patient.[28]

Irena's nightmare looks to have been conceived with *The Interpretation of Dreams* open in front of the filmmakers. "It is not surprising," Freud wrote, "that a person undergoing psycho-analytic treatment should often dream of it and be led to give expression in his dreams to the many thoughts and expectations to which the treatment gives rise," a rationale both for Irena's nightmare and the figures that appear in it. Indeed, this statement, as well as a quick précis of dream symbols including the womb, wild beasts, and the separation of a neurotic impulse into an independent figure all appear in a single paragraph of Freud's study: "wild beasts . . . represent passionate impulses of which the dreamer is afraid," he asserts. Further, such beasts "might be said to represent the libido, a force dreaded by the ego and combated by means of repression. It often happens, too, that the dreamer separates off his neurosis, his 'sick personality', from himself and depicts it as an independent person," a structure that would similarly describe the psychoanalytically charged *Dr. Jekyll and Mr. Hyde* and *The Wolf Man*.[29]

After once more shutting Oliver outside a door, Irena tosses in bed as blurry, overlapping images of (animated) black panthers slink out of her head toward the viewer. In voice-over, Dr Judd repeats, "a psychic need, a desire for death." The cats are followed by the figure of King John in mail advancing and drawing his sword. The King is also played by Tom Conway (Dr Judd), which doubles his role as savior and ultimate killer of the cat woman with his phallic sword cane, a succinct formulation of the film's ambivalence. King John/Judd presents the sword horizontally, which then dissolves into the key to the panther cage as his voice repeats:, "The key, the key." To Freud, these particular images were common dream symbols with clear meanings: "The emperor and empress (or the King and Queen) as a rule really represent the dreamer's parents," Freud said, so that King John is, in the story's terms, Irena's missing father who returns to punish her mother (called witch and cat woman by other children), leaving Irena the victim of their otherworldly struggle.[30] Stating that "All elongated objects . . . may stand for the male organ [including] . . . all long, sharp, weapons, such as knives, daggers, and pikes," Freud cites boxes, cases, and chests as womb symbols. "Rooms in dreams are usually women; . . . In this connection interest in whether the room is open or locked is easily intelligible. There is no need to name explicitly the key that unlocks the room," he concludes.[31]

The final image of the nightmare, the key she dreams, dissolves into a graphic match with the actual key in the panther cage the following day. Irena returns and again exchanges looks with the big cat as it devours a chunk of meat. This time, she avoids the zookeeper and steals the key (clinical, phallic, and material), suggesting that whatever the consequences, she takes control of her destiny; not as Judd or Oliver envisioned by renouncing her delusional thoughts, but by seizing the power to release the caged beast at her choosing. Though the narrative makes Irena the monster, this gesture epitomizes the film's unresolved tensions. On the surface, Irena is finally thwarted and punished either way. Her only alternative to a supernatural curse is blithe assurance by a husband and psychiatrist that she is merely sexually frigid, if not insane. Moreover, if Irena is mad, she will still be caged – in a mental institution. Present-day empathy for Irena is perhaps greatest in the scene where outside her presence, Dr Judd, Oliver, and Alice conspire to "help her" by having her committed. The now mutually acknowledged love between the pair is hampered because legally, Oliver and Irena's marriage cannot be annulled if she is insane. While Oliver's immediate refusal to end the marriage, seconded by Alice, is portrayed as a noble gesture, the decision to commit her now comes across as a tacitly cynical maneuver that will assure troublesome Irena's removal from their lives anyway.

In the climax, Judd's attempted seduction of Irena, a callous abuse of their association that seems driven by condescension as much as lust, partly justifies her violent response. Irena goes to him in smiling silence, the cat/spider woman laying a trap for an unworthy opponent. When he kisses her, the curse is fulfilled. Her spotlit eyes gleam like a cat's, and Tourneur reframes to depict the shadow of a big cat clawing at the doctor as he fights back with the sword, including one shot of him struggling with a real animal. Oliver and Alice return to the apartment as the visibly wounded Irena creeps away. Returning to the zoo with the stolen key, she frees the panther, which knocks her down as it bolts from the cage and leaps over the wall. Though struck and killed by a taxi, the cat becomes an expression of Irena's tragic yet defiant efforts to free herself from psychological and social strictures. Oliver and Alice come to stand over her body from which the broken blade of Judd's sword protrudes. Hardly the relieved and happy couple that usually emerges from a horror film in its classic mode, they turn away crushed rather than sanguine. Despite displaying a live leopard as the cat woman in two scenes, the film's sense of unsettling enigma remains.

As Irena and her beastly alter ego lie dead, the film's final shot complements the opening epigraph with lines from John Donne that evoke Irena's dualism, and finally the film's: "But black sin hath betrayed to endless night / My world, both parts / and both parts must die." Though the quotations that bookend the film each speaks of "sin," by emphasizing the Freudian undercurrent (even if its on-screen adherent is repudiated as patronizing and morally suspect), *Cat People* consistently advances a more "scientific", i.e., modern and skeptical, method of interpretation. Both parts of Irena "must" die because as yet, no alternative to the constraints of the larger society can be directly represented in a movie such as this, only imagined and alluded to in an "endless night" of black shadows and uncertain explanations. *Cat People* finally suggests much more than mere hobgoblins lurking, however artfully, just off screen.

Post Script: Theme and Variations

As the first RKO horror programmer under Lewton's supervision, *Cat People* exerted a strong influence on the ones that followed, despite subsequent stories that usually repudiated occult explanations in less ambiguous terms. Though even more shadowy and ominous than *Cat People*, *The Seventh Victim* (1943) reveals a murderous cult of all-too-human Satanists at the center of its bleak vision. Still, in what logically would have made it a kind of "prequel" to *Cat People*, Lewton recast actor Tom Conway and explicitly identified him as the same character, the ill-fated Dr Louis Judd. Even if considered simply an in-joke, the sinister shrink's reappearance as one of the cultists in *The Seventh Victim* expands the sense of hopelessness and unfathomable mystery in a universe where evil, whatever its source or definition is omnipresent.

Cat People's excellent sequel merits more discussion than space permits, but we can point out themes in *Curse of the Cat People* (1944) that revisit similar conflicts.[32] Echoing the ambivalence toward marriage, child rearing, and working women found in the original, when the sequel opens, Oliver, "a plain, ordinary Americano" and Alice, "the new type of other woman," are adjusting poorly to parenthood. Alice is usually seen at home in an apron and no further references to her career are heard. The union has produced a troubled daughter, Amy (Ann Carter), who becomes enthralled by an old photo of Irena. Though the status of Irena's ghost, visible only to Amy, remains ambiguous, the dreamy child's repeated problems at school so estrange Oliver he half-seriously disavows her paternity: "[Amy] could almost be Irena's child," he fumes in frustration. Increasingly shunned by peers and punished by her parents, Amy becomes entwined in a sad emotional rift between a senile old lady (Julia Dean) and her embittered adult daughter played by Elizabeth Russell, the "cat woman" of the original, and an indispensable presence of haunted loveliness in four Lewton films. The women's torment inside a dark gothic manor just a block over from the outwardly perfect middle-class home Oliver and Alice have made parallels Alice and Amy's relationship and anticipates its future: "You are not my [daughter]!" the confused Mrs Farren (Dean) repeats to the anguished Barbara (Russell). A mirror by the door of the dark house that doubles the image of Mrs Farren and Amy, or Amy and Barbara, reiterates the motif. Irena's ghost obligingly vanishes at the happy ending, suggesting the "healthy" end of Amy's fantasies, but, as in the first movie, a strong sense of unresolved conflicts remains.

CHAPTER 8

HORROR IN "THE AGE OF ANXIETY": *INVASION OF THE BODY SNATCHERS* (1956)

For more than a decade after World War II the horror film nearly disappeared. Around 1950, science fiction abruptly assumed horror's place as the most popular form of the fantastic film on American movie screens. Science-fiction films varying widely in budgets and ambition appeared throughout the 1950s, giving the genre sustained commercial viability for the first time in Hollywood history.[1] Despite its crass, exploitation title, *Invasion of the Body Snatchers* (1956) offered one of the most sophisticated and enduring takes on the genre during the Cold War's most dangerous era. The plot concerns the gradual takeover of a small American town by alien seedpods that duplicate and then replace the residents one by one, turning them into emotionless cogs devoid of passion or objective. Unlike other science-fiction movies of the time, *Body Snatchers* has no flying saucers, radioactive behemoths, or bug-eyed aliens. Instead, the movie used low-key lighting, inventive compositions, and a rapid pace to conjure a surreal sense of nightmare as the handsome, levelheaded protagonist is steadily reduced to wild-eyed hysteria. Though part of the science-fiction boom, the film's similarity to traditional horror in both tone and visual style offers an opportunity to probe the connections and key differences between these related genres. *Body Snatchers* conveyed a new kind of

FIGURE 16 Subterranean realms: Dr Miles Bennell (Kevin McCarthy) discovers the duplicate pod of Becky forming in a coffin-like box in the cellar. *Invasion of the Body Snatchers* (1956, Allied Artists)

horror for a world threatened with nuclear annihilation, a terror expressed not only in shrieking flight but also as social and psychological numbness.

Invasion of the Body Snatchers has achieved both a cult following and a measure of critical respect few other postwar science-fiction films possess. This is due in large part to the craft that acclaimed producer Walter Wanger and then-promising new director Don Siegel brought to a low-budget production from the second-rank studio Allied Artists, a bravura interpretation through performance, camerawork, and editing of a well-scripted story. *Body Snatchers* succeeds first as an emotionally engaging, visually accomplished film, which made it far easier for critics to look beyond the juvenile title to observe a knowing parable of contemporary social anxieties. Still, critics eager to parse the sociopolitical trends and conflicts it touches often ignore the movie's visual sophistication. Here we will discuss *Body Snatchers* in relation to its interplay between visual style and genre conventions, as well as the historical context.

Invasion of the Body Snatchers opens with a police car hurrying to an emergency room where cops and a psychiatrist (Whit Bissell) confront an apparent madman, Miles Bennell (Kevin McCarthy), who claims that alien invaders have taken over his hometown. In flashback, Dr Bennell returns to Santa Mira, California from a medical convention confronted with reports of numerous patients claiming their loved ones are somehow different, changed, even impostors. A terrified boy runs from his mother, claiming she isn't his mother at all. A woman worries that her favorite uncle has turned cold and distant. Recently divorced, Miles renews his relationship with an old flame, Becky Driscoll (Dana Wynter), also divorced and back in town. Jack (King Donovan) and Teddy Belicec (Caroline Jones) call Miles to see something fantastic: a mysterious corpse, seemingly a double for Jack, laid out on their rec room pool table. The group later discovers several embryonic figures gestating from large seedpods in Miles' greenhouse. Realizing they have stumbled onto an alien plot to enslave the town by creating artificial duplicates that take over when a person falls asleep, the four attempt to escape Santa Mira. When their friends succumb, Miles and Becky run from a mob trying to absorb them into the alien horde. Becky is overtaken and Miles flees onto the highway where he discovers a truck loaded with pods bound for San Francisco. Back at the hospital, the doctors dismiss his story until a truck driver is brought in from an accident, dug out from under a load of strange pods. A relieved Miles hears the psychiatrist telephone the FBI, apparently just in time.

Perhaps the most fascinating aspect of the critical response to the film is how commentators have divided on essential questions about its supposed politics. About as many regard the movie as an endorsement of McCarthy-era paranoia as believe it attacks the anticommunist witch-hunt and resists pressures for social obedience. Moreover, the fear of atomic war underpinning much 1950s science fiction resonates here too. *Body Snatchers* has become a Rorschach pattern that reveals contradictory American fears of communist attack or subversion; and/or of a passive decline into conformity and suppression of individuality.[2] Such fears were prompted not only politically, by the hunt for alleged domestic subversives, but socially, by an increasingly bureaucratized and impersonal corporate economy. There is good evidence for both interpretations in the film. The well-known circumstances of the movie's production contribute to this discrepancy. With shooting finished, the studio insisted on the framing scenes to give the bleak story an upbeat ending. Wanger and especially Siegel strongly objected to this change, but the director eventually shot it to maintain some control over the finished film once it was clear Allied Artists was going to add it anyway. Siegel preferred the original ending, in which a frantic Miles, running through a traffic jam and unable to alert anyone in the film to the imminent danger of the pods screams, "You're next!" directly into the camera, throwing the problem squarely at the audience.[3] In the released version, although the movie has focused on the threat of deadening conformity and passivity at all levels of society, the closing frame abruptly asks the audience to retain faith in traditional institutions. Ultimately, the movie's ideological ambiguity has only added to its luster as one of the most provocative pop cultural documents of the 1950s.

The Thing (1951) had ended with a reporter warning the world by radio to "Keep watching the skies!" – to remain on guard against another invasion of bloodsucking aliens that was sure to come. *Body Snatchers* starts with a visual and aural evocation of this moment. The opening credits appear over a dark sky filled with roiling clouds as the low, threatening calls of French horns punctuated by timpani rolls and dissonant brass chords announce the approach of some menace from above. While firmly in the tradition of the emerging science-fiction genre, this image is misleading because the film will locate the true threat in decidedly earthbound surroundings. Where the Martians glimpsed in *The War of the Worlds* (1953) resembled squat, cyclopean frogs, the pods of *Body Snatchers* are our family, friends, and neighbors, almost the same but missing the sparks of personality and emotion. Similarly, the first scene, where policemen and doctors confront a hysterical man who has seen something that unhinged him, evokes movies such as *Them!* (1954), where a traumatized girl is the only survivor of humanity's first encounter with . . . giant radioactive ants. A village posse forming to hunt down the Frankenstein monster with torches and pitchforks became an emblematic scene of 1930s horror. Fifties science fiction required police, military forces, and Big Science coordinated by the federal government to counter an alien threat. (And so the decisive call to the FBI at the movie's end.) But *Body Snatchers* will still gradually incorporate the expressionistic shooting style of prewar horror to emphasize the hero's subjective terror and set the conventions of horror and science fiction in tension.

As noted in Chapter 1, a crucial difference between science fiction and horror lies in the scale of the threat. The monster's danger in horror is usually localized and individual, whereas in science fiction the peril swiftly moves from the immediate area to the nation or even the entire world. Natural pests multiplying like vermin or virus, the pods are actively expanding from the conquest of Santa Mira to the surrounding region. Yet the movie's shooting title, taken from Jack Finney's source novel, was simply *The Body Snatchers*. Allied Artists added "invasion" to exploit similar science-fiction titles of the time.[4] *Sleep No More*, a title Kevin McCarthy suggested, might have positioned the movie as a traditional horror film by indicating a descent into the psychic depths, which, as we saw in *Cat People* (1942), was a particular feature of horror in the previous decade. For such an approach to work in the 1950s, however, the monster's reach must extend beyond a few victims to a genuinely apocalyptic threat of total destruction. Typically, the sympathetic Miles Bennell becomes the audience surrogate; his move from good-humored local doctor to broken hysteric conveys the doom enveloping the individual victim. In this, visual style remains a compelling factor. Once the developing body of the first "blank" is seen at Jack and Teddy's house, Siegel moves into the deep shadows and distorted framings of actors and spaces familiar from expressionist horror.

As the flashback begins, a high-angle crane shot takes in the woodsy, small-town depot where Miles arrives home on a sunny day. His voice-over explains: "At first glance, everything looked the same. It wasn't. Something evil had taken possession of the town." From this alone we can understand why Siegel opposed the framing scenes which, coupled with the additional voice-over narration, revealed the danger far too quickly. Still, to set the tale in everyday reality, it is the hero's arrival by train, in place of a spaceship's ominous descent, that signals discovery of this invasion. Kevin McCarthy's characterization of Miles anchors the film's definition of the normal. Well-adjusted and content in his life as village physician, when asked about the urban medical convention, for instance, Dr Bennell quips: "They wept with envy when I read my paper." This is not someone easily given to "paranoia" or "hysteria," the two words now most commonly applied to the McCarthy era. And even Miles' nurse, Sally, who called him back and meets him at the train, expresses professional concern, not terrible apprehension about the many locals repeatedly calling and visiting the office with unspecified complaints they will discuss with no one but the doctor.

When young Jimmy Grimaldi flees from his mother apparently because, she says, he doesn't want to go to school, Miles takes her at her word but also notices that the family's roadside vegetable stand, thriving before he left town, has been boarded up. "Too much work," Mrs Grimaldi shrugs. Sally's note that the Grimaldis had been among the patients eager to see him the previous week signals something amiss, yet the vegetable stand might really be the most interesting thematic element. Besides paralleling the alien plant life turning people into "vegetables," Mrs Grimaldi's sudden disinterest in hard work and individual initiative lends the tale a subtle economic undercurrent. "Less than a month ago it was the cleanest and busiest stand on the road," Miles' voice-over pronounces, putting more stock in the abandonment of free enterprise than a child frightened of his own mother. Those seeking a right-wing anticommunist message to the film could see the Grimaldi family becoming collectivist "pods" no longer motivated to work for themselves and now expecting a state command-economy to care for them. Yet given that the flashback began with Miles returning home from the city to find the small town in crisis, it might also suggest how small businesses and traditional ways are steadily failing under the totalizing power of an urban-based consumer culture. This populist fear of large concentrations of power and authority (here represented as the pods) was common to both left- and right-wing ideologies of the period.[5]

Conventional shot composition and lighting continue in our introduction to daily life in Santa Mira. Bright sunlight and unremarkable angles initially mark the scene where Miles, now reunited with Becky Driscoll, visits her cousin Wilma and hears her describe how her Uncle Ira now seems only a facsimile of the man who raised her. Aided by the actors' sidelong glances, Siegel inserts angles that invest shots of an old man mowing the grass in the distance with foreboding. Uncle Ira turns to look back at them only once, yet Miles and the audience grow wary. Still, he is not ready to accept Wilma's story. "The trouble is inside you," he gently opines. Wilma trusts her perceptions, but similarly questions her own sanity. Miles ironically assures her that "Even these days it isn't as easy to go crazy as you might think." A more pointed exchange occurs later when he consults Dr Danny Kaufman. To Miles' question about what is causing this apparent "epidemic of mass hysteria," the psychiatrist responds: "Worry about what's going on in the world, probably." These remarks and others granting that anxiety and uncertainty is socially widespread even before we discover the pods indicate how *Invasion of the Body Snatchers* actually acknowledges the surrounding political climate and the threat of atomic war. That is, rather than a buried subtext, these fears are really right on the surface.

Puzzling incidents give way to the irrationality of nightmares once Miles and Becky enter the Belicec's shadowy home and see what appears to be the stiff body of a man laid out, with surrealist logic, on Jack's pool table. Teddy believes the man resembles Jack, that it seems to be turning into his duplicate. Yet its unformed features and smooth fingers without prints also merit their designation of the figure as a "blank." That it seems to be at once a corpse and a gradually developing embryo combines images of birth and death. As they inspect the body, Siegel employs a variety of high and low angles and high-contrast lighting, decisively slipping into the visual and thematic conventions of the horror film, with or without the "invasion."

Rather than just an obligatory subplot, Miles' romance with Becky carries considerable thematic importance as it counters the cool contentment of the pods with the emotional as well as erotic attraction between the couple, expressed in frank terms for mid-1950s Hollywood. Earlier, as Miles and Becky headed to dinner, they kiss for the first time and she flirtatiously asks whether his compliments are "an example of your bedside manner." "No ma'am, that comes later," Miles slyly responds. As the menace spreads, Miles and Becky engage in what seems like increasingly desperate kissing and embracing in order to prove their basic humanity to the aliens and finally to themselves. Leaving the Belicec's to watch over the developing blank, Miles drives Becky home, where they again flirt in the semi-darkness. The moment's sexual promise is ended by a shadowy figure ascending from the basement. When Becky's father emerges from some mysterious task in his workshop, it marks the first of several episodes in which the protagonists are startled by basement activities, moments always linked to the pods or their conspiracy. But the appearance of Becky's father in the midst of what seemed like the initiation of sex between his daughter and her lover also carries an Oedipal threat of punishment and guilt amplified by the motif of "subterranean realms" Freudian dream theory equated with the unconscious. In fact, what started as a love scene between the couple ends with Becky and her father going upstairs to bed as Miles heads home alone. This scene's placement between two key episodes involving the blank at the Belicec's is more than expository. It heightens the psychosexual undercurrents of the story that are nearly as important as its political resonance.[6] Indeed we would not consider *Invasion of the Body Snatchers* so closely related to the horror genre if it did not probe such psychosexual pressure points.

Siegel links these scenes by a dissolve from the father and daughter climbing the stairs to a closeup of the blank's head with Jack and Teddy dozing in the background. The cuckoo clock that had startled Becky earlier sounds again to signal the passage of time and reiterate the threat. The uncanny atmosphere of twilight sleep, indeed sleep itself as a central metaphor, continues in the darkened house as the blank's eyes flicker open. When Teddy sees this and screams, the shock cut to her face is shot with a wide-angle lens that both expands and distends the visage of the frightened woman. In a moment evocative of the monster's birth in Whale's *Frankenstein*, she cries, "It's you! It's you!," after a shot of the blank's twitching hand, which now bears the same cut in the palm the real Jack had suffered earlier. (Recounting the event to Miles she even repeats, "It's alive! It's alive!") Because Siegel employs the pronounced lens distortion in the midst of the wide-screen composition, the stylized treatment of Teddy's face underscores the subjective emotions identified with expressionism: "The Scream" of 1956. Such visual inventiveness keeps the film working at a level that seems at once commonplace and bizarre, the key to its major themes.

After the Belicec's report Miles fears for Becky's safety, associating her father's late-night activity in the basement with the awakening blank. Hereafter an increasingly hallucinatory logic prevails, a point where the film's short shooting schedule became a virtue rather than a limitation. Miles races to Becky's house but instead of simply knocking, he decides to break into a basement window and inspect the area himself. ("I was going to ring the bell, then I had a hunch I had better be careful," his voice-over recounts.) In the darkened cellar, he lights a match and spots a wooden chest clearly suggesting a coffin, opening it to find a duplicate of Becky forming inside a sticky cocoon, once more uniting imagery of birth and death. Siegel's low-angle reaction shot of the unnerved Miles repeats the lens distortion of Teddy's scream. At this, he charges upstairs and takes Becky from her bed, an action, which, juxtaposed with the earlier introduction of her father, suggests a rescue (or seizure) of the woman from the dangerous patriarch.

The appearance of this second blank followed by Miles pulling the real Becky from her bed provokes a question I have never seen raised in discussion of this movie. What exactly is the relationship between the developed pod and the person it duplicates? In tales of malevolent possession such as *The Exorcist*, an outside presence overtakes the victim's mind and body. If this happens in *Body Snatchers* – consider the title itself – why does the pod need to grow a double of its host? Does the blank physically copy a victim then somehow steal his or her mind when the person falls asleep? This seems to be the implication. But if so, what happens to the original human body? Becky even asks this when they discover a pod opening in the greenhouse. Miles hurriedly speculates, "When the process is completed probably the original is destroyed or disintegrates." This may seem like a thoroughly academic question, the kind we are not supposed to ask of such a fantastic tale, but even movies of the time about giant ants and reborn dinosaurs provided some explanation, however implausible, for the mechanism. For

Body Snatchers, this inconsistency works as a central feature of its night-mare vision.

The film's abrupt shifts in location, the rapid progression of events only loosely motivated, the sudden appearance or disappearance of different people, the transformation from love object to terrible threat are all characteristics of the dream experience. When they return to Jack's house to look for the blank, for instance, it has of course vanished and will not return until Jack himself is taken over. Miles summons Danny Kaufman and all three men return to Becky's basement in search of her blank. Dr Kaufman turns condescending, going along with the search simply to prove it misguided. The shrink takes the same tack Miles had used with Wilma – the problem is within you. But now we too have begun to suspect those who insist any peculiar occurrence is a delusion. The conspiracy seems to be spreading, its scale all the more frightening for its still unknown ends. This impression is furthered when the trio, finding no duplicate of Becky, is discovered by her father, whom we already distrust. The arriving policeman, Nick Grivett, also seems angrily dismissive of Miles and Jack, claiming that their odd corpse has already been located and taken to the morgue after being found – in a decidedly creepy tableau – on a farmer's burning haystack. If a psychiatrist and the local police, but, crucially, the father of the hero's love interest are all in this together, it still suggests the persecution mania of a disturbed mind as much as an insidious and broad-based plot.

Accordingly, careful direction and portrayal of the pods themselves is a crucial stylistic and thematic element. Once transformed, pod people are not entranced zombies or puppets speaking in monotone. Unlike the alien-possessed children in *Village of the Damned* (1960), eyes aglow with silver luminescence, the pods look and behave unremarkably. When Becky's father surfaced from the basement, he hospitably invited Miles for a nightcap. Even considering the importance of sexual desire as a sign of the human, Uncle Ira noticed the attractive Becky in her low-cut dress, saying to Miles, "Great having Becky back, eh boy?," with a complicit wink. That the pods are "passing" well as normal humans, making it difficult to know in retrospect just when each person was overtaken, marks the film's thematic precision. When Danny Kaufman later tells the captive Miles that after the transformation one is "reborn into an untroubled world," he speaks with quiet conviction rather than zealotry or menace. Paradoxically, pods are more unnerving to the extent they appear less distinctly "other."

Although we expect scenes shot at night in dank cellars as settings for horror films, Siegel stages several equally unsettling episodes in bright daylight – an effect sustained by the film's quickening pace. The sunny morning after the midnight rescue of Becky, she is, interestingly enough, happily engaged in the domestic chore of cooking breakfast for the group at Miles' house. All are trying hard to believe it was indeed a shared nightmare from which they have just awoken. But in the midst of affectionate repartee, Miles and Becky are once more startled by noise in the basement. This time, they find a gasman reading the meter, an incident that now seems more ominous for its very ordinariness.[7] By the light of that same clear day, succeeding scenes revealing the abrupt reconciliation of Jimmy Grimaldi and his mother, and Wilma with Uncle Ira only deepen Miles' unease. The film's manipulation of night/ day further suggests the contrast of horror/science fiction, especially if we recall Vivian Sobchack's distinctions about the monster's individual versus social threat in the two related forms. The scenes beginning with and immediately following the discovery of the blank at Jack's mainly feature the expressionist visuals and psychological emphases of horror; once Miles and Becky are fleeing from a mob through the streets and hills surrounding Santa Mira, the story takes on more elements of science fiction. It is not a question of computing the "right" category for the movie but of recognizing the divergent concerns of each genre and what this alteration reveals.

The visual texture of expressionist horror dominates the scene that night at Miles' home. The two couples try to relax and chat over martinis and steaks grilled in the backyard – a quintessential postwar American tableau – again half-believing their experience was illusory. But considering that a bump in the basement on a bright morning set everyone on edge, it is unlikely that another night will bring comfort. The air of forced conviviality evaporates when Miles discovers not one but four large seedpods stacked in his greenhouse, bubbling with foam as they start to open. When Miles first enters the structure, Siegel positions the camera inside in long shot to watch him come through the door, often a way to imply the presence of an unseen peril. High-contrast lighting accentuates the low angles and canted framings when he hears the pod's strange pop. As the group gathers round the spectacle, they are bathed in crosshatched shafts of light cutting through the roof and sides of the greenhouse. Reprising the oblique angles and wide-angle lens distortion in closeups, Siegel transforms a banal domestic space into a shadowy womb about to birth a monster. In another moment reminiscent of *Frankenstein*, they see an arm break out from an oversized pod. Another pop makes a rising torso visible. Moreover, when the frightened Jack tries to attack the pods, he fetches a pitchfork, the weapon of choice for enraged villagers in Universal horror movies of decades past. Miles stops Jack from striking but later, when he realizes this pod is his duplicate, the hero grabs the pitchfork himself and plunges it into the pod, leaving the tool's handle protruding like a stake in a vampire.[8]

As the scene continues, however, the tale slides back into the realm of science fiction – the threat is clearly expanding to society at large and Miles, grasping this, attempts to summon help from outside authorities. His realization that the local telephone operator is stalling his call to Los Angeles now seems unequivocal evidence that "they" have taken over the phone lines, so he orders Jack and Teddy to flee to a neighboring town to spread the alarm. While they wait for the connection, Becky asks Miles where the pods come from, provoking a reply that recaps other science-fiction plots and once more alludes to the atomic threat as an underlying explanation for the strange invasion of Santa Mira: "So much has been discovered in these past few years anything is possible. It may be the results of atomic radiation on plant life, or animal life – some weird, alien organism, a mutation of some kind." Much had been discovered all right, foremost the atomic bomb, which meant that the total destruction of civilization was now possible for the first time in human history. Giant bug movies pointed directly to atomic terror in a ludicrous way. *Invasion of the Body Snatchers* uses careful visual design to make the point at a more indirect level, which has seemed to increase its effectiveness and longevity.

The balance of the film involves Miles and Becky's panicked attempts to escape Santa Mira. They drive, run, and hide in different sections of town, affirming that their worst fears are realized and virtually no real people remain. The most famous and chilling episode here is Miles' surveillance of Sally's home. Peeking through a window, he observes his and Becky's closest relatives and friends – Sally, Wilma, Uncle Ira, and others sitting calmly in the living room. When Becky's father asks Sally whether her baby is asleep, she flatly responds, "Not yet, but she will be soon. And there'll be no more tears." Holding one of the pods, he asks, "Shall I put this in her room?" "Yes," the new mother responds coolly, "in her playpen." The awfulness of this moment has barely sunk in when Nick Grivett's hand grasps Miles' shoulder. "We've been waiting for you, Miles," he intones, invoking the aura of inevitable defeat that often predominates in nightmares. Though Miles escapes in the car with Becky, the fatalistic mood has been fixed.

Foremost, the pods are mounting an attack on emotion itself, substituting a catatonic sameness not only for love and passion but also even for pain, anger, curiosity, and dissatisfaction, the range of emotions that in the largest sense lead to striving and change. Individuality is supplanted by unquestioning surrender to "podism," an outside ideology that seemingly fulfills (or negates) every need. This is the point where uncertainty about the nature of that ideology has led to debate about whether it represents Stalinist totalitarianism or reactionary fear of anything outside the ordinary. What is perhaps most disturbing here is how quickly, and to a large extent willingly, people succumb. The opportunity to surrender seems highly attractive. Danny Kaufmann's assurance that a pod is "reborn into an untroubled world" completes the string of oblique references to the peril of life in the Atomic Age. Moreover, Miles' scoffing reply, "[a world] . . . Where everyone's the same? What a world!," could alternately refer to the theoretically classless society of state communism or contemporary America where pressures for political and social conformity were strong and growing.

Before their capture, Miles and Becky surreptitiously overlook the town's main square from his office window. On another sunny morning, Siegel depicts an open and increasingly organized effort to spread the pods' influence. Large groups of people converge in the square, joining police assembling around farmers' trucks stacked with seeds ready for distribution. Officer Grivett uses a loudspeaker to assign people to missions in surrounding towns. Extreme long shots allow the couple a commanding view that only underscores their impotence. After their capture, we finally get an explanation for what has occurred: Dr Kaufmann explains that, "less than a month ago, Santa Mira was like any other town. People with nothing but problems. Then out of the sky came a solution. Seeds, drifting through space for years, took root in a farmer's field. From the seeds came pods which have the power to reproduce themselves in the exact likeness of any form of life."

"Out of the sky came a solution" has a quasi-religious ring, one that may return us to the utopian promises of a totalitarian ideology. However, this explanation departs from that offered in other 1950s science-fiction movies. Unlike the man-made peril of atomic mutants – variations of the scientific overreaching that makes *Frankenstein* a common ancestor of both horror and science fiction – pods are a natural hazard, plants that reproduce in the peculiar manner of their species. That is, pods are not "evil" in the conventional sense of the term as used in either genre. Taken at face value as plant life, they know no moral or social taboos to breach, unlike the monsters in horror; and they bear no relation to the alien invaders in *The War of the Worlds* or *The Thing*, intelligent aggressors with rational designs on the Earth. Of course, it is unlikely we would still care about this movie if critics just took pods at face value! Instead, pods have become a suggestive metaphor precisely because of the vagueness of their "true" meaning. As such, what *people* do or become as pods remains the issue.

We return to the social canvas of science fiction when, after overpowering their captors, the protagonists walk into the pod-filled streets of Santa Mira trying to act as if they have been converted. But when Becky reveals her emotions by crying out when a dog is nearly run over in the street, the entire populace turns to chase them down. The pursuit is filmed outdoors in natural light, and punctuated by the blasts of a warning siren that recalls Civil Defense drills in the early Cold War years for a "national emergency," the euphemism for the threat of imminent nuclear attack. Yet Siegel's climactic reprise of expressionist visuals occurs as they hide from the mob in an abandoned mineshaft. By now they have been awake for more than two days but know that sleep will be fatal. The dark cavern, with its shimmering pool of water they splash on their faces to stay awake, returns us to the realms Freud identified with the womb and/or the unconscious, bringing together the film's metaphors of sleep, nightmare, and the annihilation of identity.

Before leaving to investigate music playing in the distance, Miles admonishes Becky to stay awake – though we know she won't. When he returns, Becky is a pod, revealed when they kiss for the last time. As Miles draws back in fright, Siegel cuts between closeups of each, again using a wide-angle lens that exaggerates the effect of Miles' sweat-stained face and widening eyes. Notably, unlike the calm demeanor of other pods, Becky's closeups portray her with a lowered jaw and cold, threatening glare. "I didn't know the real meaning of fear until I kissed Becky," Miles says in voice-over, an unintentionally funny line that evokes the gender conflict present in much postwar science fiction.[9] When she calls out to the other pods, betraying the man she loved, shot compositions in the shadowy mineshaft further suggest Miles' subjective vision; as if we are inside the mind of a man broken by panic, exhaustion, and hopelessness. His final flight onto the highway where he finds outbound trucks loaded with seedpods seems anticlimactic in comparison.

This is where Siegel wanted the movie to end, and where the studio asserted control. The flashback's close reiterates the nightmare motif with a clichéd flute glissando and a wavy dissolve into Miles finishing his account to the psychiatrist at the hospital. When an ambulance attendant mentions seedpods, the madman's tale suddenly makes sense, prompting the shrink to telephone the FBI. Yet this is the Bureau of the 1950s, of Director J. Edgar Hoover's obsession with domestic subversion, a context that has made many critics perhaps too willing to accept the ending's preferred effect. Al LaValley contends that Siegel sought to undercut the "happy ending" by holding the camera on Miles in the last shot, the protagonist collapsing with a goofy smile of relief as we hear the psychiatrist's off-screen voice.[10] That is, the director again chose a particular visual strategy to imply that we remain in Miles' subjective haze; and thus to suggest that perhaps this catharsis or rescue is no more trustworthy than other such moments in the film's main body.

Ever since Susan Sontag's essay "The Imagination of Disaster" (1965), critics have ascribed the rise of Hollywood science fiction to the Cold War backdrop, arguing that atomic anxiety and fear of communist invasion were the barely concealed subtexts of many such films, discussions that seldom fail to name *Invasion of the Body Snatchers* as the preeminent 1950s science-fiction movie that's really "about" the Cold War. As the genre arose in a period that also witnessed a cycle of lurid anticommunist dramas and Korean War combat films that warned of an international communist onslaught, it is not surprising that the tangible and fantastic threats became virtually interchangeable. *Body Snatchers* was produced between *I Married A Communist* (1949) and *I Married A Monster From Outer Space* (1958). *Invasion U.S.A.!* (1952), a low-budget exploitation movie depicting a Soviet assault of the American mainland, came after alien invasions in *The Thing* and *The Day the Earth Stood Still* (1951). *Invasion U.S.A.!* also began with a framing scene, a group of people thrust into a collective nightmare by a stranger they encounter in a bar, an oracle that brings them out ready to heed his warning about the communist enemy. The framing device recurred when Warner Bros. and the Pentagon teamed to produce the propaganda short *Red Nightmare* (1962), which imagines an American town fallen to Soviet domination and one man's resistance as his family and friends willingly give in. Like Miles Bennell, the hero is awakened relieved and ready to confront the danger. A deep cultural anxiety accompanied the end of the unpopular Korean War in 1953, provoked by reports that large numbers of American prisoners of war had collaborated with their communist captors after subjected to torture and "brainwashing"; the term first entered popular usage at this time. The brainwashing scare proved to be greatly exaggerated, yet exposed a heretofore unsuspected fear that American soldiers, and thus average Americans, were highly susceptible to thought-control.[11] Like the people of Santa Mira victimized by the pods, the American POW's brain was "washed" clean, making him a "blank" that could be rewritten with communist ideology.

Siegel's movie retains its interest not for its presumed positions on the social and political conflicts of its day but for its suggestive, allegorical quality, ambiguity conveyed foremost through cinematic style, its deft blending of science-fiction themes with the look of expressionist horror. Indeed, *Body Snatchers'* controversial production history echoes that of the work that established expressionist aesthetics as the foundation of the horror film, *The Cabinet of Dr. Caligari*. Its visual debt to *Caligari* is most evident in the murky interiors of rooms or cellars where pods are discovered, and canted, night-for-night chase scenes when a distorted and truly paranoid atmosphere surrounds the hero. Standard interpretations claim that the closing frames – the revelation of Francis as the true madman in *Caligari*, Miles' vindication and deliverance in *Body Snatchers* – instantly negate the visual patterns and fatalistic tones of the main body of each tale, a dubious proposition at best. Without a doubt *Invasion of the Body Snatchers* touched raw nerves in American society of the mid-1950s; its cinematic sophistication in conjuring a pessimistic mood of disquiet and crisis has insured its continuing importance.

CHAPTER 9

SLAUGHTERING GENRE TRADITION: *THE TEXAS CHAIN SAW MASSACRE* (1974)

Perhaps no single work better illustrates the dynamic cultural status of the horror film in the last 30 years than *The Texas Chain Saw Massacre* (1974), a disturbing work of cinematic virtuosity. Produced independently by young Austin, Texas filmmakers and released to the exhibition margins of drive-ins and urban grind-houses, the film shocked and offended but kept earning profits.[1] As it became a favorite on the midnight movie circuit in the late 1970s, the undeniably terrifying film was denounced by a chorus of feminists and cultural conservatives as vile and misogynistic pornography, and championed by leftist critic Robin Wood as one of the few horror movies to invoke "the authentic quality of nightmare."[2] *Texas Chain Saw Massacre* and other works of its type upended the genre conventions and ideological assumptions established in horror's classic period in the 1930s. Like the watershed *Psycho* before it, *Chain Saw Massacre* depicted the monsters as recognizably human, though its backwoods cannibal family was visibly more bizarre than the handsome Norman Bates. Along with its shrewd and deliberate visual style, it epitomized trends for chaotic violence in exploitation horror. Like Romero's *Night of the Living Dead* (1968), its frightening narrative intensity permits little emotional respite for victims or viewers. Thematically, *Chain Saw Massacre* continued to

FIGURE 17 Family portrait: post-*Psycho* horror films increasingly blurred distinctions between monster and family. *The Texas Chain Saw Massacre* (1974, Bryanston Distributing Co.) *Producer and Director:* Tobe Hooper

identify the American family as the locus of monstrosity and terror, perhaps the most crucial and disturbing development of the genre in this period.

Texas Chain Saw Massacre appeared amid larger changes in American cinema of the late 1960s through the early 1970s. Movies of this period, including a spate of grisly horror films, unspooled in an atmosphere consumed with anguish over violence in American culture touched off by the Vietnam War, urban race riots, and traumatic political assassinations. By turns brilliant, confused, and incoherent, filmmakers tried to respond. Some critics charged that hucksters simply used the relaxation of censorship in 1968 for cynical exercises in gratuitous nudity and pointless bloodshed. Indeed, at times from roughly 1968 through 1975, at least in terms of graphic violence and sexuality, it was often difficult to tell the difference between a mainstream movie and a marginal or "underground" film. For the horror genre, Warner Bros.' blockbuster *The Exorcist* (1973) epitomized this now fluid relationship between studio pedigree and a film's assault on audience sensibilities.[3] At the other end of the budgetary spectrum, films like *Night of the Living Dead*, *Last House on the Left* (1972), *Deranged* (1974), et al., unfolding in utterly banal surroundings, seemed at first glance crudely made and morally debased. Their onscreen horrors were as real as the demented mass murderers (especially Ed Gein, Charles Whitman, Richard Speck, and Charles Manson) haunting America's imaginative landscape. Studio movies such as *Bonnie and Clyde* (1967), *The Graduate* (1967), *Easy Rider* (1969), and *M.A.S.H.* (1970) succeeded by embracing stylistic innovations from the European art cinema and appealing to an increasingly disaffected youth audience.[4] Yet many exploitation pictures similarly displayed startling formal changes while drawing on a deep wellspring of social and political alienation.

The Texas Chain Saw Massacre wastes little time with plot development and characterization, often sure signs of a horror film's offhandedness or commercial cynicism, but here an asset to the story's feverish mood. Five young friends, Sally Hardesty (Marilyn Burns), her wheelchair-bound brother, Franklin (Paul Partain), Jerry (Allen Danziger), Kirk (William Vail), and Pam (Terry McMinn) are driving through rural Texas when they hear radio reports of crazed ghouls digging up corpses in a local cemetery. They stop to investigate whether Grandfather Hardesty's grave has been desecrated. Assured it wasn't, they travel to the grandparents' abandoned farm, but not before picking up a threatening Hitchhiker (Edwin Neal) who slices himself and Franklin with a knife before the screaming kids kick him out. At the farm, their van runs out of gas. Searching for more, they stumble on another farmhouse inhabited by a psychotic family of former slaughterhouse workers who slay them one by one until only Sally remains. Leatherface (Gunnar Hansen), the masked, chain saw-wielding brother is the most fearsome killer of the group, which also includes the Hitchhiker they had picked up, and a brother called the Old Man (Jim Siedow).[5] After harrowing sessions of pursuit and torture she manages to escape and flag down a passing truck.

Lacking stars and a large promotional budget, an exploitation movie like *The Texas Chain Saw Massacre* had to pull in customers with little more than a sleazy title, a feat it deftly accomplished. But consider the rich associations in these few words. Texas in the American imagination meant the rural South with its tragic dynamics of race and class; but it also symbolized the West itself, with all the accumulated cultural mythology from cattle drives and Indian fighting to the Alamo.[6] Throughout the Vietnam era, many Westerns inverted the genre's prior assumptions with the frontier disappearing under the advance of modernity, and violent struggle often bringing only fruitless carnage rather than a promise of individual and social renewal.[7] It would have been extraordinary indeed if frontier motifs referenced even indirectly in a horror film at this point had done anything other than continue those revisionist trends with still bleaker irony and violence.[8] *Chain Saw Massacre* invokes the bountiful landscape of countless Westerns only to portray its menace and frightening decay. The cattle business, a familiar Western motif, underpins the movie, whose unemployed slaughter-house workers obsolesced by industrial technology roughly parallel the aging gunslingers of the late Western overwhelmed by the closing of the frontier. *Chain Saw Massacre* depicts its socially dispossessed figures implicitly retaliating by butchering – and eating – young travelers associated with the anti-war counterculture.

Star of the show, the chain saw itself connotes the urban/agrarian conflict as a tool commonly used by the rural working class for small chores, as well as one that can be employed for destruction on a mass industrial scale in logging – or the slaughterhouse industry to cut up carcasses. This outlandish juxtaposition of functions – versatile tool become ferocious weapon – occurs when the cannibals reduce their victims to meat. A massacre is by definition the heartless slaughter of people unable to defend themselves. For Americans in the early 1970s, that word had become inseparably linked with the My Lai Massacre in Vietnam, where American soldiers gunned down 300–400 unarmed Vietnamese civilians, including women and children, an event still raw in public consciousness after the publicized 1970–1 trial of one of its leaders, Lt. William Calley, Jr. In three gripping words, a low-budget horror movie managed to grab patrons and call up some of the bitterest social and political schisms of the day. Still, these pointed references may register less forcefully on first viewing than the film's brutality conveyed by vivid cinematic style.

An air of factual reporting counters the title's promise of chaotic butchery. The movie begins with a solemn narrator (John Larroquette) reading a printed crawl that claims the events about to be depicted were true. Moreover, this quasi-documentary introduction supports the definite article in the title: *the* Texas chain saw massacre, the one everybody has heard about. This was all clever hype, and expertly blended into the film's look, but like any potent legend only partly connected to reality. The story was loosely inspired by the case of rural

Wisconsin lunatic Ed Gein, whose exposure as a grave robber and serial killer in 1957 revealed he had transformed his victims' skin and body parts into "grisly works of art" – the description used in the opening radio reports in *Chain Saw Massacre*.[9] The Gein case begat Robert Bloch's 1959 novel *Psycho*, which became the basis for Hitchcock's influential film. The title "August 18, 1973," following *Chain Saw's* spoken introduction, emulates those in *Psycho's* first shot that establish specific day, time, and place of the story as if detailing facts in a crime report. The function in both is to set up a horror tale that will break completely from supernatural foundation. (Hitchcock's *Psycho* ends in a police station; *Chain Saw Massacre's* fourth scene shows a sadly mundane vista of cops and gawkers around the cemetery crime scene.) *The Texas Chain Saw Massacre* was "true" only in the way it blended certain actual occurrences filtered through formulae of media and fiction, the very logic and method of genre development.

Director Tobe Hooper's hand is assured from the start. Disturbing sound effects, a key stylistic feature, begin over the fade to black following the narration, effects that sustain an oppressive air that will be split in the movie's second half by Leatherface's racing chain saw and the screams of its victims. The first sounds are a shovel digging steadily in the earth and labored breathing. We listen in blackness for some twenty seconds until the screen is lit by photoflashes allowing glimpses of a badly decayed corpse's hands, legs, and skull. The click and whirr of cameras plus low electronic tones punctuated by what might be rusty hinges groaning accompany the cuts. In conjunction with glances at the melting dead, these sounds not only record what's happening now – presumably the corpses being photographed by the authorities as evidence – but simultaneously present the atrocity's initial stage when the robbers (implicitly the Leatherface clan) defiled the graves. The combination initiates a subjective and fatalistic mood.

This gloomy opening recalls James Whale's *Frankenstein*. There the grave robbers at least claimed a noble purpose. What Mary Shelley's Doctor famously called his "filthy workshop of creation" aimed for nothing less than human immortality. *Chain Saw Massacre's* tableau simply depicts degenerate madness, yet still one with an aim, however obscure, as indicated by the purposeful arrangement of the dead. From a closeup of a corpse's rotting face, Hooper's camera recedes into a low-angle view that frames a pair of corpses wired to a headstone in a copulatory position. Framed against a hazy, yellow-orange sky, the placement of skulls and limbs suggests both terrible agony and wild passion. A radio broadcast describes the scene, fusing banal reportage and meticulous style.

It's a disturbing sequence brilliantly realized through camerawork, editing, and superb sound design; as well as a vivid statement of a major theme – the grisly conversion of sexual energy into aggression and murder.

After a brief credit sequence over abstract shots of solar eclipses tinted blood-red, Hooper introduces his young characters with an establishing shot depicting a familiar sight along Texas highways, a dead armadillo upended in the bright sunlight, heat waves blurring the background as their van pulls off the road. Thus associated with this stiff, hapless creature, the travelers seem just as anonymous, ineffectual, and doomed. They remain largely indistinct as characters, even Sally, with whom we will share the movie's terrifying second half. (The radio news continues over this sequence, blandly detailing incidents of domestic violence, a collapsing office building, a couple charged with starving a child chained in the attic – reports that convey a generalized sense of social breakdown, particularly within the traditional family.) Pam only briefly stands out as she reads from an astrology magazine that describes the dark sign of Saturn in retrograde, which, as Robin Wood suggests, foreshadows the literal Saturnalia, the awesome patriarch's slaughter – and consumption – of his "children" the movie will depict.[10] Talk of the zodiac connects with the unnaturally tinted sun in the opening credits, which, coming after shots of disinterred corpses, suggests the universe itself conspires against this group.

Before any dialog commences, though, the van stops so Franklin can relieve himself beside the road. A crude ramp of boards to unload his wheelchair and a coffee can for the task anchor the tale in everyday reality. For all its gore, *Night of the Living Dead* offered viewers a shred of emotional distance in its tale of a ravenous zombie army, a conceit that could be experienced as a grisly fairy tale even if set in the Pennsylvania countryside. *Chain Saw Massacre*'s impact accrues from the sense that however unfathomable in origin, these events could actually happen in this place – an effect sustained by a "documentary realism" in settings and location overlaid with careful stylization. In characterizing Franklin, script and performance avoid the usual condescension to the disabled. As he pees, the roar of a passing semi-truck startles him, sending his wheelchair into an uncontrolled slide down the embankment. Franklin's slow-motion tumble down the hill, presumably sloshed with his own urine, is an opportunity neither for humiliation nor pity. Since he was unhurt, it becomes simply a funny moment among friends still essentially enjoying themselves on a trip. Like everything else in the film's opening minutes, however, Franklin's fall also feels like a harbinger of doom.

After the brief cemetery stop, our attention stays with the quirky Franklin who babbles on, to his friends' annoyance, about the heat, his uncle – also a slaughterhouse worker – and most disturbingly, techniques for slaughtering cattle. "They bash 'em on the head with a big sledgehammer. They usually wouldn't kill 'em on the first lick," he explains with relish over eerie shots of cattle in the slaughterhouse pens they pass, now paralleling the group with meat on the hoof and associating Franklin with the butchers. Whining and needy though he is, Franklin seems to be the movie's protagonist, even if his wide-eyed, childish fixation on killing cattle hardly describes a stalwart hero. Indeed, emphasis on Franklin in the film's first half roughly corresponds to the time Hitchcock devotes to Marion Crane in *Psycho*, shattered here when Leatherface eviscerates the helpless man and Sally becomes our identification figure. Franklin perhaps recalls Stoker's mad Renfield, a connection suggested when they stop for the creepy Hitchhiker and Franklin himself intones, "I think we just picked up Dracula."[11] Worse, this version of the tale will have no wise Van Helsing or heroic male collective to combat the evil.

The multiple associations in the film's title cohere in the Hitchhiker's introduction. Hooper makes a visual allusion to the Western with an extreme long shot depicting the van slowing as the man runs toward it, the vehicle standing on a ribbon of land at the bottom of the frame with the upper three-quarters picturing blue skies and floating clouds – a composition we might find in a John Ford film. Where such wide vistas in the Western usually connote the beauty of the landscape and its limitless possibilities, here it only furthers the sense of isolation and threat. A thin man with beard stubble, long, scraggly hair and jumpy demeanor, the Hitchhiker resembles deranged cult leader Charles Manson, a connection made by some initial reviews. The red marks on his face, like war paint, recall the Indian motifs favored in counterculture attire; also the fur-covered bag from which he pulls freakish souvenirs – snapshots of cattle he killed during his slaughterhouse days. Although the term "hippies" was rapidly losing currency by 1974, the kids in the van are almost reflexively understood as part of the counterculture by virtue of their long hair, floral prints, and jeans alone. Simultaneously, the Hitchhiker personifies the threat of nihilistic violence that President Nixon's conservative "silent majority" had come to project onto the youth movement, especially after the December, 1969 arrest of the Manson family for the bloody Tate–LaBianca murders in Los Angeles, just days before the Rolling Stones' free concert at Altamont Speedway ended in the murder of a fan directly in front of the stage. However, because *Chain Saw Massacre*'s hallucinatory quality both allows and encourages diverse associations of characters and events – the fundamental logic of dreams and nightmares – it seems equally valid to interpret it as Robin Wood does, as a tale of a counterculture youth set upon by murderously reactionary elements of the traditional order.

Classical horror films assumed the monster was anathema to social "normality," the nuclear family in particular. Drawing parallels between Franklin and the Hitchhiker, *Chain Saw Massacre* begins with that previously inviolable barrier cracking. Avid discussion between the two about the sledgehammer versus the retractable bolt-gun for slaughtering cattle creates a creepy rapport. Hearing the weird man's family "has always been in beeves," however, Franklin quips, "A whole family of Draculas," describing almost exactly what they will soon encounter. Where the gothic is characterized by the lingering menace of an oppressive past, the Hitchhiker and his kin seem positively atavistic. His primitivist threat to a group of modern, urban characters is conveyed by fetishistic acts including the Polaroid photo he takes of Franklin, then burns with a flash of gunpowder when they refuse to buy it (another foreshadowing of the group's destruction); and the giggling, methodical drawing of his own blood and Franklin's, acts more ritualistic than lethal. (He opens his own palm with Franklin's pocketknife, then cuts Franklin's arm with the straight razor he pulls from his boot, a "blood brother" rite that bonds the two.) These acts, alongside the many "grisly works of art" attributed to the Leatherface clan, intimate a bizarre devotional statement of some kind. This parallels not only Ed Gein's perversions but the Manson family slayings where the cultists scrawled cryptic phrases ("helter skelter" most notoriously) on the walls in their victims' blood, supposed references to secret messages the leader claimed the Beatles were sending to him in their music. That this madness emanates from a *doppelgänger* of the nuclear family – a ghastly fugue from Ed Gein to Norman Bates, the Addams Family to the Manson family – shatters the boundary between monster and domestic sphere.

When the Hitchhiker is ejected from the van, Hooper returns to the extreme long shot with which he was introduced, the sense of imminent danger undiminished by the man's expulsion as he smears blood across the side, in retrospect a mark to alert his brothers at the gas station up ahead to target this group. Yet from inside the van, the travelers see only the Hitchhiker running alongside, spitting wildly at them, a gesture seemingly both relentless and futile. The killers' predatory logic contrasts with the ignorance of their victims – macabre designs experienced emotionally as randomness and near-delusion. What the film increasingly presents as Sally's slide into Hell will end with her narrow escape in a fashion nearly as abrupt and ludicrous as its beginning. The departure from reality begins at the decrepit gas station run, as we soon realize, by the cannibals, a setting analogous to the remote frontier outposts in Westerns that offer a tenuously "civilized" oasis in a hostile environment – but whose operant genre reference is the forsaken Bates Motel.

Jim Siedow's grinning and chilling performance as the Old Man matches the eccentric energy of Ed Neal's Hitchhiker and Paul Partain's Franklin to give *Texas Chain Saw Massacre* unnerving characters along with the carnage. As proprietor of the gas station that fronts for the evil house nearby, the Old Man is the movie's most direct figuration of Ed Gein/Norman Bates, though his ingratiating manner barely conceals his ravenous drive to consume new victims. When the hysterical Sally later races into his arms escaping Leatherface, he cozens her by speaking lovingly and hugging her, like the father figure he seems to be, then as quickly begins tormenting her. This begins as Sally vainly grabs a knife to protect herself, and he easily disarms her with a broom and thrusts her into a burlap sack. Driving back to the house, he alternately reassures her and prods her sadistically with the broom handle as she writhes on the truck floor, as low-angle shots and moving patterns of light on his face impart a queasy menace.

The first gas-station scene opens, however, with a balding, slightly stooped young man who shuffles out with rag and bucket to clean the windshield, though not before taking several meaningful glances upward at the mist-covered sun. As the group and the Old Man debate whether to wait or keep looking for gas, he becomes slightly comic as he wheels his bucket back and forth in front of the van. This comic counterpoint may be missed as Hooper keeps the window-washer mysterious by filming him through the windshield, his face obscured by soapy water. Although a different actor (Robert Courtin) plays this mute figure, who otherwise appears only in this scene, he is implicitly Leatherface with-out his mask, making a mundane contribution to the family business.[12] In any case, the semihuman killer himself gets a couple of comic moments later, even after his grisly slaughter of the helpless travelers. These rare bits of humor release just enough tension to keep the audience off balance.

Temporarily out of gas, the place does have one amenity, homemade "barbecue" that Franklin eagerly samples. For a movie whose icons are a screaming woman impaled on a meat hook and a saw-waving maniac with a mask of human skin, *Chain Saw Massacre*'s references to cannib-alism are somewhat oblique. The monsters are so physically aggressive and the film's pace so quick once the killing begins, we may be too caught up initially to register the obvious – the jobless workers have literally substituted people for cattle. By the time the shrieking Sally flees to the gas station's illusory safety, point of view shots of fat sausages roasting over a fire in a red-saturated hearth seem like veritable glimpses of Hell and indirect confirmation of our darkest suspicions. Explicit depiction of zombies chomping human flesh in *Night of the Living Dead* – especially young Karen Cooper chewing on her mother's severed arm – initiated the cannibalism theme in post-1968 horror, signaling as directly as possible the pervasive sense of familial and social self-destruction and collapse that ran through the genre in the 1970s.[13]

Hooper continues to invest a sunlit summer day with awful portents at Grandpa Hardesty's abandoned farm. The director again employs the long shot as the kids climb out of the van, the camera viewing them from a distance before tracking laterally through tall weeds to suggest they are already watched by a dangerous presence. The now decaying two-story house where the Hardesty siblings spent childhood days transfers the traditional functions of the haunted castle to rural Texas and invites the symbolism of psychic regression conveyed by the gothic. Inside, Kirk disturbs a squirming clutch of arachnids ("daddy longlegs") on the ceiling, their menace underscored by a looming inserted closeup and unnaturally amplified scuttling, nature itself as the threat again. Hooper and Paul Partain combine for a weird moment as Sally happily leads the others upstairs on a tour of her childhood rooms, stranding Franklin downstairs. In low-angle shots, the deserted Franklin angrily glares up at the friends above and not only mocks their laughter but spits impotently at the ceiling. This mad, funny gesture exposes a previously unsuspected rage and further parallels him with the seething Hitchhiker spitting at their van. Like other such moments in the film, it's an inspired non sequitur that adds to the aura of insanity. Yet the scene ends with Franklin's discovery of a bone fetish hanging in the house, directly recalling the Hitchhiker's tangible threat.

Chain Saw Massacre's first act steadily builds a mood of pure hostility and dread; all the more effective in that the protagonists remain largely oblivious right up to the moment of their deaths, beginning with Pam and Kirk's search for a swimming hole that leads to the monster family's house. As the laughing couple pass through fields of tall grass, conventions of exploitation movies in the early 1970s lead us to expect a gratuitous scene of sexual titillation, motivated perhaps by skinny-dipping in a pond they discover, but which never occurs. Although nude frolics just before bloody mayhem became the hoariest convention of the slasher cycle from *Halloween* (1978) forward, sexual expression is non-existent in *Texas Chain Saw Massacre*, the erotic drives exclusively channeled into horrific violence. *Psycho*'s often criticized ending scene, where a psychiatrist gives a long, clinical account of Norman's aberration, provides a simplified explanation of why his unfulfilled sexual desires and Oedipal fixation on his domineering mother twisted into murderous violence – a point Hitchcock had already made unforgettable in the single most famous scene of his career with the frenzied, phallic stabbing of Marion in the shower. Yet during Sally's dinner-table ordeal, a scene of similarly great power, the genre's dialectic of sexual desire and violence pivots in an unexpected, equally disturbing direction. When Sally hysterically offers to submit to any perverse sex acts they desire in exchange for her life, she is met with virtual incomprehension, so fully committed is the family to pointless terrorizing and ultimately, cannibalism.[14]

Pam and Kirk's final journey contains one of the film's richest moments when they hear a small engine running and decide the occupants of a nearby house will have gas. With even the weird music now withheld, the generator's low sputter invokes a region simultaneously empty, dead, and highly dangerous. Hooper and co-writer Kim Henkel say they initially conceived the story as a variation of the fairytale of Hansel and Gretel, the abandoned children captured by a witch who intends to fatten and eat them. However, whether conscious or not, surrealist art, especially Salvador Dali's "The Persistence of Memory" (1931), also inspires thematic and visual elements in the film, and for this sequence in particular.[15] In a famous phrase, Freud, the greatest intellectual influence on the surrealists, spoke of "the timelessness of the unconscious." The painting, one of Dali's best known works, depicts four pocket watches in a stark, mental landscape with a bare tree sprouting from a tabletop and lonely, seaside cliffs in the distance. Three of the watches are drooping, suggesting melting and, inevitably in Freudian terms, impotence. A wilted timepiece also overlays a phallic, organic shape that might be a dead animal (it's actually a stylized profile of the artist himself). But most famously, in the midground, a pocket watch gone limp drapes over the limb of the dead tree, picturing the end of time. Hooper alludes to Dali's painting when Kirk and Pam pass a ripped blue tent pitched beside a bare tree hung with metal household objects – rusty pans, cups, and coffeepots gently clinking in the breeze. The obliterated campsite also vaguely recalls the Western; yet Hooper closely references Dali's witty rendering of unconscious memory with an inserted close up of a pocket watch run through by a long nail, also hanging from a branch.[16] This entrance into a nightmare region where time stops refutes the "factual" claims of the opening. In genre terms, the nail in the watch recalls the stake driven through a vampire's heart, the method of destroying this traditional monster, transformed instead into another omen of the cannibals' relentless aggression. The nail also foreshadows the crucifixion that will soon occur in the movie's most notorious scene, in which Leatherface plunges the screaming Pam onto a meat hook and leaves her dangling, shocked and dying, arms reaching up feebly against the fatal pressure.

The lower left section of "The Persistence of Memory" depicts a swarm of ants that congregate atop a watch as if it were a piece of rotting fruit. Given the more direct allusion to Dali in the campsite tableau, it seems possible Hooper had earlier echoed this motif, another sign of a voracious universe, when Kirk disturbs the nest of arachnids in the farmhouse. In surrealist art, not only the frustration of sexual desire but often its expression came at psychic and physical costs of violence, decay, and death. The humor and eroticism in such works may exist alongside dreadful images of dismemberment and brutality. Indeed, the ant swarm, a frequent motif in Dali's work, also appears in his famous collaboration with director Luis Bunuel on the avant-garde film *Un Chien Andalou* (1929) where a close up depicts ants spilling out of a hole in a man's open palm.[17] But the surrealist short's most indelible moment is an extreme close up of a woman's eyeball seemingly slit open by a straight razor–like the one the Hitchhiker cut Franklin with and holds to Sally's throat as Grandpa slurps blood from her finger. Hooper further alludes to Bunuel's appalling image during Sally's torture with increasingly closer and more stylized shots of one fragile eyeball distended in stark terror. For all the proclamations of irrationality defining surrealism – or latter-day variants like *The Texas Chain Saw Massacre* – as works of art they more often reveal an articulate plan in most every device or effect.

More prosaically, this segment includes Kirk's uncomprehending discovery of dusty autos hidden beneath camouflage netting, a parallel to the swamp behind the Bates Motel where Norman sank his victims' cars. The evil house itself is suffused with gothic menace. Kirk finds what appears to be a human tooth on the porch and taunts Pam with it, recalling Johnny scaring Barbara in the first scene of *Night of the Living Dead*; Kirk's smug sadism precedes his similarly ironic death. As he ventures in, a blood–red hallway decorated with human and animal bones arranged liked trophies augurs his fate. More chillingly, pig squeals and grunts equate him with livestock. Hooper largely shoots the killing in shadowy long shot, though a quick montage depicts Leatherface, in butcher's apron, emerging and raising a mallet to fell Kirk with one heavy blow, the body collapsing, feet spasmodically kicking the floor. Upon Leatherface's second whack, we recall Franklin's description of slaughtering cattle: "They usually wouldn't kill 'em on the first lick . . . They'd start squealin' and freakin' out . . ." As a fatalistic chord resounds, Leatherface yanks Kirk inside the hallway and slams a metal sliding door that merges the industrial slaughterhouse with domestic space – another surreal, thematically precise juxtaposition.

Before Pam's ghastly death, Hooper climaxes the film's steady development of dread when she trips and falls into what one can only call with the greatest irony, the monster family's "living-room". A tour de force for art director Robert A. Burns, the room offers a vivid rendering of the nausea-inducing sights that met those who entered Ed Gein's farmhouse.[18] She lands on her hands and knees on a floor carpeted with chicken feathers and bones, a revolting mass of filth and decay. A wide lens and moving camera underscore Pam's silent fright as she surveys the scene, merging objective detail with subjective terror. The charnel room holds piles of randomly discarded body parts and meticulously wrought constructions – decorative mixtures of human and animal bones, a dangling human skull with a cow's horn thrust through the jaw, a sofa trimmed in scapulas and skulls. Still, perhaps the most genuinely surreal touch is a sullen white hen improbably wedged in a canary cage. The caged chicken, with its low, threatening squawks, completes the film's parade of ominous creatures living or dead we have seen throughout. Angles on the bird's blinking eye reverse with shots registering Pam's mute horror. (These shots foreshadow the montage of Sally's terror-filled eye in her coming ordeal.) The spell is broken when Pam flees the room, only to be grabbed by Leatherface and dragged to the meat hook. This gruesome interlude between the murders actually intensifies the subsequent shock.

The emotional jolts *Chain Saw Massacre* can still inspire are such that spectators often believe on first viewing that the movie is even more graphic than it really is. Outrageous violence is on display, no mistake; but so is formal control. The introduction of the chain saw itself occurs just after the assault on Pam during which we see Kirk's body lying on a table as Leatherface runs across the room to grab and start the machine. Instead of finishing Pam, he lays the whining saw against Kirk's body, implicitly beheading him – though a low angle camera position partly obscures the view. Moreover, when the monster wrestles Pam into the kitchen, the shot begins with the meat hook looming in the foreground. But in a series of quick cuts as he hoists the struggling woman upward, the killer's back actually blocks our view of the supposed impact of her body on the hook. When Leatherface splatters Franklin with the chain saw, the assault occurs in heavy nighttime shadows and silhouettes with Franklin's back to the camera, so that the roaring saw and what seems to be sprays of blood convey the horror without having to see it up close.[19] A shot of his dropped flashlight hitting the ground artfully substitutes for the fate of assorted body parts. If Hooper borrowed themes and motifs from *Psycho*, he also assimilated The Master's lessons in shaping form to involve and manipulate the audience at will. One may finally be appalled or disgusted by the film, but describing it as either "crude" or "gratuitous" is demonstrably false.

Jerry's murder condenses elements of the first two, a swift dispatch that climaxes an anarchic killing spree. As he enters the now empty kitchen and opens the freezer (that looks distinctly like a casket with a double-compartment lid), Pam's blue, twitching body springs up, a grotesque "funhouse" scare seconds before Leatherface smashes him with a mallet. But in a finally more bizarre moment, Leatherface retreats to another room and sits by the window, agitated, pounding his head, rocking back and forth. This suddenly allows us a better look, to see the parched, crudely stitched mask as the camera moves in on his eyes and mouth, tongue licking his teeth. His reaction is nearly unreadable – anything perhaps from fatigue to indifference, a hint of remorse or virtually post-orgasmic exhilaration. The effect is unnerving, as if "we" have suddenly been left alone in the death house with this implacable thing. Hooper says he thought of the Old Man as flickering between rationality and the total insanity driving his brothers – perhaps a thread necessary for a director to help an actor find something to play in an underwritten character, yet finally less important to viewers. Our sense of Leatherface as a character is even more schematic.[20] Indeed, the search for coherence and logic in what we witness is largely frustrated throughout, much to the enhancement of the film's overall effect.

After Franklin's death, Hooper embellishes the long, harrowing pursuit of Sally with moving camera, quick cutting, and jagged lighting effects as she struggles through brush, races around and into the house, and crashes through a second story window to escape. The tall, hefty Gunnar Hansen's Leatherface is a freakish leviathan of great speed, while as Sally, Marilyn Burns' awkward, flailing terror elicits empathy and shock, as if we are actually witnessing the assault and cannot intervene. Their graceless running and stumbling makes the sequence so "real". It is common now to hear *Texas Chain Saw Massacre* called a "slasher movie", an anachronistic term that as yet speaks to the impact it had on the film cycle that mushroomed not five years later. The successive murders of four young friends plus the relentless chase of the "final girl" by the psychotic prefigure crucial elements of the slasher sub-genre. But later slasher films were interested only in the number and variety of murder episodes; Chain Saw Massacre extends Sally's ordeal far beyond the chase itself. Moreover, unlike the typical explanations for the psycho's vengeance in the slasher cycle (or Hitchcock's Psycho), Chain Saw Massacre gives little or no coherent grounds for the killers' actions from grave robbing to cannibalism.

During Sally's pursuit, she finds the mummified remains of Grandma and the ancient, barely breathing Grandpa seated in wing chairs, like discovering the corpses of the dour farm couple in Grant Wood's "American Gothic". The tableau includes a small stuffed dog at their feet, fur peeling back from its skull, macabre humor that points up the essentially domestic nature of scenes inside the dark house. With Sally's capture, we are forced to confront the monsters as characters, most of all as family, with their all-too-recognizable bickering and yelling. The Old Man's railing at the Hitchhiker precedes the film's one true comic line when he spots the front door Leatherface splintered during the chase, damaged as if by unsupervised children: "Look what your brother did to that door!". (Shocked laughter and the awkward hustling of Sally into the house can obscure his next line, "He's got no pride in his home?!") This sense of family itself as the monster crystallizes around the dinner table, as if Norman Rockwell were gang-raped by Dali and Hogarth.

Hooper alternates between long shots that picture Sally's entrapment within the shadowy, bone-filled house, and close ups of her and her tormentors from eccentric angles that render the sequence highly subjective. The nadir seemingly comes when Leatherface slices her finger and thrusts it into Grandpa's mouth to drink her blood, a primal image that connotes rape, oral sex, a baby suckling, and vampirism.[21] At this Sally finally blacks out, but the film gives only the briefest relief. From a series of shots of the house, the windmill, and the moon racked into focus, she slowly awakens – to the drone of a fly – to find herself still at the table, still surrounded by the monsters. The nightmare continues – a remarkable dramatic feat that evokes the timelessness symbolized by the nail through the watch. Had she revived on some baroque torture device (a la The Pit and the Pendulum) it might have been more bearable, for the audience at least, because so melodramatically conventional. Instead, Sally's steady surrender to panic and hopelessness as the cannibals enact an insane version of a family dinner keeps this horror in the realm of the plausible. During this segment, Hooper often shoots the cannibals looking directly into the camera, increasing the sense of mutual threat to Sally and the audience. The overall visual conception and the actors' energized performances are so overwhelming, we may even miss that her hands are tied to another of Robert Burns' dark creations – an "arm chair" actually made of human arms.

In a family without women, the monsters destabilize and manipulate traditional gender roles, a major facet of the contemporary horror film from *Psycho* forward. At the dinner table all three killers abruptly assume new dimensions.[22] Leatherface appears in a wig and make-up (not completely evident), now almost comically broad and less agitated, even pausing to stroke and kiss the top of Grandpa's head. The Old Man becomes passive and appears guilty as well as giddy at the prospect of Sally's imminent death. The now openly sadistic Hitchhiker transforms into the cold patriarch berating the Old Man, who apparently cannot bring himself to participate in the actual killing: "He ain't nothin'; he's just the *cook*! Me and Leatherface do all the work!". This provokes a weird moment of involuntary sympathy for the Old Man, contemptuously ordered to keep his place, implicitly as the woman of the house. Though he manages the (admittedly novel) retort, "Shut up, you bitch-hog!", he is visibly intimidated. Yet this episode gives way to hallucination as the group suddenly starts laughing among themselves, at Sally, at who knows what, their chortles slightly out of synch and mixed with random interjections of pig squeals.[23] Such contradictory moments manage at once to define important themes and perpetuate the feel of drug-induced delirium.

Hooper conveys Sally's terror with closer and closer views of her screaming face, moving in with a macro lens to depict her eyelashes, pupil, and finally just huge close ups of capillaries laced in the eyeball. Although I suggested this sequence alludes to *Un Chien Andalou*, there is no threat to Sally's eyes, per se; rather, extreme close ups of the eye capture her complete physical vulnerability and terror. This step-frame montage of her face and eyes (there are actually two during the ordeal as Sally grows more dissociated) contrasts with a more famous sequence, solarized shots of astronaut Dave Bowman's eyes as he passes through the "star gate" in *2001: A Space Odyssey* (1968). There we have little sense of what he is experiencing which renders the sequence both formally and thematically abstract; Hooper's editing fully elaborates Sally's pain and fright. Despite excessive histrionics and gore that could derail it into camp, Sally's torture remains one of the most emotionally harrowing scenes ever presented in the genre.

At the climax, the Hitchhiker proposes that Grandpa have the honor of administering the fatal blow, seconded by the Old Man who assures Sally that Grandpa is so skilled, "it won't hurt a bit". But as Sally is held down and hit by the enfeebled man's glancing blows, the others surround him shouting, "Come on, Grandpa, kill the bitch!, kill the bitch!", as if encouraging a clumsy toddler. Alongside the sick comedy of Grandpa repeatedly dropping the hammer, this episode connects diverse themes. As recounted by the Old Man, Grandpa was in his day something like the John Henry of the stockyards, legendary for his physical prowess and passionate devotion to sledgehammering cattle. Indeed, the parallel with the folktale of railroad worker John Henry, "a steel drivin' man", according to the folksong, extends to Grandpa and his scions that were also bested and replaced by technology. Big-hearted John Henry dies in his contest with a machine; the cadaverous Grandpa is perhaps the clan's ultimate fetish, as Christopher Sharret observes, a literally decaying vestige of the past, abandoned by industrial capitalism.[24] The family's depravity is conveyed through the pathetic failure of the patriarch's once-mighty phallic hammer now become comically impotent. But again anticipating the slasher cycle, this social as well as physical impotence is avenged through vicious, sexualized violence against nubile young women.

Upon Sally's sudden escape, with a second berserk crash through a window, she emerges outside as the sun is rising, suggesting we are all slowly awakening from the nightmare, though the play with horror genre conventions up to now should at least make us wary. The immediate discovery of a busy highway just in front of the house where cannibals have been claiming victims for years also seems in equal parts promising and bizarre. The partial return of normalcy marked by passing vehicles dangles salvation, though the movie's indirect portrait of society at large via the initial radio reports was hardly reassuring. Hooper maintains the pace, however as Leatherface wounds himself with the saw and the Hitchhiker is run down by a skidding semi-truck, whose driver grabs a wrench and fights Leatherface, before just fleeing off-screen. We last see the traumatized, blood-drenched Sally in the bed of a speeding pick up that halted during the melee, still screaming in senseless terror even as it dimly registers she has somehow escaped. Yet significantly, Hooper ends the movie with shots of Leatherface dancing wildly in the road, backlit by the rising sun, swinging the roaring saw.

Sally is alive, yes, but there is no catharsis here. Her escape is nearly as capricious as the senseless killing of Ben at the end of *Night of the Living Dead*. Both climaxes leave a profound and depressing sense of irresolution, refusing coherence, closure, and safety. In *Living Dead*, traditional symbols and figures of civil, religious, or scientific authority, the ultimate solution to the monster's rampage in traditional horror films, are either dismissed or virtually become the "monsters" themselves in the careless shooting of heroic Ben; in *Chain Saw Massacre*, such figures or institutions are absent entirely. More importantly, Leatherface lives, too. This may be another instance of Hooper varying Hitchcock: *Psycho's* final images picture Norman/Mother's awful grin lap-dissolved over a fleeting skull image and the chain wrenching Marion's car out of the swamp.[25] But unlike Norman, held by the police and already inter-rogated and "explained" by a psychiatrist at this point, Leatherface is still at large, flaunting his insatiable saw in a dance that might just as easily celebrate anarchic freedom and ferocious power as express frus-tration at Sally's escape. Moreover, we have cyclically returned to the ominous daylight that did nothing previously to inhibit "a whole family of Draculas", and no explanation, no summing up of what it all means is forthcoming.

With its contemporary locations and all-too-human monsters, *The Texas Chain Saw Massacre* continued American horror's definitive move away from the expressionistic settings established by the Universal classics of the 30s and Hammer's European gothicism of the 60s. Although *Chain Saw Massacre* was redolent of its time with its pervasive atmosphere of social crisis and reversal of longstanding genre conventions, it was hardly bound to that moment. By the 1980s, Leatherface had joined a new monster pantheon that included Michael Myers, Jason Voorhees, and Freddy Krueger, whose likenesses began appearing on shirts, posters, and toys. Leatherface returned in three uneven sequels and an expen-sive remake in 2003. Mirror opposite of the original, the $10 million film from New Line Cinema, produced by blockbuster maven Michael Bay (*Armageddon*, *Pearl Harbor*) and starring Jessica Biel as the Sally character, opened in 3,016 theaters, grossing $29 million its opening weekend. The remake begins and ends with grainy black and white film footage supposedly from a police investigation of the crimes; and features scenes in a packing plant of the "Blair Meat Company", both likely nods back at *The Blair Witch Project* (1999) for elements that the low-budget sleeper had extracted from the original *Chain Saw Massacre*, notably the "documentary" framework and discovery of weird fetishes in the woods. Moreover, because of TV beauty Jessica Biel's star power, which often equals invulnerability, we never believe she will die. She even rescues a baby from the cannibals, a bit lifted from *The Hills Have Eyes* (1977). Bloody carnage aside, the remake is finally much more similar structurally to classical horror films than the original.

Though in most aspects Hooper's *Chain Saw Massacre* does not reflect the stalk and slash mode, its influence was nearly as profound as *Psycho* on those later films in its image of the family as monster as much as for its intense, graphic violence. Yet like many subsequent horror films, its lack of closure both reflects and intensifies its emotionally and ideologically disturbing themes. The continuing reliance and commercial popularity of this open-ended formula (a convention like any other, once recognized as such) is only partly explained by the increasing need for cheap, pre-sold sequels in Hollywood production since the 1970s. Robin Wood argues that the return of the monster in a slightly different version of the original tale (e.g., *Bride of Frankenstein* [1935], *Dracula Has Risen From the Grave* [1969]) is qualitatively different from the profound lack of a satisfying restoration of "normality" within the fictional world of contemporary horror films. Certainly the new slasher pantheon, in exalting even blank, mute characters like Michael Myers or Jason Voorhees invites important questions about the nature of "identification" in such movies, issues that have occupied a variety of critics since *Halloween*. Still, the possible social functions and meanings of these newer monsters clearly can, and probably should be separated from the films that first presented them. *The Texas Chain Saw Massacre* has lost little of its power to frighten and disturb, reactions that spring from its masterful control of film form and manipulation of audience expectations.

CHAPTER 10

HALLOWEEN (1978): THE SHAPE OF THE SLASHER FILM

For mid-twentieth-century moviegoers, the notion of a horror film brought to mind gothic settings and supernatural creatures like Dracula or the Wolf Man. Increasingly after 1978, however, the common impression of a horror film for a younger generation most likely meant the gory slaughter of contemporary American teenagers by a deranged serial killer in everyday surroundings. The movie that crystallized these shifts was John Carpenter's *Halloween*, whose huge box office spawned a derivative cycle that soon became a thriving sub-genre generally known as the slasher film. Though Carpenter's hit had a number of antecedents, most obviously *Psycho*, to which it alluded in several ways, the film's most pertinent elements – episodes of highly sexualized violence inflicted with primitive weapons, a sole survivor's struggle to escape – resonated anew with its target audience. The slasher cycle also elicited sustained condemnation in the mainstream press, outcries against the foreboding social implications of unfettered media violence that dovetailed with feminist protests against demeaning images or violence against women in commercial media, activism that flowed from the social movements of the 1960s. As the defining work of a simultaneously popular and controversial horror

FIGURE 18 Final girl: Laurie (Jamie Lee Curtis) prepares to fight as Michael Myers breaks into the closet where she has hidden. *Halloween* (1978, Compass International). *Producer:* Debra Hill. *Director:* John Carpenter

cycle, *Halloween* occasioned a significant transitional moment in the genre's history.

The starting point for most discussions was *Halloween*'s extraordinary prolog in which the audience experiences the vicious stabbing of a naked young woman in first-person camera, as if becoming the killer. When *Friday the 13th* (1980) and other films copied the technique, critics charged that this strategy stimulated the most base and morally irresponsible reactions that encouraged viewers to identify with the murderer rather than the victim; and did so in starkly gendered terms where the killer's phallic weapon inflicted an implicitly "just" punishment on sexually independent women.[1] Indeed, constant devotion to illicit sex, illegal drugs, and general adolescent irresponsibility became the hallmarks of slasher victims. Meanwhile the heroine, or "final girl," as Carol J. Clover termed her in an influential essay, seemingly survives because she represses these very impulses and desires, in particular retaining her virginity.[2] Michael Myers and subsequent slashers, following the Norman Bates example, can only express sexuality through brutal violence. Abstinence and rectitude evidently give final girls the power to fight back and survive. (At her death, Marion Crane had been sexually active and a thief.) As the cycle flourished on the cusp of the conservative Reagan 1980s, these thematic currents brought social and analytical issues of gender and sexuality to the forefront of discussion in a way that made the slasher cycle appear perhaps more socially urgent than the merits of most examples would suggest. As often happens, though, the movie that sparked this profitable cycle displayed far greater formal and thematic integrity than its many imitators.

Halloween's simple, linear plot laid down the pattern for the slasher cycle. On Halloween night in 1963, a 6-year old and deeply insane Michael Myers watches his older sister Judith in sexual play with a boyfriend, then brutally stabs her to death. Wearing a clown costume and still clutching the knife, he is discovered outside the family home just afterwards by his puzzled parents. Fifteen years later, the adult Michael (Nick Castle) escapes the mental institution and is pursued back to his hometown by his frantic psychiatrist, Dr Sam Loomis (Donald Pleasence). Donning a white rubber mask, the shadowy killer begins stalking a local high-school girl, Laurie Strode (Jamie Lee Curtis). While Laurie is babysitting two children on Halloween night, Michael slays her friends Annie (Nancy Loomis), Lynda (P. J. Soles), and Bob (John Michael Simms). Gradually realizing what is happening, Laurie fights for her life against the mute but relentless killer. As Michael closes in, Dr Loomis appears and repeatedly shoots the murderer, who falls from a second-story window. Yet when he looks down, the seemingly ghostly stalker has vanished again.

Briefly described in this way, *Halloween* seems to epitomize the quick and greedy exploitation movie bent solely on pointless shocks that came to mark the mainstream critical consensus about "horror films" in general. In fact, the movie exudes masterful attention to craft and mood that belies its low (around $340,000) budget. *Halloween* allied Val Lewton's controlled economy of expression with the emotional and violent intensity of post-1968 horror. Unlike the many rip-offs and imitations that followed, including several *Halloween* sequels with which Carpenter had little to no involvement, the original relies far more on suspense than graphic bloodletting. What became at best a problematic moment in the genre's history flowed from *Halloween*'s skillful treatment of new motifs, notably the sex and violence dialectic focused around contemporary teenagers; and its transfer of familiar gothic conventions into contemporary settings. Carpenter's pointed variations of key narrative and formal aspects of *Psycho* completed the process.

John Carpenter (b. 1948), who made amateur horror-fantasy movies as a teenager and then as a student at the University of Southern California, was part of the first film-school generation of directors in the "New Hollywood" of the late 1960s and 1970s. Like the French New Wave filmmakers who preceded them by a few years, the American "movie brats" often referenced favorite films of the past in the process of working their own variations on the thematic or narrative patterns of those older works. Yet where some found inspiration in the auteurs of European art cinema (Bergman, Fellini, etc.), Carpenter remained committed to Hollywood genre movies, particularly the work of Howard Hawks and Alfred Hitchcock. Michael's vengeful, sexually charged knifing of his sister in her bedroom that opens *Halloween* parallels Norman Bates' off-screen slaying of his mother and stepfather ("In bed," as the Fairvale sheriff's wife pruriently whispers) that initiated his madness. Yet Carpenter's *hommages* are also more direct. Not only does Donald Pleasence's Dr Sam Loomis take his name from that of Marion Crane's lover (John Gavin), a far more important reference to *Psycho* figures in casting Janet Leigh's own daughter, Jamie Lee Curtis as Laurie, the would-be victim who not only battles but survives her deranged attacker.[3] The generational passage symbolized by this astute gesture describes that of the genre itself in the 1970s but also self-consciously underscores the familial basis of horror in *Halloween* and subsequent slasher films.

In this regard, we should note that *Psycho* itself, though a highly profitable and instantly famous movie, was not generally considered a milestone of the "horror film" until well into the 1970s.[4] True, it did immediately inspire imitations from producers associated with the genre, particularly William Castle's *Homicidal* (1961) and several knock-offs from Hammer (*Maniac* [1963], *Paranoiac* [1963], etc.), the kind of exploitation fare Hitchcock himself initially referenced. Yet because it lacked occult foundation *Psycho* was deemed a "thriller," or as the director's fame merged with the ascending popularity of the auteur theory, foremost as a "Hitchcock film."[5] Moreover, while the often loosely defined notion of the thriller may link to the horror film, the former often rates higher critical praise for marshaling suspense through understatement and restraint – the seemingly opposite approach of exploitation horror.[6] But as many horror films from the late 1960s forward increasingly located uncanny disturbance within the family, *Psycho*'s preliminary domestic implosion, along with its explicit violence and unmistakable gothic elements, came to seem indistinguishable from the genre's evolution. Even so, *Psycho*'s concern with guilt-crippled adults at the end of the 1950s versus *Halloween*'s focus on randy teens in the late 1970s attests to the historical and social ground that had been traversed in the intervening years.

Halloween's vivid promotional graphic, a screaming Jack O' Lantern alongside a fist plunging a bloody knife, accompanied the tagline, "The Night *He* Came Home." Its emphasis on the home as a fount of monstrosity aligned it with major horror films of the decade from *The Exorcist* to *The Hills Have Eyes*. Yet in the year of its release, the modest *Halloween* competed strongly at the box office with two star-laden, Oscar-winning dramas seeking to confront the Vietnam experience: the muddled but compelling *The Deer Hunter* (1978); and a weepy tale of veterans facing the physical and emotional wounds of war whose title, *Coming Home* (1978), echoed *Halloween*'s ad line. Note too that the (often disdainful) term "body-count movie" became a nickname for slasher horror, correctly recording how similar movies after *Halloween* increased the number of victims while intensifying the awful nature of their deaths. The term seemingly derived from the theatrical trailer for the original *Friday the 13th*, which flashed moments from each of its 13 murders alongside an ascending numerical tally. But recall that the phrase "body count," meaning enemy dead, originated in the Vietnam War's lexicon of euphemisms that couched the awful reality of mechanized slaughter in the tidy columns of business accounting. Applied to this horror cycle, the term suggests it was in fact the war that had come home, that the slasher film was another indirect reprocessing of Vietnam's impact on American culture, the accompanying tremors set off by the women's movement in particular.

Halloween's credits proceed beside a flickering Jack O' Lantern set against a black background, as ominous bass chords sound beneath a jangling 5/4 melody that seems to count down to an inevitable doom. Yet Carpenter immediately establishes the beckoning pull of a moving camera as the film's most important visual technique. A slow track-in moves us closer to the pumpkin's glowing eye until we seemingly enter and emerge on "the other side" in "Haddonfield, Illinois, 1963," suggesting a literal passage through the flames of hell and arrival in a world, like that of most nightmares, at once familiar and uncannily threatening.[7] The controversial prolog continues this motion in a way that associates the spectator with the stalker, as the track-in becomes a subjective point-of-view shot attached to the consciousness of we as yet know not who or what, making a furtive approach to a two-story frame house. Because the dark house itself seems less than inviting it is not immediately clear whether "we" are the monster or a potential victim about to fall prey to imprudent curiosity. The audience's role as co-conspirator or guilty witness is complicated also by what we observe, a young couple necking inside the doorway, their muffled voices anxiously discussing how long parents will be away. As in the opening of *Psycho* when Hitchcock's camera moves from an aerial view of the city into a hotel window to spy on a couple's afternoon tryst, we are both titillated and discomfited by the intimate scene we have been "made" to watch.

The approach to the house – accompanied by raspy breathing and footsteps – begins a four-minute-long take sequence that depicts the stalker watching the couple through a window as they kiss on the couch and hurry upstairs, while he enters, takes a knife from a kitchen drawer, and climbs the stairs to commit the murder. Though Carpenter hides a cut when Michael puts on the clown mask, the effect is of a continuous long take that fixes attention on the physical and psychological presence of a dangerous intruder. While some critics interpreted the subjective camera as an unambiguous merging of murderer and spectator, the film's larger method often confuses our identification with the camera to build tension that adds a sense of grim inevitability whenever the moving/stalking camera appears – yet only in part.[8] Once Laurie becomes the film's major character, we maintain close emotional and optical identification with her point of view (and/or with the persistent Dr Loomis, the effect is quite similar) through the most conventional albeit skillful patterns of Hollywood style shooting and editing.

In any case, *Halloween*'s prolog guaranteed that the camera/killer/audience's role in tracking unsuspecting victims would be the most characteristic visual and narrative device of this film and many it would inspire; the alternate term "stalk and slash" is perhaps the most accurate if ungainly description of a cycle in which the act of stalking is nearly as important as the serial murders. Moreover, this stylistic emphasis on the killer's methodical surveillance separates these films from *Psycho* or *The Texas Chain Saw Massacre*, which depicted random victims stumbling into traps carefully laid by patient if no less mad butchers. Michael, Jason Voorhees, and their cohorts were highly aggressive, restlessly hunting and destroying victims, at least some of whom were surrogates for particular individuals who had wronged the maniacs in the past. Yet if there is an over-explained logic to Norman Bates' crimes, an earlier scenario that motivated his pathological violence (a thread continued in most slasher movies), such basic information is almost entirely lacking in *Halloween*, adding to its atmosphere of encroaching doom. In the end credits, the killer is referred to only as "The Shape," a designation that suggests this monster is finally no tormented mental case but an ambiguously ghostly figure. This allowed *Halloween* to break new ground while keeping one foot in the gothic tradition.

Besides the voyeuristic threat, the killer's peek through the window initiates other pertinent themes when the boyfriend puts on a clown mask to tease the girl. "Are we alone?," he asks, faintly detecting the labored breathing. "Michael's around here someplace," his negligent babysitter, later identified as his sister Judith, allows, as if nonchalantly discussing the family dog, and implying the mask belongs to a child. Indeed, the masked and ever-silent Michael is associated with both children and animals, the latter most memorably after pinning Bob to the kitchen wall with a long knife then studying the result with a tilt of the head, a gesture we attribute to piqued curiosity in dogs. The couple's play with the mask underlines the theme of childhood innocence giving way to adolescent sexuality (even fetishism), then twisting into murder. Young Michael's Halloween costume might have been almost anything, but in a film of this title the final choice would inevitably matter. Carpenter pointedly selected the emotionally complex – and androgynous – figure of the Clown, confirmed when an arm encased in a green and white satin sleeve with ruffled cuff removes a knife from a kitchen drawer, then reclaims the discarded mask with its red phallic nose just before the murder. In this *Halloween* seemingly extends a fleeting moment in *The Exorcist* when Chris MacNeil, walking through autumnal streets, smilingly observes costumed children trick-or-treating shortly before the Devil possesses her own daughter. As underscored by the mask motif, it is the appearance of innocence that's false. The eroticizing of both childhood and violence in this sequence deepens the spectator's distressing sense of involvement initiated by the subjective camera.

Carpenter integrates these disparate themes when the killer dons the clown face, the camera itself now masked to look through eyeholes, which further blurs distinctions between Judith's boyfriend and brother, her killer and the spectator. Before this though, we watch as the swaggering boy comes back downstairs tugging on his shirt and half-smilingly promising to call tomorrow. (He seems rather proud of himself considering he has been upstairs about one minute!) As a chiming clock signals that Judith's time is up, illicit sex and gruesome violence intertwine as the intruder follows a trail of clothing that leads to the girl sitting naked before a mirror, humming while brushing her hair. It is notable that in this initiating instance, the boyfriend is spared and the killer's rage vented exclusively on the helpless girl for reasons we must take, literally, at face value. The camera swings right to take in the rumpled sheets on the bed – seemingly quick confirmation and indictment of her activities – then pulls left to commit the brutal stabbing with amplified strikes of the knife as she falls screaming to the floor with blood-spattered breasts.

The sudden return to objective camera outside with the climactic revelation that the killer is a rather plain child, though one with a blank stare, completes the spectator's disorientation. The consciousness that initiated the acts we experienced remains divided and ambiguous, its motivations forever mysterious. Although this sequence became metonymically equated with the slasher cycle as a whole, it stands alone in both power and execution. As with Hitchcock's shower murder, the lingering shock of *Halloween*'s bravura opening will not require a repetition nearly as intense in the rest of the film. Carpenter builds tension later by conventionally inserting shots of Michael's point of view, but never again forces the audience to "become" the killer in such a sustained fashion. Our identification transfers primarily to Laurie, who will wound Michael with small but precise and effective phallic weaponry of her own, a knitting needle and a hastily straightened clothes hanger. Even so, as critics charged, *Halloween*'s stylized opening immediately answers the expression of female sexuality with merciless violence.

Frightened yet resilient young women were often the protagonists of gothic fiction, but only rarely in traditional horror films. This changed after *Halloween*. Although veteran character actor Donald Pleasence got top billing over then-unknown Jamie Lee Curtis and gets nearly as much screen time, our attention stays mainly on Laurie. Dr Loomis is really the Van Helsing figure, the wise man with special knowledge and insight pursuing the monster, though here with growing fear and declining confidence. (He is the opposite of *Psycho*'s self-assured clinician.) Loomis' inability to marshal others to recognize Michael's exceptional threat echoes many post-1968 horror films in which traditional authorities are ineffectual or absent. Unlike the shrugging doctors in *The Exorcist* who torturously poke and prod Regan then conclude her symptoms are all psychosomatic, Dr Loomis has already abandoned rational science after years of studying the silent Michael whom he pronounces "pure evil." Yet this recognition will not defeat the monster. The victory, partial at best, is in Laurie's survival, which, though aided by Loomis, obtains from the ways she dynamically negotiates Michael's evolving threat through both thought and action.

Halloween's working title, "The Babysitter Murders," foretold a sensational crime story, a premise delivered then upended by the heightened style and macabre revelation of the prolog. However, for the next hour, Carpenter relies entirely on suspense and suggestion rather than explicit violence. On a stormy night, Loomis' arrival at the mental hospital where Michael is housed to find patients wandering the grounds outside hauntingly depicts the breakdown of institutional control and rationality itself. The white-gowned figures in the headlights, stumbling aimlessly through the rain, contrast with Michael's apparently methodical preparation for this moment. We may imagine that he has slain numerous guards and doctors in his escape but this is left to speculation. Instead, The Shape's furtive appearance as another gowned figure scrambling on top of the car driven by Loomis' nurse subverts expectation – Carpenter's canny method throughout – when a brawny arm smashes the window and drags her out, terrorizing but not killing her. Loomis' anguished "The evil is loose!" as Michael drives away reveals his basic weakness and allows the story's deeper resonance to develop in the battle between Laurie and the monster.

In what became a convention of the slasher film, Laurie is indeed identified as a virgin, albeit a reluctant one dismayed by her lack of social skills and sexual experience relative to her brash, promiscuous friends. Babysitting becomes a key motif as it occupies the heroine in trustworthy acts of proto-homemaking and motherhood. In one of many needling references to virginity, Annie jokes that Laurie "must have a fortune stashed away in babysitting money," her repression channeled into rigid responsibility as a mother in training. By contrast, leaving to meet a boyfriend, Annie dumps her young charge, Lindsey, on Laurie who is already sitting Tommy, so that Lynda and Bob can use the now-empty house for beer-fueled sex, events that lead to the deaths of all three teens. However, Laurie's intelligence is underlined too, as when she delivers a thoughtful analysis of a literary theme (one describing fate as an inescapable "force of nature") in English class. The scene concludes with her first sight of Michael, standing outside the school staring at her. Laurie's fate is not inevitable, as indicated by her battle to survive. However, she is portrayed as solitary and dreamy, qualities that feed a sense that Michael may be a product (even a projection) of her troubled imagination. In drawing these strands together, part of *Halloween*'s disturbing charge comes from the ways Michael is constructed as Laurie's fantasy lover.[9]

Skillful editing, especially control of point-of-view shots, builds suspense by keeping the monster visible only to Laurie, though she usually spots him while in the company of others. Yet each encounter concludes with dialog or action that offer the monster as her mate. This commences at Laurie's introduction, walking from her home and making plans with Tommy for babysitting that evening as they approach the deserted Myers house on an errand for her father, a realtor trying to sell the infamous landmark. Here and in subsequent passages through the neighborhood, Carpenter uses a combination of long shots and long takes as she walks, an otherwise conventional plan that in light of the prolog's subjective, moving camera implies Laurie is already under surveillance. This is confirmed as the camera observes them from the house's darkened interior, activating off-screen space to imply Michael's presence. Though Laurie dismisses the boy's fears about the "spook house" as she approaches to drop off a key, the monster's silhouette suddenly appears inside. The three figures from the prolog – reckless teenage girl, her conceited boyfriend, and child/killer – reappear in distorted reflection as Laurie, Tommy, and the adult Michael. Continuing down the street alone she sings softly, "I wish I had you all alone, just the two of us," as Michael steps into frame outside still watching her. (Her song is ironically answered by Blue Oyster Cult's "Don't Fear the Reaper" playing on the radio as Annie and Laurie drive and the stolen station wagon driven by Michael slips around a corner to follow them.) Laurie's "wish" will be granted in their climactic confrontation.

The perverse courtship continues with similarly well-crafted episodes as when, walking home with Annie, she spots Michael staring at her by a hedgerow up ahead. When Annie goes to the spot, he has of course vanished, and she derisively calls back to Laurie, "He wants to talk to you. He wants to take you out tonight." Michael substitutes for the never-seen Ben Tramer, a boy Laurie confesses she would like to go out with. (Tommy later spots Michael's dark silhouette across the street as Annie informs Laurie she told Ben of Laurie's interest in him.)[10] Returning to her room, the billowing white curtains from the open window visually anticipate what Laurie sees looking down – Michael gazing up at her from amid white sheets blowing on a clothesline. In subsequent conversation with Annie – after a start from a ringing telephone – their discussion includes Annie's jokes about obscene phone calls and another reference to Laurie's virginity: "You're losing it, Laurie" / "I already lost it" / "I doubt that." Later, Laurie suggests the voyeur might have been an elderly neighbor, Mr Ridder: "He can still watch," she insists. "That's probably all he *can* do," Annie deadpans. Both accounts blandly describe neurosis brought on by frustrated sexuality, both hers and the man's. In a 1981 interview, Carpenter summarized his reaction to criticism of the film's association of female promiscuity and murder: "Ironically, the one girl in the film who does not fool around . . . is the one who stabs him and over and over with this long knife! She's as repressed as he is getting rid of this sexual energy. And no one sees this."[11] Despite the director's correct account of the movie's portrayal of its female protagonist, there remains an undeniable erotic teasing built around female sexuality in all the murders.

In that same interview, Carpenter called director Dario Argento "brilliant," admiringly citing the Italian's stylish horror movies of the past decade. *Psycho*'s importance aside, Argento's films from *The Bird With the Crystal Plumage* [*L'Ucello dalle piume di cristallo*] (1970) through *Deep Red* [*Profondo Rosso*] (1975), and especially *Suspiria* (1977) – all successfully distributed in the United States by major studios – remain little noticed influences on the horror cycle that seemingly emerges full-grown with *Halloween*. Argento's first four movies concern insane killers (both male and female, though the murderer's identity as well as gender is hidden through most of each) who stalk and slay particular victims with a variety of phallic weapons.[12] *Deep Red*'s prolog depicts a domestic slaying of a parent witnessed by a child, reiterating the *Psycho* lineage. *Suspiria*'s monster is an ancient witch and the plot entails a number of explicitly supernatural horrors, yet its two most spectacular murder scenes play like the work of a driven, largely unseen maniac, particularly the ghastly massacre of two female students in their upper-floor apartment. (The camera floats through the air toward the building and the attack begins at the window, yet the murders still seem to be committed by a human agent.) The killer's depiction as only muscular arms and hands (traditionally supplied by Argento himself) precedes Carpenter's staging of Michael's asylum escape. Argento's own throbbing electronic score likewise drives the film, and the Italian maestro was years ahead of Carpenter in unsettling the audience through sustained identification with a prowling camera assumed to be the killer's vision. Carpenter seemingly absorbed these lessons, achieving comparably impressive results in far more ordinary settings and with minimal gore.

Though *Halloween* and its progeny were denounced as cynical, even "immoral," Argento's vision was far bleaker, its universe unremittingly hostile in ways that exceed the depredations of a single anomalous psychopath. Argento's films too are densely plotted, their twists often unsatisfying in conventional terms for their cursory, often wildly illogical "explanations." *Halloween* denies important back-story we would like to know but offers an engrossing plot, a strategy of theme and variation that tricks the audience and sustains the fatalistic mood. The escaping

Michael attacks the nurse in the car but spares her, yet finally kills Annie inside her car. Prior to this, in a variation of the prolog, Michael stalks Annie outside the house, with lengthy episodes of subjective camera, watching her remove her stained clothes in the laundry room, though with back turned so we see no nudity. In one of *Halloween*'s most famous images, The Shape becomes multiple "ghosts," costuming his cadaverous white mask with a white sheet and the glasses of the just-murdered Bob, impersonating Lynda's lover before killing her – though not until she enticingly lowers the bedsheet to reveal her breasts, linking her with Judith. After Laurie spots Michael below her window, Annie's strange chewing noises on the phone and jokes about obscene calls rhyme with Laurie mistaking the sounds over the phone of Lynda being strangled by Michael for groans of passion between Lynda and Bob. Michael draws progressively closer to Laurie in a struggle that promises to fuse sex and violence, yet she survives because she soon anticipates his moves and turns his own weapons against him.

As in many horror films, *Halloween*'s steady pace suppresses logical questions such as why no one except Dr Loomis is apparently bother-ing to search for a criminally insane escapee; or how this ominous figure can stand exposed on the streets in broad daylight and scarcely be noticed by anyone. Amplifying the sense of subjective delusion, the lonely streets of Haddonfield seem virtually deserted both day and night save for Laurie, her friends, and the stalker, who remains at once a looming threat and elusive wraith. *Halloween* shows few adults besides Sheriff Brackett (Annie's father) and Dr Loomis. Where are Laurie's parents after her dad's fleeting appearance? Her house is deserted; nor do we see the parents of the kids she's babysitting. Except for the boy threatened by Michael after bullying Tommy, the latter is the only other character who sees The Shape, reinforcing the sense that the killer is a half-imaginary eruption of troubled and neglected psyches. One of the film's most haunting images is Tommy's view from across the street of Michael' slowly carrying Annie's limp body from the garage, up the steps and right into the front door of the house where she was killed. In a story built on the bloody destruction of adolescents in dark and empty middle-class homes, the parallel failure of police and medical science portends an assault on a near-defenseless society. When Loomis visits the cemetery to search for the grave of Judith Myers, the caretaker's interrupted tale of another horrible domestic tragedy prefigures the dis-covery of the missing tombstone that will reappear in the bed along with Annie's body, a baroque tableau of the self-destruction of the nuclear family that no one in the story can arrest.

At the time of *Halloween*'s 1978 release, the recent phenomenal success of *Close Encounters of the Third Kind* and *Star Wars* suggested that effects-heavy science-fiction epics had decisively eclipsed low-budget horror. Besides its own box-office triumph, *Halloween* quietly rebuts this notion within the film by costuming Tommy for the holiday in a white flight suit with black tool belt that recalls Luke Skywalker's white judo outfit. The comic books he shows Laurie underscore his passion for science fiction, titles like *Laser Man*, *Neutron Man*, and *Tarantula Man*. Yet in the midst of this he fearfully asks about the Boogeyman, suggesting that futurist rationality may yet be overtaken by pagan dread. Laurie responds to the effects of domestic and social breakdown by becoming the tale's most capable "parent," swiftly acting to save Tommy and Lindsey by putting herself in danger; and the hero who confronts the monster. Yet her transition from hesitant wallflower to quick-witted survivor is all the more remarkable considering the explicit 1950s cultural references surrounding her as she babysits on Halloween night, motifs that initially situate her as an idealized homemaker of the postwar years. The Atomic Age allusions in the titles of the comic books Tommy must hide from his disapproving mother evoke the mid-1950s controversy over the EC comics line whose notorious titles included *Tales From the Crypt* and *Weird Science*. Similarly, the children sit glued to the television watching Eisenhower-era movies, *The Thing* (1951) – which Carpenter would successfully remake in 1982 – and *Forbidden Planet* (1956). Though these might not seem proper choices for Halloween-night programming, scenes excerpted from each depict a phantom creature stalking its prey. Laurie appears throughout in an apron, making popcorn and helping the children carve pumpkins – no women's liberation this. But the story's gothic foundation suggests that her struggle to escape an oppressive threat from the past also includes such limited and predetermined social roles, whether as neurotic hausfrau or even the dubious "liberation" of her oblivious friends. Though only 18 at the time, Jamie Lee Curtis' mature mien heightens this effect. In her performance, Laurie becomes a rare commodity for the slasher film – a character with depth who seems capable of self-awareness and growth.

Laurie defends the children and survives through nerve and intelligence, refusing the status of traumatized victim. Sensing something is wrong with Annie and Lynda, she puts the children to bed ("Sleep tight, kids," she whispers, unconvinced) before locking the door and venturing across the street to investigate. Notably, Carpenter gives Laurie several handheld point-of-view shots as she approaches the neighboring house, a technique routinely used to convey instability and apprehension as characters enter dangerous terrain, but also suggesting through the same camera style of the prolog that she is acquiring something of the purposefulness and force that gives Michael his awful power. Upon discovery of her friends' deaths, Michael wounds her with a knife and knocks her over the banister. Stumbling into the street, she screams for help at another house but the owners refuse to open the door – a chilling evocation of the indifference of adult authority that the film has previously only implied.[13] Barely escaping back to Tommy's house, she realizes Michael is already inside, simply conveyed by another economical cut to curtains blowing at an open window. In keeping with the story's domestic setting, Laurie answers Michael's slaughter of Judith with a knife pulled from a kitchen drawer with decidedly domestic utensils, first stabbing him in the neck with a knitting needle, then straightening a clothes hanger to gouge him in the eye. Yet she also attacks him with his dropped knife while she crouches in the closet, thrusting up into his chest in gestures that literally invert his stabbing of the seated Judith.

As children like to hide and play in closets, this primal location seems steeped in the psychology of childhood itself, not inevitably connected to molestation or abuse, yet easily incorporable into terroristic scenarios: retreat to a (paradoxically) womblike enclosure to escape threatening adults ("giants" or "Boogeymen") who may be actual parents or thinly disguised surrogates. Laurie's retreat to the closet places *Halloween* at the intersection of the horror film and the domestic melodrama. One of the most famous examples of the latter is D. W. Griffith's *Broken Blossoms* (1919), where Lillian Gish cowers in a closet from a drunken, brutish father battering the door with an ax, finally running in panicked circles, filmed from directly above so she resembles a frantic animal. The closet is also the site of ongoing torture for the helpless girl in *Sybil* (NBC, 1976), the harrowing made-for-TV movie about child abuse and insanity. Brian De Palma referenced Griffith's overhead shot in *Carrie* when her religiously unhinged mother drags her to a closet to atone for imagined sins – the same spot to which the dying Carrie slinks with the mother's body as her telekinetic powers pull down the house around them, a remarkable womb/tomb image. Carpenter similarly shoots high-angle shots looking down on Laurie trying to melt into the wall as Michael breaks through the flimsy doors. *Halloween* initially depicts Michael as a child, yet the tale is so immersed in fractured family conflicts and the glaring absence of protective authorities that the connections to earlier examples are easily traced.

Just before the first assault on Laurie, The Shape's pallid mask eerily materialized from black shadows behind her. Carpenter stages variations of this composition in each subsequent attack, placing Laurie in the foreground looking away as we see past her to Michael's appearance or revival in the background, pulling the audience deeper into the predicament and refuting facile claims that we are formally driven to identify with the killer. Moreover, the simple fact remains that movies are made to be consumed by audiences. Though the final scenes highlight Laurie's courage in fighting Michael, as a movie character she also engages in unlikely behavior calculated to make audiences squirm and talk back to the screen. Not once but twice after barely surviving and disabling the maniac, she drops her weapons and turns her back on the thing which has already proven itself nearly invulnerable. Of such perennially effective techniques are classics made. Yet these moments surely "force us," as much as any work of fiction can, to root for this sympathetic human being, not the skull-faced hulk that won't stay dead.

At the climax, Loomis shoots Michael as he strangles Laurie, though not before she strikes him in the head, knocking off the mask. A glimpse of a young man's face, with cauliflower ear and one drooping eye, seemingly confirms that Michael is human. He replaces the mask just as Loomis hits him with the first shot. The sense of the killer as a mortal psychopath disappears with the doctor's look out the window to find nothing where the killer's body should have been. In this, *Halloween* continued the dominant trend of horror in the 1970s, refusing closure and catharsis. Laurie summoned the strength to fight for her life but The Shape is gone in the night, free to continue its murderous spree. Nearly reduced to a childlike state herself, Laurie cries, "It *was* the Boogeyman." Upon Loomis' grim confirmation, "In fact, it was," Carpenter ends with a montage of darkened rooms and desolate houses seen previously, ending on the façade of the haunted Myers house, the most basic gothic emblem, all overlaid with the same unsettling musical theme of the opening and the sound of Michael's heavy breathing. The evil lives, seemingly ubiquitous.

Halloween refined particular tropes that began with *Psycho* and advanced through many horror films of the Vietnam era and its immediate aftermath – the increasing problematizing, or crisis in gender roles, capital punishment of sexual expression, the violent breakdown of the family. Against the backdrop of tumultuous social crisis in 1968, the catatonic Barbara in the low-budget *Night of the Living Dead* and a ravaged woman bearing the Devil's child in the slickly produced *Rosemary's Baby* signaled the veritable death of the ideal (read: passive) woman slated for last-minute rescue in earlier horror films. Thereafter, from expensive movies such as *The Exorcist* and *The Omen* (1976) to exploitation fare like *It's Alive!* (1974), with its murderous baby-monster, the genre resonated anxiety about women's changing roles, compounded by the bitterly divisive *Roe v. Wade* decision in 1973.[14] To the extent *Halloween* implies that Michael might be a projection of Laurie's own repressed desires to destroy the very friends who insult and intimidate her, she suggests an ambivalent heroine/monster like the protagonist of *Carrie*, a forerunner of the slasher cycle in its focus on disruptive adolescent sexuality. Given the strength of the direction and performance of Laurie in *Halloween*, however, assorted critical predictions of inevitable spectator, especially male spectator, complicity in misogynistic violence seem unpersuasive – at least in this case. Yet particularly in the nearly unredeemable *Friday the 13th* series, which rapidly converted the mad butcher into the star with no moral or psychological counterweight, the slasher cycle plunged into highly questionable realms.

Halloween and others in which hearth and home generate the monster proved popular and profitable. Formal differences aside, had this message been either unpalatable or foreign to their audiences, teens and young adults in particular, these films would have had little impact. Yet even the most formulaic of numbered sequels contained ambiguous implications: Are the clueless teens of slasher movies truly liberated or simply cast adrift by adults in a social system that no longer seems capable – or perhaps even worthy – of self-defense? Academics and journalists alike recognized the centrality of gender shifts to the slasher cycle, though often disagreeing considerably on the larger implications of these changes. "The night *He* came home" was also the night she fought back; this occurred less forcefully in most sequels and imitations that followed. The careful attention to form that John Carpenter and associates brought to *Halloween* upheld the best traditions of the genre, those in which frightening images and complex, often contradictory themes do not simply disturb but also expose deep psychological and social fissures.

CHAPTER 11

RE-ANIMATOR (1985) AND SLAPSTICK HORROR

The domination of the horror genre in the first half of the 1980s by the stalk-and-slash formula and increasingly grisly special effects that often superseded narrative, set the stage for a movie that rejected the former and transcended the latter, an outrageous work that was both traditional and boundary-shattering. Stuart Gordon's *Re-Animator* (1985), a variation of the *Frankenstein* myth, won a special prize at the Cannes Film Festival and became a box-office hit despite being released unrated, a move that often limits access to advertising and theater bookings. *Re-Animator* exemplified the splatter era that exhibited spectacles of bodily destruction traceable to Grand Guignol productions. But it also adapted the Parisian theater's strategy of "hot and cold showers" to jolt audiences by chasing violence with sexual titillation, mixing medical horrors and absurdist comedy. "Audiences are always looking for an excuse to laugh while watching horror films," Stuart Gordon once observed, "so you've got to provide some for them so they won't laugh in the wrong places."[1] His insight suggests that the horror director's careful control of humor – usually thought to mean avoiding comedy altogether – can shape an audience's experience as much as the orchestration of shock and suspense. Still, most attempts to combine comedy and horror fail on both counts.

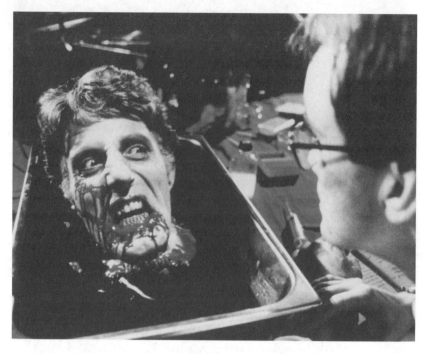

FIGURE 19 Going head to head: Herbert West (Jeffrey Combs) revives his decapitated nemesis Dr Carl Hill (David Gale) to initiate the absurd and gory climax of *Re-Animator* (1985)

Re-Animator's success lay in synthesizing stylistic and thematic strains of classic and contemporary horror while hewing to the principle of social transgression inherent in the most audacious horror and comedy.

Re-Animator encapsulates more than a century of horror tradition. Its production design juxtaposes bold, saturated colors with the genre's typically shadowy, high-contrast lighting, most notably in syringes of mad doctor West's bright yellow-green reagent glowing against black backgrounds – a look that evokes both postwar science-fiction laboratories and four-color comics. Indeed, Gordon freely grants the lighting and compositional influence of artist Bernie Wrightson, who drew both color and black-and-white comics, including Warren horror magazines in the 1970s. This distinct visual approach further separated *Re-Animator* from the realist settings of low-budget slasher movies, harking back instead to Hammer's *Curse of Frankenstein*, whose subdued palette set off splashes of bilious reds and blues. Minus a few establishing shots, *Re-Animator* plays in claustrophobic interiors that recall expressionism's self-contained worlds. Still, Gordon's visual style knowingly accentuated the story's play with familiar gothic tropes, including the miraculous reagent that raises the dead, a plot device no more specific than Shelley's fleeting account of how Frankenstein built his creature or Universal's vague postulate that body parts plus lightning somehow produce artificial life. The myth's enduring interest lies in the idea and the treatment, which for *Re-Animator* means mounting increasingly grotesque displays. Indeed, *Re-Animator*'s devotion to both grisly spectacle and sardonic humor makes it one of the truest cinematic expressions of the Grand Guignol aesthetic.

Re-Animator concerns Herbert West (Jeffrey Combs), a medical student who discovers a reagent that can restore life to the dead. His experiments lead him to Dr Carl Hill (David Gale), a senior researcher he believes stole the work of West's late mentor. Fellow-intern Dan Cain (Bruce Abbott) takes West as a roommate against the wishes of his girlfriend, Meg Halsey (Barbara Crampton), daughter of the college Dean (Robert Sampson). West draws Dan into his work and in the hospital morgue they revive a corpse that goes berserk. Coming to investigate, Dean Halsey is killed by the thing, then also reanimated in a catatonic state. Intending to steal the formula, Dr Hill tries to blackmail West, who instead beheads him with a shovel. West then injects Hill's head, which returns to life . . . conscious and talking! A wild climax ensues in the morgue after Dr Hill, somehow coordinating his separated head and body, kidnaps Meg. West and Dan stop the beheaded Hill in the midst of a bizarre rape attempt on Meg but the evil doctor uses the reagent to make a dozen corpses rise up to attack them. In the mêlée, West and Hill are killed and Meg mortally injured. After she dies, Dan administers the reagent. We hear her screams as the screen fades to black.

The script was derived from a finely plotted if grim novella by H. P. Lovecraft (1890–1937) called "Herbert West – Reanimator," serialized in a pulp magazine in 1922, which Gordon read while searching for a horror project that could propel him from a directing post with Chicago's experimental Organic Theater to Hollywood. Lovecraft's writing for pulps like *Weird Tales* in the 1920s and 1930s greatly influenced the postwar generation of horror fans and writers including Robert Bloch and Stephen King. He is best known for a series of stories including *The Dunwich Horror* grouped as "The Cthulhu mythos," set around the fictional New England town of Arkham, a dark Yoknapatawpha where an ancient race of malevolent gods threaten to erupt in the modern world. But where many Lovecraft stories conjure a bleak atmosphere with an undercurrent of sexual dread, Gordon's *Re-Animator* would flaunt sexuality and gore. This was not a radical revision, since in Lovecraft's retelling of *Frankenstein* an obsessive doctor's aim to raise the dead succeeds only too well when the experiments empty an ancient cemetery and a horde of revitalized corpses tears him apart. Yet on film, *Re-Animator* joins those versions of the myth that expose its camp undertones such as *Flesh for Frankenstein* (1973) or *The Rocky Horror Picture Show* (1975), carefully perching between the astonishing physical grossness of the former and the ribaldry of the latter.

Comedic takes on horror are sometimes condescending in a shallow way that does little justice to the power of the form. The most successful examples from *Abbott and Costello Meet Frankenstein* (1948) to *Shaun of the Dead* (2004) work at the serious business of comedy foremost and seldom belittle the genre itself. Such movies also shrewdly decline to mix laughs and genuine fright as the attempt usually flounders on issues of audience identification and sympathy: We need to empathize with the victims in horror while comedy requires some emotional distance for us to laugh at the misery or pratfalls suffered by hapless characters. *The Evil Dead* trilogy and Peter Jackson's *Dead Alive/Braindead* (1992) are closer to *Re-Animator* in their relish of splatter effects, yet all might be termed slapstick horror for their celebration of violent knockabout that also avoids emotional engagement with the victims. *Re-Animator*'s sustained commitment to frighten initially adds comedy obliquely; nervous laughter arises from psychological discomfort, as when West hurriedly arms himself with a croquet mallet while searching for the reanimated cat in his dark basement laboratory. Even with the unseen cat's defiant shrieks echoing on the soundtrack, we wince at the thought of him smashing the animal with a children's toy. Susan Sontag argued that "the essence of camp is its love for the unnatural; of artifice and exaggeration," a definition easily encompassing the plot and treatment of *Re-Animator*, which revels in its own excesses.[2] Still, the movie's early scenes balance emotional identification and detachment until West's decapitation of Dr Hill, from which point ludicrous episodes of mayhem prevail.

Re-Animator's opening promises a fairly conventional genre experience. Screams coming from a locked room of a Swiss medical institute summon officials to find West injecting a serum into prostrate Dr Gruber, whose violent reactions include bulging eyes that ooze and spray blood as he collapses. That this gruesome scene transpires before several shocked witnesses – policemen, nurse, school administrator, representatives of social order all – establishes the genre's typical break from "normality." But Gordon has not set all the terms of the story. When the nurse charges that West killed Gruber, a closeup accentuates light glinting on his glasses and wide eyes, as he emphatically responds, "No . . . I gave him *life!*" evoking Colin Clive's passionate Dr Frankenstein. Immediately after, the credits steer the movie in a self-conscious direction as a new yet unmistakable arrangement of Bernard Herrmann's pulsing opening theme for *Psycho* plays over a series of anatomical diagrams in vivid hues of blue, yellow, and violet, gliding and dissolving imagery that recalls the eerily abstract credit sequence of *Vertigo*. These Hitchcock allusions serve as a wry distancing device that reiterates the sense of genre history evoked by West the mad scientist, and hint at a witty undercurrent.

The movie indeed but hints at humor for the next 20 minutes as Gordon smoothly introduces the other major characters and establishes a charnel-house atmosphere through examination and dissection of cadavers in the medical school, scenes that look gruesomely authentic thanks to the director's research with pathologists in city morgues in Chicago and Los Angeles. Dan Cain delivers a corpse to the morgue where a number of bloated or mutilated bodies lie partly exposed under sheets or wrapped in plastic. Finishing this grim task, he meets Dr Hill working on the head of a cadaver, including a cringe-inducing closeup of a cotton swab probing deeply into a hole in its temple. Meg's introduction and a brief sex scene, by now a genre convention yet one that followed the alternation of violence and sex programmed by the Grand Guignol, precede West's classroom confrontation with Hill amidst a more graphic clinical dissection. Hill demonstrates removal of the brain, peeling back a cadaver's hair and scalp to expose the skull – a process that makes his students squirm, all except icy Herbert West, who sits unmoved, expressing contempt by snapping pencils in odd rebuttal to Hill's lecture on the 12-minute limit of brain death. The mutual hostility between the pair sets up the genre's common revenge scenario, though we have no idea the lengths to which each will go in baroque acts of annihilation against the other. Still, *Re-Animator* proceeds with straightforward intentions to shock, a tack it will never entirely abandon.

Anyone who sees *Re-Animator* once remembers two things: the freakish attack on Meg and Jeffrey Combs' hilarious portrayal of Herbert West.[3] Thin and bespectacled, Combs conforms to Lovecraft's description, though he skillfully plays against a boyish face with a jaw carefully set below intense, darting eyes, expressions of a visionary both disciplined and impatient. A deep voice and clipped delivery paint West as a doctor whose yearning to overcome human mortality stands beside a barely concealed disdain for those – most – he considers his intellectual inferiors. Creepy West serves as the monster in the movie's first half, the pre-occupied, condescending medico with empty smile who interrupts Dan and Meg's lovemaking, virtually forces his way into the house, and eagerly claims the basement for undisclosed work, typical marks of the dangerous dreamer. Yet the actor's physical preparation frames his deadpan delivery throughout increasingly absurd situations. When Dan protests that West could have left a note before anguished Meg found her cat frozen in his mini-refrigerator, his forceful retort lends weight to his protestations of innocence: "And what would a note have said, Dan? 'Cat dead – details later'?" Combs' dry yet engaging performance is crucial because we have to like West, or least be intrigued just a little so Dr Hill can gradually emerge as the true and greater monster.

The founders of the Grand Guignol chose the name to emphasize that its plays would manipulate actors like virtual "puppets," transforming human beings into toys through meticulous rehearsal and technical effects that seemingly subjected real bodies to mortal slapstick as in *The Man Who Killed Death* (1928), which anticipated *Re-Animator* with a tale about the head of a guillotined convict kept alive by scientific apparatus. The derivation of the name suggested too that on this stage story logic would often be secondary to the execution of violent shocks. The Grand Guignol viewed human nature pessimistically, emphasizing its cruelty, lust, and often fatal pettiness. Despite West's menace in the early scenes, he is overshadowed by Dr Hill, who has less medical talent but deeper pits of cynicism. Like Frankenstein, West sublimates all sexual urges through his work, regarding Hill's ardor for Meg as final proof of his rival's shallowness. Hill's venality, undisguised by a refined manner, is caught by West's sneering putdown when he interrupts the rape of Meg: "You steal the secret of life and death and here you are trysting with a bubble-headed co-ed!" Still, *Re-Animator* upholds the Grand Guignol's amoral, spare-no-one principle in the fate of Dean Halsey, a bit grouchy but surely undeserving of being bashed and chewed by a reanimated corpse, lobotomized, and finally torn to pieces by other zombies. The same for the lovey, guileless couple Dan and Meg who seem only slightly less helpless than Brad and Janet of *The Rocky Horror Picture Show*. They too will suffer or die in the climax, in contrast to the survival of those, like them, celebrated in classic-style horror films.

Direction and performance provide opportunities to laugh, as Stuart Gordon suggested, but humor often abuts atrocious gore. Dr Hill's classroom dissection introduces the bone saw, a medical instrument that will become a hideous comic prop when West uses it to re-kill the corpse he and Dan revive in the morgue. Amidst the frenzied thing's bloody assault of Dean Halsey, including biting off his fingers, a rack focus reveals West poised with the tool behind his dumbstruck friend, sighing, "Dan – Look out," as he steps up to grind the whining saw through the corpse's torso with the disdain one might reserve for squashing a bug. This gory effect will actually be topped several times, perhaps most hideously when West decapitates Dr Hill with a shovel, knocking him down then grinding the blade into the man's throat in closeup, accompanied by awful crunching and gurgling sounds. Another close up of blood-spattered West angrily proclaiming, "Plagiarist!" precedes a shot of the head rolling away from the twitching body, a joke not quite cathartic given the explicitness of the atrocity. Yet the scene moves confidently in this new direction when West uses a letter spike to steady Dr Hill's head in a tray. His sudden inspiration to test the reagent, arrived at by Combs with a mix of scientific curiosity and not a little sadism, turns fully comic when Hill's severed head indeed revives and croaks out, "You . . . bastard!" as West dutifully records the words in his laboratory journal. One admires the deft progression from a standard horror tale to splatter movie to inspired black comedy. After this, we are ready to accept and enjoy the absurdity of Hill's headless body shuffling up to seize West and knock him unconscious, as it promises an even more extravagant finale.[4]

In his provocative study *Laughing, Screaming: Modern Hollywood Horror and Comedy*, William Paul argues that the common proximity of these two seemingly disparate emotional responses, a phenomenon noted by Freud and others, marks the outward physiological reactions to experiences that momentarily overwhelm our rational faculties. "The fun of horror films follows the fun of the fun house by creating an odd pleasure in disorientation, a challenge to the participant's sense of mastery . . . Fun house pleasure is not found solely in its terrors, and I think the same must be said of horror movies."[5] Paul argues that the most trangressive horror and comedy effects occur in the "festive" experience of an audience taking in the spectacle together, enjoying a collective release from social strictures and conventions, and reveling in recognition of truths otherwise denied or suppressed. (Anyone who feels disappointment after watching a recommended comedy alone on home video is likely to experience the truth of this point negatively, by lack of engagement. Horror films viewed alone, however, tend to remain unnerving for obvious reasons.) *Re-Animator* follows a structure of shock and dry joke from Herbert West, to greater gore and drier response that builds to the moment of unhinged gross-out comedy when Dr Hill's severed head attempts to perform cunnilingus on Meg, bound nude and spreadeagled on an operating table – a moment that never fails to unleash howls, whoops, groans, and vocal expressions of all kinds from most any audience.

Viewers may be too overwhelmed by the manifest offensiveness of the image to realize its wicked visual pun, one commiserate with exploitation horror's roots in the grimly ironic and often liberating comedy of the lowly and oppressed. At a time when horror films were already under fire for violence against women this was a bold move, though the scene challenges simple emotional reactions as much as critical reductions. One can only compare it to such extraordinary and excessive images as the eyeball slicing in *Un Chien andalou* (1929) or Divine's pursuit of the defecating dog in *Pink Flamingoes* (1972) for sheer visceral punch and intellectual incomprehension. Yet the scene's patent absurdity separates it from emotionally intense screen rapes, such as the excruciating torture of the girls in *Last House on the Left* or Sally's ordeal in *The Texas Chain Saw Massacre*. Gordon keeps the camera back far enough to prove Chaplin's dictum that the long shot is for comedy, the closeup for tragedy; while with only whimpers and screams, Barbara Crampton's fearless performance registers the victim's terror and revulsion while maintaining the slightly exaggerated edge that marks the performances of Combs and Gale throughout. Still, *Re-Animator*'s steady escalation of gory slapstick permits laughter here that recognizes the forces of Eros and literal carnality extended to the last degree. The promotional line for *Bram Stoker's Dracula* (1992) conventionally assured us that "Love never dies." *Re-Animator* shows that lust doesn't either, evoking the insatiable, super-heated desire of pornographic fantasy in one of the strangest clashes of genres and tones in a commercial movie.

West's appearance briefly restores the movie's more familiar comic tone when he again confronts his nemesis with sharp one-liners ("You'll never get credit for my discovery. Who's going to believe a talking head? Get a job in a sideshow!"). The resumption of West and Hill's glaring antagonism, even in this now wholly bizarre state, allows the audience to recover before the climax, which erupts when Dr Hill directs the corpses to arise and attack. West's sideshow reference evokes the horror film's lineage from *The Cabinet of Dr. Caligari*, but *Re-Animator*'s finale emphasizes the "show" foremost. Indeed, a feel of the movie musical appears when on Dr Hill's silent command the mangled bodies sit up in unison as if on cue. The moment recalls another horror picture show, Michael Jackson's influential music video for "Thriller" (1983), where the singer and a troupe of the living dead get up and get down. Gordon mounts a frenzy of blood and guts that epitomizes 1980s splatter alongside the fiery cataclysm that traditionally engulfs the monster and its domain from the earliest gothic literature forward.

Re-Animator was released by Charles and Albert Band's Empire Pictures, an exploitation enterprise that, like AIP in previous decades, turned out a string of inventive horror and science fiction movies (*Ghoulies* [1985], *Trancers* [1985], *Puppet Master* [1989], etc.) on a shoestring. As AIP's regular director Roger Corman had shown, the trick to effective exploitation filmmaking lay not only in devising an outrageous concept but also in getting most of a modest budget up on the screen. Gordon and producer Brian Yuzna managed the limited resources for makeup and special effects to make only a handful of zombie extras seem like an overwhelming force. Simple devices like quick cutting, flashing strobes, and fog machines energize glimpses of the naked things with assorted wounds, burns, and gaping surgical openings that surround the protagonists. Makeup effects, like one zombie sent to the morgue with tubes and lines still attached to his body, prove genuinely gruesome even as sight gags continue. The bored security guard, not too concerned about the commotion inside the morgue until Hill's headless body staggers out, sticks around to see the doctor's crushed, bloody head fly into the hallway and splat against the wall. The final comic shock follows West's double injection of reagent into Hill's body that bursts its chest and transforms the intestines into thrashing tentacles that grasp and squeeze West like a bulbous python, a weirdly phallic yet anal image that culminates *Re-Animator*'s absurdist dance of gore and burlesque.

Even so, the bloody final episode of Dan hacking off the arm of a charred corpse with an ax as it strangles Meg maintains the quickening pace with a repeat of Dan's introduction in the emergency room where he and a team work in vain to resuscitate her. When Dan tries the reagent, the screen fades to black except for the green fluid disappearing under the syringe's plunger, an effect reminiscent of cartoon animation that, with the accompanying return of the *Psycho* theme and Meg's final screams, ring down the curtain. Closing with an implicit opening to further terrors, the coda upholds the grim, unresolved endings of contemporary horror, by this time virtually a genre convention. Still, the shock show of outrageous humor and ghastly effects in the climax finally turn *Re-Animator* away from too bleak a feeling after all. On the contrary, the aesthetic of the Grand Guignol, of flailing human "puppets" and grotesquely inventive effects overlaid with an amoral dedication to punishment for all conveys the fun-house effect William Paul describes; or perhaps a sense of the frightening, exhilarating, even nauseating feel of another carnival staple, the roller-coaster. Indeed, *Re-Animator* offers one of the surest examples of the "ride" critics too frequently claim for bloated action movies whose thrills often encompass no more than rapid cuts and a booming soundtrack. The history of the horror genre shows it can encompass a broad range of tones while maintaining the central drive to frighten and disturb. *Re-Animator* demonstrates that whatever style a horror movie adopts, witnessing the filmmakers' complete dedication to go to extremes – psychologically, stylistically, thematically – remains one of the genuine pleasures of the form.

CHAPTER 12

DEMON LOVER: *BRAM STOKER'S DRACULA* (1992)

Throughout its history, the horror genre has largely consisted of low- to medium-budget movies produced at the margins of the industry where extravagant production values and big stars were rarely found. For many critics and fans, however, this has amounted to a strength rather than a drawback as horror's low status permits formal and ideological challenges to the conservative status quo, celebrating alternatives to narrowly defined identities; while indirectly exposing staid or corrupt social values. Expensive horror movies may or may not win commercial success but are likely to divide critical and fan opinion in substituting middlebrow "seriousness" for social transgression. *The Exorcist*'s huge popular success came by filling a polished, major studio production with the gross-out effects of exploitation movies. While picketed and denounced by the religious right, its mostly negative reviews in the mainstream press took a condescending tone that attacked the poor taste and gullibility of the audience. Kubrick's *The Shining* (1980) drew a similarly mixed response. Prestige horror remains a risky undertaking aesthetically, commercially, critically. So it was with Francis Ford Coppola's opulent production of *Bram Stoker's Dracula* (1992), a solid hit that won three Academy Awards, yet met much resistance from genre aficionados. However, Coppola's version combines

FIGURE 20 Androgynous and orientalist motifs: Gary Oldman's introduction as the shape-shifting Count in *Bram Stoker's Dracula* (1992, Columbia). *Producer and Director:* Francis Ford Coppola

lush studio-era production design, vintage special effects techniques, and a cast of major stars to present *Dracula* as a gothic romance epic, returning in this sense to the genre's origins. Its increasingly explicit Christ allegory illuminates rarely treated facets of the vampire myth and other implications of Stoker's character in ways both provocative and confused.

In 1897, Stoker's novel conventionalized the popular definition of what a vampire is and does. Indeed, the vampire's omnipresence in twentieth-century popular culture is less an issue of evolution than of variation on this model. Although 1920s theatrical versions and Bela Lugosi's indelible 1931 film portrayal reinforced aspects of Stoker's tale, the story proved flexible enough for significant changes, including the almost alien monster of Murnau's *Nosferatu* (1922), a resilient female vampire-hunter in Columbia's wartime potboiler *Return of the Vampire* (1943), and a more frankly sexual and predatory Dracula in Hammer's 1958–72 series starring Christopher Lee. Despite the title, Coppola's film, like most adaptations follows Stoker's plot in some aspects, certainly more closely than most, while diverging greatly from it in others. Yet it is precisely in these original variants, primarily the fifteenth-century prolog and its subsequent redirection of Stoker's scenes, that its contemporary pertinence lays. *Bram Stoker's Dracula* typifies the ambivalent or even sympathetic portrayal of the vampire common in the past

20 years, a motif that permits audience indulgence in his supernatural powers, particularly the seeming sexual irresistibility of the undead. Yet the film's fidelity to Stoker's late Victorian outlook on gender tends to nullify the image of the monster as social and sexual radical that had animated the genre since the late 1960s. As interpreted by perhaps the most acclaimed Hollywood director of his generation, *Bram Stoker's Dracula* cautiously circumscribed the vampire as both aggrieved rebel and traditional threat.

The project originated in the late 1970s in the desire of screenwriter James V. Hart to produce a faithful adaptation of the novel. He was, however, affected by the 1977 Broadway revival starring Frank Langella that made the Count a sexy, appealing lover, and in John Badham's revisionist 1979 screen version, ultimately triumphant over Dr Van Helsing. The decade also saw growing popular awareness of the historical figure who had partly influenced Stoker, a fifteenth-century Romanian prince, Vlad Tepes, dubbed Vlad the Impaler. Information on Vlad cataloged by Leonard Wolf as well as Radu Florescu and Raymond T. McNally's biographical research, including photos of the Prince's ruined castle in Transylvania, ironically lent greater credence to Stoker's fictional creation.[1] Indeed, Hart and Wolf collaborated for several years trying to develop a screenplay that drew on Vlad Tepes and other aspects of vampire lore.[2] Stoker's biographers give less weight to the Vlad connection, emphasizing the literary influences of John Polidori's *The Vampyre* (1819) and J. Sheridan Le Fanu's lesbian-tinged vampire novel *Carmilla* (1872) as well as the Count's resemblance to Henry Irving, the foremost Shakespearean actor of his day, founder of London's acclaimed Royal Lyceum Theater, and the man for whom Bram Stoker worked as theater manager and assistant for many years. All of these elements would appear in the 1992 adaptation, along with allusions to *Nosferatu* and Carl Theodor Dreyer's *Vampyre* (1932). Structurally, the plot recalled Universal's *The Mummy* (1932) about an ancient Egyptian priest seeking his reincarnated love in modern times, itself a close variation of the Lugosi *Dracula*. Francis Ford Coppola's *Bram Stoker's Dracula*, screenplay by James V. Hart, had numerous authors befitting a character whose prevalence had been expanding for nearly a century.

Hart came to the novel in his late twenties and was struck by its many characters and plot elements never found in movie versions. This includes the full complement of four young male heroes who fight Dracula under Dr Van Helsing's leadership and the return to Transylvania at the end, which climaxes with what Coppola rightly terms "an enormous John Ford shootout" subsequently filmed with particular reference to *Stagecoach* (1939).[3] Nonetheless, the movie's framing story with Gary Oldman's Christian knight Prince Vlad battling Moslem invasion, the suicide of his wife Elisabeta (Winona Ryder) upon false news of his death, and the Prince's denunciation of God that seemingly wills his transformation introduced elements unknown to Stoker.[4] Sold with the line "Love never dies," the film's romance between Dracula and Mina (Ryder) in 1897 partly shifted to concerns of the woman's picture, making the female characters more prominent and the story's gender dynamics more explicit if no less problematic. The romance plot was also a new solution for the need in earlier adaptations to keep more of Dracula in the story. Theatrical and film versions usually condensed the novel's convoluted plot and multiple locations for matters of narrative and budgetary economy, in the process losing suggestive aspects of the tale. David Pirie notes that in the 1960s, Hammer settled on the opposite strategy, keeping Christopher Lee's Count off screen for long stretches, concentrating instead on the vampire's effect on the Victorian family and society, especially the women.[5] Yet Hammer's approach was really Stoker's originally. The Coppola/Hart method gave Dracula ample screen time and made him a more complex character, preserving the vampire's larger social impact while showcasing settings and special effects that foreground the history of cinema itself. *Bram Stoker's Dracula* is a love story as well as oblique commentary on the character's cultural evolution.

Coppola's first feature after attending the UCLA film school was the low-budget chiller *Dementia 13* (1963), made for AIP under the tutelage of Roger Corman, a bloody, post-*Psycho* exploitation of ax murders and family breakdown in an Irish castle whose own inventive prolog indicated a director of promise. Coppola's subsequent place as the foremost "movie brat" director of the 1970s was secured from manipulation of the traditions and genres of the studio era. From its title forward, *Bram Stoker's Dracula* declares it is as much involved with the means of telling a familiar story as with the plot itself. With Anthony Hopkins narrating and ominous score overlaid, Vlad's clash with the Turks emphasizes stylization of lighting, sets, and costumes rather than spectacle. Prince Vlad's distinctive armor, dark red and striated as if exposing the muscle structure beneath the skin of a brawny hero, also makes him seem nearly cadaverous at the outset; while his helmet resembles the head of a horned devil or a wolf, the latter subsequently depicted as Dracula's alter ego. The rich costumes and painterly lighting often recall a stage production, but Coppola never succumbs to the veritable staginess that hamstrung Universal's *Dracula*. Along with moving camera and crisp editing, the prolog renders the battle via images of backlit warriors in the foreground and obvious cutout silhouettes of troops and banners in the background that may recall the flatness of medieval art but more directly emulates the abstraction of combat in Orson Welles' expressionist *Chimes at Midnight* (1966). Upon Dracula's appearance in 1897, this same diorama-like depiction of the battle with shadow puppets reappears as purely representational illusion observed by modern Londoners in an amusement arcade, one that also includes exhibition of the Cinematograph, slyly noting that even at the moment of the novel's publication, the legend of Dracula would be perpetuated by this modern technology.

The prolog begins with the fall of Constantinople, rendered with a canted view of smoke and flames behind the dome of Hagia Sophia and a slow-motion shot of its Greek cross crashing to the pavement below. The operant color of lighting and flames is deep red, the film's major chromatic motif that initiates its many uses and symbols of blood. Coppola's montage also includes the horn-like shadow of the Moslem crescent advancing across a map of southern Europe. Although I argue the film is ultimately not heavily invested in the xenophobia that later critics have found in the novel, unquestionably once Vlad the Christian warrior becomes Dracula the vampire his threat is marked through orientalizing imagery that extends to the Far East in the long red kimono and Kabuki hairstyle worn in his modern introduction. (As Keanu Reeves' Jonathan Harker travels by train into Transylvania, overseen by Dracula's huge leering eyes in the blood-orange sky, he writes in his journal, "The impression I had was that we were leaving the West and entering the East.") Though defeating the Turks but then renouncing his faith, the undead Vlad becomes a more insidious incarnation of Eastern menace. In so forcefully amplifying this subtext of the novel, the movie invites a reading in terms not of late Victorian England but of late twentieth-century America. Its debut soon after the 1990–1 Gulf War may suggest a reactionary anti-Islamic angle on the clash between Western characters – including a Texas cowboy – and the evil undead.[6] Without denying the validity of such interpretations of the novel or film in terms of racial and/or international conflict, we must emphasize that these elements are generally not part of the popularized impression – or appeal – of *Dracula* in its many variants.[7] The story's macabre mix of sex and violence remains its most direct and potent attraction.

What Bram Stoker took most directly from Vlad was his honorific title rather than his nickname "The Impaler." In contemporary Romanian, *dracul* means "devil" but in the fifteenth century it also connoted "dragon," and designated Vlad's membership like that of his father in the crusading Order of the Dragon.[8] The dual impression of the historic Vlad as valiant champion and heartless tyrant is paralleled on screen, where Vlad's tenderness for Elisabeta contrasts with his savagery in battle, in a gory victory over enemies who are not simply killed but impaled on lances and left horribly wriggling, anticipating the traditional fate of the vampire. In the final segment, Vlad discovers Elisabeta's death by suicide and in his fury renounces God, stabbing the cross on the altar above her body that releases a stream of blood. When he catches some in a chalice and drinks, shouting, "The blood is the life!," this unholy communion seems to bestow the curse of the undead. Stoker wrote Dracula as an antichrist figure, absorbing much of the inverted Christian lore of vampirism that often goes unnoticed in the myth. With the same vibrant imagery, Coppola increasingly depicts Vlad not as *dracula* ("son of the devil") but as Christ, in a contradictory ending that is neither Stoker's nor that of subsequent versions, a muddled view of Vlad Dracula as dark "redeemer."

There is no particular virtue in fidelity to a literary source if an adaptation fails to engage the audience in the familiar terms of the screen. Rather than Stoker's fairly labored introduction of the modern characters, the film swiftly presents Renfield, Jonathan, and Mina, enhancing their well-known back-story with the stylistic panache of the prolog. We meet the disturbed Renfield (Tom Waits) in the asylum proclaiming allegiance to an unseen "master" in a high-angle shot enhanced by a wide-angle lens distortion in which pale blue lighting, the patient's odd garment, and the padded walls around him recall the clashing lines of *The Cabinet of Dr. Caligari*. Jonathan appears in an office receiving the assignment to meet Count Dracula and Mina gets no special introduction beyond our recognition that Winona Ryder had just played Elisabeta. But when the couple discusses their delayed marriage (a harbinger of dangerous disturbance in the classic film versions of *Frankenstein* and *Dr. Jekyll and Mr. Hyde*) and then kiss, a stream of turning peacock feathers with their unique blue/black "eye" patterns intrudes between them and the camera, suggesting they are already watched by a powerful presence. The final feathery eye lap dissolves into the opening of a railroad tunnel, the camera traveling along the tracks to convey Harker's journey. With evident awareness of the narrative pitfalls of earlier versions, the film avoids Harker's stops at country inns and foreboding encounters with nervous locals who pointlessly warn him away from the character we most want to see.

Coppola's stylization of virtually every sequence continues using narrative techniques of German silent films, especially montages of overlapping dissolves. Moreover, Harker's train is obviously a miniature model as is the Westenra family manor; while Dracula's castle, like Universal's in 1931, is a combination of model and matte paintings. Everything becomes purely an image. Stoker's use of the epistolary structure conveys the novel's plot in a series of letters and journal entries by the English characters. This profoundly literary device becomes another visual motif, superimposing images of writers, their pages, and surroundings in expressly cinematic form that turns the written words into images. The first overlapping image appears at Vlad's victory, when he calls Elisabeta's name and her face hangs in the air beside him, an appropriately ethereal ideal; when he reads her suicide note the image of her fatal plunge is superimposed over the page. Yet this cinematic translation upholds Stoker's clash between nineteenth-century rationalism and a supernatural monster. The heroes use typewriters, Dictaphones, microscopes, blood transfusions, rifles – symbols of modernity that offer little protection from, let alone explanation for, Dracula's threat. Coppola's key visual trope becomes cinema itself as a storytelling medium in ways that seem to vary audience engagement and estrangement within this dark fairy tale.[9]

The novel's early chapters describing Jonathan Harker's stay at Castle Dracula contain some of the story's most lasting images and themes. These scenes display Coppola's main debt to *Nosferatu*, though he initially improves upon Murnau, who had experimented less successfully with negative film stock and fast motion to render the phantom coach that picks up the bewildered Englishman. In Coppola's scene, all shot on a sound stage, it arrives floating on a bed of mist. The eerie coachman (traditionally Dracula in disguise), garbed with a weird headpiece to resemble a large black insect, echoes Renfield's mania for consuming bugs; his unnaturally long and powerful arms that lift Harker inside portend the vampire's shape-shifting omnipotence. Like Murnau, Coppola depicts the vampire as a strange, nonhuman creature. Where Max Schreck's Count Orlok suggests a rat-man, Gary Oldman's Dracula is a pale, androgynous crone wearing double folds of white hair on top of his head and trailing the long scarlet kimono instead of swirling an elegant black cape. Japanese-born costume designer Eiko Ishioka says of Dracula's kimono, "The enormous train was designed to undulate when he rushes about his castle, like a sea of blood," and this imagery associated with the slaughter in the prolog suggests the bloodshed he threatens to unleash again.[10]

Even so, Coppola's image of the vampire, like Murnau's, is so bizarre, one nearly laughs in both at the visitor's obliviousness to it but for the strength of arresting makeup designs and the actors' performances. *Nosferatu* contains one moment that seems intentionally funny, when a closeup of Orlok reading the legal documents is framed to emphasize his beady eyes scanning the paper. In Coppola's scenes, the only apparent humor lies in perception of an actor thoroughly enjoying a sumptuous costume and the chance to do a showy accent, relishing lines as when Dracula calls Harker "a man of good . . . taste" with a twinkle in his eye. These currents intersect when Dracula seizes the straight razor after Harker cuts himself shaving and, with a broad flourish, turns away and swiftly licks the blood off the blade, a surreptitious, slightly guilty gesture that, like the analogous moment in the Lugosi version, shows recognizable human weakness in the supernatural creature. The outward appearance of physical frailty as well as gentility evaporates when Dracula perceives that Harker is laughing at the story of his ancestors and suddenly strides across the floor whipping his sword about, the berserker warrior still housed within the decadent frame.

From Dreyer's *Vampyre*, less a tale of the undead than a series of hallucinatory visions, Coppola took the idea of Dracula's malevolent shadow that moves independently of his body, striking menacing poses behind Harker that reveal the gracious host's darker intentions. The motif fits well for this telling in which Dracula's own divided self is a central theme. Moreover, these scenes intimate the vampire's bisexual appeal, a trope that appears in many variations of the myth. Dracula's kimono and distinctive coiffure carry further relevance here if we recall that male actors traditionally play female roles in the Kabuki. Oldman's desiccated Dracula dominates Harker with a combination of seduction and steely menace. Just as the creature's shadow defies the laws of physics, the vampire defies conventional codes of sexual propriety, though this version will work foremost to reunite the traditional heterosexual couple. Dracula's play with Harker ends upon his stricken recognition of Elisabeta in the oval portrait of Mina, another point taken from Murnau, not the novel.

Stoker's most sexually charged episode, previously filmed with utmost restraint, depicts Jonathan Harker's semi-helpless consort with Dracula's vampire brides, another bravura staging by Coppola in a scene both erotic and frightening, exactly as the novelist intended.[11] The blood orgy is preceded by Jonathan's view of the long shadows of three wolves just outside the window; and after he watches Dracula crawling down the vertical face of an outside wall, three rats similarly defy gravity on a beam overhead as Jonathan explores the castle. The female trio that appears are implicitly these wolves and rats, hardly an appetizing endorsement of unconventional sexuality. Still, in the montage of sensuous female forms literally rising out of the undulating covers of a huge bed to fall on Harker with bare breasts and bared teeth one is reminded of Hollywood's original master of having it both ways, Cecil B. DeMille, who in the silent era staged daring vistas of ancient decadence and then quickly countered with less thrilling – or persuasive – moral condemnation. Jonathan admits in the novel he was perversely thrilled by the prospect of being ravaged by the women, an erotic surrender diminished here by the assurance of eternal love in Dracula's discovery of his long-lost wife.

The scene might not rise above soft-core porn without including an element rarely depicted in its entirety. Dracula's angry intrusion prompts quick shots of the brides scuttling away in accelerated reverse motion, including one in which two actresses were lashed together to suggest a weird, awkward spider; or more directly to seem as if one woman is being birthed from between the legs of another. This freakish image anticipates Dracula's offer of consolation, a bag containing a squirming baby which the weird sisters seize with relish, shocking the delirious Harker. The scene displays the most direct imagery of the vampire's threat to the normative values of monogamy and family that classic-style horror labors to destroy: Jonathan and the brides enjoy a wanton sexual feast that turns literally carnal when, instead of creating a baby to nurture, they kill it and drink its blood. The scene's centrality is underscored by its mirror-opposite in England when Van Helsing (Anthony Hopkins) and three virile young men ambush the undead Lucy Westenra (Sadie Frost) and bloodily destroy her after she returns to her crypt carrying a small child she intends to devour, the reversal of the earlier scene literally rendered by shooting Lucy in reverse motion moving back into her coffin to seemingly fall asleep as they surround her. In the novel's coda, Stoker conventionally resolves this theme when, seven years after Dracula's destruction, Van Helsing, Jonathan, and Mina return to Transylvania with their child, a boy christened with the names of all the vampire hunters. That this scene does not appear in the movie indicates how the new romance plot alters and somewhat confuses Stoker's tale.

As in the novel, Dracula's appearance in London intrudes upon – and here destroys – the ongoing marriage plans of the two female characters, Lucy and Mina. Though Mina is betrothed to Jonathan at the beginning, Lucy is introduced as a sexually adventurous rich girl manipulating three eager suitors, Dr Jack Seward (Richard E. Grant), nobleman Arthur Holmwood (Cary Elwes), and the American millionaire Quincey Morris (Bill Campbell), who represent socially advantageous matches. Lucy's choice to become Lady Holmwood verifies Stoker's allegiance to traditional social hierarchy though the rapacious vampire will becomes her actual mate. Because here Dracula's attention is fixed on Mina, his ultimate destruction of Lucy is portrayed as enraged vengeance for Mina's departure to care for the recovering Jonathan in Europe. Using a jerky, intermittent shooting style, Coppola conveys Dracula's lupine point of view with a traveling shot that races across the ground as flowers wither and crawling beetles and toads evoke a creature both natural and fantastic that easily blows past Lucy's male defenders. In a sequence reminiscent of the climax of *The Godfather*, Coppola intercuts Jonathan and Mina's Orthodox wedding ceremony with Dracula's murder of Lucy in which he changes between a wolf-man form to the wizened figure we first met, to an actual wolf that rapes and tears her to death. Dracula threatens social, sexual, and natural orders alike.

Following the first attack on Lucy where Dracula appears as the snarling wolf-man, Renfield proclaims from his cell, "Master . . . I have worshipped you!" then as the camera glides over the crates of earth at Carfax Abbey, Van Helsing's voice-over explains that "contrary to some beliefs," that is, as in most movies, vampires can walk about in daylight though their powers are weakened. At this, a crate bursts apart and Gary Oldman appears as a young man, bare-chested, auburn tresses hanging at his shoulders, looking like the resurrected Christ. For those coming to see a romantic fantasy perhaps more than a horror film as such, Dracula's encounter with Mina ranks as the film's most lyrical episode. Indeed, seemingly reborn by feeding on Lucy's blood, the dapper Prince Vlad walks the streets with a sense of wonder rather than malevolence. Coppola conveys his awe with another well chosen device, initially shooting the street with a hand-cranked Pathé box camera, a close relative of the Cinematograph, adding the sound of its whirring mechanism to a slightly grainy image that emphasizes the kinship of Dracula, by some accounts the character that has appeared the most often in any movie, and cinema itself. Within this self-consciously mystical aura he spies Mina. Moreover, as Prince Vlad rediscovers his wife, composer Wojciech Kilar followed the example of Bernard Herrmann's score for *Vertigo* (1958), quoting the lush chords and melodic lines of the "Liebestod" (love-death) theme from Wagner's *Tristan and Isolde* with its ache of lost and irrecoverable love.[12] The juxtaposition of Dracula/Vlad's savaging of Lucy and his rapturous discovery of

Mina/Elisabeta, the Christ imagery in between, epitomizes the movie's contradictory themes and effects.

The rediscovery scene's multiple allusions include a sandwich board advertising Henry Irving's production of *Hamlet* at the Lyceum Theater and, within the large tent housing the Cinematograph exhibition, the shadow-puppet tableau from the prolog, both pointing to the novel's varied origins. Here Vlad enthralls and frightens Mina in a visually complicated series of shots in which the couple sits talking in the foreground while behind them, mirrors reflect multiple images of spectators watching the Cinematograph projection. The newly shot but historically plausible film excerpts we glimpse recall the story's earlier scenes. One is a trick film about a man's fantasy of cavorting with two nubile women on his lap, who then transform into his disinterested wife. This evokes Jonathan's encounter with the vampire brides and portends the possible result of his eventual union with Mina, both parties frustrated and disappointed after encounters with enthralling creatures of psychological and cinematic fantasy. Within this complex arrangement of images, illusions, and planes of action, the wolf escaped from the zoo intrudes upon the love scene, casting multiple reflections in the mirrors and exposing the inner being of a creature who himself casts no reflection. The wolf walks in front of screen images of a nude woman simply displaying her body for the camera, recalling the savage attacks on Lucy. The story's fantasy of undying romantic love stands beside these allusions to its darker truths and possibilities.

This basic contradiction recurs in the multiple uses of Anthony Hopkins, initially playing the Orthodox priest who condemns Elisabeta to perdition after her suicide, as well as the prolog's assured narrator and the troubled voice of the captain of the ship that carries Dracula to England, a division of persona and authority that also complicates our response. Similar to other versions, Dr Van Helsing's introduction begins with microscope slides of blood cells to indicate his dedication to rational science as well as a willingness to look very closely at things that escape the naked eye. Such scenes may involve the study of dangerous flora (the Venus Flytrap in *Nosferatu*) or deformed blood cells that convey the notion of vampirism as a disease to be eradicated, here specifically aligned with syphilis and other sexually transmitted diseases.[13] Yet where the wise professor is usually a father figure, there is more than a touch of sadism in this Van Helsing, one who seemingly enjoys tormenting Dr Seward about decapitating Lucy as mourners regard her coffin; or nonchalantly describing Lucy's gory destruction over dinner then embarrassing Jonathan by discussing his "infidelities" with the brides in front of Mina. The emotional ambivalence generated by this less than saintly characterization accrues from Anthony Hopkins' recent tour de force in *The Silence of the Lambs* (1991) as the viciously droll Dr Hannibal Lecter, virtually a vampire himself, conscienceless, elegant, and fascinating. A tale of a tragic Dracula and a mad Van Helsing points up the horror genre's often uncertain play with both fear and identification with the monster and his attacks on the social and psychosexual order.

The climax of *Bram Stoker's Dracula* not surprisingly presents the author's scenes and their reinterpretation. Mina is now turning into a vampire after she drank Dracula's blood from a gash on his chest and Van Helsing's group races back to Transylvania to destroy him and save her. We finally see the horseback chase that, because never represented in earlier Dracula movies, still seems strangely out of place, well-staged riding and shooting stunts from millions of B Westerns filmed on a sound stage saturated in gothic gloom. At the castle the battle becomes a sword fight between the Englishmen and Dracula's gypsy servants, inverting the prolog with Dracula's forces defeated. Yet the new elements hardly leave us with a sense of triumph. Turning ancient again, Dracula is slashed and stabbed by Jonathan Harker and Quincey Morris and retreats with Mina to the altar where we first met Vlad and Elisabeta, only this time he lays dying as she mourns. Mina's willingness to "free him" by destroying the vampire scatters the story's themes in all directions, most unsatisfying. The dying Dracula speaks Christ's words on the cross, "Where is my God? He has forsaken me" and "It is finished," yet in the film's terms it was Vlad who renounced God. Still, a heavenly ray of light falls on him and transforms him back into the young Vlad, implicitly "saved" in the afterlife.

According to James V. Hart, the movie had two disastrous previews that necessitated some revision. The ending was partly reshot to show Mina not only pushing the knife through Dracula's heart but then pulling it to cut off his head, granting him a normal human death as had been established with the destruction of the other vampires. This ending, with Mina casting her glance upward at the painting above that in the film's final shot depicts Prince Vlad and Elisabeta transcendently reunited, substituted for a final sequence in which Mina went back outside and embraced Jonathan.[14] Audiences evidently rejected this ending because the love story had concentrated all energy on Vlad and Mina. Indeed, Jonathan Harker is often extraneous in *Dracula* adaptations. In the Lugosi version, he matters so little that we follow Renfield

(Dwight Frye) to Transylvania and Harker (David Manners) is around simply to signal the classic genre finale, carrying Mina (Helen Chandler) up from the bowels of Carfax Abbey into the sunlight after Dracula's destruction. This speaks again to the primary appeal of the monster.

As we know Vlad's wife only as filtered through the sensibility of the modern Mina, Elisabeta remains an impossible ideal. Yet given the centrality of the romance plot, we can understand why preview audiences did not want to see her return to the earnest but dull Jonathan, Stoker's image of the "normal" restored. The intensity of the passion, romance, and one must be certain, sex in her encounters with Vlad/Dracula would make the conventional resolution feel forced and emotionally false. Yet as the gash in the cross on the altar seals itself and Dracula becomes human again, Mina claims that "There in the presence of God, I understood how my love [i.e. Dracula] could save us from the powers of darkness," a particularly obscure line that might also have been omitted in the re-editing, for Dracula now inexplicably seems to become Christ himself, not Stoker's antichrist figure. We are left finally with Coppola's vivid reinterpretations of the familiar story, especially Gary Oldman's Dracula as the androgynous relic, in scenes that reiterate its appeal in terms both knowing and elusive. Love in fact, often dies; Dracula does not.

CHAPTER 13

AFTERWORD:
OUR HAUNTED
HOUSES

The quotation from *Grand Guignol* playwright André de Lorde with which we began the survey of horror-genre history noted the universal experience of fear as an emotion and the variant shapes it has assumed culturally and historically. Indeed, particular phases of the horror film have drawn from the prevalent anxieties of the times that produced them. However, to say that horror films may reflect certain ideals, values, and fears of a period is not to suggest a simple or direct correlation between the form and content of a particular movie and an easily discerned set of predominant social feelings. To guess about the collective mood of millions risks claiming far too much for the predictive quality or relevance of particular mass-entertainment texts, each one only a small part of the deluge of mass-mediated messages and experiences with which people are drenched in the postmodern epoch. With these caveats in mind, we will end this survey of the American horror film with some observations about the cinema of the fantastic around the millennium, a period dominated by mutual celebration of, and anxiety about advanced, especially digital technology; and the terrorist attacks of September 11, 2001 and their aftermath. Important aspects of our communal fears and their major sources seem clear at this juncture. Have they been translated into popular formulas and genres for mass consumption?

In Chapter 1, we noted that in general, horror deals with individual fears; science fiction with collective dangers. Of course, personal and social disquiet are often in dialectical tension. The disaster-movie cycle of the 1970s including *Airport* (1970), *The Poseidon Adventure* (1972), and *Earthquake* (1974) depicted a cross-section of society imperiled, coded reactions to the sociopolitical upheavals of the Civil Rights, Vietnam, and Watergate years.[1] The late 1990s saw Hollywood attempting to revive the cycle, initially using natural disasters to motivate the display of advanced visual effects in movies such as *Twister* (1996), *Dante's Peak* (1997), and *Volcano* (1997). The later incarnations, highly expensive and gimmicky, yet still designed for spectacle rather than plausible drama or characterization, fared little better critically or aesthetically than their predecessors. What all these movies had in common, though, was a vision of social cataclysm that evoked the apocalyptic undercurrents of science fiction. The disaster movies dovetailed with a pair of end-of-the-world tales about giant asteroids threatening the Earth, *Armageddon* (1998), in which a macho crew of oil-fire-fighters turned astronauts save the world; and *Deep Impact* (1998), more about the reactions of people on Earth to the approach of doom in a truly sci-fi future where an African-American president (the ever-stately Morgan Freeman, surely as qualified to be President of the United States as Arnold Schwarzenegger is to be governor of California) organizes a solution and offers consoling wisdom in its aftermath. Yet where now was the jeopardy, the collective shudder? Communism had crumbled, the economy was booming at historic levels, and the greatest political problem seemed to revolve around obsession with the President's sex life.

Be careful what you wish for. Recalling science fiction's rise to popularity in the 1950s in the midst of the Cold War, a post-Soviet onslaught of alien invaders struck in *Independence Day* (1996), a millennial variation of *The War of the Worlds* (1953), whose nationalistic rhetoric was perhaps best caught in a scene in which, after globally devastating alien attacks, somewhere in the Iraqi desert a surviving group of British, Israeli, and Iraqi pilots – the lion and the lamb have truly laid down together – decode radio messages from Washington and wonder aloud, "What do [the Americans] plan to do?" What they do is persevere, figure out a solution, and win, just like in World War II movies, which would also enjoy a minor resurgence after Spielberg's *Saving Private Ryan* (1998), movies whose can-do determination echoed in *Armageddon* and

Independence Day, suggesting they were ultimately backward-looking despite the techno-savvy characters and digital effects.[2] However, although empty spectacle, then, *Independence Day* also foretold the future with images of Lady Liberty face down in New York harbor as the twin towers of the World Trade Center burn in the background; and the White House and US Capitol blasted by alien spacecraft, only the method now so fantastic as it seems that one or the other was the intended target of the hijacked airliner that crashed in Pennsylvania on 9/11.

The transformation of these Hollywood images from visual stunts to potent allegory ripened with Spielberg's *War of the Worlds* (2005), which drew on specific imagery from 9/11, including makeshift bulletin boards covered with photos of missing people after the aliens devastate the New York City area; and extrapolation of what the director called the frightening novelty of "the American refugee experience," first seen when stunned crowds streamed out of Manhattan on foot after the terrorist attacks. Perhaps because *Independence Day* had already updated the combat spectacles of 1950s alien invasion movies, Spielberg chose to downplay those elements to concentrate on the struggle of Tom Cruise's working-class Ray Ferrier to save his young daughter and teenage son in the midst of attack and social breakdown. Spielberg's mastery of gripping action aside, the film's most unexpectedly eerie sequence transforms our first look at the invaders into oblique commentary on the domestic debate over Bush's invasion of Iraq. When Ray and daughter Rachel (Dakota Fanning) take refuge in an upstate farmhouse, the setting turns suddenly gothic in its dark cellar, rats scurrying about, and the farmer (Tim Robbins), a mad survivalist otherwise inexplicably clad in what look like a medieval monk's robes. The scene reveals too that, like vampires, the aliens are draining human blood to fertilize their own red flora that is quickly overgrowing earthly terrain.

In the 1953 original, Dr Clayton Forrester (Gene Barry) and Sylvia Van Buren (Ann Robinson) set up temporary housekeeping in an abandoned farmhouse, a hopeful metaphor for marriage and social reconstruction, interrupted when an alien vessel smashes the house and they get their only glimpse of the cyclopean Martians. Here hiding from the invaders who surround them, Ray Ferrier and Harlan Ogilvy (Robbins) react to the unfolding calamity in ways that take on topical political dimension. "You and me – I don't think we're on the same page," Ogilvy hisses after Ferrier, fearing for the life of his child, wrests away the shotgun with which the farmer was about to shoot one of the aliens inspecting the cellar, a kind of Red State/Blue State caricature. Yet with his own family dead, the crumbling Ogilvy's former occupation as an ambulance driver in the city evokes the hundreds of firemen and first-responders killed in the World Trade Center, making him a near-ghostly figure suffused with pain and loss. Earlier Ogilvy challenged Ferrier's seeming defeatism, asking, "Are you gonna sit here? Wait for them to come and get you? Is that your plan, Ray?" Reading this as a contemporary allegory, though, Spielberg shrewdly manipulated the public personae of the two stars: Tom Cruise became a conservative icon of the Reagan years, playing the strutting fighter jock in *Top Gun* (1986); meanwhile, Tim Robbins was an outspoken liberal opponent of the Iraq invasion. The episode's climax is disturbing, if contradictory, when Ferrier silently kills the half-deranged Ogilvy to keep him quiet; then saves Rachel by destroying an alien tripod with hand grenades. Still, the gothic symbolism suffusing Ferrier's clash with Ogilvy speaks to a moment of American darkness, domestic discord amidst the confused conduct of "the war on terror" whose definition, let alone direction, remains highly contentious.

The staid haunted-house movies the major studios attempted after *The Sixth Sense* (1999), such as *Thirteen Ghosts* (2001) and *The Ghost Ship* (2002), gave little indication of the horror genre's overall health as they strained to present superficially gothic imagery through digital effects that still seemed to belong in science fiction. Notably, however, two of the most successful horror films of recent years, *The Blair Witch Project* (1999) and *The Ring* (2002), succeeded through a particular stylistic approach integral to the themes of their otherwise divergent stories, drawing on the ubiquitous presence of electronic imagery from both television and computer screens increasingly suffusing all aspects of public and private life. That all this techno-utopian dazzle might harbor implications darker than those claimed by the relentlessly cheerful promises of advertising and consumer culture had been indicated at the millennium by fears of the "Y2K" bug, an inadvertent programming quirk from decades past that prompted many people to stock extra provisions, and in some cases, weaponry against the possibility of a collapsing technical and social infrastructure. (Harlan Ogilvy assured Ray that he had large supplies of food and water on hand, presumably not amassed in anticipation of extraterrestrial invasion.) As translated from the Japanese into contemporary American anxiety, *The Ring* realized familiar gothic themes using visual technology as both means and motif in telling an unsettling story in the best traditions of the horror genre.[3]

"I hate television," claims a nervous teenager in the first line of a movie in which the monster takes its victims who watch a videotape filled with threateningly enigmatic imagery. Katie (Amber Tamblyn) and Becca (Rachel Bella) discuss hearing that others had supposedly died after watching the tape then receiving a phone call that informed the victim he or she has only seven days to live, seemingly an urban legend that typifies those now spread by internet rumors that cloud distinctions between demonstrable fact and paranoid hearsay. The opening stays in the main currents of a genre that has catered to an adolescent audience for decades, with the girls in an empty house conferring about boyfriends and drugs just before . . . something awful. But *The Ring* promises and delivers more than plodding slasher sequels or the dull postmodern cynicism of *Scream* ever offered, conjuring the torpor of the post-World War II art cinema. Gore Verbinski, a decorated director of TV commercials, might have been tempted to adopt their flash and frenetic energy but created a carefully paced, visually astute horror tale that recalls the style and themes of Antonioni's *Blow Up* (1966). Katie's mysterious death prompts her aunt, Rachel Keller (Naomi Watts), a reporter, to investigate, eventually learning the tape contains the malevolent ghost of Samara Morgan, a little girl murdered by her mother years earlier whose spirit perpetually seeks vengeance. *The Ring* unfolds as if the pale figures in the pictures that Antonioni's blasé photographer (David Hemmings) enlarges and arranges on his walls emerged to pursue and hound him to death.

The Ring's pervasive sense of entropy is caught in fleeting street scenes in the rainy city of Seattle where the American version has been set. In one, Rachel emerges from a photo shop to inspect the final pictures of Katie and her deceased friends as a sleek monorail passes overhead, a vestige of Space-Age optimism and a bright "future" long past. Later, her young son Aidan silently encounters his estranged, guilty father, Noah, hooded against a gentle rain. Water is the film's major motif, as it evokes both Samara's death in the well and perhaps amniotic fluid in a story consumed with conflicting views of motherhood and its outcomes. Family disturbance and dysfunction, central to the horror genre for decades, underpin *The Ring*'s two converging narratives: the potential reunification of Rachel, Noah, and Aidan; and the supernatural results of the violent disintegration of Anna and Richard Morgan and their demon daughter Samara. The absence of a traditional nuclear family for Rachel and Aidan is clearly at issue. On the day of Katie's funeral, frantic Rachel can't find her black dress and runs into the living room to see it already laid out, shoes as well, by her son. Aidan, who calls his mother by her first name, is shown in double image before a mirror calmly tying his necktie, a canny composition that indicates his role as husband-like child.

Still, the movie presents these issues with subtlety. Though Rachel is a busy professional and single mother, she seems highly competent in both realms. Noah is a man-child who, despite the mythic force of his name, will fail to save the world from destruction. Rachel's investigation into Anna Morgan's murder of Samara and subsequent suicide that occurred in the 1960s – the beginning of the women's movement – locates the source of monstrosity within a traditional family. Anna's inability to conceive led to the adoption of Samara, whose origins remain mysterious; her subsequent slaying of the child suggests a sort of belated abortion, an issue often close to the surface in demon-child movies that start with *Rosemary's Baby* (1968). Why the girl was banished to an isolated room – familiar, even charming but for its location in the barn loft – remains unclear. On the old hospital interview tape Samara says that Richard Morgan loved his horses more than her, which says everything and nothing specific despite the arresting imagery of her weird bedroom. Discovered by Rachel years later shortly before his spectacular suicide, Richard Morgan seems riven with guilt and fear, hardly a cartoonish patriarch.

Moreover, *The Ring* uniquely reconciles the horror film's classic and contemporary modes, essentially presenting two endings, one cathartic and traditional, the other the pessimistic, unresolved finale of contemporary horror. Either all worked out, Samara's ghost was released and Aidan's family reunited – or not. Each "ending" feels logical and complete, the contradiction only adding to the nightmare texture. Rachel plunges into the abandoned well where Samara died and in the slimy water below, retrieves the body. As she cradles what appears to be a sleeping child, it dissolves into a rotted skeleton, a gothic Pietà that in a more conventional ghost story would signal that in the arms of a genuinely "good mother" – Rachel's devotion to Aidan is never in doubt – the tormented girl had finally found peace. Later, as police and ambulances surround the cabin and Rachel sits wrapped in the obligatory blanket that means traditional authority has been reestablished, Noah says firmly, "They're going to bury her next week. It's over." Cursory familiarity with the horror genre since the late 1960s should make us wary, but the movie goes further, showing the reconstituted family driving home together, Aidan falling asleep on the backseat but looking up to see his parents clasp hands. "We set [Samara] free," Rachel says contentedly as she and Aidan drift off to sleep later in her bed. "You *helped* her?" the frightened child says with a start, initiating the fatalistic conclusion.

The Ring negotiates these divergent genre tendencies as the monster climbs out of the well on the videotape and emerges from the television to kill Noah, just as the image of the fly Rachel saw on the tape somehow passed through the screen and became real. Rachel saves Aidan by helping him make a copy of the tape that will condemn another person – possibly Beth, Noah's young girlfriend, whom Rachel observes ascending in the elevator to Noah's apartment to discover his body as Rachel flees back to her son. But the curse is implicitly passed on to the movie audience as Aidan asks in the final lines, "What about the person we show it to? What happens to them?" For Rachel Keller, like Ray Ferrier, all that matters is saving a child, the primal symbol for hope both individual and social. Still, "What is it with reporters?," Richard Morgan asked bitterly, though he might have been speaking of mediated culture generally. "You take one person's tragedy and force the world to experience it. You spread it like sickness." In *The Ring*, all our houses are haunted, all our repressed and secret sins are surfacing, and the agent of our destruction lurks behind a screen that is alternately window, mirror, womb, and tomb – perhaps the best metaphors for the functions of the horror film itself.

APPENDIX: HORROR AUTEURS

A number of important directors began careers in the 1970s dedicated in large measure to the horror/fantasy fields. The term *auteur* (French for "author") refers to outstanding directors who display distinctive visual style and characteristic themes across a body of work. The concept is often controversial because it seemingly ignores or diminishes the contributions of writers, cinematographers, production designers, actors, or other creative talents; it can also sever individual movies from the industrial, social, and historical contexts in which they were made. Used judiciously, however, auteurism can be an illuminating starting point for a variety of different analyses. The following summaries address only highlights of each director's output.

After *Night of the Living Dead*, **George A. Romero** directed *The Crazies* (1974), a more pointed Vietnam allegory about Army germ-warfare testing turning an American town into maddened killers. *Martin* (1977), the gruesome study of a serial killer who thinks he is an actual vampire, was followed by two sequels to his initial hit, the energetic *Dawn of the Dead* (1979), in which zombies assault a shopping mall, and the more downbeat *Day of the Dead* (1985), a doomsday variation depicting the implicit destruction of the entire human race before the expanding zombie onslaught. Shot in color and produced on a bigger scale, the sequels were relentlessly gory and introduced elements of dark humor. Amid the mayhem, *Dawn of the Dead* slyly compared the zombies to other less vicious but similarly mindless consumers shuffling through the mall. *Day of the Dead* includes ghastly images of screaming victims literally torn apart by the zombie horde, with guts popping and bloody pieces trailed across the floor. Romero also collaborated with Stephen King on the uneven *Creepshow* (1982), a salute to the influential EC horror comics of the early 1950s. The technically polished *Monkey Shines* (1988) was full of characteristic Romero touches of shock and irony in the tale of a paralyzed man who forms a psychic bond with a monkey trained to help care for him but which he manipulates for cold revenge. Unfortunately, owing to legal glitches, Romero and his original partners did not share in most of the profits from his first success. In order to realize some return on what had become one of the most famous horror movies ever, Romero produced a color remake of *Night of the Living Dead* (1990), directed by makeup wizard Tom Savini who had rendered gory effects for Romero's zombie sequels and other horror films of the 1970s and 1980s. This time, rather than catatonic victim, Barbara (Patricia Tallman) is a tough, gun-toting survivor like the African American hero of the original. The zombie series proved too attractive to abandon as Romero released *Land of the Dead* (2005), whose higher budget added to the apocalyptic formula of its predecessors with undertones of post-9/11 anxiety.

Brian De Palma was one of several acclaimed directors with film-school backgrounds, including Francis Ford Coppola and Martin Scorsese, whose early career included exploitation movies for AIP. De Palma's visually adroit *Sisters* (AIP, 1973), starring Margot Kidder, was a queasy tale about separated Siamese twins, one or both of who may be a demented murderer. De Palma won major box-office success with *Carrie* (United Artists, 1976), based on Stephen King's first novel. One of the most stylish and effective major studio horror films of the 1970s, *Carrie* starred Sissy Spacek as a lonely teenager with psychokinetic powers trapped between the sexual paranoia of her fanatically religious mother (Piper Laurie) and a pack of high-school oppressors. Critics sometimes unfairly dismissed De Palma as merely a Hitchcock imitator. While his admiration for the Master of Suspense is clear (Carrie attends Bates High School, clearly an ominous sign!), De Palma's horror films can be seen as commentaries on major Hitchcock themes. *Dressed To Kill* (1980), a conscious reworking of *Psycho*, drew public protests for its aestheticized images of violence against women. After the bloody gangster drama

Scarface (1983), the unrepentant De Palma directed *Body Double* (1984), which includes a woman pinned to the floor and eviscerated by a huge power drill, perhaps the goriest horror film made while major studios competed directly with exploitation movies in the decade after *The Exorcist*. The film was highly self-conscious, with allusions to *Rear Window* and *Vertigo* and witty asides on horror and pornography.

Canadian director **David Cronenberg** is the foremost purveyor of the horror variant of what Carol J. Clover terms "body genres," films in which excessive physical transformation, eruption, or rebellion of the human body against itself becomes the source of fear. Gothic exaggerations or taboo-shattering alterations of sexual activity, reproduction, birth, disease, and mutilation fill Cronenberg's work. The interconnection of sex and violence so essential to horror broke completely from metaphor in *They Came From Within* (a.k.a. *Shivers*) (1975), in which people are infected by parasitic organisms that spark uncontrollable sexual frenzy followed by murderous rage. *Rabid* (1977) featured former porn star Marilyn Chambers as an accident victim who becomes a vampire killer with a phallic probe that springs from her armpit to siphon victims' blood. In *The Brood* (1978) Samantha Eggar plays a troubled woman who begins physically manifesting her fury by growing egg sacs on her back that birth vicious little monsters. *Videodrome* (1983) commented on the obsessive nature of television viewing featuring sensuous images of probing glass fingers reaching out from the TV screen for its adoring protagonist or belching out blood and guts. Cronenberg's style of explicit gore mixed with emotional detachment and dry humor make his films so memorably disturbing.

Cronenberg's later films became more expensive but no less unsettling. *The Fly* (1986) was his effects-laden update of the 1950s cult movie. Scientist Jeff Goldblum's experiments with matter teleportation accidentally result in his body combining with insect DNA. The film was widely interpreted as an expression of the fear of degenerative diseases, especially AIDS. As the scientist gradually mutates into the fly, he shows his girlfriend (Geena Davis) "the Seth Brundel museum of natural history," a medicine chest filled with discarded body parts including his nose, ears, and penis. In the creepy sexual *doppelgänger* tale *Dead Ringers* (1988), Jeremy Irons played dual roles as insane twin gynecologists. *Crash* (1998) was Cronenberg's controversial adaptation of J. G. Ballard's novel about twisted characters who become addicted to painful sex immediately after deliberate auto wrecks. Minus any supernatural motivation and by extension, its intellectual distance, *Crash* was perhaps Cronenberg's most discomfiting film.

Italian maestro **Dario Argento** directed some of the most visually imaginative and grueling horror films of the 1970s and 1980s. Internationally distributed, Argento's films are classified as *giallo* ("yellow") in Italy, a term derived from the yellow band bordering the covers of lurid crime and horror novels published by the Mondadori company. *Giallo* can encompass routine mystery novels but more often connotes violent crime stories and, on film, gory horror that may or may not have supernatural basis. Whether an Argento monster is a psychopath (*Cat o' Nine Tails* [1971], *Four Flies on Grey Velvet* [1972], *Deep Red* (1975), *Tenebre* (1982)] or supernatural agent (*Suspiria* [1977], *Inferno* [1980], *Opera* [1987], *The Stendhal Syndrome* [1996]), his work is distinguished by expressionistic use of bright, saturated colors, complex camerawork, and adroit editing, effects that cohere to produce hideously inventive scenes of violence. *Suspiria*, a substantial US hit, influenced *Halloween* with its driving electronic music score and disembodied camera movements. Argento's baroque murder scenes often exploit sadistic overkill. In *Deep Red* [*Profondo Rosso*] a woman is drowned by repeatedly dunking her head in the scalding water of her own bathtub. In *Suspiria*, an almost invisible killer viciously assaults two women in their apartment. In the death of one, Argento shows a view *inside her body* as a knife repeatedly plunges into her heart. The massacred victim is then hanged from an upper balcony.

Like Mario Bava, Argento manipulates moving camera and unconventional point-of-view shots unattached or only ambiguously attached to any particular character, including the killer. This technique keeps the audience on edge and serves the convoluted plots in which the assumed identity (and especially gender) of the killer may change several times before the end. Argento sometimes invents almost surreal scenes. In *Suspiria*, a woman is trapped in an attic room as the killer – seen only as a probing straight razor manipulating the latch – tries to break in. She barely escapes by piling up trunks to reach a high window, but when she jumps through lands in a blue-tinted room inexplicably filled floor to ceiling with coils of wire that entangle her, allowing the killer to enter and slit her throat – an astonishing event without rational explanation. Dario Argento is one of the most original intellects to work in the horror genre.

Since *Halloween*, the prolific **John Carpenter** has averaged about a movie a year starting with *The Fog* (1980), a well-crafted Lewtonesque exercise in suggestive horror. *Escape from New York* (1981), starring Kurt Russell, was a pulpy sci-fi adventure set in a bleak future where Manhattan has become a quarantine prison island. Carpenter's fatalistic remake of *The Thing* (1982) went back to John W. Campbell's short story for inspiration. Here the invading alien is a formless organism that can assume the shape of any living host. Truly gross and astonishing makeup and mechanical effects by Rob Bottin depict the ever-changing creature's rampage. Like many directors, Carpenter had difficulty adapting Stephen King. *Christine* (1983), from King's novel about a demonic Plymouth auto, played more like a campy, made-for-TV movie. The director returned to form with the witty science-fiction romance *Star Man* (1984). *They Live* (1988) was a satiric action picture about soulless alien invaders equated with 1980s Yuppie consumerism. A sinister King-like novelist whose fiction can actually reorder the physical world dominates the effective and visually sophisticated *In the Mouth of Madness* (1995). *Village of the Damned* (1995) was Carpenter's clever remake of an eerie 1960 British science-fiction film of the same title about alien-spawned children. The always edgy James Woods starred in *Vampires* (1998), a shoot-'em-up variant of the traditional myth inspired by Hong Kong action cinema. If not every work is a complete success, one admires John Carpenter's dedication both to the filmmaker's craft and to the horror-fantasy form.

Tobe Hooper may be the Orson Welles of the horror film. After a brilliant debut the director struggled to find projects to give free rein to his anarchic talent. Hooper's suspenseful network TV adaptation of King's *Salem's Lot* (CBS, 1979) was made for a heavily censored medium that would not permit the novel's gore, let alone the nihilistic pyrotechnics of Hooper's debut. *The Funhouse* (1981) was a more fitting expression of his style that, like *Texas Chain Saw Massacre*, effectively blended real locations (a rundown carnival) and a few well-crafted sets. The smart, well-produced film riffs on *Frankenstein*, *Freaks*, and the slasher cycle. On *Poltergeist* (1982), special effects and Spielberg's commercial formulas largely outstripped Hooper's vision. Delayed from release for several years, *Lifeforce* (1985) was a stylish, post-*Alien* science-fiction tale about extraterrestrial vampires infecting London. Hooper's long-awaited *Texas Chain Saw Massacre 2* (1986) drew mixed reviews but emphasized exaggerated carnage and humor along with self-conscious commentary on the original movie and subsequent controversies over gory horror. Hooper has also been sought out regularly to direct segments of TV horror anthologies, including *Tales From the Crypt* and *Freddy's Nightmares*.

Other notable horror/fantasy directors include **Joe Dante** and **Tim Burton**, both part of the generation that grew up watching vintage Universal horror on *Shock Theater* and reading monster fan magazines.

Dante's skillfully produced *The Howling* (1981) put a contemporary slant on the werewolf myth. Curt Siodmak's script for *The Wolf Man* (1941) contained a faux "folk poem" that began: "Even a man who is pure at heart / and says his prayers by night / may become a wolf . . ." *The Howling* begins with the hunt for a serial killer (Robert Picardo) sexually obsessed with a TV newscaster (Dee Wallace) that leads to a porno theater where he transforms into a werewolf. Now even a man "impure at heart" may become a wolf, a beastly killer in either form, and unlike Larry Talbot, untroubled by conscience. References to classic horror movies abound here and in most of Dante's work such as *Gremlins* (1984), which juxtaposes riffs on 1950s science fiction with Capra's *It's A Wonderful Life* (1946). Similarly, Tim Burton, an accomplished visual stylist who draws inspiration from expressionism, gained fame with the anarchic genre comedy *Beetlejuice* (1988). An ardent fan of Vincent Price, Burton cast the actor in his last screen performance as the addled inventor who creates the title character of *Edward Scissorhands* (1990). His loving biography of legendary "worst director" Edward D. Wood, Jr (*Plan Nine From Outer Space* [1959]) in *Ed Wood* (1994) showcased Martin Landau's Oscar-winning turn as Bela Lugosi. *Sleepy Hollow* (1999) was an inventive reconception of Washington Irving's famous tale boasting richly gothic atmosphere, surprising gore, and Christopher Lee as a sinister magistrate.

NOTES

Notes to Chapter 1

1 R. H. W. Dillard, "The Pageantry of Death," in Roy Huss and T. J. Ross, eds., *Focus on the Horror Film* (Englewood Cliffs, NJ: Prentice-Hall, 1972), 36. A longer version of Dillard's essay originally appeared under the title, "Even a Man Who is Pure at Heart," in W. R. Robinson, ed., *Man and the Movies* (Baton Rouge: Louisiana State University Press, 1967), 64–70.

2 James B. Twitchell, *Dreadful Pleasures: An Anatomy of Modern Horror* (New York: Oxford University Press, 1985), 104.

3 See, for example, Devendra P. Varma, *The Gothic Flame, Being a History of the Gothic Novel in England: Its Origins, Efflorescence, Disintegration, and Residuary Influences* (London: A Barker, 1957).

4 Stephen King, *Danse Macabre* (New York: Berkeley Books, 1982), 133–4.

5 Quoted in Harold Bloom, ed., *Classic Horror Writers* (New York: Chelsea House, 1994), 110.

6 See, for example, William Paul, *Laughing, Screaming: Modern Hollywood Horror and Comedy* (New York: Columbia University Press, 1994) and Linda Williams, "Film Bodies: Gender, Genre, and Excess," in Leo Braudy and Marshall Cohen, eds., *Film Theory and Criticism: Introductory Readings* (New York: Oxford University Press, 1999), 701–15.

7   King, *Danse Macabre*, 175.

8   Walter Kendrick, *The Thrill of Fear: 250 Years of Scary Entertainment* (New York: Grove Weidenfeld, 1991). See Chapter 6, "Genrefication," 165–99.

9   Thomas Schatz, *Hollywood Genres: Formulas, Filmmaking, and the Studio System* (New York: Random House, 1981), 5.

10   Ibid., 37–41.

11   Ibid., 37.

12   Ibid., 37–8.

13   Wood published three different versions of this essay. I will draw on the last one, published under the chapter title, "The American Nightmare: Horror in the 70s," in Robin Wood, *Hollywood From Vietnam To Reagan* (New York: Columbia University Press, 1986), 70–94. This book devotes several chapters to the horror genre.

14   Ibid., 78.

15   For close comparison of horror and science fiction, see Vivian Sobchack, *Screening Space: The American Science Fiction Film* (second enlarged edn, New York: Ungar, 1987), chapter one, "The Limits of the Genre: Definitions and Themes," 17–63.

16   Ibid., 30.

Notes to Chapter 2

1   André de Lorde, "Fear in Literature," in Mel Gordon, *The Grand Guignol: Theatre of Fear and Terror* (New York: Amok Press, 1988), 113.

2   The Bible says little about the specific nature of Hell. Italian artists of the late Middle Ages and after often drew on descriptions of Hell imagined by Dante, whose portrait often appears in such murals. Creighton S. Gilbert, *How Fra Angelico and Signorelli Saw The End of the World* (University Park PA: Pennsylvania State University Press, 2003), 44–5; 87–111.

3   Valdine Clemens, *The Return of the Repressed: Gothic Horror from* The Castle of Otranto *to* Alien (Albany: State University of New York Press, 1999), 7.

4   Ibid., 49.

5   King, *Danse Macabre*, 60–1.

6   Twitchell, *Dreadful Pleasures*; see chapters three through five.

7   David J. Skal, *The Monster Show: A Cultural History of Horror* (New York: Penguin Books, 1993), 19.

8   See Stephen D. Arata, "The Occidental Tourist: 'Dracula' and the Anxiety of Reverse Colonization," *Victorian Studies*, 33:4 (Summer, 1990), 621–45.

9   For a fine biography and critical discussion of Méliès see John Frazer, *Artificially Arranged Scenes: The Films of Georges Méliès* (Boston: G. K. Hall, 1979).

10 Tom Gunning, "The Cinema of Attractions: Early Film, Its Spectator and the Avant-Garde," *Wide Angle* 8:3/4 (1986), 63–70.

11 For more recent developments in Melies criticism, including his play with gender, see Elizabeth Ezra, *Georges Méliès: The Birth of the Auteur* (Manchester and New York: Manchester University Press, 2000), especially chapter 3, "The Amazing Flying Woman."

12 This final scene is now commonly missing from circulating versions.

13 Porter, quoted in Charles Musser, *Before the Nickelodeon: Edwin S. Porter and the Edison Manufacturing Company* (Berkeley: University of California Press, 1991), 209.

14 Gordon, *Grand Guignol*, 10.

15 In Sergei M. Eisenstein's 1923 essay "A Montage of Attractions" (from which Tom Gunning adapted the notion of "the cinema of attractions"), the Soviet director approvingly cites the Grand Guignol, including an indirect reference to the plot of de Lorde's *At the Telephone* (see below). Sergei Eisenstein, *The Film Sense*, trans. and ed. Jay Leyda (New York: Harcourt Brace Jovanovich, 1975), 231.

16 For discussion of censorship in the nickelodeon period see Garth S. Jowett, "'A Capacity for Evil': The 1915 Supreme Court *Mutual* Decision," in Matthew Bernstein, ed. *Controlling Hollywood: Censorship and Regulation in the Studio Era* (New Brunswick, NJ: Rutgers University Press, 1999), 16–40.

17 "Films based on acknowledged cultural masterpieces in other media were positive proof that producers and exhibitors were uplifting and educating the audience . . . [and] . . . could demonstrate that the motion-picture show was an appropriate place for children and that they were bringing high culture to the masses." Eileen Bowser, *The Transformation of Cinema, 1907–1915* (Berkeley: University of California Press, 1990), 42, 43. See also Charles Musser, *Thomas A. Edison and His Kinetographic Motion Pictures* (New Brunswick, NJ: Rutgers University Press, 1995), 46, 48.

18 *Edison Kinetogram*, vol. 2, March 15, 1910, 3–4.

19 The *doppelgänger* theme has been discussed in critiques of the novel. See, for example, David Ketterer, *Frankenstein's Creation: The Book, The Monster, and Human Reality* (Victoria, BC: University of Victoria, 1979), 56–65.

20 Harry M. Geduld, ed., *The Definitive Dr. Jekyll and Mr. Hyde Companion* (New York: Garland, 1983), 195–7.

21 Brian A. Rose, *Jekyll and Hyde Adapted: Dramatizations of Cultural Anxiety* (Westport, CT: Greenwood Press, 1996), 38.

22 Ibid., 38.

23 E. Marsili, ed., *Albo dei Caduti nella Guerra 1915–1918* (Orvieto, Italy: Commune di Orvieto, 1922), 9.

24 For a detailed history of Ufa, see Klaus Kreimeier, *The Ufa Story: A History of Germany's Greatest Film Company, 1918–1945*, trans. Robert and Rita Kimber (Berkeley: University of California Press, 1999).

25 *The Cabinet of Dr. Caligari*'s February 26, 1920 release date has long been established, yet many historical accounts continue to use 1919. In fact, shooting began in late December, 1919 and finished in late January, 1920. David Robinson, *Das Cabinet Des Dr. Caligari* (London: British Film Institute Press, 1997), 24, 46–7. See also Siegfried Kracauer, *From Caligari to Hitler: A Psychological History of the German Film* (Princeton: Princeton University Press, 1974 [1947]), 71.

26 For analysis of the production, reception, and historical impact of the film see Mike Budd, ed., *The Cabinet of Dr. Caligari: Texts, Contexts, Histories* (New Brunswick, NJ and London: Rutgers University Press, 1990).

27 See John Willett, *The Theatre of the Weimar Republic* (New York and London: Holmes & Meier, 1988), especially chapter 4, "Revolution and the Establishment of Expressionism," 53–70.

28 See especially Robinson, *Cabinet Des Dr. Caligari*.

29 Quoted in Kracauer, *From Caligari to Hitler*, 79–80.

30 German director Werner Herzog produced an eerie remake of *Nosferatu* (1979) with Klaus Kinski. *Bram Stoker's Dracula* (1992) referenced images from Murnau, including the vampire's gravity-defying rise from his coffin. *Shadow of the Vampire* (2000) was an inspired dark comedy about the making of the famous German silent which claims that director Murnau (John Malkovich) got such a convincing performance from Max Schreck (Willem Dafoe) because the actor really was a vampire.

31 For discussion of these events, see David J. Skal, *Hollywood Gothic: The Tangled Web of Dracula from Novel to Stage to Screen* (New York: W. W. Norton, 1990), chapter 2, 43–63.

32 Michael F. Blake, *Lon Chaney: The Man Behind The Thousand Faces* (New York: Vestal, 1993), 153.

33 Sidra Stich, *Anxious Visions: Surrealist Art* (New York: Abbeville Press, 1990), 26–30.

34 Skal, *Monster Show*, 67.

35 David Bordwell, Janet Staiger, and Kristin Thompson, *The Classical Hollywood Cinema: Film Style and Mode of Production to 1960* (New York: Columbia University Press, 1985), 72–7.

36 Thomas Schatz, *The Genius of the System: Hollywood Filmmaking in the Studio Era* (New York: Pantheon, 1988). See chapter 6.

37 On production of the Spanish-language *Dracula*, see Skal, *Hollywood Gothic*, 153–77.

38 *Dr. Jekyll and Mr. Hyde* is alternately listed as a 1931 or 1932 release. Originally scheduled for early 1932, Paramount hurriedly screened the film in a limited run in Los Angeles in December 1931 to compete with the December release of *Frankenstein*, before sending it into general release in the new year. Part of the confusion also stems from the fact that for many years, Hollywood emulated the precedents of vaudeville and Broadway seasons using fall to spring release schedules for major films.

Thus *Dracula*, released in February, 1931 was part of the 1930–1 season; *Frankenstein* and *Dr. Jekyll and Mr. Hyde* fell into the 1931–2 season. The Academy Awards were also based on this system from 1927 through 1933: Fredric March's Best Actor award was for the 1931–2 season.

39 Skal analyzes this theme in detail; *Monster Show*, 148–50.

40 The making of *King Kong* by the producer–director team of Merian C. Cooper and Ernest B. Schoedsack roughly overlapped their production of *The Most Dangerous Game*, which shared some of the same jungle sets, special-effects backgrounds, and cast members, including Robert Armstrong and Fay Wray.

41 Rather than claiming *Svengali* as a horror film, however, it may be more correct to say that it continued the trend of using Germanic style to connote a prestige production. Though based on a stage adaptation of the nineteenth-century novel *Trilby*, *Svengali*'s connection to *The Cabinet of Dr. Caligari* in both set design and the sinister hypnotist figure seems clear.

42 Memorandum, John M. Stuart to Joseph I. Breen, January 15, 1935. *Werewolf of London*, MPPA/Production Code Administration files, Margaret Herrick Library, Beverly Hills, CA.

43 See, e.g., Rhona J. Berenstein, *Attack of the Leading Ladies: Gender, Sexuality, and Spectatorship in Classic Horror Cinema* (New York: Columbia University Press, 1996), 22–8.

44 Neville March Hunnings, *Film Censors and the Law* (London: George Allen & Unwin, 1967), 141–2. The "H" category was purely advisory, but some local government authorities further stipulated that such films could not be shown to children under age 16.

45 Tom Johnson, *Censored Screams: The British Ban on Hollywood Horror in the Thirties* (Jefferson, NC: McFarland & Co., 1997), 135–47. The title of Johnson's informative book is misleading, as there was no generalized ban on horror in Britain during the 1930s. Rather, persistent hostility to (largely American) horror films among some local government councils produced varying regulation that most often restricted admission to adults; in some locations, children under 16 could see "H" films if accompanied by a parent or bona fide adult guardian. Many theaters exercised the option to make specific cuts in films that satisfied local authorities and permitted wider audiences. See Hunnings, *Film Censors and the Law*, chapter 4, "The British Board of Film Censors," 126–48. Johnson summarizes these qualifications as well; *Censored Screams*, 20–1.

46 Gregory William Mank, *It's Alive! The Classic Cinema Saga of Frankenstein* (New York: A. S. Barnes & Co., 1981), 77. Skal, *Monster Show*, 202–5.

47 Trade review clippings, December 10, 1941. *The Wolf Man*, MPPA/Production Code Administration files, Margaret Herrick Library, Beverley Hills, CA.

48   For analysis of wartime horror films, see Rick Worland, "OWI Meets the Monsters: Hollywood Horror Films and War Propaganda, 1942–1945," *Cinema Journal*, 37:1 (1997), 47–65. Also see Chapter 4 in this volume.

49   Joel E. Siegel, *Val Lewton: The Reality of Terror* (New York: Viking Press, 1973), 20–1. By comparison, *Citizen Kane* (1941), produced at RKO shortly before Lewton arrived, cost about $840,000 – actually not an extravagant amount for a prestigious A picture.

Notes to Chapter 3

1   The original Japanese version of *Godzilla* opened with seamen rescuing fishermen burned by radiation of unknown origin. The episode was drawn from an actual incident in which Japanese fishermen were stricken by fallout from an American hydrogen bomb test. Unlike the reworked American release, the Japanese version is filled with direct references to the war and the atomic bombings of Hiroshima and Nagasaki such that the "meaning" of Godzilla's rampage is hardly metaphorical.

2   For discussion of these demographic and industry changes see Thomas Doherty, *Teenagers and Teenpics: The Juvenilization of American Movies in the 1950s* (Boston: Unwin Hyman, 1988), especially Chapter 6, "The Horror Teenpics," 142–78.

3   For detailed history of the social and economic shifts in film production and exhibition that shaped the genre in this period see Kevin Heffernan, *Ghouls, Gimmicks, and Gold: Horror Films and the American Movie Business, 1952–1968* (Durham NC: Duke University Press, 2004).

4   "[W]e didn't have big stars, we didn't have best-selling books, we didn't have big plays. So what did we have? We had titles, and we had artwork. And that's what we sold. So Jim Nicholson was the guy who used to be able to make that work – if he didn't come up with the titles himself, he used to be able to select titles we would get from our staff." Ray Greene, "Sam Arkoff: The Last Interview," *Cult Movies*, 36 (2002), 11.

5   Professor Quatermass's work became an "Xperiment" in Britain due to a change in the censorship system in 1951 that eliminated the old H certificate and its prohibitions on horror, and created the X certificate, meaning no one under age 16 admitted. Hammer was flaunting the movie's restrictive rating in classic exploitation style. Denis Meikle, *A History of Horrors: The Rise and Fall of the House of Hammer* (Lanham, MD: Scarecrow Press, 1996), 23.

6   Ibid., 51, 55. Hammer also made financing/distribution deals with Warner Bros. and Columbia.

7   Doherty, *Teenagers and Teenpics*, 148–9.

8   "TV Mean Terrifying Vampires," *Famous Monsters of Filmland*, 1 (February, 1958), 58–65.

9 Stephen Rebello, "*Psycho*: The Making of Hitchcock's Masterpiece . . . ," *Cinefantastique*, 16: 4/5 (October, 1986), 50.

10 Sam Arkoff with Richard Turbo, *Flying Through Hollywood By the Seat of My Pants* (New York: Birch Lane Press, 1992), 91–2.

11 This is not quite true, however, if we understand that British horror films from Hammer and its close rival Amicus were co-financed or distributed in the United States at different times through deals with Universal, Warner Bros., Paramount, and Columbia.

12 Charles Flynn and Todd McCarthy, *Kings of the B's: Working Within the Hollywood System* (New York: E. P. Dutton, 1975), 352.

13 This sadistic humor was explicit in the original cartoons. As the children busily construct a torture rack from scratch, the father gushes, "You'll see, chicks, that half the fun is in making it yourself." Charles Addams, *My Crowd: The Original Addams Family and Other Ghoulish Creatures* (New York: Fireside, 1991), 105.

14 Reminiscing on a panel with former cast members in 2001, Dan Curtis stated that among his vivid memories of working on the show was "the kids, the thousands of kids who used to swarm around outside the studio." Kathryn Leigh Scott, *Dark Shadows Memories* (Beverly Hills, CA: Pomegranate Press, 2001), 182.

15 For insightful discussion of these films see Harry M. Benshoff, "Blaxploitation Horror Films: Generic Reappropriation or Reinscription?," *Cinema Journal*, 39:2 (2000), 31–50.

16 For detailed history of the Blaxploitation phenomenon, see Ed Guerrero, *Framing Blackness: The African-American Image in Film* (Philadelphia: Temple University Press, 1993), chapter 3, "The Rise and Fall of Blaxploitation," 69–111.

17 For discussion of the film in relation to Price's career, see Rick Worland, "Faces Behind the Mask: Vincent Price, *Dr. Phibes*, and the Horror Genre in Transition," *Post Script: Essays in Film and the Humanities*, 22:2 (Winter/Spring, 2003), 20–33.

18 Roger Ebert, "Why Audiences Aren't Safe Anymore," *American Film*, 6:5 (March, 1981), 54–6. Janet Maslin, "Bloodbaths Debase Movies and Audiences," *New York Times*, November 21, 1982, Section. 2, 1, 13.

19 I am indebted here to Robin Wood, who suggests that "the overall development of the Hollywood cinema from the late 60s to the 80s is summed up in the movement from Romero's use of the Star Spangled Banner (the flag) at the beginning of *Night of the Living Dead* to Spielberg's use of it (the music) at the beginning of *Poltergeist*." Wood, *Hollywood From Vietnam to Reagan*, 182.

20 John McCarty, *Splatter Movies: Breaking the Last Taboo of the Screen* (New York: St. Martin's Press, 1984).

21 Michael A. Arnzen, "Who's Laughing Now? The Postmodern Splatter Film," *Journal of Popular Film and Television*, 21:4 (1994), 176–84.

22 Terence Rafferty, "Head-Spinning Evil Gets a New Twist," *New York Times*, September 17, 2000, Section II, 24.

23 For discussion of the longstanding disagreement between Blatty and Friedkin on this crucial point, see Mark Kermode, *The Exorcist* (2nd edn, London: British Film Institute Press, 1998), especially 100–11.

Notes to Chapter 4

1 Jason S. Joy to Will H. Hays, December 5, 1931. *Frankenstein* file, MPPA/ Production Code Administration files, Margaret Herrick Library, Beverly Hills, CA. (Subsequent references to files under film titles refer to this source.)

2 John V. Wilson to Anne Bagley, April 11, 1932. *Murders in the Rue Morgue* file.

3 Jason S. Joy to Carl Laemmle, Jr., September 13, 1930. *Dracula* file.

4 Joy to Laemmle, Jr., March 17, 1931. *Dracula* file.

5 Tom Johnson, *Censored Screams: The British Ban on Hollywood Horror in the Thirties* (Jefferson, NC: McFarland & Co., 1997).

6 Breen to Harry H. Zehner, June 9, 1937. *Frankenstein* file.

7 For close analysis of *Rue Morgue*, see Wood, *Hollywood From Vietnam to Reagan*, 80–3.

8 "Office Memorandum," C. C. Pettijohn to Jason Joy, February 26, 1932. *Murders in the Rue Morgue* file.

9 Joseph I. Breen to Harry Zehner, February 26, 1934; Breen to Zehner, April 2, 1934. *The Black Cat* file. (At this point Breen was a member of the MPPDA's Studio Relations Committee prior to the formation of the PCA in July 1934.)

10 "Memorandum," John McH. Stuart, February 7, 1935. Zehner to Breen, February 9, 1935. *Werewolf of London* file.

11 "Memorandum," John McH. Stuart, February 7, 1935. *Werewolf of London* file.

12 Breen to Zehner, February 26, 1934. *The Black Cat* file.

13 For further discussion of censorship of *Dracula's Daughter* and other 1930s horror films, see Skal, *Monster Show*, chapter six, "Angry Villagers," 161–209.

14 Breen to Zehner, October 23, 1935. *Dracula's Daughter* file.

15 Breen to Zehner, January 15, 1936. *Dracula's Daughter* file.

16 Zehner to Breen, February 5, 1936. "Memo Re Dracula's Daughter," February 6, 1936. Breen to Zehner, February 27, 1936. *Dracula's Daughter* file.

17 Breen to Mrs Katherine K. Vandervoort, November 26, 1938. *Son of Frankenstein* file. For further discussion of this episode, see Skal, *Monster Show*.

18　Breen to Brooke Wilkinson, November 7, 1938. *Son of Frankenstein* file.

19　"The war took center stage in 72 pictures that OWI analysts classified as 'war features' between December 1, 1941 and July 24, 1942." Clayton R. Koppes and Gregory D. Black, *Hollywood Goes to War: How Politics, Profits, and Propaganda Shaped World War II Movies* (New York: Free Press, 1987), 60.

20　Ibid., 59.

21　Ibid., 65–70.

22　Neville March Hunnings, *Film Censors and the Law* (London: George Allen & Unwin, 1967), 141–2.

23　"Feature Viewing," March 15, 1943. *Son of Dracula* file. (Hereafter, all citations for files under specific film titles refer to the Office of War Information files, Bureau of Motion Pictures division, Film Analysis section. Record Group 208, National Archives.)

24　"The Government Information Manual for the Motion Picture Industry," April 29, 1943, 2. Record Group 208, Box 15.

25　"Feature Script Review," April 22, 1943. *Revenge of the Zombies* file.

26　Ulric Bell to Bill Cunningham, April 26, 1943; William S. Cunningham to Lindsley Parsons, April 27, 1943. *Revenge of the Zombies* file. Bell succeeded Poynter as BMP head in 1943.

27　"Feature Review," July 23, 1943. *Revenge of the Zombies* file.

28　Gregory A. Waller, *The Living and the Undead: From Stoker's* Dracula *to Romero's* Dawn of the Dead (Chicago: University of Illinois Press, 1986), 13–18.

29　"The Government Information Manual for the Motion Picture Industry," April 29, 1943, 14.

30　Maureen Honey, who studied portrayals of women in popular fiction in relation to OWI's Magazine Bureau guidelines and as represented in print advertising, argues that "The role allocated to women in war-time propaganda . . . was a complicated mixture of strength and dependence, competence and vulnerability, egalitarianism and conservatism." Maureen Honey, *Creating Rosie the Riveter: Class, Gender, and Propaganda During World War II* (Amherst: University of Massachusetts Press, 1984), 7.

31　See Chapter 6, n.6.

32　The *New York Times* derided the movie's formulaic nature without noticing either the wartime setting or Lady Jane's unusual role. B. C., [Bosley Crowther] "Any Blood Donors?," *New York Times*, January 29, 1944, 10. The *Hollywood Reporter* opined that "The performances of Frieda Inescort and Matt Willis are outstanding, but are secondary to that of Lugosi, the master of horrors." Clippings in *Return of the Vampire* file.

33　Koppes and Black, *Hollywood Goes to War*, 145.

34　"Feature Viewing," November 1, 1943. *Return of the Vampire* file.

35　Susan Sontag, "The Imagination of Disaster," in *Against Interpretation and Other Essays* (New York: Delta Books, 1966), 209–25.

36 For analysis of cultural figurations of postwar suburban life as utopian, see Rick Worland and David Slayden, "From Apocalypse to Appliances: Postwar Anxiety and Modern Convenience in *Forbidden Planet*," in David Desser and Garth Jowett, eds., *Hollywood Goes Shopping* (Minneapolis: University of Minnesota Press, 2000), 139–56.

37 Skal, *Monster Show*, 279. For discerning analysis of various fan activities as consciously engaged and creative acts see Henry Jenkins, *Textual Poachers: Television Fans and Participatory Culture* (New York: Routledge, 1992).

38 Twitchell, *Dreadful Pleasures*, 68.

39 James Warren had actually published a short-lived men's magazine before *Famous Monsters*. Skal, *Monster Show*, 268–9.

40 Terri Pinckard, "Monsters Are Good for My Children," *Famous Monsters of Filmland*, 35 (October, 1965), 22–7. Ackerman properly noted in an introduction that Pinckard was a friend and fellow horror/science-fiction fan, so the essay was essentially a commissioned piece.

41 Ibid., 26–7.

42 *Castle of Frankenstein*, 5:19 (n.d.; *c.*1972), 3.

43 "Nabisco Picketed Over Monster Toys," *New York Times*, November 16, 1971, 50; "Monster Toys Are Dropped By Nabisco's Aurora Unit," *Wall Street Journal*, November 26, 1971, 13.

44 The best summation of 1970s anti-pornography feminist polemic is Laura Lederer, ed., *Take Back the Night: Women on Pornography* (New York: William & Morrow, 1980), which includes the statement by Robin Morgan. A recent formulation of the anti-censorship feminist argument is Linda Williams, ed., *Porn Studies* (Durham, NC: Duke University Press, 2004).

45 Stuart Elliot, "Television campaigns are creating some controversy during the Summer Games," *New York Times*, September 19, 2000, Section C, 10.

Notes to Chapter 5

1 Steve Neale, "Melo Talk: On the Meaning and Use of the Term 'Melodrama' in the American Trade Press," *Velvet Light Trap*, 32 (Fall, 1993), 66–89. Neale shows that the association of the term with romantic and domestic dramas, versions of what Hollywood once called "the woman's picture," is too limited in relation to actual film industry press usage, where even *Son of Frankenstein* (1939) was called a melodrama in some reviews.

2 It is notable in this sense that during the involved post-production process of *The Phantom*, which included reshoots and three preview screenings, comedy scenes with Mack Sennett veteran Chester Conklin were first inserted into the film then removed before the final release. Blake, *Lon Chaney*, 136–7.

3 Michael Dempsey, "Lon Chaney: A Thousand and One Faces," *Film Comment*, 31:3 (May–June, 1995), 69.

4 Blake, *Lon Chaney*, 108–10, 116–17, 132–4, 206–7.

5 David J. Skal and Elias Savada, *Dark Carnival: The Secret World of Tod Browning, Hollywood's Master of the Macabre* (New York: Anchor Books, 1995), 47–50; 101–5.

6 For analysis of MGM's regularized presentation of Chaney's star image in a series of variant but similar roles, see Schatz, *Genius of the System*, 39–42.

7 These particular Jannings roles, in fact, symbolize the exchanges between Germany and Hollywood in this period. *The Last Laugh* and *Variety* were Ufa productions; *The Last Command* a Paramount release; and *The Blue Angel* a Paramount-Ufa co-production filmed in separate German and English-language versions.

8 Sigmund Freud, *The Interpretation of Dreams*, ed. and trans. James Strachey (New York: Avon, 1965), 419, 422.

9 Skal and Savada, 111. "The Uncanny" in James Strachey, ed. and trans., *Standard Edition of the Complete Psychological Works of Sigmund Freud*, vol. XVII (London: Hogarth Press, 1955), 235.

10 Skal and Savada, *Dark Carnival*, 110–11.

11 Midget men have often been used in bawdy humor to express a paradoxically overheated sex drive and the implicit inability to satisfy a "normal" woman, lewd scenarios involving Snow White and the Seven Dwarfs being a particular favorite. Cojo's cigar is hardly innocent in this case. Consider the tasteless comedy *Little Cigars* (1973), in which a gang of midget bank robbers team up with statuesque former Playboy playmate Angel Tompkins. One can only dream of what Browning might have done with this.

12 "Like the other Chaney pictures directed by Tod Browning, this has a macabre atmosphere. If you wince at a touch or two of horror, don't go to *The Unknown*. If you like strong celluloid food, try it." Quoted in George C. Pratt, *Spellbound in Darkness: A History of the Silent Film* (Greenwich, CT: New York Graphic Society, 1973), 453. *Variety's* reviewer said: "Every time Browning thinks of Chaney, he probably looks around for a typewriter and says, 'Let's get gruesome' . . . [in *The Unknown*] . . . what momentum [Browning] has gained on paper has been lost in discretion." Quoted in Blake, *Lon Chaney*, 194.

13 Chaney's work has been neglected by contemporary criticism informed by psychoanalytic film theory, though his roles seem readily interpretable in relation to what Carol J. Clover calls "body genres," those forms including horror and pornography that depict intense physical sensation on screen and invoke comparable if less direct physiological responses in the spectator. See Clover, *Men, Women, and Chain Saws: Gender in the Modern Horror Film* (Princeton, NJ: Princeton University Press, 1992),

especially chapter 1, "Her Body, Himself," 21–64. These themes are also taken up in Linda Williams, "Film Bodies: Gender, Genre, and Excess," in Leo Braudy and Marshall Cohen, eds., *Film Theory and Criticism, Introductory Readings* (5th edn, New York: Oxford University Press, 1999), 701–15.

14 Lewis Jacobs, *The Rise of the American Film: A Critical History* (New York: Harcourt, Brace, 1939), 409.

15 *"Possibly Too Much for the Present Day,"* *Hollywood Reporter*, December 10, 1941. Clipping in *The Wolf Man*, MPPA/Production Code Administration files, Margaret Herrick Library, Beverly Hills, CA.

16 Blake, *Lon Chaney*, 285.

17 "Alice in Monsterland," *Famous Monsters of Filmland*, 1 (February, 1958), 12.

18 During the 1960s monster vogue, the Hunchback was represented in all the toys, model kits, etc. In recent years, Quasimodo has disappeared. The deaf and physically deformed bellringer is no real "monster," and no one now reflexively assigns a handicapped person to such grotesque and evil company. The Bride of Frankenstein has taken the Hunchback's place, so that a female monster joins the pantheon of cult images in merchandizing controlled by Universal.

Notes to Chapter 6

1 Mary Wollstonecraft Shelley, *Frankenstein, Or The Modern Prometheus*, 1818 text, ed. (with intro. and notes) Marilyn Butler (London: William Pickering, 1993), xx–xxxi.

2 Ibid., xlvii.

3 Ibid., xv–xx; xliii–xlvi. See also Lee Sterrenburg, "Mary Shelley's Monster: Politics and Psyche in *Frankenstein*," in George Levine and U. C. Knoepflmacher, eds., *The Endurance of Frankenstein: Essays on Mary Shelley's Novel* (Berkeley: University of California Press, 1979), 143–71.

4 For an account of Florey's neglected contributions to the pre-production of *Frankenstein* and subsequent direction of *Murders in the Rue Morgue* (1932) see Brian Taves, "Universal's Horror Tradition," *American Cinematographer* (April, 1987), 36–48. Unfortunately, Florey did not receive screenwriting credit on *Frankenstein*'s US release though his name properly appeared on prints distributed in Europe.

5 Phillip J. Riley, ed., *Dracula: The Original 1931 Shooting Script*. Universal Film Scripts Series, Classic Horror Films, vol. 13 (Atlantic City: MagicImage Filmbooks, 1990), 85.

6 Due to the stricter standards after 1934, the censors urged: "We suggest the deletion of the closing comment of the scientist where he tells the audience that 'after all *there are such things*'" (original emphasis). F. S.

Harmon to J. D. Miller, March 17, 1938. "Dracula," MPPA/Production Code Administration files, Margaret Herrick Library, Beverly Hills, CA.

7   This was apparently the film's third shot originally. When *Bride of Frankenstein* was produced in 1935, two shots from the 1931 film showing the funeral procession moving up the hill and approaching the grave were cut from the negative for the quick montage of highlights appearing at the sequel's beginning. Although other shots and bits of dialog cut from the 1931 release have been restored in recent years for home-video formats, the full opening never was, perhaps because few realized these shots had ever been present.

8   R. H. W. Dillard points to the significance of the Grim Reaper in *Frankenstein*'s cemetery scene but does not mention the equally important effigy of Christ. Whale varies this tableau in *Bride of Frankenstein*, where the monster tips over another statue in a cemetery to uncover the entrance to an underground crypt as a similar crucifixion statue bears witness. R. H. W. Dillard, *Horror Films* (New York: Monarch Press, 1976), 17.

9   Ibid., 16.

10   "The conservative appropriation of the novel as a warning against scientific research, like the conservative religious reading of *Frankenstein*, continues to this day to deflect the novel's reformist intentions. Within the terms of the novel, Frankenstein's limitation is not that he enters sacred realms but that he fails to take responsibility for his own actions." Betty T. Bennett, *Mary Wollstonecraft Shelley: An Introduction* (Baltimore, MD: Johns Hopkins University Press, 1998), 39.

11   Dillard argues for the thematic consistency of this gesture in furthering the up/down motifs in the film, connecting Fritz's comic struggle with his sock to the image of little Maria's father carrying her body through the village, one drenched sock drooping on her leg. Dillard, *Horror Films*, 30–1.

12   This theme is presented far more overtly in *Bride of Frankenstein* in the character of Dr Pretorius. For extended analysis of this genre subtext, see Harry M. Benshoff, *Monsters in the Closet: Homosexuality and the Horror Film* (Manchester and New York: Manchester University Press, 1997).

13   Among other changes, these profane lines were eliminated (obscured with a peal of thunder) by order of the PCA when Universal readied the film for re-release in 1937. See Chapter 4.

14   The neck bolts are sometimes described as the monster's electrical power intakes and, indeed, were depicted this way in later sequels, though never in Whale's two films.

15   Skal, *Monster Show*, 132.

16   Dillard, *Horror Films*, 24.

17   Whale's biographer says this scene prompted the only creative dispute between actor and director during the film's production. James Curtis, *James Whale: A New World of Gods and Monsters* (Boston: Faber & Faber, 1998), 147.

18   Clive was no longer available by then so another actor, seen only in the slightly out-of-focus distance, stands in for him in the last scene. Rudy Behlmer, *Behind the Scenes: The Making of . . .* (New York: Samuel French, 1990), chapter 1, "In His Own Image: *Frankenstein* (1931)," 18. The same last-minute salvation of Clive's character also occurred after principal photography wrapped on *Bride of Frankenstein*.

Notes to Chapter 7

1   French critics coined the term Film Noir in the mid-1950s to describe both the visual and thematic "darkening" of many Hollywood movies in the 1940s. For an introduction to the critical discussion of Film Noir see Alain Silver and James Ursini, eds., *The Film Noir Reader* (New York: Limelight, 1997).

2   Schrader contends: "Film Noir is not a genre . . . It is not defined, as are the western and the gangster genres, by conventions of setting and conflict, but rather by the more subtle qualities of tone and mood." In Film Noir, "the theme is hidden in the style, and bogus themes are often flaunted ('middle-class values are best') which contradict the style." Paul Schrader, "Notes on Film Noir," in Silver and Ursini, *Film Noir Reader*, 53, 63.

3   Although Film Noir was not dependent on the work of particular directors, Jacques Tourneur went on to make significant examples such as *Experiment Perilous* (1944) and *Out of the Past* (1947), the latter often considered one of Noir's most definitive works.

4   "[The filmmakers] have dared to be intelligent in discarding the horror spectacle that usually results from dramatizations of the Robert Louis Stevenson novel. Substituted is an adult treatment of Jekyll and Hyde for adult audiences, an absorbing study with psychological impact." "Tracy's 'Jekyll-Hyde' A Monument to Good Acting," *Hollywood Reporter*, July 22, 1941.

5   The Lewton films often include signage that indirectly comments on the plot. In *The Ghost Ship*, for example, the face of the unhinged Captain (Richard Dix) is reflected in a framed motto which reads: "Who does not heed the rudder shall meet the rock," before he smashes it down.

6   Tony Williams makes a nuanced argument considering Irena a threat to traditional family in *Hearths of Darkness: The Family in the American Horror Film* (Madison: Farleigh Dickinson University Press, 1996). See chapter 3, "Lewton or 'The Ambiguities'." Williams calls Lewton's films "macabre versions of the film noir genre," 51.

7   The portrait is Goya's *Don Manuel Manrique Osorio de Zuñiga*, painted in the early 1790s. The caged finches are said to symbolize the child's innocence; and the danger that lurks just outside, represented by the cats. Tourneur really shows only the lower third of the painting emphasizing

the cats ready to pounce on the unwary bird; in the actual painting, the black cat with glowing yellow eyes in the background appears distinctly ghostly. The painting echoes the film's motifs of cats, caged birds, and an ambiguous image of childhood innocence.

8   See, for example, Williams, *Hearths of Darkness*, 55.
9   See Carlos Clarens, *An Illustrated History of the Horror Film* (1967; New York: Paragon Books, 1979), 113; and Siegel, *Val Lewton*, 35–6. Their point about the ambiguity of the narrative is clear, but so too is the leopard.
10 Schrader, "Notes on Film Noir," 58.
11 Schrader's remaining Noir techniques, fatalistic voice-over narration, and a complex narrative chronology involving flashbacks are not used in *Cat People*. However, voice-over is important in *I Walked With A Zombie*, and the thoughts of a mute sailor conveyed in filtered voice-over are crucial to *The Ghost Ship*. Indeed, these techniques occur in some but not all of the more recognized examples of Film Noir. There is no consensus on the "minimum" number of visual or narrative elements that classify a given movie as Noir, but the importance of high-contrast lighting, baroque shot compositions, and psychologically disturbed or neurotic protagonists seem the most determinative. Ibid., 57–8.
12 Ibid., 57.
13 Ibid.
14 Ibid.
15 Ibid.
16 Siegel, *Val Lewton*, 31–2.
17 Dillard, *Horror Films*, 41–2.
18 See for example, Janey Place, "Women in Film Noir," Sylvia Harvey, "Woman's Place: The Absent Family of Film Noir," and other writers collected in E. Ann Kaplan, ed., *Women in Film Noir* (new revised and expanded edn, London: British Film Institute Press, new revised and expanded edn, 1998).
19 John Berks, "What Alice Does: Looking Otherwise at *The Cat People*," *Cinema Journal*, 32:1 (Fall, 1992), 26–42. Berks calls the zookeeper's song a "funeral dirge" but does not corroborate this identification. Ibid., 36.
20 Schrader, "Notes on Film Noir," 57.
21 Sigmund Freud, *The Interpretation of Dreams*, trans. James Strachey (New York: Avon, 1965), 436.
22 Ibid., 445.
23 Nathan G. Hale, *The Rise and Crisis of Psychoanalysis in the United States: Freud and the Americans, 1917–1985* (New York: Oxford University Press, 1995), 76–7. The mass mobilizations of men in World War I heightened public awareness of Freudian concepts. Psychoanalytic theories and practices were employed to treat the vast numbers of soldiers suffering from psychological impairments initially termed "shell shock" (now called "post-traumatic shock syndrome"). The increased dissemination of psychoanalytic

ideas occurred through the diagnosis and treatment of this initially controversial malady as it was discussed in extensive press reporting, particularly from 1915 through 1921. Chapter 1.

24 C. R. Metzger, "Synopsis: *The Cat People*," July 10, 1942. MPPA/ Production Code Administration files. We can only speculate whether this early draft used an actual quote from Freud or one concocted through artistic license. As I suggested above, the epigraph in the finished film with its reference to "the world consciousness" has a more Jungian tang.

25 Freud was actually distressed by the popular belief that his theories claimed dreams did nothing but comment on sexual matters. In the 1919 edition he wrote: "The assertion that all dreams require a sexual interpretation, against which critics rage so incessantly, occurs nowhere in my *Interpretation of Dreams*. It is not to be found in any of the numerous editions of the book and is in obvious contradiction to other views expressed in it [1919]." Freud, *Interpretation of Dreams*, 423.

26 Hale, *Rise and Crisis of Psychoanalysis in the United States*, 28, 96. Freud knew of the film and wanted no part of it, but his disciple Karl Abraham kept him informed of the progress of scripting and production. Anne Friedberg, "An *Unheimlich* Maneuver between Psychoanalysis and the Cinema: *Secrets of a Soul* (1926)," in Eric Rentschler, ed., *The Films of G.W. Pabst: An Extraterritorial Cinema* (New Brunswick, NJ: Rutgers University Press, 1990), 41–51.

27 As Friedberg notes: "*Secrets of a Soul* was not the first film to deal with serious psychological problems nor the first to attempt cinematic representation of dreams or mental phenomena, but it *was* the first film that directly tried to represent *psychoanalytic* descriptions of the etiology of a phobia and the method of psychoanalysis as treatment" (original emphasis), 45.

28 The optimism represented by a successful Freudian cure usually prevailed – at least on the surface – in Hollywood prestige dramas featuring psychiatrists and their patients such as *King's Row* (1942), *Spellbound* (1945), and *The Snake Pit* (1948).

29 Freud, *Interpretation of Dreams*, 445.

30 Ibid., 389.

31 Ibid., 389–90.

32 For further analysis of *Curse of the Cat People*, see Williams, *Hearths of Darkness*, and J. P. Telotte, *Dreams of Darkness: Fantasy and the Films of Val Lewton* (Urbana: University of Illinois Press, 1985).

Notes to Chapter 8

1 Important films released in 1950 include Eagle-Lion's expensive color production *Destination Moon* with special effects by George Pal, as well as low-budget movies including *The Flying Saucer* and *Rocketship X-M*. Major

studio releases of *The Day the Earth Stood Still* and *The Thing* followed the next year, and the boom was on.

2 Peter Biskind considers *Body Snatchers* a right-wing film in *Seeing Is Believing: How Hollywood Taught Us to Stop Worrying and Love the Fifties* (New York: Pantheon, 1983), 137–44; a similar, briefer argument appears in Nora Sayre, *Running Time: Films of the Cold War* (New York: Dial Press, 1982), 199–201. The liberal "anti-conformity" position is argued by Stuart Samuels, "The Age of Conspiracy and Conformity: 'Invasion of the Body Snatchers'," in John E. O'Connor and Martin A. Jackson, eds., *American History / American Film: Interpreting the Hollywood Image* (New York: Ungar, 1980), 203–17. By carefully considering production documents, Al LaValley critiques these approaches and favors the liberal/left reading in " 'Invasion of the Body Snatchers': Politics, Psychology, Sociology," in LaValley, ed., *Invasion of the Body Snatchers: Don Siegel, Director* (New Brunswick, NJ: Rutgers University Press, 1989), 3–17. LaValley ultimately argues for the film's ideological ambiguity. All these accounts are complementary and illuminating.

3 Guy Braucourt, "Interview with Don Siegel," in LaValley, *Invasion of the Body Snatchers*, 158–9.

4 The studio was also concerned about audience confusion with Val Lewton's RKO production *The Body Snatcher* (1945), starring Boris Karloff. LaValley, *Invasion of the Body Snatchers*, 26.

5 Perhaps punning on the plot of *Body Snatchers*, Biskind writes: "It was no accident that left- and right-wing films resembled each other like two peas in a pod. Radical films generally obscured the difference between right and left in order to create a broad-based coalition against the center." Biskind, *Seeing Is Believing*, 48.

6 For insightful discussion of this aspect of the film see Nancy Steffen-Fluhr, "Women and the Inner Game of Don Siegel's *Invasion of the Body Snatchers*," in LaValley, *Invasion of the Body Snatchers*, 206–21.

7 The gasman is played by future writer-director Sam Peckinpah, known for some of the most complex and violent films of the Vietnam era, including *The Wild Bunch* (1969), *Straw Dogs* (1972), and *Bring Me the Head of Alfredo Garcia* (1974). Peckinpah was also an assistant to Siegel on *Body Snatchers*.

8 Stuart M. Kaminsky made a similar point in an interview with Siegel. Stuart M. Kaminsky, "Don Siegel on the Pod Society," in LaValley, *Invasion of the Body Snatchers*, 155.

9 This argument about the complex interplay between "monster" and "woman" in postwar science fiction is also taken up by Biskind, *Seeing Is Believing*, 123–7; in discussion of *Them!* Cynthia Freeland devotes an insightful chapter to this issue in *The Naked and the Undead: Evil and the Appeal of Horror* (Boulder CO: Westview Press, 2000), 55–86. See also Steffen-Fluhr, "Women and the Inner Game."

10   LaValley, *Invasion of the Body Snatchers*, 15.

11   See Susan L. Carruthers, "*The Manchurian Candidate* (1962) and the Cold War Brainwashing Scare," *Historical Journal of Film, Radio, and Television*, 18:1 (1998), 75–94. See also Sayre, *Running Time*.

Notes to Chapter 9

1   For the movie's tangled production and distribution history, see Ellen Farley and William K. Knoedelsender, Jr., "The Real 'Texas Chain Saw Massacre'," *Los Angeles Times*, September 5, 1982, 4. Additional oral history interviews are in Alex Lewin, "Adventures in the Scream Trade," *Premiere*, 14:6 (February, 2001), 82–6. The most detailed version is John Bloom, "They Came. They Sawed," *Texas Monthly*, November, 2004, 162–9; 245–56. This is a straightforward, factual account not written in the voice of Bloom's comic persona, Joe Bob Briggs. These reports agree that the movie was highly profitable; and that Hooper and his partners (including much of the film's cast and crew) saw little of it.

2   Wood, *Hollywood From Vietnam to Reagan*, 90.

3   Released in late December, 1973, *The Exorcist* made most of its commercial and publicized cultural impact in the calendar year 1974, which is to say roughly coinciding with the October début of *Texas Chain Saw Massacre*. The films became linked in some media accounts.

4   See Robert B. Ray, *A Certain Tendency of the Hollywood Cinema, 1930–1980* (Princeton, NJ: Princeton University Press, 1985), especially chapter 8, "The 1960s: Frontier Metaphors, Developing Self-Consciousness, and New Waves," 247–95.

5   The given names of the characters comprising the monster family are unknown. These designations Hitchhiker, Leatherface, and Old Man appear in the end credits. Some critical accounts refer to the Old Man as "The Cook," taken from the Hitchhiker's spiteful insult during Sally's dinner-table torture. Others state that the Old Man is the father of the family. In the director's commentary on the DVD, Hooper allows that though this is somewhat unclear in the film, the Old Man was intended to be the eldest brother. In the jokey *Texas Chain Saw Massacre 2* (1986), the monsters get first names and the allegedly funny last name "the Sawyers."

6   John Wayne's iconic image looms here, as in many aspects of postwar cultural history. Three of Wayne's most important roles in this period specifically identified him as figures of Texas legend: the empire-building cattle rancher in *Red River* (1948); the hardened Indian-fighter in *The Searchers* (1956); and as Davy Crockett in his personally produced and directed version of *The Alamo* (1960). The first critic to analyze the frontier connections in *Chain Saw Massacre* is Tony Williams, "American Cinema in the 70s: *The Texas Chain Saw Massacre*," *Movie*, 25 (1978),

12–16. See also Christopher Sharrett, "The Idea of Apocalypse in *The Texas Chain Saw Massacre*," in Barry Keith Grant, ed., *Planks of Reason: Essays on the Horror Film* (Metuchen, NJ: Scarecrow Press, 1984), 274. The thread occurs in "The American Nightmare," but Wood applies it primarily in discussion of Craven's *The Hills Have Eyes* (1977), a work that develops motifs from *Chain Saw Massacre* and Craven's own *Last House on the Left*.

7 For detailed consideration of the Western in relation to American political and cultural history in this period, see Richard Slotkin, *Gun-Fighter Nation: The Myth of the Frontier in the Twentieth Century* (New York: Antheneum, 1992).

8 See, by contrast, Universal's peculiar horror-western *Curse of the Undead* (1959), in which the vampire gunslinger is finally defeated in a shootout with a preacher who engraves a cross on bullets in his six-gun. This is at base a classical Western plot with a frontier hero killing an "outlaw" to make the town safe; or, alternately, a classical horror plot with a male hero saving a woman and society from the monster.

9 Gein's capture made national headlines and was featured in stories with accompanying photos in both *Time* and *Life* magazines in December, 1957. As a child, Hooper had heard tales about Gein from Wisconsin relatives. Co-writer Kim Henkel told Bloom he researched the Gein case during the writing process.

10 Wood, *Hollywood From Vietnam to Reagan*, 90.

11 Ironic references to classic horror appear often in the revisionist horror of the Vietnam era; e.g., Johnny's taunting of Barbara in the opening scene of *Night of the Living Dead* with a Boris Karloff impression: "They're coming to get you, Barbara," he lisps, just as the first zombie appears and gets Johnny.

12 Unlike the confusion about the Old Man's relationship to the others, there is no clear evidence that the window-washer was meant to be Leatherface without the mask. However, if not Leatherface, this character's identity is another elusive aspect of a film often short on narrative explanations.

13 Other horror films that depicted cannibalism include *Deranged*, another Ed Gein-inspired tale (though whether Gein actually practiced cannibalism is unclear), the British import *Raw Meat* (1973), and *The Hills Have Eyes*. *Halloween* implies that Michael Myers is cannibalistic. *Motel Hell* (1980), a semi-parody of the cannibalism theme, flaunts major elements of *Psycho* and *Chain Saw Massacre*, attesting to the impact the two films had exerted on the genre at this point.

14 "It is striking that no suggestion exists anywhere that Sally is the object of an overtly sexual threat: she is to be tormented, killed, dismembered, eaten, but not raped. Ultimately, the most terrifying thing about the film is its total negativity: the repressed energies – represented most unforgettably by Leatherface and his continuously whirring phallic chain saw

– are presented as irredeemably debased and distorted." Wood, *Hollywood From Vietnam to Reagan*, 91.

15 Wood briefly observes, with little subsequent elaboration, "It is worth noting here that one group of intellectuals did take American horror movies very seriously indeed: the writers, painters, and filmmakers of the Surrealist movement." Ibid., 78. I submit that Tobe Hooper returned the gesture. For elaboration on the theme of this exchange, see Joan Hawkins, *Cutting Edge: Art-Horror and the Horrific Avant-Garde* (Minneapolis: University of Minnesota Press, 2000). More concerned with shifting cultural definitions of high and low, however, Hawkins' insightful study actually says little about *Texas Chain Saw Massacre* specifically.

16 Hooper was clearly determined to include this construction in the film. He shot an alternate version of this scene where Kirk and Pam find the decaying campsite in the woods and the pocket watch is nailed to a tree trunk. (The outtakes appear in the DVD special features.) In the final cut, Hooper condensed this episode substantially yet moved the conception closer to Dali's painting by hanging the impaled watch from a bare tree branch.

17 For Dali and Buñuel, this image was partly a sight gag, literally picturing the French colloquial expression, *avoir des fourmis dans les mains* ("to have ants in the hand"), to refer to the tingling sensation of a hand "falling asleep." The hole in the palm here might also refer ironically to the stigmata of Christ.

18 Burns' work on this film led to impressive contributions to *The Hills Have Eyes, The Howling* (1981), and *Re-Animator* (1985).

19 In the DVD director's commentary Hooper recounts that he spoke often with the MPAA ratings board during the shooting and editing. He originally sought a PG rating (even a PG-13 would be impossible today) to ensure the widest possible audience, which may directly explain why the film contains no nudity. He also says the ratings board indicated that particular effects, such as seeing Pam's body penetrated by the hook, would likely result in a R-rating. Hooper was pushing the envelope, but doing so in direct negotiation with the ratings system. The film's strong violence ultimately resulted in the R-rating anyway, which did not hurt its commercial success.

20 Leatherface actually wears three different masks in the film, one a woman's face (with a wig) to which, in a deleted scene, he applies makeup. This was intended to vary his "personality" in the most hideous way possible by literally changing "faces," while also referencing Ed Gein's atrocities. In the end, apart from Leatherface's unnerving closeup sequence after Jerry's murder, these elements were downplayed in favor of maintaining the film's pace.

21 Grandpa's makeup is reminiscent of the prosthetic effects Hollywood makeup artist Dick Smith designed for two seemingly dissimilar films a

few years earlier, works that, considered together, oddly anticipate motifs in *Texas Chain Saw Massacre*: Dustin Hoffman's look as the 121-year-old Jack Crabb in Penn's revisionist Western *Little Big Man* (1970) and vampire Barnabas Collins' brief reversion to his true two-century age in *House of Dark Shadows* (1970).

22 One of the opening news reports recounts the discovery of mutilated corpses with genitals removed, making even immediate confirmation of the gender of the dead uncertain.

23 This segment immediately follows Sally's choked plea, "I'll do anything you want," and the cannibals' incomprehension. Yet the interjection of montage and off-sync sound breaks linear cause-and-effect logic and thus does not signal that their laughter or Sally's delirium is a consequence of this dialog. The second montage of Sally's terror-filled eyes, however, seems directly tied to the Hitchhiker's line, "Hey Grandpa, we're gonna let you have this one!"

24 Sharrett, "Idea of Apocalypse in *The Texas Chain Saw Massacre*," 271.

25 *Psycho*'s ending is not terribly cathartic or reassuring either. As Mark Crispin Miller contends, "In the end [Norman/the audience's] whole project of absolute repression breaks down in a terminal montage of unsurpassed uncanniness, as that boyish face smiles up at us through Mother's bony rictus, and then the white car reemerges startlingly, yanked up and lunging toward us from the depths." Mark Crispin Miller, "Advertising: End of Story," in Miller, ed., *Seeing Through Movies* (New York: Pantheon, 1990), 227.

Notes to Chapter 10

1 The subjective camera was the particular target of Roger Ebert's influential article, "Why Audiences Aren't Safe Anymore," *American Film*, 6:5 (March, 1981), 54–6. In a similar vein, columnist Janet Maslin wrote: "To say [slasher films] aren't very frightening is not to say that they don't have a profound effect on those who watch them. Go see one, and you'll have empirical proof that a film like this makes audiences mean . . . Violence in the real world becomes much more acceptable after you've seen infinitely greater [sic] violence on the screen." "Bloodbaths Debase Movies and Audiences," *New York Times*, November 21, 1982, Section 2, 1, 13.

2 Carol J. Clover, *Men, Women, and Chain Saws: Gender in the Modern Horror Film*. See chapter one, "Her Body, Himself," 21–64. Other important and nuanced academic feminist analyses of the slasher cycle include Linda Williams, "Film Bodies: Gender, Genre, and Excess," in Leo Braudy and Marshall Cohen, eds., *Film Theory and Criticism: Introductory Readings* (5th edn, New York: Oxford University Press, 1999), 701–15; and Cynthia

A. Freeland, *The Naked and the Undead: Evil and the Appeal of Horror* (Boulder, CO: Westview Press, 2000).

3 Brian De Palma repeated this idea in *Body Double* (1984), whose multiple references and reworkings of Hitchcock include casting Melanie Griffith, the daughter of actress Tippi Hedren (*The Birds, Marnie*), as a blond, sexually alluring object of a phobic man's desire.

4 In 1967, Carlos Clarens wrote: "Although pathological case histories lie outside the province and proper spectrum of the pure horror film – as in the case of *M* or the horrifying *Psycho* – Michael Powell's *Peeping Tom* (1960) almost bridges the gap, concerned as it is not so much with terror as with the face of terror." Clarens, *Illustrated History of the Horror Film*, 145. Ivan Butler devotes an appreciative chapter to Hitchcock in his 1967 horror survey, but presents no rationale for why *Psycho* should be included in such a study. Ivan Butler, *The Horror Film* (London: A. Zwemmer, 1967); see chapter 9, "Hitchcock and *Psycho*," 93–101. The conceptual uncertainty of these two perceptive critics is telling. By around 1980, however, "pathological case histories" had become for many virtually the definition of the horror film.

5 Brian Davis' schematic overview of the thriller mainly discusses 1940s Film Noir and later crime movies revolving around robbery and pursuit. He devotes a chapter to "The *Psycho* Syndrome," films featuring insane killers, noting equivocally: "The *Psycho* 'school' borrows its rules from the horror genre and deliberately sets out to disturb and disorient the audience." *The Thriller: The Suspense Film from 1946* (London: Studio Vista, 1973), 103. In a more sophisticated discussion Martin Rubin argues that "The thriller can be conceptualized as a 'metagenre' that gathers several other genres [e.g. hard-boiled detective, spy, horror, disaster] under its umbrella, and as a band in the spectrum that colors each of those particular genres." He emphasizes the particular emotional reactions evoked by thrillers stressing their ambivalent pull between "anxiety and pleasure, masochism and sadism, identification and detachment." *Thrillers* (New York: Cambridge University Press, 1999), 4, 6. Consistent with these concepts, he later terms *Psycho* "a sensationally successful foray into the horror genre," 114.

6 Historical context remains vital overall. Robert E. Kapsis points out that when, around 1980, journalistic critics began to compare *Halloween* and other slasher films unfavorably to *Psycho*, they did so by praising Hitchcock's artful restraint; whereas in 1960, many critics and viewers considered the film to have exceeded prevailing standards of taste in its shocking depictions of blood and violence as well as tawdry sexuality. Kapsis, *Hitchcock: The Making of A Reputation* (Chicago: University of Chicago Press, 1992), 56–64; 165–72.

7 For an interesting discussion of the motif of eyes and vision in *Halloween*, see J. P. Tellotte, "Through a Pumpkin's Eye: The Reflexive Nature of

Horror," in Gregory A. Waller, ed., *American Horrors: Essays on the Modern American Horror Film* (Urbana and Chicago: University of Illinois Press, 1987), 114–28.

8   For analysis of different possibilities of identification or narrative uses of the ambiguous/subjective camera, see Isabel Cristina Pinedo, *Recreational Terror: Women and the Pleasure of Horror Film Viewing* (Albany: SUNY Press, 1997), 51–5.

9   *Halloween II* (1981), which picks up directly from the final moments of the original, includes Laurie's belated discovery that she too is Michael's sister and that he is repeating the pattern of his murder of Judith. Though Carpenter and producer Debra Hill co-wrote both screenplays, there is no evidence in the original that this plot point was on their minds then. Even so, the twisted domestic ties of the story easily accommodate this development, explicit or not.

10 Moreover, in *Halloween II*, Ben Tramer dies accidentally later that same night while wearing a white rubber mask, his burned body mistaken for Michael.

11 Jordan R. Fox, "Carpenter: Riding High on Horror," *Cinefantastique*, 10:1 (1981), 40.

12 For introduction to Argento's work see Maitland McDonagh, *Broken Mirrors/Broken Minds: The Dark Dreams of Dario Argento* (New York: Citadel Press, 1991). Adam Knee discusses Argento's point of view manipulation in "Gender, Genre, Argento," in Barry Keith Grant, ed., *The Dread of Difference: Gender and the Horror Film* (Austin: University of Texas Press, 1996), 213–30.

13 "It is not simply a world in which the adults are largely absent; more significantly, it is one in which that sense of human responsibility and complicity that we conventionally associate with adulthood is conspicuously missing". Telotte, "Through a Pumpkin's Eye," 127.

14 For insightful analysis of these themes in post-1968 horror films, see Vivian Sobchack, "Bringing It All Back Home: Family Economy and Generic Exchange", in Waller, *American Horrors*, 175–94.

Notes to Chapter 11

1   Remarks made at Southern Methodist University, April, 1998.

2   Susan Sontag, "Notes on 'Camp'," in *Against Interpretation and Other Essays* (New York: Farrar, Straus, & Giroux, 1966), 275.

3   The head's attack on Meg was even giddily discussed by Kevin Spacey and Wes Bentley in the award-winning *American Beauty* (1999).

4   The unrated theatrical version of *Re-Animator* removes a subplot that describes Dr Hill's experiments with mind control and the laser drill that provides more of an explanation for how he can coordinate his separated

head and body and finally direct the other reanimated corpses in the morgue. This subplot was included in the R-rated version released on home video.

5 Paul, *Laughing, Screaming*, 66–7. Paul never mentions *Re-Animator*, which would seem to be one of the surest proofs of his overall argument.

Notes to Chapter 12

1 Leonard Wolf, *A Dream of Dracula: In Search of the Living Dead* (Boston: Little, Brown, 1972); Raymond T. McNally and Radu R. N. Florescu, *In Search of Dracula: A True History of Dracula and Vampire Legends* (Greenwich, CT: New York Graphic Society, 1972).

2 Francis Ford Coppola and James V. Hart, Bram Stoker's Dracula: *The Film and The Legend* (New York: Newmarket Press, 1992), 7.

3 Ibid., 3.

4 In chapter three, however Dracula regales Harker with tales of wars fought by his ancestors, including those against the Turks. Harker notes that Dracula "spoke as if he had been present at them all," and of course we must presume that he was.

5 David Pirie, *A Heritage of Horror: The English Gothic Cinema, 1946–1972* (New York: Avon, 1973), chapter 5, "Approaches to Dracula . . . ," 82–98.

6 For a thoroughly negative political assessment of the film see Christopher Sharrett, "The Horror Film in Neoconservative Culture," in Grant, *Dread of Difference*, 253–76. Coppola is defended in David Ehrenstein, "One From the Art," *Film Comment*, 29:1 (January–February, 1993), 27–30.

7 The Hungarian-born Bela Lugosi defined the popular American image of Dracula as decidedly foreign, yet hardly "eastern," as Stoker emphasizes. Lugosi's vampire was another oily Continental roué, a stock figure of American popular culture throughout the nineteenth and early twentieth centuries. Hammer's Christopher Lee spoke in clipped British English, little different from Peter Cushing's Van Helsing.

8 Kurt W. Treplow, *Vlad III Dracula: The Life and Times of the Historical Dracula* (Oxford: Center for Romanian Studies, 2000), 8, 10.

9 For discussion of these effects in the work of Coppola and "The New Hollywood" directors of the 1970s, see Robert Ray, *A Certain Tendency of the Hollywood Cinema, 1930–1980*, chapter 12, "*The Godfather* and *Taxi Driver*," 326–60.

10 Coppola and Hart, Bram Stoker's Dracula, 38.

11 It is surely incorrect to assume that Stoker or his Victorian readers were unaware of the sexual implications of this scene. For analysis of the novel on this point, see Phyllis A. Roth, "Suddenly Sexual Women in Bram Stoker's 'Dracula'," and Christopher Bentley, "The Monster in the

Bedroom: Sexual Symbolism in Bram Stoker's 'Dracula'," in Margaret L. Carter, ed., Dracula: *The Vampire and the Critics* (Ann Arbor, MI: UMI Research Press, 1988). For droll dissection of the scene, see King, *Danse Macabre*, 73–5.

12 In this regard, it may not be coincidental that as both Elisabeta and Mina, Winona Ryder typically wears garments of rich green, the same color often worn by Kim Novak's ghostly Madeleine in *Vertigo*. When Scotty (James Stewart) and Madeleine visit the giant redwoods, he translates the species' Latin name as "always green, ever living."

13 Both Ehrenstein and Sharrett associate this episode and Van Helsing's lecture to medical students with the ongoing AIDS epidemic.

14 Remarks by James V. Hart at the Deep Ellum Film Festival, Dallas Texas, November 19, 2005.

Notes to Afterword

1 For consideration of these films see Peter Lev, *American Films of the 70s: Conflicting Visions* (Austin: University of Texas Press, 2000), chapter 3, "Disaster and Conspiracy," 40–59.

2 For analysis of *Independence Day* along these lines in relation to the Clinton years, see Michael Rogin, Independence Day: *or How I Learned to Stop Worrying and Love the Enola Gay* (London: British Film Institute Press, 1998).

3 For insightful analysis of *The Ring* and other recent Hollywood remakes of Asian horror films, see Kevin Heffernan's forthcoming article, "*Kaidan* Ghosts and *Gaijin* Monsters: Hollywood and the Re-Making of Contemporary Asian Horror."

INDEX

Note: Film and play titles are shown in italics with year of release/production. Book, and other literary/artistic, titles are in italics with author's name and year of publication/production.

Abbott, Bruce 245
Abbott and Costello Meet Frankenstein (1948) 77, 246
Abby (1974) 97
ABC 91, 92, 93, 138
Abominable Dr. Phibes, The (1971) 8, 97–8

abortion 143
Absalom, Absalom! (William Faulkner 1936) 29
Academy Awards 20, 59, 108, 154, 253
Ackerman, Forrest J. 85, 139, 141, 155
Adams, Julia 80
Addams, Charles 92
Addams Family, The 92, 111, 138–9, 141, 215
advertising 85, 86, 141; come-ons 81; move that often limits access to 243; sexist images in 142
Aelita, Queen of Mars (1924) 49
African-Americans 95, 111, 267, 274; mobilizing for the war effort 130; rash of low-budget movies with 96
AIDS 111, 275
AIP (American International Pictures) 80, 81, 84, 86, 88, 90, 95, 96–7, 102, 104, 107, 112, 154, 155, 175, 51, 256, 274
Air Force (1943) 128
Airport (1970) 267
Alien (1979) 12, 102, 115
alien invasions 77–8, 206, 193, 195, 267, 277
All Quiet on the Western Front (1930) 55
allegory 3, 12, 49, 54, 206–7, 273; Christ, explicit 254; nuclear doom 95
Allied Artists 78, 81, 194, 196, 197
Almost Married (1931) 120

Amazing Colossal Man, The (1957) 78
American Film Institute 156
American Gothic (Grant Wood 1930) 222
American Werewolf in London, An (1981) 108
Amicus 97
Amityville Horror, The (1979) 102
androgyny 233, 259
Ankers, Evelyn 70
Annabel Lee (Edgar Allan Poe 1849) 42
anthology films 88, 89–90, 91
anticommunist witchhunt 195
antiheroes 96–7
antitrust litigation 76
Antonioni, M. 270
anxiety 7, 138, 182; age of 77, 193–204; atomic 206; sexual, adolescent 81; women's changing roles 242
Apparition, The (1903) 33–4
Applause (1929) 59
Argento, Dario 114, 237, 276
Aristotle 13–14
Arkoff, Samuel Z. 80, 81, 88, 102
Armageddon (1998) 267
Armstrong, Robert 63
art-cinema style 4, 91, 210
Arzen, Michael A. 111
Asian movies 115, 116
Astin, John 92
At the Telephone (1902) 38
atomic bombs 77, 78, 203; fear of war 195
Atwill, Lionel 64, 69
Auden, W. H. 77
audiences 137; fright experienced by 16; identification and sympathy 246; manipulation of 113, 226; smaller and younger 80; teenage 142; urban black 96; youthful 90
Audrey Rose (1977) 100
Aurora toy company 141
auteurism 3, 5, 107, 230, 273–8
avant-garde 4, 44, 57, 159, 219
Avenging Conscience, The (1914) 42–3

B movies 72, 126
Baby Boom generation 76, 137, 155
Baclanova, Olga 62
bad deaths 8, 12

Badham, John 100, 255
Baggot, King 41
Baker, Rick 85, 107–8
Ballard, J. G. 275
Band, Charles and Albert 251
Banks, Leslie 62
Bara, Theda 156
Barker, Clive 106, 107
Barry, Gene 268
Barrymore, Drew 113
Barrymore, John 41, 64
Bat, The (1926) 146
Batman Forever (1994) 112
Battle of Britain (1940) 129, 132
Bauhaus 65
Bava, Mario 89–90, 114, 276
Bay, Michael 225
Beast From 20,000 Fathoms, The (1955) 78
Beast With Five Fingers, The (1946) 75
Beatles, The 138, 215
Beauty and the Beast myth 148
Beck, Calvin T. 140
Bedlam (1946) 74
Beetlejuice (1988) 278
Beginning of the End, The (1957) 78
Bell, Ulric 131
Bella, Rachel 270
Bells, The (1926) 50
Belmore, Lionel 167
Benham, Henry 41
Benjamin, Richard 17
Bergman, Ingmar 91, 230
Bergquist, Lillian 131, 135–6
Berks, John 186
Bewitched Inn, The (1897) 33
Bible 118, 140, 182
Biel, Jessica 225
Billy the Kid vs. Dracula (1966) 5
Biograph Company 38
Bird With the Crystal Plumage, The (1970) 237
Birds, The (1963) 95
Bissell, Whit 81, 195
Black Cat, The (1934) 65, 66, 88, 124, 125
Black Christmas (1974) 104
black comedy 19, 63, 249
Black Dragons (1942) 128
Black Sabbath (1963) 90

Black Sunday (1961) 89
Blackenstein (1973) 97, 103
Blacula (1972) 96–7
Blade (1998) 117
Blair, Linda 2, 100
Blair Witch Project, The (1999) 113–14, 225, 269
Blake, Michael F. 148
Blatty, William Peter 100, 114
Blaxploitation 96–7, 111
Blind Bargain, A (1922) 51
Bloch, Robert 86, 212, 245
blockbusters 100, 210, 225
Blood Feast (1963) 90
Blow Up (1966) 270
Blue Angel, The (1930) 149
Blue Oyster Cult 236
BMP (OWI Bureau of Motion Pictures) 129, 130, 131, 132, 134, 135
Bodeen, DeWitt 73
"body-count movies" 231
Body Double (1984) 275
"body genres" 275
Body Snatcher, The (1945) 74
Body Snatchers, The (Jack Finney 1955) 197 *see also Invasion of the Body Snatchers*
Boehm, Carl 87
Bogdanovich, Peter 95–6
Boles, John 163
Bond, James (III) 111
Bone Collector, The (1999) 113
Bonnie and Clyde (1967) 94, 210
"Bonus Army" demonstrators 121
Boorman, John 100
Bottin, Rob 277
Bowie, David 111
Bowman, Dave 223
Boy and His Dog, A (1975) 102
Boyle, Peter 98
brainwashing scare 206
Bram Stoker's Dracula (1992) 111, 250, 253–65
Breen, Joseph I. 121, 123, 124, 125, 126, 127
Bride of Frankenstein (1935) 66–7, 82, 161, 165, 166, 226
Bride With White Hair, The (1993) 115
Britain 95, 122–3; government ban on horror movies (mid-1942) 129

British Board of Film Censors 67, 123, 126
Broadway 53, 54, 55, 57, 255
Broken Blossoms (1919) 240
Brood, The (1978) 275
Brooks, Mel 98, 127
Browning, Tod 5, 55, 56, 57, 62, 144–56, 157
Buffy the Vampire Slayer (1992) 111
Bullitt (1968) 94
Buñuel, Luis 219
Burning, The (1981) 11
Burns, Marilyn 210, 221
Burns, Robert A. 220, 223
Burnt Offerings (1976) 100
Burr, Raymond 78
Burstyn, Ellen 100
Burton, Tim 85, 277, 278
Bushman, Francis X. 156
Butler, Marilyn 159
Byron, George Gordon, Lord 66, 158, 159, 165

Cabinet of Dr. Caligari, The (1920) 38, 44–7, 48, 49, 50, 51, 57, 58, 61, 116, 145, 160, 163, 188, 207, 250, 258
Cagney, James 154, 155
Calley, Lt. William 211
Campbell, Bill 262
Campbell, Bruce 110
Campbell, John W. 277
Candyman (1992) 107
Cannes Film Festival 243
cannibals 99, 208, 216–18, 219, 224
canon formation 3–4
Capra, Frank 278
Carmilla (J. Sheridan Le Fanu 1872) 255
Carnival of Souls (1962) 91
Carpenter, John 11, 85, 101, 104, 107, 227, 229–37, 239–42, 276, 277
Carradine, John 75, 88, 130, 155
Carreras, James 82
Carrie (1976) 27, 29, 101, 240, 242, 274
Carter, Ann 74, 191–2
Carter, Jimmy 104
Castle, Nick 229
Castle, William 81–2, 86, 87, 88, 96, 115, 154, 230
Castle of Frankenstein (magazine) 137, 140–1, 154

Castle of Otranto, The (Horace Walpole 1764) 6, 12, 27, 29, 30
castration 99, 148; symbols of 149
castration anxiety 63, 144
Cat and the Canary, The (1927) 50, 54, 146
Cat o' Nine Tails (1971) 276
Cat People (1942) 14, 73, 176–92, 197
  see also Curse of the Cat People
catharsis 13–14, 19, 20, 206, 241, 271
Catholic Legion of Decency 65, 66, 121
CBS 91, 92, 138, 277
censorship 7, 8, 11, 14, 39, 66, 84, 125, 130, 187; end of (1968) 5, 38, 209; major change in the system 121; nascent motion-picture business seeking to protect itself from 160; politically appointed boards 122, 126; strict, *Frankenstein* the chief cause of 122–3
Chambers, Marilyn 275
Chandler, Helen 265
Chaney, Lon 50–5, 70, 71, 85, 98, 144–56
Chaney, Lon Jr. (Creighton Chaney) 70–1, 75, 77, 84, 88, 129, 154, 155, 179
Changeling, The (1980) 100
Chaplin, Charles 250
characters; clown 149; comic 159; deformed servant 9; iconic 30; mad scientist 9, 54, 75; psychotic slasher 9; werewolf 9; wise elder 9 *see also* Dracula character; Frankenstein Monster; King Kong character; Jekyll and Hyde characters; Mummy character; Phantom of the Opera character
Child's Play (1988) 106–7
Chimes at Midnight (1966) 257
Chinese Revolution (1949) 77
Christian tradition 26, 161, 258
Christine (1983) 277
Christopher, Dennis 109
Chrome and Hot Leather (1970) 97
"cinema of attractions" 33, 43, 107
Cinematograph 32, 257, 262, 263
Civil Rights movement 4, 90, 94, 138, 267
Clark, Bob 103, 104

Clarke, Mae 163
Clemens, Valdine 28–9
Clifford, John 91
Clive, Colin 57, 58, 63, 66, 161, 247
Clockwork Orange, A (1971) 102
Close Encounters of the Third Kind (1977) 102, 239
Clover, Carol J. 228–9, 275
Cobb, Lee J. 115
Cold War 77, 78, 156, 193, 206; Civil Defense drills in early years 205; repeated confrontations and crises 91; science fiction's rise to popularity in the midst of 267; sublimated anxiety 136
Colonial 78
Columbia 72, 73, 81, 132, 254; Censor warning notes sent to 126; television division 84
Columbine High School shooting rampage (1999) 143
Combs, Jeffrey 108, 245, 247, 249, 250
comedy 82, 84, 146, 246; absurdist 110, 243; attempts to combine horror and 243–4; black 19, 63, 249; gross-out 250; haunted-house 50, 53, 54; mixed with extreme violence and gore 110; romantic 16, 115; sick 224; thriller 55 *see also* slapstick
Coming Home (1978) 231
Communion ritual 63
communism 77; crumbled 267; international onslaught 206; theoretically classless society of 204; threat of 136
Conquest of the Pole, The (1912) 35
Conway, Tom 178, 189, 191
Coogan, Jackie 92
Coppola, Francis Ford 253–4, 255, 257, 258, 259, 260, 262, 265, 274
copulation symbols 149
Corman, Roger 88–9, 91, 95, 96, 251, 256
Costner, Kevin 115
counter-culture movements 21
Courtin, Robert 216
Crampton, Barbara 245, 250
Crash (1998) 275
Craven, Wes 99, 106, 109, 113
Crawford, Joan 144, 147, 151

Crazies, The (1974) 273
Creature From the Black Lagoon, The (1954) 79–80
Creature Walks Among Us, The (1956) 80
Creeping Unknown, The see Quatermass
Creepshow (1982) 274
Crime in the Madhouse, A (1925) 37
critics 3, 7, 12, 14, 71, 176, 257; feminist 89; leftist 208; rapprochement between audiences and 4; social, radical 21
Cronenberg, David 107, 275
crucifixes 134, 219
Cruise, Tom 112, 268
Cruze, James 41
Cuban Missile Crisis (1962) 92, 137, 156
cult movies 78, 99, 194
cultural conservatives 208
cunnilingus 250
Cunningham, Sean S. 104
Curse of Frankenstein (1957) 19, 82–3, 84, 88, 154, 244
Curse of the Cat People (1944) 73–4, 191
Curse of the Undead (1959) 19, 20
Curse of the Werewolf (1961) 84
Curtis, Dan 92–3
Curtis, Jamie Lee 101, 104, 229, 230, 234, 239
Curtiz, Michael 64
Cushing, Peter 82, 83, 84, 88, 96, 155

Dagover, Lil 49
Dali, Salvador 218–19
Dance of the Vampires (1967) 93
Dante, Joe 82, 85, 137, 277, 278
Dante's Peak (1997) 267
Danziger, Allen 210
Dark Shadows (1966–71) 92–3
Daughters of Darkness (1971) 96
Davis, Geena 275
Dawley, J. Searle 39–40
Dawn of the Dead (1979) 108, 273, 274
Day of the Dead (1985) 273–4
Day the Earth Stood Still, The (1951) 77–8, 206
DC/National Comics 141
Dead Alive/Braindead (1992) 246
Dead and Buried (1981) 11
Dead Child, The (1918) 37

Dead Hate the Living, The (2000) 7
Dead Ringers (1988) 10, 275
Deadly Mantis, The (1957) 78
Dean, Julia 192
death 7–8, 23, 276; fear of 7, 26, 146; monster as personification of 7; talisman against 112; wish to conquer 165
Deathdream (1974) 103
Decla 44, 45
Deep Impact (1998) 267
Deep Red (1975) 237, 276
Deer Hunter, The (1978) 231
Def By Temptation (1990) 111
"deflowering" 172
Dementia 13 (1963) 256
DeMille, Cecil B. 261
demon-child movies 100, 271
demons 27, 28, 35, 93; family assaulted by 104; half-animal 43; muscular 26; sadomasochistic 106; vampiric female sexual 111
Dempsey, Michael 148
Deneuve, Catherine 93, 111
De Palma, Brian 27, 142, 240, 274–5
Der Januskopf (1920) 47
Der Müde Tod (1921) 47, 49, 54
Deranged (1974) 210
Destiny (1921) 47, 49
detective genre 28
determinists 14
Devil 25, 28, 34, 100, 125, 233
Dickinson, Angie 142
Dillard, R. H. W. 5, 161–2, 172, 185
Direct Cinema documentary 4
directors *see* Antonioni; Argento; Barker; Bava; Bogdanovich; Boorman; Brooks; Browning; Burton; Capra; Carpenter; Castle; Coppola; Corman; Cronenberg; Curtiz; Dante; Dawley; Franco; Fuest; Hitchcock; Hooper; Julian; Lucas; Mamoulian; Murnau; Pabst; Polanski; Reeves (M.); Robson; Romero; Scorsese; Siegel; Spielberg; Tourneur; Waggner; Welles; West; Whale; Wise
disaster-movie cycle (1970s) 267
Dismute, Paul 148
Disney, Walt 112
divorce rate 112

domestic subversion 205–6
Donne, John 191
Donovan, King 195
doppelgängers 31, 47, 99, 107, 174, 215
Double Indemnity (1944) 177
Dr. Jekyll and Mr. Hyde (1908/1911/
  1913/1920) 18, 41–2; (1931) 41,
  59–61, 112, 120, 124, 157, 167, 189,
  258; (1941) 60, 69, 179
Dr. Jekyll and Sister Hyde (1972) 96–7
Dr. Strangelove (1964) 111
Dr. X (1933) 4, 64
Dracula (Bram Stoker 1897) 17, 30, 122,
  159, 254, 255, 256, 257
Dracula (1931) 5, 19, 55, 56–7, 59, 64,
  67, 68, 120, 121–2, 128, 135, 144,
  157, 160, 165; (1938) double feature
  (*Frankenstein*) re-release 126, 161;
  (1979) 100–1, 112; (1994) 112 *see also*
  Billy the Kid vs. Dracula; *Bram Stoker's
  Dracula*; *Horror of Dracula*; *House of
  Dracula*; *Taste the Blood of Dracula*
Dracula character 2, 4, 13, 31, 39, 105,
  106, 146, 153; imitation of scenes
  from 109, 112
Dracula: The Vampire Play (1927) 57,
  135, 161
Dracula Has Risen From the Grave (1969)
  226
Dracula 2000 (2000) 117
Dracula's Daughter (1936) 58, 67, 125–6
Dracula's Greatest Hits (comedy LP)
  138
Dragonfly (2002) 115
Drake, Frances 63
Dreadful Pleasures (James Twitchell 1985)
  6, 30
Dream of a Rarebit Fiend, The (1906)
  35
dreams 33, 149; characteristics of 201;
  Freudian theory often located in 188;
  rooms in 190
DreamWorks 115
Dressed to Kill (1980) 142, 274
Dreyer, Carl Theodor 4, 91, 260
Driller Killer (1979) 105
drive-ins 80, 90, 208
Du Maurier, Daphne 29
Dunwich Horror, The (H. P. Lovecraft
  1928) 245–6

Duvall, Shelly 102
DVDs (Digital Video Discs) 114

Earles, Harry 62–3, 150
Earthquake (1974) 267
Easy Rider (1969) 210
Ebert, Roger 101
EC Comics 118, 139, 239, 274; *Tales
  From the Crypt* 140
Eck, Johnny 62
Ed Wood (1994) 278
Edeson, Arthur 157
Edison, Thomas 18, 32, 160
Edison Company 35, 39–40, 174
Edward Scissorhands (1990) 278
Eggar, Samantha 275
Elwes, Cary 261
"Emergo" 81, 96
Empire Pictures 251
Empire State Building 64
Englund, Robert 106, 109
epic myth 49
Eros 250
eroticism 219; attraction 199; drives
  218; fear 28; morbid 124; oral 31;
  teasing built around female sexuality
  237
Escape from New York (1981) 276
European experimental cinema 57
evil 187, 241; attitudes about the nature
  of 119; character who recognizes 9;
  instances and figures of 23; questions
  about the nature of 3
Evil Dead trilogy 246
Evil Dead 2 (1987) 110–11
Exorcist, The (1973) 2, 97, 100, 104,
  210, 231, 233, 234, 242, 253, 275;
  (2000) 114–15
Exorcist II: The Heretic (1977) 100
exploitation movies 4, 21, 80–1, 85, 97,
  99–100, 103, 210; competing with
  mainstream features 94; conventions
  of 217; degrees of carnage 107;
  gross-out effects of 253; most
  unnerving (1970s) 106; new career
  as star 87–8; response to growing
  competition for 88; sex and violence
  22, 105; startling formal changes 210;
  trick to effective filmmaking 251
export licenses 131

expressionism 51, 54, 157–75, 176; established as foundation of horror film 207; subjective emotions identified with 200 *see also* German Expressionism

eyes 223; closeups of 128, 134; huge leering 257; mutilation of 37, 107; "window of the soul" 162

Fade To Black (1980) 109

fairy tales 23, 49, 140, 148; story as variation of 218

faits divers 36

Fall of the House of Usher, The (Edgar Allan Poe 1839) 12, 29

Famous Monsters of Filmland (magazine) 85, 137, 139–40, 154, 155

Fanning, Dakota 268

fantasy 22–4, 33, 43, 44, 47, 63, 91, 106; adventure 64; epic 116; romantic 115, 262; wartime settings for tales 130; wish-fulfillment 148

Farrow, Mia 93

fascism 128, 129, 131

Faulkner, William 29

Faust (1927) 47, 49

Faust legend 34

fear(s) 6, 7, 13, 25, 56, 138, 151; childhood 106; communal 266; communist invasion 206; eroticism and 28; psychosexual 23; reactionary 204; sexual penetration 180; social 120, 316

Feher, Friedrich 45–6

Fellini, Federico 230

female sexuality; erotic teasing built around 237; expression of 234; fear and containment of 89

feminists/feminism 3, 89, 142–3; film denounced by 208; protests against demeaning images 227

fertility symbols 167

fetishes/fetishism 224, 225, 233

fight-or-flight reflex 146

Film Noir 3, 177–8, 186; stylistic elements that characterize 183, 184, 187; visual motif common to 184

Finney, Jack 197

First Amendment protection 94

Fisher, Terence 82, 83, 84

Flash Gordon (1936) 77

flashback 45, 197, 198

Fleming, Victor 60

Flesh for Frankenstein (1973) 246

Florescu, Radu 255

Florey, Robert 57, 61, 75, 159, 160

Fly, The (1986) 11

Flying Saucer, The (1950) 78

flying saucers 136

Flynt, Larry 142

Focus on the Horror Film (anthology 1972) 4–5

Fog, The (1980) 276

Foley, Charles 38

Forbidden Planet (1956) 78, 239

Ford, Harrison 115

Ford, John 214, 255

Fort, Garrett 57, 159

Foster, Jodie 113

Four Flies on Grey Velvet (1972) 276

Fox 54, 55, 120

Foxy Brown (1974) 96

Fra Angelico 26–7

Francis, Jan 101

Franco, Jess 114

Frankenstein, or the Modern Prometheus (Mary Shelley 1818) 30–1, 66, 158–9, 162, 165, 166, 170, 171, 172, 174, 175, 212, 245

Frankenstein (1910) 18, 39–40, 160, 174; (1931) 5, 18, 19, 20, 24, 40, 49, 55, 57–8, 66, 68, 120, 122–3, 157–75, 258; (1938) double feature (*Dracula*) re-release 126, 161; *see also Abbott and Costello Meet Frankenstein; Castle of Frankenstein; Curse of Frankenstein; Flesh for Frankenstein; Ghost of Frankenstein; I Was A Teenage Frankenstein; Presumption; Son of Frankenstein; Young Frankenstein*

Frankenstein Meets the Wolf Man (1943) 69, 71, 113

Frankenstein Created Woman (1967) 82

Frankenstein Monster character 2, 30, 39, 47, 69, 105, 154; comic-strip ads 141; grinning copy of 92; Karloff's close identification with 64, 153; key to how and why it has outshone all others 168; variation of the myth 108, 243

Freaks (1932) 62–3, 66, 120, 121, 124, 144, 150
Freddy vs. Jason (2003) 115
Freddy's Nightmares (TV series 1988) 277
Freeman, Morgan 113, 267
French New Wave 4, 230
Freud, Sigmund 6, 12, 13, 14, 15, 31, 149, 176–92, 205, 218, 249
Freudianism 60, 63, 151, 191; dream theory 199; impotence 218; motifs 70; nightmare sequence 75
Freund, Karl 47, 49, 57, 61, 63
Frid, Jonathan 93
Friday the 13th (1980) 10, 18, 104–5, 108, 228, 242; scenes evoking 143; theatrical trailer for 231
Friday the 13th Part II (1981) 142
Friday the 13th Part V (1985) 105
Friedkin, William 100
Fright Night (1984) 111, 112
From Beyond (1986) 108
From Dusk Till Dawn (1996) 17, 111
Frost, Sadie 261
Frye, Dwight 56, 57, 159, 161, 165, 265
Fuest, Robert 97
Fulton, John P. 59
Funhouse, The (1981) 109, 277
fun-house effect 252

Gale, David 245, 250
Galeen, Henrik 47, 48
gangster movies 65, 66
Garbo, Greta 149
geiger counters 78
Gein, Ed 86, 113, 210, 212, 215, 216, 220
gender 82, 229, 276; late Victorian outlook on 255
gender conflict 205
gender dynamics 256
gender roles 119, 186; crisis in 241; feminine 133; inversion of 186; monsters destabilize and manipulate 223; shifts in 134, 178
genital symbols 149
Genovese, Kitty 141
genre movies 15–18; growth and development of 18–22
genrefication 17, 18, 39

George, John 147
German cinema 11, 149; narrative techniques of silent films 258
German Expressionism 6, 43–50, 58, 145, 158, 159, 160, 168, 183; Hollywood's adoption of 174; two major offshoots of 177
Ghost of Dragstrip Hollow, The (1959) 80
Ghost of Frankenstein, The (1942) 70, 71, 73
Ghost Ship, The (1943) 73, 178; (2002) 269
ghosts 10, 12, 28, 34, 50, 53, 93, 192; materializing in color 81–2; multiple 238; nocturnal torment by 33
Ghoulies (1985) 251
giallo films 113, 276
Giger, H. R. 102
gimmicks 81, 82, 96, 154
Gish, Lillian 240
Godfather, The (1972) 100, 261
Godzilla (1954) 78–9
Goetzke, Bernhard 49
Goldblum, Jeff 275
Goldwyn, Sam 64
Golem, The (1920) 47, 65, 160
Goodman, John 82
Gordon, Mel 36
Gordon, Stuart 108, 243–8, 250, 251
gore 20, 81, 82, 90, 113, 213, 275; excessive 111, 223; explicit 275; extreme 91, 110
Goth rock music 143
gothic literature/fiction 5, 6, 8, 10, 12, 27–30, 39, 234
Government Information Manual for the Motion Picture Industry, The 129, 130, 133
Graduate, The (1967) 210
Graduation Day (1981) 104
Grand Guignol 36–8, 39, 61, 82, 107, 111, 140, 147, 245, 251; alternation of violence and sex programmed by 247; Hammer-style 88; spectacles of bodily destruction traceable to 243
Grant, Richard E. 261
Grau, Albin 48
Great Depression (1929) 55, 56, 57, 65, 77, 121, 122; horror cycle initiated 157

Great Train Robbery, The (1903) 35
Great War (1914–18) 43–4, 65
Greek mythology 12, 31
Greer, Rosie 97
Gremlins (1984) 111, 278
Griffith, D. W. 38, 42–3, 240
Grim Reaper 7, 113
Gropius, Walter 65
gross-out effects 11, 108, 250, 253
gruesome pictures/subject-matter 120–7,
    161
Gulf War (1990–1) 257
Gung-Ho (1944) 128
Gunning, Tom 33
Gwynne, Fred 92

H (horrific) ratings category 67, 123
Hale, Nathan G. 187
Hall, Charles D. 58, 98, 157
Hall, Grayson 93
Hall, Jon 72
Halloween (1978) 10, 11, 101, 102, 104,
    105, 106, 109, 113, 142, 218, 227–42
Halloween II (1981) 104
Halperin, Victor and Edward 61
Hamilton, George 17
Hamilton, Suzy 143
Hammer Films 19, 74, 82, 84, 90, 95,
    96, 97, 154, 175, 244, 256; Dracula
    series (1958–72) 254; knock-offs from
    230; new star system 155; photos of
    topless actresses movies 140
Hand, The (1981) 111
Hands of Orlac, The (Maurice Renard
    1920) 63, 75
Hands of Orlac, The (1924) 47
Hansel and Gretel 218
Hansen, Gunnar 210, 221
Happy Birthday To Me (1981) 104
Harris, Marilyn 171
Hart, James V. 255, 264
Harvey, Herk 91
haunted houses 29, 50, 53, 54, 115,
    241, 266–72; dwelling itself becomes
    monster 102; metaphor for individual
    human mind 24
Haunting, The (1963) 90, 115; (1999) 119
Haunting of Hill House, The (Shirley
    Jackson 1959) 90
Hawks, Howard 230

Hays, Will H. 120, 121
He Who Gets Slapped (1924) 149
Hefner, Hugh 139
Hell 8, 27, 43; expressionist vistas of 49
Hellraiser (1987) 106
Hemmings, David 270
Henkel, Kim 218
Henry, O. 91
Herlth, Robert 49
heroes 93; African-American 21, 274;
    monsters and 20, 112; reluctant 95;
    tragic 93
heroines 228–9
Herrmann, Bernard 86, 105, 247, 262
Heston, Charlton 103
Hills Have Eyes, The (1977) 99, 225, 231
Hilton, Daisy and Violet 62
Hitchcock, Alfred 3, 18, 29, 74, 85–7,
    95, 101, 105, 113, 115, 142, 212,
    214, 218, 221, 222, 225, 230, 232,
    234, 247, 274
Hobart, Rose 59
Hogarth, William 74
Holden, Gloria 67
Hollywood 4, 19, 41, 50–5, 129, 189;
    adoption of German expressionism
    174; attempt to revive the disaster-
    movie cycle 267; B movies 27; brief
    experiment with 3-D movies 79, 88;
    censorship 8, 11, 66, 94; debut of
    gory, Italian-style detective drama
    112–13; depictions of non-Western
    peoples 130; digital revolution 116;
    expressionism 157–75; first foray into
    the zombie theme 61; five largest
    studios engaged in monopolistic
    activities 76; German filmmakers
    migrating to 50; "golden age"
    of horror 55–69, 158; greatest
    competition in Europe 44; major
    studios releasing expensive, star-driven
    fright films 115; major studios
    remained aloof from horror 90;
    shooting and editing style 232;
    slow to capitalize on youth audience
    80; socially critical, revisionist
    genre filmmaking 102; stamps
    commemorating classic monsters 153,
    175; targeting urban black audiences
    96

Hollywood Reporter, The 71, 154
Holocaust 77, 93, 140
Holt, Jack 181
home video 85, 114
Homicidal (1961) 230
homoerotic undercurrent 165–6
homosexuality 67, 125, 138; socially
   mandated repression of desires 182
Hong Kong 115, 277
Hooper, Tobe 99, 104, 212, 213,
   215–26, 277
Hoover, Herbert 121
Hoover, J. Edgar 205
Hopkins, Anthony 112, 256, 261, 263,
   264
Hopkins, Miriam 59, 60
Horrible Experiment, The (1909) 37
Horror of Dracula (1958) 19, 83, 254
House of Dracula (1945) 75, 189
House of Frankenstein (1944) 75
House of Usher (1960) 88
House of Wax (1953) 88, 98
House on Haunted Hill, The (1958) 81,
   87, 96; (1999) 115
Howling, The (1981) 278
Hudson, Kate 115
Hull, Henry 66, 124–5
humor 13, 66, 219, 248, 260, 277;
   blend of horror and 68; careful
   control of 243; dark 108, 274;
   macabre 108; mixed with spectacles
   of excessive gore 111; self-conscious
   109
Hunchback of Notre Dame, The (1923) 50,
   52, 144, 146, 148, 155 *see also*
   Quasimodo
Hunger, The (1983) 111
Hunter, Kim 74
Hustler magazine 142
hydrogen bomb testing 78

I Know What You Did Last Summer
   (1997) 113
I Married A Communist (1949) 206
I Married A Monster From Outer Space
   (1958) 206
I Still Know What You Did Last Summer
   (1998) 113
I Walked With a Zombie (1943) 73, 74,
   178

I Was A Teenage Frankenstein (1957) 5,
   80, 81
I Was A Teenage Werewolf (1957) 80, 81,
   112, 137, 154
iconography 17–18, 143, 157; popular
   41
id 187
illusions 32, 33, 34
imagery 268; advertising 143; Christ
   263; flag 104; gothic 12; orientalizing
   257; phallic 179; retrograde 130;
   water 187
Impossible Voyage, The (1904) 32
impotence 150, 218, 224
In the Mouth of Madness (1995) 277
incest 65, 124, 151
Incredible Melting Man, The (1977) 108
Independence Day (1996) 267–8
Inescort, Frieda 72–3, 132
Inferno (1980)
Inn Where No Man Rests, The (1903) 33
Interpretation of Dreams, The (Sigmund
   Freud 1900) 149, 179, 189
Interview With the Vampire (Anne Rice
   1976) 112
Invasion of the Body Snatchers (1956)
   78–9, 193–207
Invasion U.S.A.! (1952) 206
Invisible Agent (1942) 72
Invisible Man, The (1933) 59
Invisible Man Returns, The (1940) 69
Invisible Ray, The (1936) 65
Iranian hostage crisis (1979–81) 103
Iraq 268, 269
Irons, Jeremy 275
Irving, Henry 255, 263
Irving, Washington 278
Ishioka, Eiko 259
Island of Dr. Moreau, The (H. G. Wells
   1896) 61–2
Island of Lost Souls, The (1933) 61–2, 66,
   124
Isle of the Dead (1945) 74
It Came From Beneath the Sea (1955) 78
It's A Wonderful Life (1946) 278
It's Alive! (1974) 242

Jackson, Michael 250–1
Jackson, Peter 246
Jackson, Shirley 90

Jacobs, Lewis 153–4
James, Henry 12
Jane Eyre (Charlotte Brontë 1847) 74, 93
Jannings, Emil 149
Janowitz, Hans 46, 47, 51
Japan 77, 78, 115–16; propaganda 130, 131
Jason Goes to Hell: The Final Friday (1993) 106
Jason X (2001) 115
Jaws (1975) 100
Jekyll and Hyde characters 4, 15, 24, 30, 31, 39, 47, 66, 70, 92, 103 *see also* *Dr. Jekyll and Mr. Hyde*; *The Strange Case of Dr. Jekyll and Mr. Hyde*
John Henry folktale 224
Jolie, Angelina 113
Jolly Corner, The (Henry James 1909) 12
Jones, Caroline 92, 195
Jones, Dorothy B. 135
Jones, Duane 95
Joy, Jason S. 120, 121–2, 123, 124
Julian, Rupert 52

Kane, Carol 104
Karloff, Boris 10, 40, 50, 57, 58, 61, 64–5, 66, 68, 70, 74, 75, 84, 85, 88–9, 92, 95, 96, 124, 128, 153, 155, 157, 159, 162, 168, 169, 172, 174, 175; novelty record featuring comic impersonations of 137
Kendrick, Walter 6, 16–17, 18, 39
Kerr, Frederic 163
Kerry, Norman 147, 148
Kidder, Margot 274
Kidman, Nicole 112, 115
Kilar, Wojciech 262
Kilmer, Val 112
Kinetoscope 32
King, Stephen 2, 8, 14, 30, 85, 102, 245, 274, 277
King Kong (1933) 23, 63–4; (1976) 107
Klein-Rogge, Rudolph 49
Korean War (1950–3) 77, 206
Krauss, Werner 45–6, 47, 188
Kreimheld's Revenge (1924) 49
Ku Klux Klan 90
Kubrick, Stanley 101, 102–3, 111, 253

Laemmle, Carl 52, 54, 55, 160
Laemmle, Carl Jr. 55, 67
Lanchester, Elsa 66, 67
Land of the Dead (2005) 274
Landau, Martin 278
Landon, Michael 81
Lang, Fritz 49, 54, 63
Langella, Frank 100, 112, 255
Langenkamp, Heather 106, 109
Larroquette, John 211
Last Command, The (1928) 149
Last House on the Left (1972) 11, 21, 99, 210, 250
Last Laugh, The (1924) 65, 149
Last Warning, The (1929) 55
Laughing, Screaming (William Paul 1994) 249
Laughton, Charles 61–2
Laurie, Piper 274
LaValley, Al 206
Lee, Christopher 82, 83–4, 88, 155, 254, 256, 278
Lee, Roland V. 68–9
Le Fanu, J. Sheridan 255
Leigh, Janet 2, 86, 101, 230
Leni, Paul 50, 54–5, 62, 66, 146
Leroux, Gaston 52
lesbianism 67, 96, 255; strong undertones 125
Levine, Ted 113
Lewis, Al 92
Lewis, Herschell Gordon 90–1, 107
Lewis, Matthew Gregory 27
Lewton, Val 11, 73, 74, 90, 94, 176–92, 229, 276
libido 189
Lifeforce (1985) 277
liminal figures 9
Living and the Undead, The (Gregory A. Waller 1986) 112 *see also* *Night of the Living Dead*; *Return of the Living Dead*
Lloyd, Danny 102
Lloyd Webber, Andrew 53
Lloyd's of London 81
Logan's Run (1976) 102
Lom, Herbert 84
London After Midnight (1927) 50, 51, 146, 156
Lonely Villa, The (1909) 38
Loomis, Nancy 229

Lord of the Rings trilogy (2001–3) 23, 116
Lorde, André de 25, 37–8, 266
Loring, Lisa 138–9
Lorre, Peter 63, 75, 88, 89, 155
Lost Boys, The (1987) 17, 111, 112
Lost World, The (1925) 64
Love at First Bite (1979) 17
Lovecraft, H. P. 108, 245–6, 247
low-budget films 61, 78, 107, 176, 194, 211, 225, 241, 256; exploitation-style 21–2, 206; minor cult figure in 108; slasher 22, 244
Lucas, George 85, 102
Lucky Pierre (1961) 90
Lugosi, Bela 2, 13, 47, 56–7, 61–2, 64, 65, 68, 69, 70, 71–2, 77, 84, 85, 123–4, 127, 128, 132, 134, 135, 146, 153, 155, 157, 159, 254, 255, 260, 278; comic impersonations of 137, 138
Lumière, Auguste and Louis 32
Lust for a Vampire (1971) 96
lycanthropic form 179, 185

M (1931) 63
Macabre (1958) 81, 154
McCarthy, Kevin 79, 195, 197
McCarthy-era paranoia 195
McCarty, John 107
McCrea, Joel 62
McDowall, Roddy 111
McGee, Vonetta 97
McMinn, Terry 210
McNally, Raymond T. 255
MacNeil, Chris 100
Mad Love (1935) 38, 63
Mad Monster, The (1942) 72
Madhouse (1974) 97
Madsen, Virginia 107
magic 23, 32, 33
makeup artists 11, 55, 82, 85, 103, 107 *see also* Baker; Blake; Pierce; Savini; Westmore
Mamoulian, Rouben 59, 60, 61, 66, 112, 157, 167
Man-Made Monster (1941) 70
Man of A Thousand Faces (1957) 154–5
Man Who Killed Death, The (1928) 248
Man Who Laughs, The (1928) 55

Maniac (1963) 230; (1980) 107
Manners, David 265
Manson, Charles 99, 210, 214, 215
Mao Zedong 77
March, Fredric 59, 60, 103
Mark of the Devil (1970) 11
Marshall, William 96
Martians 23, 78, 196, 268
Martin (1977) 273
M.A.S.H. (1970) 210
Maslin, Janet 101
Matheson, Richard 91, 93
Matinee (1993) 82, 137
Matrix, The (1999) 116
Maurey, Max 36, 37
Mayer, Carl 46, 54
medium-budget features 81, 88, 155
Melford, George 57
Méliès, Georges 32–5, 36, 39, 49, 117
Melmoth the Wanderer (Charles Maturin 1820) 12
melodrama 145
Menzies, William Cameron 120
Metenier, Oscar 36, 37
Metropolis (1927) 47, 49–50, 57, 160
MGM (Metro-Goldwyn-Mayer) 38, 50, 54, 55, 60, 63, 69, 75, 78, 90, 93, 120, 144, 149, 179; reputation for glossy production values and glamorous stars 62
microcepholites 62
midgets 62
Midnight Cowboy (1969) 94
Milland, Ray 97
misogyny 208, 242; media 142, 143
Mondadori company 276
Monk, The (Matthew Lewis 1796) 12, 27, 28
Monkey Shines (1988) 274
Monogram 72, 73, 128, 130
Monster, The (1925) 54, 146
"Monster Boomers" 137
Monster Mash, The (song) 137, 138
Monster on the Campus (1958) 80
monsters 118–43; classic, stamps commemorating 153, 175; most famous 55; sympathetic, compelling 167; teenage 76–143; undying 1–24, 137

montages 60, 78, 219–20, 241, 257; extended 188–9; overlapping dissolves 258–9; sensuous female forms 261; step-frame 223
Montmartre 36
Moreland, Mantan 130
Morgan, Robin 142
Moss, Gene 138
Most Dangerous Game, The (1932) 62, 124
motifs 27, 63, 99, 102, 145, 199, 219, 233, 260; adapted 42; cultural 6; *doppelgänger* 107; expressionistic 68; Freudian 70; gothic 29, 68; musical 105; new, skillful treatment of 229; Old Testament-derived 98; permitting audience indulgence 255; visual 161, 184
Motion Picture Herald 121
"movie brats" 230
MPPDA (Motion Picture Producers and Distributors Association) 120, 121
Mr. Sardonicus (1961) 82
Mr. Wu (1927) 51
Mrs. Miniver (1942) 134
Mummy, The (1932) 4, 61, 63, 154, 255; (1959) 84; (1999) 117
Mummy character 137, 154
Mummy's Hand, The (1940) 69
Mummy's Tomb, The (1942) 70
Mumy, Billy 91
Munch, Edvard 46, 113
Munsters, The 92, 138
Murder My Sweet (1944) 177
Murders in the Rue Morgue (1932) 61, 123–4
Murnau, Friedrich W. 47–8, 49, 54, 55, 59, 65, 254, 259, 260
musicals 16
Mussolini reference 122
Musuraca, Nicholas 73
mutilation 37; genital 148; interwar period obsession with 63
Mutual 42
My Bloody Valentine (1981) 104
Mysteries of Udolpho, The (Ann Radcliffe 1794) 12, 27
Mysterious Retort, The 34 (1906) 34
Mystery of the Wax Museum (1933) 64, 88
mythology 23; cultural 210–11

Nakata, Hideo 116
Napier, Alan 181
narratives 26; destabilizing 7, 119; *Dracula*-inspired 134; emotionally involving 43; secular, parallel to religious traditions 8; techniques of German silent films 258
"national emergency" 205
National Organization of Women 141
naturalism 36
Nazism 50, 77, 93, 132; racist doctrines 130, 131
NBC 143, 240
Neal, Edwin 210, 216
Neale, Steve 145
Near Dark (1987) 111
necrophilia 65, 124
Neeson, Liam 115
neighborhood theaters 80, 85
neoclassical phase 20
Neubabelsberg 44
New American cinema 4
New Hollywood 4, 230
New Line Cinema 115, 225
New York Times 114
New York WOR-TV 84
Nicholson, Jack 89, 102, 103
Nicholson, James H. 80, 81
nickelodeon 39–43
Niebelungen saga 49
Night of the Living Dead (1968) 8, 11, 21, 94, 95, 99, 103, 111, 139, 208, 210, 213, 217, 219, 224–5, 241; color remake (1990) 274; sequels 107, 273
Night Stalker, The (1972) 93
nightmare/delirium sequence 179
Nightmare on Elm Street, A (1984) 106, 109
nightmares 9, 13, 187, 188–9, 190, 198, 231; collective 206; one of the few horror movies to invoke "the authentic quality of" 20; symbolically coded 15
Nike 143
Nixon administration 100, 214
North By Northwest (1959) 86
Nosferatu, A Symphony of Terror (1922) 47, 48–9, 57, 160, 162, 254, 255, 259, 260, 263

nuclear threat 91–2, 137, 156, 194
nudity 90, 94, 139; crass exploitation of 105; frolics before bloody mayhem 217–18; soft-core 142

O'Bannon, Dan 110
O'Brien, Willis 64
Of Mice and Men (1939) 70
Old Dark House, The (1932) 12, 58
Oldman, Gary 256, 259, 260, 262, 265
Olivier, Laurence 100
Omega Man, The (1971) 101–2
Omen, The (1976) 100, 242
Opera (1987) 276
Organic Theater 245
Orion Pictures 102
Orvieto 43
Oscars 59, 100, 112, 134, 231, 278
Osment, Haley Joel 115
Others, The (2001) 115
Otterson, Jack 68
Ouspenskaya, Maria 70
Outer Limits, The (1963–5) series 91
outlaw biker movies 97
OWI (US Office of War Information) 128, 129, 130, 136; Overseas Branch 131 *see also* BMP

Pabst, G. W. 149, 188–9
Paramount 41, 50, 55, 59, 61, 66, 78, 86, 93, 95, 104, 120
Paramount case (US Supreme Court 1948) 76, 94
Paranoiac (1963) 230
Paris Opera House 52
parodies 109
Parsons, Lindsley 130, 131
Partain, Paul 210, 216, 217
pastiche 109
Pathé box camera 262
Patrick, Butch 138
Paul, William 249, 252
PCA (Production Code Administration) 66, 67, 69–70, 94, 121, 123, 124, 125, 129
Peake, Richard Brinsley (1823) 159
Pearl Harbor 71, 128
Peck, Gregory 100
Peeping Tom (1960) 8, 87
Penalty, The (1920) 51

Pentagon 206
Perkins, Anthony 86, 105
Persistence of Memory, The (Salvador Dali 1931); 218–19
Peter Pan (J. M. Barrie 1904) 112
Peter Pan (1955) 112
Pfeiffer, Michelle 115
phallic associations 70, 89, 144, 179, 190, 251; clown mask 233; displays of prowess/skill 150, 152; probe that springs from armpit to siphon blood; 275; weaponry 60, 189, 218, 224, 228, 234, 237
Phantasm (1977) 107
Phantom Lady (1944) 177
Phantom of the Opera, The (1925) 50–1, 52–3, 58, 64, 144, 146, 148, 155; (1943) 53, 69, 154; (1962) 84
Phantom of the Opera character 2, 50, 52, 153
Philbin, Mary 52
Phillips, Augustus 40
Picardo, Robert 278
Pickett, Bobby 137
Pierce, Jack P. 55, 57, 58, 66, 70, 82, 108, 154, 157, 159, 168, 175
Pinckard, Terri 139–40, 141
Pink Flamingoes (1972) 250
Pirie, David 256
Pit and the Pendulum, The (1961) 10, 88, 89, 141, 222
Pitt, Brad 113
Pitt, Ingrid 96
Plan Nine From Outer Space (1959) 278
Planet of the Apes series (1968–73) 101, 103
Plato 14
Playboy 139, 142
Pleasence, Donald 229, 230, 234
plots 12, 45; conventionalized, emotionally excessive 145; familiar in the realm of popular melodramas 42; haunted hotel 33
Poe, Edgar Allan 12, 28, 29, 38, 39, 42–3, 47, 61, 88, 91, 155
Poelzig, Hans 65
Polanski, Roman 93
Polidori, John 159, 255
political assassinations 209
Poltergeist (1982) 104, 277

pornography 275; hard-core 142; soft
96, 261; marches against spread of
142; vile and misogynistic 208
Porter, Edwin S. 35
Poseidon Adventure, The (1972) 267
postmodernism 108–12, 113, 116
"Poverty Row" chillers 72
Powell, Michael 87
Poynter, Nelson 129
Prana-Film 48
PRC 72
Presumption: or, The Fate of Frankenstein
(1823) 159
Price, Vincent 82, 87–8, 89, 94, 97–8,
137, 141, 155, 278
Prom Night (1980) 104
propaganda 128, 129, 132, 133, 136;
Japanese 130, 131; shorts 206
prostitutes 42, 59–60, 61, 87
Psycho (Robert Bloch 1959) 86, 212
Psycho (1960) 2, 8, 9, 12, 18, 21, 74,
85–7, 92, 93, 94, 99, 101, 105, 112,
208, 214, 222, 223, 225, 226, 241;
borrowed themes and motifs from
221, 230, 237, 251; conscious
reworking of 274; imitation of
famous scenes from 109, 142;
influence of 113; opening/opening
theme 232, 247
Psycho II (1983) 105
Psycho III (1986) 105
psychoanalytic theory 6, 15, 75, 180, 183,
189; first movie to attempt coherent
dramatization of 149; illustrated in
dramatic form 188; popularization of
176; public familiar with 187
psychological horror 6, 7, 13, 15
psychopaths 10, 106, 113, 241, 276 *see
also* sexual psychopaths
psychosexual themes 63, 75, 93, 153
pulp magazines 27, 245
Puppet Master (1989) 251
Purloined Letter, The (Edgar Allan Poe
1845) 28

Quasimodo 50, 52, 147–8, 156
Quatermass Xperiment, The (1955) 82
Queen of the Damned (2002) 116
quest myth 23
Quigley, Martin 65–6, 121

Rabid (1977) 275
racism 107; overt 131; portrayals of 128,
130
Radcliffe, Ann 10, 28 *see also Mysteries of
Udolpho; Sicilian Romance*
Raimi, Sam 110
Rains, Claude 59, 69, 70, 154
Randian, Prince 62
Randolph, Jane 73, 178
rape 26, 28, 84, 99, 222; bizarre
attempt 245; emotionally intense 250;
pornography and 142; ritualistic 93
rape-murder 83
Rasulala, Thalmus 97
Rathbone, Basil 69, 88, 127
ratings 93, 94; H category 67, 123
Raven, The (1935) 65, 128; (1963) 89
Reagan administration 104, 115, 155,
229, 269
Re-Animator (1985) 19, 108, 110,
243–52
Rear Window (1954) 85, 113, 275
Rebecca (Daphne Du Maurier 1938) 29
Rebecca (1940) 10, 29, 93
Red Nightmare (1962) 206
Reed, Oliver 84
Reeves, Keanu 257
Reeves, Michael 11, 95
Reimann, Walter 44
religious right 142, 253
remakes 20, 53, 69, 107, 154, 274;
clever 115, 277; expensive 225;
fatalistic 276–7; glossy 115; uninspired
84
Remick, Lee 100
Rennie, Michael 78
Repulsion (1965) 93
Return of the Living Dead (1985) 110
Return of the Vampire (1943) 72, 132–6,
254
revenge 90, 171, 172; common 247;
methodical and savage 99; psychotic
105
Revenge of the Creature (1955) 80
Revenge of Frankenstein (1958) 83
Revenge of the Zombies (1943) 72, 73,
130, 131
Rice, Anne 2, 112, 116
Ring, The (2002) 11, 115–16, 269–72
Ring Two, The (2005) 116

Ringu (1998) 115
RKO 62, 63, 68, 70, 73, 154, 176, 191
Road to Mandalay, The (1926) 51
Robbins, Tim 268, 269
Robinson, Ann 268
Robinson, Arthur 49
Robson, Mark 73, 74
Rocky Horror Picture Show, The (1975) 99, 246, 248
Rodriguez, Robert 111
Roe v. Wade (US Supreme Court 1973) 242
Rohrig, Walter 44, 49
Rollerball (1975) 102
Rolling Stones 214
Romania 132
romantic comedy 16, 115
Romero, George A. 94, 99, 103, 107, 108, 110, 208, 273–4
Roosevelt, Franklin D. 56, 129
Rose, Brian A. 41
Rosemary's Baby (1968) 93–4, 100, 241, 271
Rosse plays 36
Royal Lyceum Theater 255, 263
Russell, Elizabeth 181–2, 192
Russell, Kurt 276
Ryder, Winona 256, 258

sadism 127, 223, 249, 263; barely disguised undertones of 62; exploited 276; outrageous scenes of 94; sexual 8, 141; undertones/undercurrents of 61, 83
sadomasochist qualities 106, 147, 148
Salem's Lot (1979) 277
Sampson, Robert 245
Sangster, Jimmy 82
Sarandon, Susan 111
satanists 65, 74, 93, 100, 124, 191
Savada, Elias 148, 149, 150
Saving Private Ryan (1998) 267
Savini, Tom 103, 107, 108, 274
Saw (2004) 8
Scalps (1983) 11
Scanners (1981) 8
Scarface (1983) 275
Schatz, Thomas 18, 19, 20, 21
Schrader, Paul 178, 183, 184, 187
Schreck, Max 48, 259

Schufftan, Eugen 49
Schwarzenegger, Arnold 267
science fiction 23–4, 34, 47, 154, 196, 202, 203, 205; apocalyptic undercurrents of 267; blending of expressionist horror with 207; effects-heavy epics 239; fear of atomic war underpinning 195; first major epic 49; *Frankenstein* a common ancestor of horror and 204; gothic 64; landmark of 159; rise of 76–117, 136, 206, 267
Scorsese, Martin 274
Scott, Ridley 102
Scream, The (Edvard Munch 1893) 46, 113
Scream (1996) 19–20, 113, 270
Scream Blacula, Scream (1973) 97
Screen Gems 84, 85, 154
Seastrom, Victor 149
Seattle Censorship Board 124
Secrets of a Soul (1926) 149, 188–9
self-consciousness 4, 19, 20, 111, 115, 275; comic 135; historical 109
Selig Polyscope Company 41
Sellers, Peter 111
Selznick, David O. 74
September 11 (2001) 266, 268
sequels 49, 66, 69, 82, 84, 97, 106, 107, 109, 154, 184, 226, 229
serial killers 86, 106, 107, 113, 212, 273, 278
Serling, Rod 91
Seven/Se7en (1995) 113
Seventh Victim, The (1943) 73, 74, 178, 191
sex: beer-fueled 235; children's increasing awareness of the mysteries of 138; illicit 228, 233; implied 126; initiation of 199; obsession with 267; oral 99, 222; painful 275; perverse acts 218; pleasures of 139; premarital 115
sex and violence 9, 26, 87, 94–104, 142, 218, 227, 257; alternation of 247; exploitation horror 22, 105; focused around contemporary teenagers 229; interconnection of 275; relatively high degrees of 81; struggle that promises to fuse 238
sexual psychopaths 87, 101

sexual themes: arousal 73, 176;
dysfunction 148; fear of penetration
180; frank 254; frigidity 190;
frustration 167, 219; gratuitous
titillation 217; identity 111;
interpretations 31; irresistibility of the
undead 255; morbid suggestiveness
66; obsession 278; perversion 125;
repression 60; revolution (1960s and
1970s) 96; sadism 8, 141; taboo-
shattering alterations 275 *see also*
psychosexual themes
sexuality 187; adolescent 233, 242;
expressed only through brutal
violence 229; fear and compelling
curiosity about 138; frustrated 62,
236; graphic 209; open 19, 96;
perverse 121; restrained 113;
unconventional 261 *see also* female
sexuality
sexually transmitted diseases 263
Shaft (1971) 96
Shakespeare, William 5
Sharret, Christopher 224
Shaun of the Dead (2004) 246
Shelley, Mary (Wollstonecraft) 30–1, 40,
58, 66, 82, 158–9, 162, 165, 166,
170, 171, 172, 174, 175, 212, 245
Shelley, Percy Bysshe 66, 158, 159
Shining, The (1980) 102–3, 104, 253
Shivers, *see They Came From Within*
Shock! Stations/Theater telecasts 84–5,
154, 156, 277
Shyamalan, M. Night 115
Siamese twins 62
Sicilian Romance, A (Ann Radcliffe 1790)
27
Siedow, Jim 110, 216
Siegel, Don 79, 194, 195, 196, 197,
198, 199, 200, 202, 205, 206
Siegfried (1923) 47, 49
Silence of the Lambs, The (1991) 112–13,
264
"silent majority" 214
Silent Night, Deadly Night (1974) 104
Silent Running (1972) 102
Simms, John Michael 229
Simon, Simone 73, 178
Siodmak, Curt 70, 278
Sisters (1973) 274

sitcoms 92
Sixth Sense, The (1999) 20, 115, 269
Skal, David J. 30, 51, 137, 148, 149,
150, 156, 169
Skeleton Key, The (2005) 115
Skulls, The (2000) 143
slapstick comedy 110, 243–52
slasher films 2, 19, 21, 101, 104–7, 108,
111, 142, 221–2, 244; conventions
of 217–18, 235; forerunner of 242;
most popular series (1980s) 115; new
pantheon 226; novel variation of 109;
parodied 143; postmodernist revival
of 113; supernatural basis apparently
absent in 10; *Sleepy Hollow* (1999) 278
Smith, Kent 73, 178
Smith, Roger 155
Snuff (1976) 142
So Proudly We Hail! (1943) 134
soap opera 92–3
Sobchack, Vivian 24, 202
Soles, P. J. 229
Son of Dracula (1943) 69, 71, 129
Son of Frankenstein (1939) 68–9, 126,
127, 173
Son of Kong (1933) 68
Sontag, Susan 136, 206, 246
Sorcerers, The (1967) 95
sound 49, 55; early experiments with
59; disturbing effects 212
Soviet Union 49, 77, 78, 206
Soylent Green (1973) 102
Spacek, Sissy 274
Spacemen Annual (magazine) 139
Spacey, Kevin 113
special effects 107, 277; digital 116;
father of 33; increasingly grisly 243;
limited resources for 251; one of
the great triumphs of 64; vintage
techniques 254; visual 49
Speck, Richard 210
Spielberg, Steven 85, 102, 104, 267,
268, 269, 277
splatter movies 11, 99, 107, 108, 243,
249, 251
Stagecoach (1939) 256
Stalinist totalitarianism 204
stalk-and-slash model 142, 232, 243
stalkers 2, 87, 109, 132, 238
Star Man (1984) 277

star system 155
Star Wars (1977) 23, 102, 239
Star Wars Episode II: Attack of the Clones (2002) 116
Steadicam 103
Steele, Barbara 89
Stefano, Joseph 92
Steinbeck, John 70
Stendhal Syndrome, The (1996) 276
Step-Father, The (1987) 112
Stevens, Leslie 92
Stevens, Onslow 75
Stevenson, Robert Louis 30, 31, 41
Stich, Sidra 51
Sting, The (1973) 100
Stoker, Bram 17, 30, 31, 48, 56, 122, 133, 159, 214, 253–65
Stoker, Florence 48
Strange, Glenn 75, 77
Strange Case of Dr. Jekyll and Mr. Hyde, The (Robert Louis Stevenson 1886) 30, 61, 41–2
Struss, Karl 59
Student of Prague, The (1926) 47
Sugar Hill (1974) 97
Sunrise (1927) 54, 59
Superfly (1972) 96
supernatural 9, 10, 12, 31, 134, 276; creatures 227; powers 23, 255
Supreme Court 7, 94
surrealism 51, 218–19
suspense 11, 90, 145, 229; building 235–6; critical praise for marshaling 230; one of the most effective devices of 185
Suspiria (1977) 237, 276
Svengali (1931) 64
sword and sorcery films 49
Sybil (1976) 240
Sydney Olympic Games (2000) 143
symbolism/symbols: cat 181; dream 189; femininity and fertility 167; Freudian 149; gothic 269; phallic 144, 152; psychic regression 217; religious 8; sexual 102; womb 190
System of Dr. TarrTarr and Professor Fether, The (1912) 38

20th Century-Fox 78, 101
28 Days Later (2003) 116

2001: A Space Odyssey 101, 223
tabloid newspaper reports 36
taboos 3, 138, 204, 275
Tales From the Crypt (TV anthology) 277
Tales of Terror (1962) 88
Tallman, Patricia 274
Tamblyn, Amber 269
Tarantula (1955) 78
Targets (1968) 95–6
Taste the Blood of Dracula (1969) 96
Tate–LaBianca murders 214
Technicolor 52, 64, 69, 154
technological innovations 49, 79
Teenage Caveman (1958) 80
Teenage Zombies (1959) 80
Teenagers from Outer Space (1959) 80
telekinetic powers 240
television 76, 84, 85, 91–2, 108–12, 114, 275
Tell-Tale Heart, The (Edgar Allan Poe 1843) 42
Tenebre (1982) 276
Terrible Night, A (1896) 33
terror 6, 11, 140, 162, 223, 250; atomic 203; distinguishing between horror and 10; locus of monstrosity and 209; psychological 79, 194; psychological escape from 13; sexual 144; subjective 196, 220; technological 77
Terror, The (1963) 89, 96
Terror Train (1980) 104
Texas Chain Saw Massacre, The (1974) 8, 19, 99, 101, 111, 142, 143, 208–26, 232, 250, 277; (2003) 20, 225
Texas Chain Saw Massacre 2 (1986) 277
Thanhouser, E. 18, 41
Théâtre Libre 36
Theatre of Blood (1973) 97
Théâtre Robert-Houdin, Le 32
Them! (1954) 78, 196
Thesiger, Ernest 66
They Came From Within (1975) 275
They Live (1988) 277
Thing, The (1951) 77, 196, 204, 206, 239; (1982) 107, 277
Thing With Two Heads, The (1972) 97, 107–8
Thirteen Ghosts (1960) 81; (2001) 115, 269
This Gun For Hire (1942) 177

This Island Earth (1955) 78
Thrill of Fear, The (Kendrick 1991) 6
Thriller (1983) 250–1
thrillers 55, 63, 230
THX-1138 (1971) 102
Tigon 95
Tingler, The (1959) 82, 87
Todd, Tony 107
Toho 78
Tonkin Gulf Resolution 138
Toolbox Murders, The (1978) 105
Top Gun (1986) 269
torture 26, 33, 62, 206, 210, 219, 206, 240
Tourneur, Jacques 73, 74, 176, 180, 183, 184–5, 186–7, 190
Town That Dreaded Sundown, The (1977) 104
Townsend, Stuart 116
Tracy, Spencer 41, 60, 179
trailers 81, 231
Trancers (1985) 251
Transylvania 255, 257, 261, 264, 265
trick films 32–5, 39, 42, 49, 64
Trip to the Moon, A (1902) 34–5
Twilight Zone, The (1959–64) TV series 91–2, 140
Twins of Evil (1971) 96
Twister (1996) 267
Twitchell, James 6, 30, 138
Two Thousand Maniacs (1964) 90–1

UA (United Artists) 77, 97, 274
Ufa (*Universumfilm Aktiengesellschaft*) 44, 47, 50, 54, 55, 57, 65
UFOs (unidentified flying objects) 78
Ulmer, Edgar G. 65
Un Chien Andalou (1929) 219, 223, 250
undead 7, 17, 48, 96, 122, 257
"underground" film 210
Unholy Three, The (1925) 51, 150
Uninvited, The (1944) 115
United Nations 129, 131
Universal 12, 18, 19, 41, 49, 50–9, 61, 65–79, 85, 105, 120, 124, 127, 155, 157, 159, 161, 165, 171, 174, 175, 177, 184, 245, 255, 256; concerns and strategies 160; expressionistic settings established by 225; Hammer's new accounts of horror classics 84; popular series of models depicting monsters 141; products built around classic monster characters 138; re-released *Dracula* coda with *Frankenstein* (1938) 161; *Shock!* vintage horror movies 154, 277; tribute to, and lampoon of 1930s horror films 98; Universal-International 154
University of Texas 96
Unknown, The (1927) 14, 51, 144–56
urban race riots 209
US Department of Health, Education, and Welfare 155
US Postal Service 153

Vail, William 210
Vampire Chronicles, The (Anne Rice 1970s) 116
Vampire Lovers, The (1970) 96
Vampirella (comic-book heroine) 141
vampires 8, 9, 28, 48–9, 50, 51, 92, 97, 111; ambivalent or sympathetic portrayal of 254–5; bisexual appeal 260; homoerotic undertones of the myth 67; iconic image of 157; lesbian 96; method of destroying 219; rarely treated facets of the myth 254; Russian variation 90; sexual undercurrent of the myth 89, 122 *see also Buffy*; *Dance of the Vampires*; *Dracula*; *Interview With the Vampire*; *Lust for a Vampire*; *Return of the Vampire*; *Vampyre*
Vampires (1998) 277
vampirism 222, 258; associated with *Peter Pan* story 112; metaphor for lesbianism 67
Vampyre, The (Byron 1819) 159; (rev. Polidori 1819) 159, 255
Vampyre (1932) 4, 255, 260
Van Helsing (2004) 117
Van Sloan, Edward 61, 159, 160, 161
Variety (1925) 149
Variety magazine 71
Vasari, Giorgio 26
Veidt, Conrad 45, 46, 47, 55
Verbinski, Gore 270
Verne, Jules 35
Vertigo (1958) 86, 247, 262, 275

victimization 36, 48, 51, 69, 122, 206; feminine screams suggesting 181; worst fears realized 11; young women 105
Videodrome (1983) 275
Vietnam War 4, 22, 94, 96, 100, 103, 156, 241, 267; allegory 273; angry references to 140; impact on American culture 231; My Lai Massacre 211; violence in American culture touched off by 209
Village of the Damned (1960) 201; (1995) 277
villains 15, 29, 38, 51, 65, 102
Villarias, Carlos 57
violence 7, 10, 15, 59, 145, 151, 161, 250, 274; chasing, with sexual titillation 243; comedy mixed with 110; domestic 61, 213; eroticizing of 233; explicit 11, 230; gory 11, 139; graphic 10, 82, 93, 97, 184, 209, 226; limits of 66, 121; misogynistic 242; movies that set new precedents for 124; reactionary 21; real-world 142; sadomasochistic 179 *see also* sex and violence
violent computer games 143
virgin/whore dichotomy 42
virginity 229, 235, 236
virgins 17, 31, 112, 138
visual effects 42, 49, 102
Vlad the Impaler (Vlad Tepes) 255, 256, 257–8, 259, 262–3, 264, 265
Volcano (1997) 267
Von Sydow, Max 100
voodoo 130, 131

Waggner, George 70
Wagner, Richard 262
Waits, Tom 258
Walking Dead, The (1936) 64–5
Wallace, Dee 278
Waller, Gregory A. 112, 133
Walpole, Horace 6, 27, 28
Walthall, Henry B. 42
Wanger, Walter 194, 195
War of the Worlds, The (H. G. Wells 1898) 23
War of the Worlds, The (1953) 78, 196, 204, 267, 268

War of the Worlds (2005) 268
Warm, Hermann 44, 49
Warner Bros. 64, 66, 88, 99–100, 206, 210
Warning Shadows (1923) 49
Warren horror magazines 244
Warren, James 85, 139, 141
Washington, Denzel 113
Washington 121, 267
Watergate 93, 100, 103, 237
Waterloo Bridge (1931) 57
Watts, Naomi 270
Waxman, Franz 166
Waxworks (1924) 47, 54
Weaver, Sigourney 102
Wegener, Paul 47
Weimar Republic (1919–32) 44, 49, 56
Weine, Robert 45, 46
Weird Tales (pulp magazine) 245
Welles, Orson 257, 277
Wells, H. G. 23, 61
were-cats 176
Werewolf of London, The (1935) 66, 70, 124–5
werewolves 24, 30, 71, 93, 132, 278 *see also American Werewolf in London*; *Curse of the Werewolf*; *I Was A Teenage Werewolf*; *Werewolf of London*
Wes Craven's New Nightmare (1994) 109
West, Mae 66
West, Roland 54, 146
West of Zanzibar (1928) 51
Westerns 3, 16, 216, 264
Westmore, Bud 155
Whale, James 5, 57, 58, 62, 66, 68, 157, 158, 159–60, 161, 162, 164, 168, 200, 212
What Lies Beneath (2000) 115
When A Stranger Calls (1979) 104
White Zombie (1932) 61, 64
Whitman, Charles 96, 210
Wild Angels, The (1966) 97
Wild Bunch, The (1969) 94
Wilder, Gene 98–9
Wilkinson, Brooke 126, 127
Williams, Larry 129–30
Williamson, Kevin 113
Willis, Bruce 115
Willis, Matt 132
Wise, Robert 73, 74, 90

witches 11, 70, 93, 181, 188, 189, 218, 237

Witchfinder General/Conqueror Worm (1968) 11, 95

Wizard of Oz, The 23

Wolf, Leonard 255

Wolf Man, The (1941) 70, 71, 75, 154, 185, 189, 278; *Cat People* shows indebtedness to 179

Woman in the Moon, The (1928) 47

womb 190, 205, 240, 272

women: evisceration of 142, 275; sexually independent 21; violence against 250, 274; young, victimization of 105

Women Against Violence Against Women 142

women's liberation movement 101

Wood, Edward D. 278

Wood, Grant 222

Wood, Robin 20–2, 174, 208, 213, 215, 226

Woods, James 277

World Trade Center 268, 269

World War I, *see* Great War

World War II 69–75, 136, 186; death toll 77; resurgence of horror genre 127; social patterns 178

Wray, Fay 63, 64

Wrightson, Bernie 244

Wynter, Dana 195

xenophobia 257

Y2K bug 269

Yale Skull and Bones Society 143

Yeats, W. B. 5

Young Frankenstein (1974) 98–9, 109, 127

Yu, Ronny 115

Yuzna, Brian 251

Zardoz (1973) 102

Zehner, Harry 126

Zola, Émile 36

zombies 8, 9, 21, 95, 99, 107, 108, 110, 131, 136, 251, 273–4; cycle popular in the war years 130; explicit depiction, chomping human flesh 217; paramilitary posse hunting 103 *see also I Walked With a Zombie*; *Revenge of the Zombies*; *Teenage Zombies*; *White Zombie*

Zombies of Sugar Hill, The (1974) 97

Zuccari, Taddeo 26